SON OF VENGEANCE

Son of Vengeance

Searching for the Legendary Apache Rafael

Bradley Folsom

UNIVERSITY OF OKLAHOMA PRESS : NORMAN

This book is published with the generous assistance of the Kerr Foundation, Inc.

Library of Congress Cataloging-in-Publication Data
Names: Folsom, Bradley, 1979– author.
Title: Son of vengeance : searching for the legendary Apache Rafael / Bradley Folsom.
Description: Norman : University of Oklahoma Press, [2022] | Includes
bibliographical references and index. | Summary: "Draws on English- and Spanish-
language sources to prove that Raphael was indeed a real person, an Apache raised
by a Spanish priest, and explores how and why this man who straddled two social
and cultural worlds, Native American and Spanish, became a legendary figure
whose criminal exploits were said to include killing hundreds of people in northern
New Spain between 1804 and 1810"—Provided by publisher.
Identifiers: LCCN 2021056659 | ISBN 978-0-8061-9067-9 (hardcover) |
ISBN 978-0-8061-9068-6 (paperback)
Subjects: LCSH: Rafael (Apache Indian), active 1804–1810. | Apache Indians—
Mexico—Biography. | Outlaws—Mexico—Biography. | Indian outlaws—
Mexico—Biography. | Apache Indians—Mexico—Ethnic identity. | Indians of
Mexico—Cultural assimilation. | Mexico—History—Spanish colony, 1540–1810. |
Mexico—Race relations—History—19th century. | BISAC: HISTORY /
Latin America / Mexico | HISTORY / Modern / 19th Century
Classification: LCC E99.A6 R213 2022 | DDC 979.004/97250092 3[B]—dc23/
eng/20220610
LC record available at https://lccn.loc.gov/2021056659

The paper in this book meets the guidelines for permanence and durability
of the Committee on Production Guidelines for Book Longevity of
the Council on Library Resources, Inc. ∞

To Mabel

CONTENTS

MAPS

ACKNOWLEDGMENTS

The onset of the COVID-19 pandemic shuttered universities and restricted international travel, closing the doors to many avenues of research and complicating what was already a challenging project. Thankfully, I was fortunate to have the help of kind-hearted archivists from the Nettie Lee Benson Latin American Collection, the University of Texas at Arlington, and the Archivo Histórico del Estado de Durango who promptly responded to my email requests and assisted in some last-minute research by photocopying needed documents. Miguel Vallebueno of the Archivo Histórico del Estado de Durango was particularly helpful in this regard. I also owe a debt of gratitude to archivists for the governments of Mexico and Spain, the Church of Jesus Christ of Latter-Day Saints, and the University of North Texas. Without their monumental efforts to digitize historical documents, this book would not have been possible.

I was also fortunate to have friends and colleagues like Sarah Hambrick, Paul Conrad, Ryan Schumacher, and Todd Smith who were willing to read early manuscript drafts and provide feedback. Mark Santiago offered extremely helpful advice as a press-appointed reader, as did my editors Joe Schiller and Kent Calder. Sonja Sonnenburg, Albert Nungaray, Diego Neave, Ian Watson, Lisa Stallings, and Willem De Reuse assisted with various aspects of writing and research, and I received guidance and encouragement from Donald Chipman, Randolph Campbell, and Carlton Maxwell. My friends and family deserve the most praise for putting up with my eccentricities and tolerating my long work hours. Thank you, Dana Folsom, Geoff Folsom, Heather Folsom, Barbary Phy, Raymond, Alyssa, Mabel, Brent Cline, Robert Walters, Jason Bates, Richard Mowrey, Chael Sirois, and K. J. Ellis.

Finally, I want to thank the librarian at the University of Texas at El Paso who opened the microfilm room for me over Christmas break 2019. As most in academia are aware but choose to ignore, adjuncts, who now teach the majority of classes at universities, often make less than starting primary school teachers in the worst-paid states. Even more problematic, an adjunct's hope for advancement and full-time employment relies on publishing, an endeavor in which they must compete with tenured professors who have one-third the workload, three times the pay, and who have summers off and receive regular sabbaticals for writing and research. This arrangement means that if an adjunct were to carve out a few dollars for a motel and schedule a research trip during Christmas break only to find that the library they were visiting unexpectedly closed their archive room, it might result in permanent resignation to the academic proletariat. Fortunately, I was able to temporarily avoid such a fate thanks to a kind-hearted librarian who understood my situation, opened the microfilm room, and sat patiently as I went through dozens of rolls of microfilm. Unfortunately, I was so busy working that I never got your name, but I hope you read this.

NORTHERN MEXICO abounds with legends and myths about men and women who possess supernatural abilities and martial prowess. For example, children in Sonora learn about Primer Montezuma, a mysterious figure who once called the region home and could perform amazing feats of strength and courage. As the story goes, Primer Montezuma once intentionally allowed himself to be eaten by a giant monster, which had been terrifying locals. Once inside the beast, he cut out its heart, burrowed his way through the creature's insides, and then burst out of its anus to freedom, killing the monster in the process. There are also tales of Juan Tigre, a half-man, half-feline who moved with catlike silence and had the strength of a mountain lion. Legend says that Juan Tigre killed his own father to free his imprisoned mother, and he later bit off the ear of a "Wildman" who challenged him to a fight. As a reward for his gallantry, a local leader made Juan Tigre his heir and gave the hero permission to marry his three beautiful daughters.[1]

Whereas Juan Tigre and Primer Montezuma are generally seen as good, or at least brave and admirable, some of the supernatural humans of Mexico's north were known to be evil and treacherous. For example, there are dozens of versions of the crying woman legend told throughout northern Mexico. In many of these, La Llorona, as she is often called, cries out for help from the center of a lake where it appears that she is drowning. When would-be rescuers, usually men, swim out to save her, La Llorona drags them to the bottom of the lake, where they drown as a reward for their attempted heroism. Even more threatening is El Cuco, a sometimes hairy, sometimes formless, always horrible shapeshifter who kidnaps and eats children who refuse to behave. For this reason, parents invoke El Cuco's name whenever they need to set wayward sons and daughters on the right path.[2]

In a similar vein, mothers in Chihuahua warn their children that if they do not go to sleep, "I will call Rafael." According to tales passed down from the nineteenth century, Rafael or Rafaelillo as he is sometimes called, was a real person who was once "a terror to their region." He would emerge from the peaks of the Sierra Madre Occidental and descend upon remote, unsuspecting Mexican villages where he used "a thousand disguises and strategies" to gain the trust of the local populace. He ate alongside the villagers, played games with them, and even attended their church services. Once the villagers let down their guard and accepted the outsider as one of their own, Rafael revealed his true nature and robbed the town of its silver, horses, women, and children, escaping afterward to one of his hideouts in the Sierra Madre. Owing to his cunning and trickery, the villagers could do nothing to track down Rafael, and they had to resign themselves to losing their livelihood and loved ones to the mysterious stranger.[3]

Details of Rafael's story vary from one telling to the next. In some versions, Rafael conducted his attacks alone. Other times, his two wives, one Indian and one white, and his brother José Antonio accompanied him on his raids. Rafael's ethnicity is left out of some versions of the story, while others describe him as "a merciless Apache warrior," who operated on primal instincts and had few ties to civilized society. In these tellings, Rafael cruelly tortured his victims for pleasure, an "Apache chief who stands out for the outrages, injuries, and deaths he caused."[4]

Other versions of the story portray Rafael as a cross between a bandit seeking financial gain and a warrior for social justice, a predecessor to Francisco "Pancho" Villa, the controversial revolutionary who created his own legends in the same region. Just as Villa's level of maleficence varies depending on who is telling his tale, Rafael is sometimes described as a benevolent, Robin Hood–like figure who stole only from the wealthy and killed only those who deserved to be killed. He bore no ill will toward the poor and downtrodden and was instead simply a hero acting out against the cruel, oppressive Spaniards who ruled over northern Mexico in colonial times. As one chronicler phrased it, "his violence only affects property, but respects human life."[5]

There is no consensus on whether Rafael was a real person. Some writers believe him to be more Juan Tigre than Pancho Villa, with one researcher claiming, "the majority of Mexican historians believe that *el Indio* Rafael did not exist, and they explain him as a myth passed down through anecdotes recounted from one generation to the next." Those who fall into this camp see Rafael as folk legend who, like El Cuco, is nothing more than a "boogeyman" created by parents to scare the children of northern Mexico into obedience.[6]

Others are even less definitive, calling Rafael "enigmatic and contradictory," but refusing to take a stand on whether or not he was once a real person. For example, while researching the Tepehuan tribe of the Sierra Madre, historian Jesús Ángel Ochoa Zazueta frequently asked locals whether they believed Rafael ever actually existed and "they always answer with a smile accompanied by a curious shrug of their shoulders." Still others, such as historian Gildardo Contreras Palacios, occupy a middle ground, claiming that Rafael was "a little real and a little legend." Only a handful of true believers feel that most, if not all, of the legends about Rafael actually happened.[7]

Unfortunately for those who doubted his existence, Rafael was real and many of the most fantastic aspects of his legend do not diverge much from historical fact. Indeed, from 1804 to 1810, Rafael and José Antonio, his companion and fellow Apache, waged an unprecedented and brutal war against the Hispanic population of what is today Chihuahua, Coahuila, Durango, and Zacatecas. The scale of their brutality was something never seen before or since in the region, with contemporary observers estimating that the two Apache men killed between 200 and 1,800 men, women, and children over the course of their rampage.[8]

Even accepting the lower figure, this means that Rafael and José Antonio were among the most prolific killers in North American history. The war they fought against the Spanish military and the Hispanicized population of what was then known as New Spain, far eclipses the Jicarilla War, Victorio's War, Geronimo's War, and many other more famous Apache conflicts of the nineteenth century in terms of bloodshed and duration. In fact, Rafael alone likely killed more people than Geronimo, Victorio, and Mangas Coloradas combined, and if the higher estimates of the number of deaths he and José Antonio caused are to be believed, they killed 1 percent of the population of northern New Spain over the course of six years.[9]

Rafael was able to achieve these terrible distinctions because he held a unique position in Spanish society. Although he was born of an Apache mother, he was raised by a Catholic priest in a Spanish settlement in northern New Spain. This allowed him to learn the Spanish language, customs, and the ways in which the Spanish military operated. He then used this knowledge to develop countermeasures to escape capture. This included dressing in numerous disguises to blend in with the local Hispanicized Indian population, making him a shapeshifter that could adapt to multiple cultures.

Although the Spanish often regarded Indians as unintelligent, or *sin razon*, Rafael earned his pursuers begrudging respect with his creativity and resourcefulness. For example, Spanish soldiers marveled when they discovered that

Rafael shoed his horse with leather horseshoes, which allowed his animal to move much more swiftly, quietly, and steadily through the rugged mountains of the Sierra Madre than the soldiers' iron-shoed horses ever could. Rafael's ability to evade the Spanish military's best laid traps and reemerge hundreds of miles away also baffled and impressed his pursuers, leading one contemporary observer to remark that Rafael was as "terrible as Napoleon was to Europe, with the difference being that one destroyed with his infernal armies and the other with only two men . . . employing unparalleled cleverness and strategy."[10]

This comparison is apt because Napoleon was one of the reasons Rafael was so successful in his raids. At the beginning of the nineteenth century, the Spanish government claimed Mexico as part of its vast American empire that stretched from the southern tip of South America to what is today the southern border of Canada. Controlling an area this size taxed Spain's resources, and the United States, annexation of the Louisiana Territory in 1803 only made things worse. The onset of war with Britain in 1804, and Napoleon Bonaparte's decision to use French military forces to depose the Spanish king in 1808 further complicated matters, as did the initiation of Mexico's War of Independence in 1810. With Spain so focused on dealing with these matters, the nation could not mobilize to stop a marauding Apache.[11]

Spain's problems left the officer in charge of northern New Spain, Commandant General Nemesio Salcedo, with little in the way of firearms, funds, and manpower to deal with Rafael and his band, leading Salcedo to develop his own complex strategies and inventions to capture the Apaches. Describing Rafael and José Antonio as "the most inexorable, elusive, fierce, and cunning men imaginable," Salcedo designed a grid-search pattern for his soldiers to root out the raiders, which was very similar to the one United States officers would use a century later when seeking to arrest Geronimo and his Apache band. The commandant general also required towns to form militias and establish night watches to defend against Rafael, and he made it illegal for anyone to travel outside of towns unless they carried a weapon. To meet the demand for firearms this created, Salcedo designed a gun that could be produced cheaply and locally, and he drew up plans for a cannon that could be fired from the back of a mule so his soldiers could better conduct military operations in the Sierra Madres. Unfortunately for those threatened by Rafael, Salcedo was in charge of all of the Internal Provinces, a military subdivision of northern New Spain made up of what is today Texas, New Mexico, Coahuila, Sonora, Sinaloa, Durango, and Chihuahua, and he could not concentrate all of his forces to capture Rafael as he had to watch for possible invasions from Britain, France, and the United States.[12]

These external threats not only prevented Salcedo from properly combating Rafael, but along with the Mexican War of Independence that consumed Mexico from 1810 to 1821, they have served to overshadow the horrors of Rafael's rampage and led historians to largely ignore the legendary figure. Indeed, Rafael has been the subject of only one scholarly article, which was published in an obscure Mexican historical journal in 1938. Several histories of northern Mexico include brief asides about Rafael, but the war of independence and discussions of the threat of invasion from the United States far eclipse references to the Apache who was more dangerous to the people of the north than any other foreign or domestic individual.[13]

Scholars may also have overlooked Rafael because of the difficulty required in researching the Apache leader. Rafael left behind no memoirs, letters, or other written communication by which to tell his story. Nor did he or José Antonio dictate their experiences for others to write down. This differentiates them from later and more famous Apache leaders such as Geronimo and Victorio who committed many of their hostile acts in the late nineteenth century during a time of free press and greater access to news, and when a large audience was curious about their activities. Likewise, historians meticulously conducted numerous interviews with Geronimo and Victorio's contemporaries. Journalism, publishing, and the study of history simply did not exist in such profusion in Mexico's Internal Provinces in Rafael's day.[14]

This lack of firsthand insight has left potential researchers dependent on documents written by Spanish soldiers, government officials, former captives, surviving victims, and others who had a vested interest presenting Rafael in a negative way. As Edwin R. Sweeney noted in his biography of Apache leader Mangas Coloradas, this reliance on enemies "presents tremendous problems for the historian." Because it is often in the best psychological and political interests for a soldier, victim, or government official to dehumanize the person with whom they are in conflict, accounts from such persons can contain falsehoods or exaggerations. Soldiers usually had little interest in learning the motivation or reasoning of people who they were sent to apprehend or kill, meaning clues to Rafael's way of thinking are in short supply. Owing to cultural taboos, Spanish reports are also often light on the type of prurient details that can serve as narrative punctuators to a history, such as descriptions of violent acts and things of a sexual nature.[15]

Making matters worse for historians, many Spanish records from Rafael's time are now inaccessible, missing, or destroyed. During the U.S.-Mexico War, American soldiers burned archives throughout northern Mexico that likely contained information about Rafael. For example, in 1846, one American soldier in Ciudad Juárez, "saw a great many of the public documents, government papers and archives destroyed. The papers were taken out of pigeon holes, packages and books, torn out and used by the soldiers for all kinds of purposes, such as kindling fires and for private purposes." Considering that Rafael spent time near that city, it seems likely that at least some records of his activities ended up at the bottom of a latrine.[16]

Unintentional fires have also taken their toll. In 1810, Commandant General Salcedo asked Secretary Juan José Ruiz de Bustamante to collect and catalog all "reports, official announcements, diaries, and other notices" concerning the "hostilities, robberies, and murders executed in this province at the hands of the Apache Indians Rafael and José Antonio." Bustamante carried out his assignment dutifully, collecting enough bureaucratic correspondence, soldier dispatches, and captive testimonies to fill three boxes and one full file on Rafael's activities. It seems that he had local officials send original reports from their archives, leaving no copies of important descriptions of Rafael in their place; many archives contain references to documents about Rafael, but the documents themselves are missing. In what would serve as a catalogue to the collection, Bustamante then described each document he collected in a calendar of events, which totaled the number of people Rafael's band had killed, injured, and captured. The catalogue and boxes were later stored in the Archivo General del Estado de Chihuahua in Chihuahua City, likely in either the Comandancia General or the Comandancia de las Provincias Internas collections. These documents remained in their respective boxes until 1941, when a fire broke out in the archives, destroying most of the collections.[17]

Fortunately, not everything was lost. In the mid-nineteenth century, then Commandant General José Merino came across the files Bustamante had assembled concerning Rafael and decided to add the catalogue to *Apuntes históricos*, a collection of interesting historical documents about Chihuahua he put together in 1856. Although Merino claimed that "this testimony has been taken literally from the authentic manuscript" and that he did not "retouch it," he seems to have included only Bustamante's summaries of the reports and not the original, much more-detailed reports themselves. Testimonies from captives, campaign diaries, and other documents that might provide deeper insight into Rafael's personality were also left out of *Apuntes historicos*. In spite of these omissions, the catalogue provides a wealth of information that cannot be found elsewhere, including rumors that Merino had heard about Rafael in the years since Bustamante assembled his report.[18]

There are other surviving contemporary documents concerning Rafael, but unfortunately, they are scattered across remote, poorly catalogued archives in Mexico, the United States, and Spain, and even someone with an unlimited budget would find it difficult to explore all these locations. Thankfully, researchers have photographed many of these archives for microfilm and digital collections, and many are even available to search online. However, owing to the sporadic nature of Rafael's attacks and the great distances he would cover from one raid to the next, searching entire microfilms or digital catalogues may only reveal one or two references to Rafael, if any. Digital searches for Rafael are also nearly impossible to conduct successfully considering that the Spanish often referred to him simply as "Rafael," one of the most common names in New Spain. Other times, they forwent his name entirely in their reports, calling him and José Antonio simply "enemigos," "Apaches," or a variety of other ambiguous terms that could apply to thousands of others in northern New Spain.[19]

The vast distances over which Rafael raided, the Spanish practice of naming towns after saints and geographical features, and Mexico's widespread renaming of towns in the nineteenth and twentieth centuries have also added to the confusion and made things even more difficult for those seeking out documents about Rafael in remote archives. For example, surviving records indicate that Rafael raided a town named San Pablo in 1807. Not only is there a San Pablo, Chihuahua; a San Pablo, Durango; and a San Pablo, Coahuila that are all within an area frequented by Rafael, but there is also a Maríano Balleza, Chihuahua, which was called San Pablo before later being renamed after a hero of Mexican independence. This means that searching through hundreds of pages of local parish records to confirm that Rafael conducted an attack in one location might yield no results because the attack actually occurred in a different location of the same name or with a different name than it had in the early 1800s.[20]

A lack of secondary scholarship is another obstacle to writing about Rafael. Until recently, few histories have explored the relationship between the Apaches and the Spanish in the last years of colonial rule. Books about the Apaches have tended to focus on the late nineteenth century and the United

States military's efforts to defeat the Apaches and force them on to reservations. These works rarely contain substantial discussion of the time before the arrival of the Americans. In the early twentieth century, Spanish borderlands historians began exploring Spain's interactions with native people along New Spain's northern frontier, but these works tended to focus on the mid-to-late eighteenth century when warfare between Spain and the Apaches was at its height. Perhaps because the two decades between 1790 and 1810 were relatively peaceful when compared to previous and subsequent times, historians largely ignored these decades.[21]

Fortunately, historians like William B. Griffen, Mark Santiago, Paul Conrad, Mathew Babcock, and Lance Blyth have gone to great lengths to point out that while the northern New Spain may have been more peaceful in the 1790s and early 1800s than previous and subsequent decades, the relationship between Spain and the Apaches continued to be complex. Griffen's multiple works concerning Apache-Spanish relations in the late eighteenth and early nineteenth centuries reveal a reciprocal relationship wherein both Spain and the Apaches used war and trade for political gain. Conrad's dissertation "Captive Fates: Displaced American Indians in the Southwest Borderlands, Mexico, and Cuba, 1500–1800," shows that Spain continued to take hundreds of Apaches as prisoners of war during this time. Babcock's *Apache Adaptation to Hispanic Rule* and Lance Blyth's *Chiricahua and Janos* make clear that Spain had to go to great lengths to maintain peace with the Apaches and even when it seemed their efforts were successful, the Apaches often broke this peace based on the slightest of pretexts and returned to hostilities. Mark Santiago's *A Bad Peace and a Good War* also shows that there was a forgotten war within this "peace" by detailing a Mescalero Apache uprising that took place from 1795 to 1800.[22]

This book seeks to supplement these works by highlighting a forgotten conflict fought between Spain on one side and the mysterious Rafael and his small group of followers on the other. The title of the book is a derivation of a quote from an 1808 newspaper article, wherein a Spanish observer described Rafael and his companions as "sons of vengeance." The author believed that it was the Apaches' inherent vengeful nature that was to blame for Rafael's attacks on the Hispanic population of northern New Spain. Like other Spaniards of the time, he saw the conflict as senseless, comparing Rafael's actions to a "barbaric, terrible plague" and "the wrath of heaven." Spain was guilty only of trying too hard to civilize the Apaches.[23]

As this work will make clear, there is little question that revenge motivated Rafael and, in many ways, a "son of vengeance" moniker is apt. However, Rafael's attacks were not born of inherent bloodlust, and the Spanish were not innocent of any wrongdoing. Instead, Rafael and the war he waged developed from deep-rooted cultural misunderstandings, a history of conflict between the Spanish and the Apaches, and personal circumstances that were unique to Rafael. Although Apache cultural expectations certainly contributed to Rafael's ultimate decision to wage war, he also fought to gain material goods and to redress personal grievances.

The subtitle, "Searching for the Legendary Apache Rafael" is meant to indicate that much of the book is devoted to cataloguing Spanish efforts to track down and defeat Rafael. It also intends to highlight the difficulties in researching a subject based on sources that are often vague, confusing, and contradictory. Indeed, because the book relies heavily on parish records, folklore, secondhand stories, legends, local histories, and other sources that one might avoid if other documentation were available, there are multiple passages throughout the book that discuss how research was conducted. This is done so the reader can understand certain conclusions, and to open the door for future authors to add to Rafael's story.[24]

Finally, the title indicates that the book is also a hunt for who Rafael was as a person. In a perfect world, the biography section of bookstores would be filled with detailed descriptions of everyday people in society, not just books about elites. Unfortunately, it seems that the only non-wealthy people who receive attention and documentation, especially prior to the twentieth century, were those who broke the rules and caused the upper class to be afraid. Therefore, this book seeks to explain why someone would take a path of death and destruction. What motivated Rafael to commit deeds that others, including his own kinsmen, would find reprehensible and unconscionable? How and why did one of the most prolific killers in history do what he did? In the search for answers to these questions, this book will attempt to avoid passing moral judgement on its subject and will leave such matters to the reader.

CHAPTER ONE

Son of Vengeance,
1781–1804

O N OCTOBER 15, 1804, Rafael stood before a tribunal of military officials and local elites in Guajoquilla, a burgeoning town of some two
thousand inhabitants on the northern frontier of New Spain. The
tribunal sat in judgement because the local military commander, José María de
la Riva, suspected Rafael of "providing intelligence to hostile Apaches." This
was a grave charge considering that Spain had been in a near constant state of
war with the semi-nomadic horse-riding Apaches over the past two centuries, a
war that had claimed thousands of lives on both sides and continued to prove
deadly. Indeed, death records from Guajoquilla indicate that on August 23,
1804, "enemy Apaches" killed local resident Joaquín Befarano, and a little over
a week before the trial, José Ricardo Silva "died at the hands of the enemies."
Riva may have felt that Rafael was complicit in these deaths.[1]

If found guilty of aiding hostile Apaches, Rafael, or El Indio Rafael as he was
known throughout Guajoquilla, faced severe punishment. The tribunal might
sentence him to hard labor in the mines of the Sierra Madre Occidental, the
jagged, volcanically mantled mountain system that loomed over Guajoquilla
and stretched from Central New Spain to what is today the American Southwest. Although imposing, the mountains contained innumerable deposits of
gold and silver, and because Spain had come to depend on this mineral wealth
to fuel its vast overseas empire, local officials often sent convicts to serve as
a cheap source of labor in mines. Should the tribunal find Rafael guilty, he
might spend the next few years or even the rest of his life working to benefit
the same government whose laws had imprisoned him.[2]

However, it was more likely that a guilty verdict would see Rafael locked in
a *collera*, or chain gang, and deported south to the capital of New Spain, Mexico City, and ultimately to the colony of Cuba, where local plantation owners

would put him to work harvesting sugarcane. Considering the difficult two-thousand-mile land and sea journey, the humid and disease-filled environment of Cuba, and the horrendous treatment prisoners faced on sugar plantations, deportation to Cuba was tantamount to a death sentence. Because of this, the Spanish usually reserved such punishment for Apache prisoners of war. Officials had come to realize that if they put Apaches to work in the mines of the Sierra Madre, there was a good chance the prisoners would escape, flee to their nearby homeland, and return to committing hostilities against the Spanish.[3]

It is likely that the local magistrate presiding over the tribunal saw deportation as a suitable punishment because Rafael had been born to an Apache mother. Spanish officials considered this problematic because according to nineteenth-century logic, Apaches had an "inherent barbarism" and a "natural inclination toward evil" that might manifest itself if given the opportunity. Making matters worse, Rafael had spent at least some of his early years as a member of an Apache *ranchería*, living a lifestyle that differed greatly from the Europeans and Hispanicized Indians who made their home in Guajoquilla. As many Spaniards of the time judged it, someone raised as an Apache "could not accept civilization" or peacefully live under Spanish rule. They certainly would not comply with a prison sentence in a local mine, and so it was best to ship them off to distant Cuba.[4]

In spite of what his accusers thought of him, by the time of the tribunal in October 1804, Rafael no longer resembled an Apache, or at least not the ones usually sent to Cuba as part of a collera. Indeed, by 1804, Rafael could easily pass as one of the tens of thousands of Hispanicized Indians who called northern New Spain home. He spoke Spanish well, wore European-style clothing, and worshipped the same Catholic god as the tribunal members. He may even have known how to read and write, something that few in Guajoquilla could claim.[5]

RAFAEL'S HISPANICIZATION owed to years of tutelage under Rafael Nevares, the chaplain of the Primera Compañía Volante, a cavalry unit stationed in Guajoquilla whose job was to track down Apaches whenever they raided nearby Spanish settlements. As chaplain, Nevares provided religious services for soldiers in the local *presidio*, the stone and adobe fortification at the center of Guajoquilla that served as the Primera Compañía Volante's home. Owing to the lack of educated clergymen on the frontier, Nevares also acted as the priest for the non-military settlers of Guajoquilla, performing mass and providing baptisms and funeral services in the small presidio chapel. However, Nevares saw himself as more than a soldier or priest in a remote frontier outpost; he was, as one historian would later describe him, "a man of piety, vision, and learning, with dreams he turned into reality."[6]

Nevares shared a dream that many men of the cloth had held since the Spanish arrived on the northern frontier: he wanted to convert an Apache to Christianity in the hopes that they might convince other Apaches to abandon their barbaric ways. Since the sixteenth century, belligerently Christian and aggressively self-assured Spanish missionaries had used gifts of European goods and promises of salvation to lure the Indians of the Sierra Madres—including Yaquis, Tepehuanes, Tarahumaras, Ópatas, and Pimas—into their churches to teach them Catholicism and the Spanish way of life. Although it took state funding and centuries of effort, by the time of Rafael's trial, most of these Indians had adopted at least some aspects of Christianity and European values and had come to accept Spanish rule.[7]

The fiercely independent Apaches were another matter. Unlike the Sierra Madre Indians, who were predominantly agricultural and sedentary before missionaries ever arrived in their villages, the Apaches were primarily hunter-gathers who rarely remained in one place for long. They were also efficient warriors. Since the adoption of the European horse, they had come to dominate the Southern Plains of North America, displacing rival tribes and creating a hunting, trading, and raiding network that at one point stretched from Louisiana to deep within the interior of New Spain. Indeed, by the middle of the seventeenth century, Spanish settlements in the Sierra Madre came under regular attack from Apaches seeking to steal European goods and livestock.[8]

Spain tried to send missionaries to end these raids and win the Apaches over to the Spanish way of life, as they had done with the Indians of the Sierra Madre, but the Apaches quickly rankled under the restrictions of the Catholic Church. Apache culture placed a greater emphasis on individual freedom than perhaps any other New World peoples, and the Apaches did not need the missionaries' gifts as much as other Indians considering that they could use their equestrian skills to raid Spanish settlements for needed goods. Because of this, Spanish missions built to cater to the Apaches remained empty and converts few.[9]

By the late eighteenth century, Spain had largely abandoned any hope of using religion to reign in the Apaches. Instead, government officials spent money on soldiers, like those of the Primera Compañía Volante, to defend existing settlements and bring war to the Apaches whenever they attacked. Even with Spain's technological advantages, campaigns were rarely effective. As one traveler described the problem with Apache raiding, "by the time the news of the disaster reaches a place where means of resistance or retribution are at hand, the Indians have put a safe distance between themselves and the smoking ruins, where relations may search for the corpses of their kindred."[10]

It is unclear how Rafael came to be under Nevares's care, as sources say only that "he lived from his earliest years in the Guajoquilla presidio," but he may have arrived as a prisoner of war. Beginning in the 1780s, it became official Spanish policy for soldiers to place Apache children they had captured in battle in the homes of prominent Spaniards and secular church leaders, so they could "raise them up and educate them Christianly." The hope was that if they got to the Apaches young enough, they "would be ignorant of their origin." Nevares may have taken Rafael in while the Primera Compañía Volante was on campaign, or soldiers escorting a chain gang from the frontier to Mexico City may have placed him in the chaplain's care. One such collera passed through Guajoquilla on January 21, 1789, with ninety-eight shackled Apache prisoners captured during recent campaigns. Soldiers distributed upward of twenty-five of this number to local Spanish families for them to raise. It is very possible that Nevares took possession of Rafael at this time or that he received him from one of the many other colleras that would pass through Guajoquilla in the 1780s and 1790s.[11]

The treatment Apache children received in their new homes varied. Despite Spanish laws banning Indian slavery, many adoptive families put Apache children to work and maintained them in servitude their entire lives, justifying their actions as necessary to keeping the Indian's savage nature in check. Others accepted Apache children as full members of their family and treated them as they would their own natural-born progeny.[12]

It is impossible to know to which end of this parental spectrum Nevares fell, but sources of the time say that the chaplain "with the greatest zeal and constancy tried to civilize [Rafael] and make him known to Jesus Christ." Evidence suggests that the chaplain taught Rafael the intricacies of the Spanish language, and he may have educated Rafael alongside other children in a public school that Nevares began running out of his home in 1795. Nevares also took Rafael on campaign with him and the soldiers of Guajoquilla, and if he were like other officers at Guajoquilla, he encouraged the adopted Apache to serve in the military. The chaplain spent so much time with Rafael that the people of Guajoquilla took to calling the young Apache "Rafaelillo," meaning "Little Rafael." He also came to be known as "El Indio Rafael," or "The Indian Rafael."[13]

Nevares was not alone in raising Rafael, as his brother Buenaventura Nevares and Buenaventura's wife Petra joined him in this endeavor. It was they who "were in charge of teaching him the Christian doctrine." Eventually, the Nevares family's efforts paid off and Rafael consented to baptism. This may have taken place in October 1800 when church records list Father Nevares as baptizing an "adult Apache" named José Francisco Rafael. It was common for converting Indians to adopt the first or last name of their caregivers as a sign of reverence.[14]

Other than this "adult" description and general assumptions that can be made based on physiological milestones, there is nothing to indicate how old Rafael was at the time of his baptism. In his history of Guajoquilla, Héctor M. Bernal Vázquez argued that Rafael was born in 1781, making him eighteen or nineteen years old in 1800. Bernal Vázquez based his assessment on unverifiable documents, so this age is questionable, but there is little doubt that Rafael had reached physical maturity by this time.[15]

Although few sources describe Rafael's appearance, those that do portray him as awe-inspiring and handsome. The most detailed contemporary description says he was "of normal build, beautiful face, aquiline nose, brown eyes." The use of "beautiful" and "aquiline nose" descriptors together is interesting considering that the "aquiline nose" modifier was commonly associated with Indians, and Spanish society often portrayed Indians as less desirable than Spaniards. This could speak to Rafael's attractiveness, his mystique, or both. Whatever the case, Nevares saw his handsome and intelligent Apache protégé as a model spokesman for the transformative power of Christ.[16]

THE PROCESS by which Rafael went from being Nevares's star pupil to standing before the tribunal accused of "providing intelligence to hostile Apaches" cannot be understood with certainty, but it likely involved the arrival of a different group of Apaches at Guajoquilla around the same time as Rafael's baptism. At the end of the eighteenth century, the Spanish implemented a period of aggressive campaigning in which they allied with the Apaches' Indian enemies the Comanches and conducted a brutal war intent on driving the Apaches into extinction or submission. With the Comanches pressuring from the north and east and the Spanish from the south and west, the Apaches found themselves crushed between two opposing forces. In one year alone, the Spanish killed some 328 Apaches and took another 365 prisoners. Because these numbers do not include Apaches killed or captured by Comanches, who could often be more ruthless than their Spanish allies, this number was certainly much higher. Indeed, over the course of the 1780s and 1790s, it is likely that the Spanish and Comanches collectively killed or captured thousands of Apaches.[17]

This led an increasing number of Apache bands to approach Spanish presidios asking for a cessation of hostilities. The Spanish were wary of such offers because they had attempted to make peace with the Apaches in the past, but history had taught them that these accords lasted only until the Apaches found the arrangement inconvenient. However, fighting Apaches was expensive and peace preferable, and so Spanish officials developed a plan wherein presidio commanders could authorize peace if the surrendering Apaches agreed to give up their nomadic ways and live adjacent to the presidio under the supervision of Spanish soldiers. Any *Apaches de paz* or *Apaches establecidos de paz*, as the Spanish would come to refer to them, who left the *establecimiento* area without the permission of the presidio commander would be treated as hostile, hunted down, and either killed or imprisoned, as would those found associating with Apaches who refused to make peace.[18]

In exchange for these concessions, the Spanish would protect Apaches de paz from the Comanches and would supply the Apaches with weekly rations of corn and beef to ensure that they no longer needed to hunt and raid for sustenance. Apache headmen and lesser chiefs, or *capitancillos*, would also receive textiles, tobacco, medals, alcohol, and occasionally firearms and gunpowder as gifts for their subservience. Unlike missions, there would be no requirement for the Apaches to convert to Catholicism or adopt Spanish language and customs. Apaches could continue to live in teepees or wikiups outside presidios, worship multiple gods, practice polygamy, wear little to no clothing, and otherwise engage in various supposedly hedonistic practices that the Spanish had forced other Indians to abandon when colonizing New Spain.[19]

As one Spanish official summarized this arrangement, "the Indians' crude and gross ways are to be tolerated and their impertinences overlooked despite the inconveniences they may cause. The Spaniards are to get to know the Apaches not only to draw them in but also to learn their secret intentions. Because it is of great interest for the Indians to remain in Spanish camps on the frontier and for others to join them, the officer in charge is given the special responsibility of carefully managing the Apaches' arrogant and delicate character." Indeed, outside of maintaining peace, the only thing the Spanish expected Apaches de paz to do was serve as scouts whenever Spanish soldiers went on campaign against Apaches who refused to enter establecimientos.[20]

Costumes Mexicains. Cacique Apache des Bords du Rio Colorado dans la Californie by Claudio Linati 1828. Apache dress differed from one band to the next, and owing to contact with the Spanish, Apaches often wore European-style clothing and carried firearms. Courtesy Amon Carter Museum of American Art.

At some point in 1800 or shortly before, thirteen Apaches would agree to these terms and settle at the Guajoquilla presidio. This included the Capitan-cillo Ysquiñe dit jane, two *gandules* (Apache warriors), two Apache women, seven children "older than 7," and one *criatura* (infant) under the age of seven. Not much is known about the origins of this group, but they were likely Mimbres Apaches, a subset of the modern Chiricahua Apache people who hailed from the Mimbres River area of what is today southern New Mexico. Although most who the Spanish referred to as Apaches spoke a derivation of Athabaskan and could claim a common ancestry, the Apaches were not a politically cohesive group and there could be significant cultural differences between Apaches in one geographical area and another. Prior to making peace, the Mimbres Apaches, or Mimbreños, tenaciously raided Spanish settlements throughout New Mexico and Nueva Vizcaya. One Spanish officer called the Mimbreños "daring," and noted that "in spite of the losses which they have suffered from our arms in punishment for their daring, they have not given up their ancient intrepidity."[21]

The Guajoquilla establecimiento was a much smaller community of Apaches than could be found at other establecimientos de paz. The presidio at Janos, for example, hosted 408 Apaches, El Norte 800, and the Carrizal presidio 254. Evidence suggests that the Apaches at the Guajoquilla had originally settled at the Carrizal establecimiento, but the officer in charge had reassigned them for either personal or logistical reasons. Sometimes presidio commanders moved Apaches to separate two warring rancherías and other times to lessen the resource drain on a single presidio. Perhaps most likely, Spanish officials sent the Mimbres Apaches to Guajoquilla so the Primera Compañía Volante could use them as auxiliaries when tracking hostile Apaches.[22]

RAFAEL'S UNDERSTANDING of both Spanish and the Apaches' Athabaskan language meant that he likely served as a translator and cultural liaison between the newly arrived Apaches and the soldiers of the Primera Compañía Volante. Considering that Apaches de paz had recently been raiding the Spanish them-selves, they made excellent auxiliaries when on campaign against those Apaches who refused to make peace. Establecimiento Apaches could identify common raiding trails, scout watering holes, read distant smoke signals, and otherwise track their cultural brethren better than Spanish soldiers. Translators allowed soldiers to make use of this knowledge, and they served as diplomats. Presidio commanders looked to translators to explain new policies, and Apaches de paz needed someone to speak for them if the Spanish failed to provide promised rations or otherwise disregarded the terms of the peace.[23]

Considering the importance of translators, Father Nevares may even have encouraged Rafael to serve in the position, believing that the Apaches de paz would see him as an example of what they could achieve if they accepted the Christian god into their lives. This is what happened with fellow Apache-turned-Christian, José Reyes Pozo. In 1779, Spanish forces captured Pozo when he was fourteen and placed him under the care of prominent Sonoran family, who raised the Apache and taught him Spanish and Catholicism. On reaching adulthood, Pozo became a translator for the Spanish military, and in 1785, he received assignment to the Bacoachi Presidio, soon to be the site of an establecimiento de paz.[24] Pozo's superiors felt of the incoming Apaches, "it would be opportune for them to see, meet and have contact with one of their own nation, [who had been] raised and was esteemed by our people, was employed as a soldier [and] would find it easy to change their impressions." The bet seemed to pay off, as the new Apaches soon came to revere Pozo for his intimate connection to the Spanish world, with its advanced technology that the Apaches did not fully understand.[25]

An increase in Apaches requesting baptism in 1801 and 1802 suggests that Guajoquilla Apaches de paz came to regard Rafael with a similar level of reverence, and as Nevares had hoped, they sought to emulate him by converting to Christianity. For example, in January 1802, Nevares baptized "adult Apache" José Antonio. This was almost certainly the same José Antonio who would later stand trial with Rafael for providing intelligence to hostile Apaches and who would join Rafael in his raids. Sources describe José Antonio as taller than Rafael but thin, with a "narrow face, normal nose and brown eyes" and a proclivity for wearing oversized shirts. Although legends sometimes portray José Antonio as Rafael's blood brother, this was probably not the case. Instead, he was likely one of the two gandules who arrived when Guajoquilla became home to an establecimiento.[26]

That same month, Nevares also baptized an Apache infant named Jesús María Rafael, and evidence suggests that the child was Rafael's son. Nothing is known about the boy's mother or how she and Rafael began a relationship, but she may have been the "adult apache woman" María Jesús Josefa, who Nevares baptized on Christmas Day, 1801. Considering that this was only a week before Jesús María's baptism (January 1, 1802), María Jesús Josefa may have sought her own baptism out of fear of losing her life during childbirth, as Apaches sometimes converted when close to death as means of hedging their bets to enter the Christian afterlife. Also speaking to the possibility that María Jesús died during childbirth, as well as the close link that Rafael shared with the Nevares family, is the fact that the mother and father would not be the one to care for Jesús María. Instead, Rafael Nevares's brother Buenaventura Nevares "purchased it to raise in his house and in order to confirm it." The influx of baptisms coupled with what appears to be an Apache voluntarily giving a child over to the Spanish to raise no doubt pleased Rafael Nevares, and the news almost certainly fed his dreams of being the instrument that would bring Christianity to the Apaches.[27]

UNFORTUNATELY FOR THESE DREAMS, the reality was that despite Nevares's "zeal and constancy," "he never received more than hope and promises" from Rafael or the other Apaches at Guajoquilla. It seems that since the arrival of the Apaches de paz, Rafael had found himself trapped between two vastly different worlds, each offering distinct advantages and disadvantages. Life with the Nevares family and the Spanish meant security, access to luxury goods, and the benefits of advanced agriculture, but it also meant restriction. The Catholic Church dictated that Rafael act a certain way, remain monogamous, attend church services, and humble himself before those he might not respect. The racist system Spain had implemented upon arriving in the New World also meant that no matter how much he excelled, Rafael's Apache ancestry dictated that he would never receive the same rights as Europeans.[28]

Life with the Apaches de paz, on the other hand, promised both danger and excitement. The loose legal restrictions of Apache culture might see Rafael die if he got into an argument with the wrong person, but the Apaches were much less judgmental when it came to social and religious matters. Even though the Spanish forbid them from leaving the area around Guajoquilla, the Apache way of life was much freer and closer to nature than living in a small adobe building in the center of town. The Apaches' looser mores also meant that merit and military prowess served as more of a determinative of status than heredity or upbringing, and all indications are that Rafael excelled on the battlefield.[29]

Speaking to this conclusion, by 1804, the establecimiento Apaches had come to refer to him as *Jasqueldatsil*. The meaning of this name is unclear, but it may stand for "one who stands above" or "one who is angry all the time." What is known is that Apaches reserved the "Jasque" modifier only for "those who have more than once given outstanding proof of their fitness and courage," indicating that Rafael had earned the respect of his peers, perhaps after having displayed daring while on campaign against hostile Apaches. With such praise, it makes sense that the more time Rafael spent with the Apaches de paz, the more he came to resent his years with Nevares and longed for a return to the life he had lived as a child.[30]

Rafael's counterpart, José Reyes Pozo, faced a similar mental struggle. "He could not sleep comfortably" within the confines of the Bacoachi presidio, and he failed to connect with his fellow soldiers on an emotional level. They treated him differently than they would Spaniards or other Hispanicized Indians and believed that his Apache ancestry would lead him to betray them one day. The Apaches de paz at Bacoachi, on the other hand, held no presumptions and embraced Pozo's dual nature as both a Spaniard and an Apache. Accordingly, Pozo spent more and more time with Bacoachi Apaches until he eventually determined that he wanted no part of the Spanish world. In 1790, the man who the Spanish hoped would convince the Apaches to turn Spaniard instead falsely claimed that the soldiers of Bacoachi were planning to massacre the Apaches de paz, encouraged the Apaches to break the peace with Spain, led his new family away from the presidio, and began to wage war against the same Spaniards who had raised him since he was fourteen.[31]

RAFAEL WOULD MAKE A SIMILAR CHOICE, although the circumstances of his decision are not as well documented as what happened with Pozo. Rafael's later actions suggest that while he was encouraging the Apaches de paz at Guajoquilla to undergo baptisms, he was also joining them in sneaking away from the presidio to conduct raids on nearby ranches for cattle and horses for personal use and trade. This was a common behavior among establecimiento Apaches and one that Spanish officials looked down on but tolerated to a degree. They understood that the rations they provided to Apaches de paz were often insufficient, and it benefitted the long-term peace to look the other way when Apaches stole a few head of livestock and harmed no one.[32]

It seems that Rafael conducted these clandestine raids with José Antonio and another Apache named Side, which may translate to "one with a scar." History would come to know Side by his nickname "El Chinche." "Chinche" roughly translates to "the biting one" in Spanish, and the term often refers to biting and stinging insects such as gnats and mosquitoes, but it is most used for lice. It is unclear if Chinche earned this name because he had a reputation for biting, if he were a pest, or if he was simply infested with lice. The latter would make sense, considering that lice were a constant problem for Apaches on the frontier. To rid themselves of the parasites, Apaches would often plaster their hair in a poultice made from yucca root, sit in a sweat lodge for long periods of time, groom one another for hours on end, or place bedding on anthills in the hopes ants would kill any hidden lice. As someone with the nickname Chinche might attest, these methods were not always successful in removing the unwanted pests. Chinche may also have earned his nickname based on his physical appearance. As opposed to the handsome Rafael and tall José Antonio, Chinche possessed a "low, fat, dark face, round, flat, black eyes, gray hair."[33]

Chinche was most likely the second of the two gandules listed on the 1800 Guajoquilla census, but one historian contends that he was a member of a different ranchería who befriended Rafael and José Antonio during one their excursions from the Guajoquilla presidio. Perhaps he was an Apache de paz from a different establecimiento who traded stolen livestock with Rafael and José Antonio. Chinche may also have been one of the "hostile Apaches" to whom the Spanish would accuse Rafael of "providing intelligence." Whatever the case, Chinche would find himself locked up beside Rafael and José Antonio and put on trial in October 1804.[34]

WITHOUT TRIBUNAL RECORDS, it is impossible to know the specific allegations Rafael and his two companions faced, but the most likely explanation is that Spanish officials caught them communicating or trading stolen livestock or horses with Apaches who refused to make peace with Spain. Although some presidio commanders might overlook indiscretions such as these, the commander of Guajoquilla, José María de la Riva, did not. A hardnosed and experienced Indian fighter, Riva saw trading or providing information to hostile Apaches as a betrayal of trust, believing that it undermined Spain's efforts to maintain peace. Just six years before, after hearing rumors that two Apaches de paz were providing information to hostiles, Riva remarked, "if the bad faith of both capitancillos and their communication with the enemies" turned out to be true, "they are to be pursued and attacked where they are found."[35]

The charges against Rafael, José Antonio, and Chinche might have been much more than just Riva wanting to set an example. Riva may have linked two recent deaths in Guajoquilla to Rafael. He might also have believed that Rafael and his companions were part of a conspiracy. In late summer 1804, rumors swirled throughout the frontier that Apaches de paz from multiple establecimientos were meeting in secret to plan a rebellion, and they planned to involve hostile Athabaskan groups in their conspiracy. There is little available information on this potential rebellion, and it may have been a product of a paranoid Spanish official's imagination. A lack of evidence would not have precluded accusations, and with Pozo's recent turn, rumor alone may have been enough for Riva to bring Rafael, José Antonio, and Chinche up on charges. Spanish officials would later admonish one presidio commander—who may or may not have been Riva "for anticipating an attack on his fortress by attacking the chiefs of the supposed conspiracy" before they had even done anything.[36]

Whether being proactive or reactive, Riva had Rafael, José Antonio, and Chinche placed in shackles and locked in the Guajoquilla presidio jail until a tribunal could determine their guilt. This greatly upset the Apaches considering that they understood that a guilty verdict would lead to deportation to Cuba. Over the years, a handful of Apaches had escaped colleras and returned to the frontier with descriptions of the long, disease-filled journeys to Veracruz spent shackled to other prisoners. Because no Apaches had returned to their homeland after reaching Cuba, imagination amplified the horrors that one faced on the island, leading many Apaches to determine that they would rather die than make the journey.[37]

In addition to mental suffering, Rafael, and especially José Antonio and Chinche, had to endure a justice procedure to which they were unfamiliar. As Apaches saw things, it was the responsibility of aggrieved parties to mete out punishment, not a government institution. If someone robbed, raped, killed, or attempted to kill another person, the victim or their family members could demand restitution from the person who committed the act. If the perpetrator refused to atone, provided insufficient payment for their crime, or if the aggrieved party were particularly angry, they could choose to harm or kill the offender as a means of "getting even." If the victims successfully enacted revenge, both parties might drop the matter, or the original perpetrator or their family might seek to avenge the act of revenge.[38]

As could be expected, such frontier justice often led to an expansion of bloodshed. For example, after an argument broke out during a heated game of hoop-and-pole, one Apache man stabbed another. This then led that man's family to attack the assaulter. Afterward, the assailant's family sought revenge, and before the day was out, at least twenty-two Apaches lay dead. However perpetually violent this process, it was one that Apaches understood, not the judicial system the Spanish had forced upon them.[39]

THE WAY IN WHICH the Spanish conducted judicial proceedings varied greatly from one location to another. Usually, however, provincial governors assigned an *alcalde mayor* to conduct a *sumaria* wherein the alcalde investigated charges, took witness testimony, and compiled evidence against the accused. This evidence would then be presented to some form of jury. Likely owing to his role as a translator for the soldiers at Guajoquilla, Rafael would stand before a tribunal made up of military officers and prominent soldiers. After this jury consulted evidence, they would hear from a governor-appointed legal defender whose job was to offer counterevidence and dispute witness testimonies. Once this was completed, the jury rendered their verdict and, if they found the defendant guilty, the local magistrate issued a sentence they felt suited the crime. There were no minimum or maximum sentences, so the accused might face light or harsh punishments based on the whims of the magistrate.[40]

Rafael's trial likely occurred in a similar manner to that of José María, a young Apache who had been raised by Spaniards "from his earliest youth" in the village of Santa Rosa in the neighboring province of Coahuila. In 1807, José María stood before a tribunal on charges that he had burglarized a house and stolen horses, clothing, and weapons. This was not the first time José María had faced criminal charges. He had gone before a tribunal on previous occasions, been found guilty, and received punishment.[41]

When José María's 1807 trial began, witness after witness testified that the young Apache was a well-known horse and weapon thief, and reports indicated that he had even stolen from the Spanish man who had raised him. A search of José María's personal trunk turned up several stolen items, confirming suspicions and sealing the youth's fate. As punishment, the local magistrate sent José María to Mexico City for rehabilitation and work detail. The decision relieved local leaders who worried that if José María had been found not guilty and freed, his Apache ancestry and "natural inclination towards evil" would lead him to become an apostate, join with hostile Apaches, and "become the worst pirate of the frontier."[42]

It is possible, especially considering that this trial took place three years after Rafael's, that the people of Santa Rosa concerns about José María came about because of what happened in the aftermath of Rafael's trial. Unlike the 1807 trial, the 1804 tribunal had "no thought of the future" when deliberating over Rafael and his cohorts' guilt. Instead, the jurors in Rafael, José Antonio, and Chinche's trial seem to have carefully considered the evidence and found

it lacking. They determined that the three were not guilty of the charges presented against them, and the local magistrate ordered the Apaches released
from their bonds.[43]

Four years in the future, a resident of the northern frontier would criticize
the tribunal members for their not guilty verdict, saying that the men "should
have feared this result, knowing that these barbarians are sons of vengeance."
Of course, this observer was operating with the benefit of hindsight. He knew
that the day after the tribunal found them not guilty, Rafael, José Antonio,
and Chinche would grab Rafael's child, leave Guajoquilla, and begin a war on
the Hispanic population of northern New Spain that would last for years.[44]

ACCORDING TO ONE contemporary newspaper account, Rafael "called to
arms to avenge the grievance" of having been locked in shackles and forced to
stand trial. The idea that someone would exact vengeance after being found
not guilty of a crime might seem illogical, but it makes sense considering
that Apaches viewed violence and revenge as necessary to maintaining social
order. It provided a form of "spiritual fulfillment" and a means of restoring
the "moral and psychological balance" to Apaches who felt they had been
wronged. As one anthropologist studying the Apaches in the early twentieth
century described it, "revenge is a burning issue for the Apaches and it haunts
his every thought until it has been fulfilled."[45]

While contemporary sources point to revenge as the prime motivator,
Rafael, José Antonio, and Chinche's choice to leave Guajoquilla may have
been a rational economic and material decision. The Spanish had recently
placed greater restrictions on the Apaches and reduced their rations, leading
many Apaches de paz to determine that "the conditions agreed to when they
came to seek peace have not been fulfilled, and their ration has dwindled in
violation of a pact that should have been observed solemnly as an example to
instill in them the proper notion of the honor and rectitude of the Spanish."
Why remain at Guajoquilla if the Spanish were not meeting their end of
the truce? They could better acquire the necessities of life through raiding,
and although this carried risk, their recent trial made clear that so did living
peacefully with the Spanish.[46]

There were also almost certainly personal reasons for Rafael leaving Guajoquilla and the Nevares family. Rafael, like the Apache Pozo, may have come
to realize that no matter how much he conformed to Spanish society, it would
not accept or trust him because of his ancestry. Individuals who transition from

one culture to another at young age, as Rafael would have after Nevares took him in as a child, sometimes experience "violent social reversions" and "psychic conflict," wherein they act out aggressively, completely reject their adopted culture, and return to that of their roots. Such "violent social reversions" are more pronounced when the adoptive culture is racist or bigoted, as Spanish society was toward Indians in the nineteenth century.[47]

For their part, the Spanish did not blame their policies, legal system, or social norms whenever adopted Indians returned to their native ways. Instead, to Spaniards, such behavior justified their racism. Although there were optimists like Father Nevares who believed that Apaches could become Spaniards, others believed that genetic or cultural factors precluded Apaches from ever adopting their way of life, even those taken in as children. One observer noted of young Apache males placed in the care of Spanish families, "boys as a rule, run away as soon as they have reached a certain age." Another went into greater detail, remarking, "the children are assigned to good masters, though scattered throughout the State, so as entirely removing them from tribal influences, they are treated with great humanity. But even after years of captivity, many of these Apache children, although brought up as privileged members of the family, will escape and flee to the mountains, such is their inherent barbarism."[48]

Some historians apply this inevitability argument to Rafael's decision to leave the Spanish world, albeit with greater nuance than someone from the nineteenth century. For example, historian Gildardo Contreras Palacios argues that instead of revolting for a specific reason, Rafael and José Antonio simply "could not accept civilization." Another speculated that Rafael left because he could not endure seeing his son raised like a Spaniard. Whether as sons of vengeance, economic opportunists, or inherent barbarians, Rafael, José Antonio, and Chinche forever abandoned their lives as Apaches de paz and became Apaches of war.[49]

CHAPTER TWO

The Rebel from Guajoquilla,
October 1804–April 1805

IN OCTOBER 1804, two soldiers from the Segunda Compañía Volante approached three *paisanos* and asked them if they had seen a group of Apaches de paz who had recently left the Guajoquilla Presidio. As the soldiers may have informed the paisanos, a term the Spanish used for the subsistence-level farmers and ranchers who made up most of the population of the northern frontier, the Apaches they sought had stolen horses from the sprawling eighty-seven-thousand-hectare Hacienda de Canutillo before taking twenty-two horses and mules from the neighboring Hacienda de Tierra Blanca. They had then raided the Hacienda del Torreón for more animals the following day. Perhaps most frightening, the Apaches had just killed three men traveling through Frijoles Gorge and stripped them of their clothes. If the paisanos could provide any information, the soldiers might be able to prevent a similar fate from befalling them. The leader of the three paisanos responded that they had seen no one and explained that he and his companions could be of no help because they were "coming from work and tired." With this, "the company sent them on their way."[1]

Only later, as the soldiers were riding off, would it dawn on them that they had just "encountered three Apaches dressed like paisanos." Rafael, José Antonio, and Chinche had killed the three men in the Frijoles Gorge and worn their clothes to fool the soldiers. Although the revelation came too late for the soldiers to confront the Apaches, they reported what had happened to José María de la Riva at Guajoquilla. Riva asked the soldiers to be more vigilant in the future, noting "the measures taken to persecute the enemies have been very good, but in war there is nothing worse than carelessness and confidence."[2]

The encounter with the soldiers of the Segunda Compañía Volante would be the first known instance of Rafael using a disguise and his knowledge of

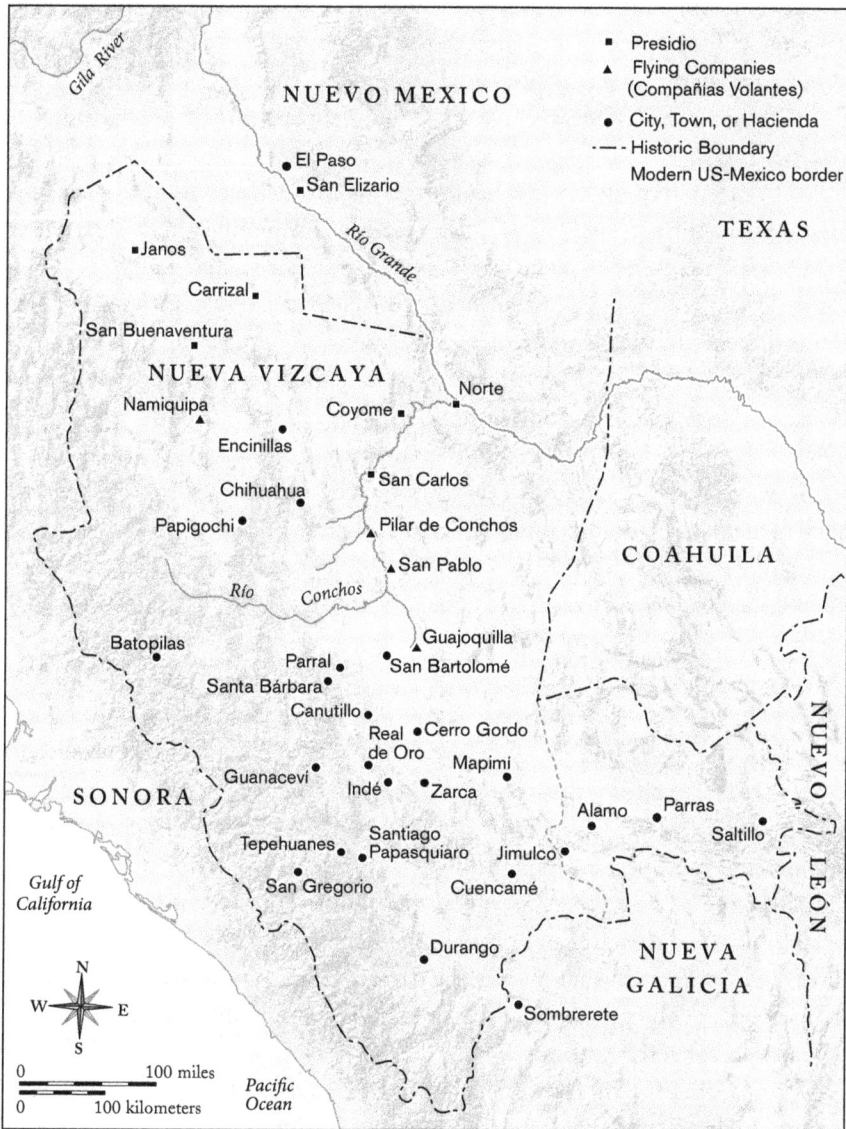

Map of Nueva Vizcaya based on a 1792 map by Juan de Pagazaurtundua. The map encompasses all areas Rafael is known to have operated. Place names and jurisdictional boundaries vary across sources and many locations have different names than they do today. Map by Ben Pease, cartographer.

Spanish language and customs to evade capture, but it would not be the last. As the following months and years would demonstrate, Rafael would become a master at adopting new identities to take advantage of the "carelessness and confidence" of the Spanish military. He would also employ deception to profit from the ignorance of the average settler on New Spain's northern frontier.[3]

RAFAEL AND HIS BAND had begun raiding on October 16, 1804, the day after their acquittal. Their first stop after leaving Guajoquilla was the Hacienda del Canutillo and the Hacienda de Tierra Blanca where they stole horses and mules. They likely sought the animals out of necessity—horses would allow them to better escape any Spanish patrols sent out after them, mules could carry cargo, and both were a food source—but also as tradable commodities. As Rafael, José Antonio, and Chinche almost certainly knew from previous experience rustling, there were many Spanish ranchers in northern New Spain who "were always eager to enhance their own herds and happy to swap items such as blankets, hats and clothing, coffee, tobacco, kettles and pots and pans, and salt" for stolen animals. Rafael's band could also trade horses and mules to hostile Apaches or those on establecimientos willing to engage in illegal commerce.[4]

In this way, Rafael and his companions adopted the identity of rustlers, or *abiegos*. In the late eighteenth and early nineteenth century, northern New Spain was home to innumerable abiego *quadrillas* or "gangs" who lived in the countryside and either stole directly from local ranchers or served as cultural middlemen between Apaches and Spaniards willing to trade in contraband. Disaffected mestizos, escaped criminals, deserters, and apostate missionary Indians often made up these abiego gangs, but members also included former establecimiento Apaches and other semi-nomadic Indians who had lived on the fringes of Spanish society. For this reason, Spanish officials often referred to members of abiego gangs as "Apaches" even though many abiegos had no Athabaskan ancestry.[5]

When Captain Riva first learned about the raids on Canutillo and Tierra Blanca, he dispatched two-man patrols from the Primera, Segunda, and Quarta Compañías volantes to investigate, likely assuming unidentified abiegos or hostile Apaches had stolen the animals. He would learn the true identity of the perpetrators when on October 18, a group of these soldiers found two gravely injured boys who informed them that they had been saying their evening prayers the previous night when three riders approached. The boys, perhaps having lived or worked in Guajoquilla, recognized the men as "the three Apaches who were established in peace at the presidio." Rafael and his companions met this acknowledgment by stabbing the two boys with their lances and leaving them for dead, and indeed one of the boys would die shortly after providing the soldiers with information. The soldiers sent the news to Captain Riva, who then warned local civic and military officials to be on the watch for three Apaches.[6]

Having worked with the Primera Compañía Volante, Rafael recognized that Spanish soldiers would be after him, and it was almost certainly for this reason that his band killed the three paisanos in Frijoles Gorge and took their clothes. There are no records of what Rafael wore when he left Guajoquilla, but traditionally Apaches adorned themselves in sleeveless, close-fitting deer-leather vests and leggings. However, having been raised by Rafael Nevares and with the Apaches de paz having acquired clothing as gifts or through trade, it is probable that the band wore a mixture of European and Indian garments. Whatever their dress, it was likely distinctive and recognizable not only to soldiers, but also locals as being something that Apaches might wear. As the two soldiers from the Segunda Compañía Volante discovered, the drab wool or cotton clothing stolen from the three paisanos made Rafael's band unidentifiable to anyone who did not know them personally.[7]

Although the new disguises fooled the two-man patrol from the Segunda Compañía Volante, the Apaches would not be as lucky when approached by Sergeant José Báro and a soldier from the Quarta Compañía Volante on October 22, 1804. Although the details of what happened in this encounter are unavailable, it seems that the twenty-four-year-old Báro saw through the paisano disguises, recognized Rafael, and a battle ensued. Rafael's band managed to kill Báro's partner in the melee, but Báro survived and fought back, eventually forcing the Apaches to flee. Rafael managed to "carry off the firearms and saddled horse of the dead soldier" but left behind sixteen animals stolen in their recent raids. Báro also captured Rafael's son.[8]

Báro brought the boy, the body of the fallen soldier, and the recovered animals to the nearby San Pablo Presidio, where he reported what had happened to the "primer alferez" or first lieutenant of the Quarta Compañía Volante, Pedro Ruiz de Larramendi. Larramendi was a well-experienced Indian fighter who had once killed a Lipan Apache with his bare hands. He had also worked with Apache auxiliaries and knew the methods Rafael's band would use to evade detection. After sending a report to his superiors informing them of

Báro's encounter, Larramendi gathered some of his men, and they set off to avenge their fallen comrade. Although it is unclear what happened to Rafael's son at this time, officials likely returned him to the custody of his adopted parents, the Nevareses.[9]

On October 24, Larramendi tracked the Apaches to the Ojuelos Ranch where he discovered that Rafael's band had injured, but not killed, twelve and fifteen-year-old girls. The soldiers then traveled to the Sierra de la Tinaja where they found the body of a local ranch owner and his ten-year-old son. On approaching the ranch house, they discovered that the ranch matriarch and her three daughters were still alive. When Larramendi asked the woman what happened, she told him that it was Rafael who had lanced her husband and son. The band had then approached the woman and her three daughters, but "speaking in Castilian, they told her that they did not want to kill her and instructed her: march into your house with your three children." Unable to locate the Apaches, Larramendi and his men continued to search the surrounding countryside over the following days. Unfortunately for them, they would soon learn that Rafael had uncovered a new method of evading Spanish forces.[10]

IN NOVEMBER 1804, what appeared to be three presidio soldiers approached a group of paisanos traveling near Guajoquilla. The paisanos recognized the men as soldiers because of their distinct uniforms. As envisioned by Spanish bureaucrats, presidio soldiers were supposed to be outfitted in blue trousers of shag or cloth. They would also wear a blue, long-sleeve shirt, over which would be worn a thick quilted leather vest made of seven buckskins. The vest was meant to replace the hot, unwieldy steel armor worn by Spaniards when they first reached northern New Spain while still providing sufficient protection from arrows fired by mounted Indians. By 1804, the hide vests had become so commonplace that soldiers on the frontier were commonly known as "*cueras*," or leather jackets. Soldiers also usually wore "a round hat with a narrow brim and crimson band on the crown." Officers distinguished themselves with gold patches on their collars.[11]

It is unclear if the three men's uniforms met this standard, but it would not matter if they did, as uniforms rarely looked like they were supposed to on the frontier. Soldiers usually purchased their own uniforms, and owing to irregular pay, distance from manufacturing centers, and corrupt shopkeepers who overcharged because they held a local monopoly on textiles, few on the frontier could afford to meet regulatory standards. This meant that soldiers

Drawing of a presidio soldier as envisioned by Ramón de Murillo circa 1804.
Owing to poor conditions on the frontier, soldier uniforms rarely met standards.
Original located in the Archivo de Indias, Seville, Spain, Sección Mapas y Planos,
Uniformes nos 57.

often went about hatless, with off-color shirts, irregular vests, and pants that
were ripped beyond repair. Officers had to tolerate such unseemliness because
there were often more soldiers on the northern frontier than complete uniform sets. As one observer noted, "there is much tolerance of dressing out of
uniform, such that with the impropriety of their dress they end up looking
ridiculous." Therefore, even if the paisanos noticed that the three men were
wearing incomplete or dirty uniforms, it would not have seemed out of place.[12]

Nor would the paisanos have had any reason to question the three soldiers'
dark skin. During the early colonial period, Spain had forbidden Indians or
mestizos, those of mixed-race ancestry, to serve in the military, preferring to
employ only those exclusively of European ancestry. This policy stemmed from
long-held racist beliefs about the intellectual capacity of non-whites. It also

came from a fear that if they were to provide Indians and those of mixed-race ancestry with firearms, they would turn them on the Spanish, a legitimate concern considering the oppression that these groups had faced under Spain. An increase in the number of children born to interracial couplings, the onset of the Apache wars, and the realities of life on the frontier forced Spain to reassess its policies in the eighteenth century. With few full-blooded Europeans willing to serve, the Spanish increased the number of mestizos in the ranks of the military. Owing to the ever-difficult situation with the Apaches, Spain had even formed two companies of Hispanicized Ópata Indians, and one company made up of Pimas. Therefore, the sight of dark-skinned soldiers would not have seemed strange to the paisanos.[13]

If, for whatever reason, the paisanos suspected that the three soldiers were not who they appeared to be, their suspicions would have been alleviated when the leader of the soldiers asked them in fluent Spanish if they had heard anything about a group of Apaches who had just killed two men and stolen their horses near the Guanaseví River. Wanting to be helpful, the paisanos offered up everything they knew, including the direction they had seen a different group of Spanish soldiers traveling in pursuit of the Apaches. In fact, the only thing that offered the paisanos pause was when the three men set off in the opposite direction after learning which way their fellow soldiers had gone.[14]

Only later would the paisanos learn that the "soldiers" they had spoken to were Rafael, José Antonio, and Chinche. They were also the same Apaches who had just killed the two men near the Guanaseví River, and their "questions were stratagems they used to learn the course taken by the troops and flee from an encounter with them." Unbeknownst to Larramendi or any of the other Spaniards pursuing them, Rafael's band had either taken uniforms when they left Guajoquilla or found uniforms among the items they had recovered from the soldier they killed at the end of October.[15]

THE TWO MEN ON THE GUANASEVÍ were not the only victims of Rafael's band in November 1804, nor were the paisanos the only ones to be fooled by the Apaches' new disguises. That same month a young man, or *muchacho*, as he is described in sources, named José Onofre was walking near Ronsevalles when the three Apaches, likely posing as soldiers, approached him and asked him what he knew about the surrounding countryside. Although Onofre's response has been lost to time, it seems that Rafael found whatever the young man said to be valuable because the Apaches kidnapped Onofre and took him with them on their next raid at a set of ranches near the villa of San Miguel de Bocas, where they captured some forty head of cattle.[16]

Shortly thereafter, Rafael's band came across two traders and attempted to rob them. The traders resisted and tried to fend off the Apaches, but ultimately lost their lives. However, the skirmish provided enough of a distraction for Onofre to escape and make his way to a nearby encampment of soldiers, who set off to locate the Apaches and recover the stolen cattle.[17]

Like mules and horses, cattle could be dealt to contraband traders, although they did not command as high of a price as mules or horses. For this reason, Apaches "center their interest on horses, mules, and burros; but if they cannot have these animals, they take whatever cattle they come across." Apaches also disliked dealing with cattle because they were often difficult to round up, especially in remote areas of northern New Spain where cows went without exposure to humans for much of their lives. Soldiers also found it easier to track stolen cattle than horses or mules, as cows left deep indentations in the soil, trampled brush, and broke branches off trees when they passed. Additionally, an experienced tracker could tell what direction a herd was heading by the smell in the air or by following distinctive signs left by pregnant cattle. Making matters worse for would-be rustlers, cattle get stuck in mud, wander away from trails, stampede at inopportune times, and otherwise move slower than horses and mules.[18]

For these reasons, Corporal José Moreno and a group of soldiers, acting on Onofre's information, were able to follow Rafael's trail into a canyon in the nearby Tularillo Mountains. The Apaches recognized that they were being pursued and decided to kill their cattle. As Spanish officer Manuel Merino y Moreno wrote in 1804, when Apaches "know that superior forces are coming after them, they kill everything they are driving and escape on the best mounts." Such measures hastened escape and disincentivized pursuit by taking away the financial incentive to push farther. Although this could be accomplished by simply leaving the cattle behind, Apaches took a more lethal approach out of spite and an understanding of ownership that differed greatly from the Spaniards. In general, Apaches saw stealing as an acceptable transfer of property from one person to another and believing that a stolen animal was now their rightful property, they did not want the original owner or anyone else to have what they felt was theirs.[19]

The slaughtering of their cattle may have been a measure to not only hasten their escape and disincentivize pursuit, but also a means to physically block Moreno. A traveler passing through the region three years after these events heard a story about a group of soldiers who pursued Apaches into a canyon that was so narrow it was impossible for two riders to ride abreast. The passage was made even more difficult because the Apaches had strategically killed some of their cattle in one of the narrowest parts of the canyon. The carcasses not only created a physical barrier, but an olfactory one as the soldiers' horses refused to go near the decaying animals, making it impossible for the soldiers to proceed any farther. Whether or not this was the same instance, Moreno called off the pursuit and returned the handful of surviving animals he was able to recover to their owners.[20]

MORE THAN A MONTH LATER, on December 23, 1804, Rafael and his band reached Ojo Caliente, a clear, warm spring located some twenty-five miles southeast of the village of Carrizal, itself some one hundred miles south of El Paso. Outside of being home to Presidio de San Francisco de Conchos, Carrizal was a relatively unimportant outpost, serving only as a stopover for traders traveling to and from New Mexico. By extension, the Ojo Caliente was an even more unimportant stopover in reaching this stopover, and few visited the location except to water their horses before crossing the flat, dry Chihuahua Desert to the north. Certainly no one came to the Ojo Caliente to bathe. Although purported to be the perfect temperature, the spring had a "great number of leeches in it, some of which are of gigantic size, swimming and crawling through it."[21]

The leeches and Rafael's band were joined that day by a group of Mimbres Apaches from the establecimiento de paz at the Carrizal Presidio. Little is known about this particular group of Mimbreños, but they likely had a previous relationship with Rafael, or at least José Antonio or Chinche. Indeed, Spanish records indicate that the Apaches de paz who settled at Guajoquilla had previously made their home at the Carrizal establecimiento.[22]

This preexisting relationship may have served as the impetus for the December 23, 1804, meeting at Ojo Caliente, as Rafael would later claim that certain "Apaches de paz, established in Carrizal . . . protected and assisted him." It was common for establecimiento Apaches to exchange rations and gifts they had received at the presidio—such as tobacco, guns, and firearms—for cattle, mules, and horses that unincorporated Apaches or abiegos had stolen from Spanish ranches. The rustlers received items they could not steal or make themselves, and the establecimiento Apaches supplemented their diet or acquired better mounts than the ones available at the presidio. Apaches de paz could even turn in the horses and livestock that they received in these exchanges to Spanish authorities, pretending that they had forcibly taken the animals from the rustlers in the hopes of receiving rewards for their efforts.[23]

Considering these benefits and that Spanish officials had already accused the Carrizal Apaches of exchanging contraband earlier in 1804, the idea that the meeting at the Ojo Caliente was for trade makes sense, but the leader of the Mimbreños, a capitancillo named Ultin, would later dispute Rafael's account of events. Instead, Ultin claimed that he had received permission from the commander of the Carrizal presidio, Lieutenant Colonel Alberto Maynez, to go hunting, and after arriving in the area of Ojo Caliente "the three enemy Apaches attacked them . . . and carried off Ultin's wife as a captive."[24]

At least some of Ultin's story is true. As part of their peace agreement with Spain, establecimiento Apaches often requested permission from presidio commanders to leave the location around the presidio to go hunting. Unless the commanders suspected that the Apaches would use the time to raid or conduct illegal trade, they usually approved these requests and issued a passport for ten to twenty days that the Apaches could present to Spanish patrols they came across. Although the Spanish suspected the Carrizal Apaches of engaging in illegal trade, Maynez had indeed issued a passport to Ultin, perhaps hoping that by hunting, the Apaches could supplement their rations. It is also plausible that Rafael, José Antonio, and Chinche would attack fellow Apaches. It was common for different Apache bands and rancherías to go to war with one another, and the Guajoquilla Apaches's previous history with the Apaches at Carrizal might indicate animosity between the two groups.[25]

Further speaking to Ultin's version of events is the fact that he would immediately return to Carrizal and report having encountered "the rebels from Guajoquilla" to Lieutenant Colonel Maynez. Ultin would also ask for permission to take some of his warriors, chase down Rafael, and recover his wife. Maynez denied the request. It is unclear why he did so but considering that the Apaches at Carrizal were already under suspicion of illegal trade, he may have believed that Ultin was fabricating his story and had instead been meeting with Rafael to receive illegal goods.[26]

Whether the meeting took place for trade or Rafael happened upon the Carrizal Apaches at Ojo Caliente and decided to attack them will remain a mystery, but there is no question that Rafael left Ojo Caliente with one of Ultin's wives. The woman goes unnamed, but Spanish sources refer to her as "La India," the first of multiple members of Rafael's gang who would bear this name.[27]

Following the capture of La India, Rafael's band made camp at the peak of Cerro Cabeza de Oso for the next month. The choice of the Cerro Cabeza de Oso was appropriate, considering that Apaches "always occupy the steepest canyons in the mountains, surrounded by the most difficult passes for approaching the site where they are located. That site is chosen, as a general rule, adjacent to the greatest heights in order to command the surrounding valleys and plains." As the highest peak in the area, Cerro Cabeza de Oso certainly fit these parameters. There were a limited number of paths to reach the peak so lookouts could keep watch for approaching patrols, and the jagged canyons surrounded the mountain would slow an enemy's ascent and block the light of campfires to only those within the enclosed area. The Cerro Cabeza de Oso also towered over the neighboring Hacienda del Canutillo and the settlement of Las Nieves, meaning it was near to potential raiding targets.[28]

ON FEBRUARY 14, after more than a month with no news on Rafael, Spanish officials received word that three Indian men and an Indian woman raided the Hacieda de Cacaría and the Estancia de Garate. The rustlers then proceeded to the Rancho de Chupaderos where they killed eight workers and severely injured a woman. As they would later learn from this sole survivor, the perpetrators were Rafael and his band. It is difficult to comprehend how Rafael's band could overpower and kill a group twice their size, but, considering that many haciendas and *ranchos* were thousands of acres in size or more, they likely did not attack the workers all at once. It is also likely that the paisanos were unarmed, considering that firearms were a luxury that few in northern New Spain could afford.[29]

Even if the workers were armed, they may not have had a chance to use their weapons owing to a strategy that Rafael and his companions would employ many times. Wearing either soldier uniforms or local dress, the Apaches would ride up to potential victims, usually "shepherds and poor people of the field" and "greet them submissively and courteously." Rafael would then dismount his horse and offer his hand for a handshake. Local custom required that such greetings be met in kind, and when this happened, Rafael grabbed the extended appendage and immobilized his target. This allowed José Antonio and Chinche to pull out their lances and drive them through the victim. As one observer noted, "they were able to do this even with groups of three or more owing to the irresolution and surprise of the technique and the lightning speed with which they killed."[30]

The following day, February 15, don Nicolás Corral and a *mozo*, a term meaning servant or young boy, would fall victim to this practice when they were approached by "four men dressed as soldiers" while traveling on the road from San Gerónimo to La Taya. The leader of the soldiers—actually Rafael—called to the two men in Spanish to speak with them and after they complied, the "soldiers" lanced and killed Corral, but the young mozo managed to escape. A few days later in the Escondida Gorge, Rafael's band found and killed Manuel Fernández as he was out making charcoal. They also killed Juan José Herrera, who was in the area herding livestock.[31]

News of the new spate of attacks reached the intendant governor of Durango, Brigadier General Bernardo Bonavía, who sent Ensign Lucas Valenzuela and men from the Segunda Compañía Volante to investigate the crimes and determine if Rafael, José Antonio, and Chinche were responsible. Valenzuela was a trusted and well-respected veteran soldier who had served in the military for thirty-three years. A mestizo native of nearby San Juan del Río in what is today central Durango, Valenzuela had risen through the enlisted ranks due to his "well-known" valor, "good" conduct, and "significant" dedication before receiving an officer's commission. This set him apart from many officers on the frontier, who had earned their ranks through wealth and family connections. Also, unlike most officers, Valenzuela lacked a formal education, and, according to service records "he did not know how to write," evidenced by the incongruous nature of his signature.[32]

During his career, Valenzuela had conducted thirty campaigns against enemy Apaches, personally killing some thirty Apaches in the process. He had also recovered more than one thousand animals and rescued at least ten captives from hostile Apaches. Perhaps most important to Bonavía and the Spanish officials who wanted to see Rafael stopped, Valenzuela had previously served in the Primera Compañía Volante, and records show him traveling with three Apache auxiliaries in Guajoquilla in 1800. Considering how few Apaches resided at Guajoquilla, it is very possible that these auxiliaries were Rafael, José Antonio, and Chinche. Perhaps Bonavía chose Valenzuela because he recognized that the veteran soldier would know the habits of Rafael's band better than anyone else.[33]

When Valenzuela reached the sites of the February 14 and 15 attacks, he located the mozo and the female survivor from the Rancho de Chupaderos and asked them about their experiences. The descriptions convinced Valenzuela that it had indeed been Rafael and his band who had committed the crimes, but the survivors also told him something that he did not expect to hear: the Apache woman, who was supposed to be a captive, had participated in the assault. Indeed, the injured woman from Chupaderos reported to Valenzuela that "La India was the one who attacked her, stabbing her numerous times with her lance without stopping. She left only when the injured woman was bleeding out, but not before taking her rosary and removing her shawl and petticoat." The mozo's report of "four men dressed as soldiers," seemed to confirm the Indian woman's involvement.[34]

Why would Ultin's wife participate in the attacks? There are many possible explanations, but the most likely one is that she lanced the woman on Rafael's orders as part of an initiation ceremony. Apaches sometimes required recent captives to kill enemies to prove their loyalty to the band. Often this meant that during raids, the main members of the band would kill the major threats, usually adult men, but leave "women and children, who were always reserved until the last because they could do no harm to the savages." The Apaches would then order their captives to execute the helpless victims.[35]

It seems that at this point, the Spanish realized that Rafael would continue to be a problem, because on February 24, 1805, Valenzuela received a promotion to lieutenant of the Segunda Compañía Volante, and he took command of a contingent of soldiers whose primary assignment was to capture or kill Rafael. Officials assigned soldiers from other flying companies to hunt down Rafael as well, some of whom would spend years searching for the band as their primary duty. Although it is difficult to keep track of exactly how many soldiers received this assignment at a given time, at one point, Rafael kept "about 300 Spanish dragoons continually employed."[36]

EITHER RECOGNIZING THAT THEIR DISGUISES were compromised or spooked by Valenzuela's pursuit, Rafael's band made no attacks until March 18, when they robbed three "Christians" traveling near Piedras Azules, stripped them of their possessions and clothes, but otherwise left them unharmed. It is unclear why Rafael's band chose to spare this particular group, but as one observer remarked, Apaches "are accustomed to spare the lives of those who fall unresistingly into their hands. But such captives are stripped, as are the slain, and their clothing distributed amongst the Apaches." Apaches sometimes freed those who provided what they want without hesitation, reserving death only for those who resisted.[37]

Likely wearing their newly acquired clothes as a disguise, the band then raided the Embudo Ranch, where they captured livestock and took an unnamed child as a captive. He rode with the band for the next six days. Rafael then returned to attack the Hacienda del Canutillo on the morning of March 25, 1805, taking ten animals, three saddles, and other "spoils and pillage." Once again, witnesses would say that Ultin's wife participated in the raid, stealing several garments. The Apaches also took two additional captives, Ignacio Mata and thirteen-year-old José Salvador Bueno Laicano.[38]

Why would the Apaches take Mata, Laicano, and the unnamed child as captives? Unlike Ultin's wife, who as an Apache had likely played a role in the raiding economy in the past, the new captives were Spanish or Hispanicized Indians who might be a hinderance to raiding. Spanish officials suspected that Rafael wanted to use the captives' knowledge of nearby towns and the habits of townspeople to better raid and avoid soldiers. As the Spanish saw it, Rafael specifically chose poor male Indian and mestizo children and teenagers because they were often disaffected with the system and susceptible to influence. If these boys happened to be *ladinos*, meaning those who had grown to resent Christianity and Spanish rule, all the better. The Spanish believed that it would not take much for these ladinos to become willing participants in the Apaches' crimes, and before long they would even adopt their "barbarous customs."[39]

The Spanish were almost certainly correct in their assessment, at least concerning Rafael's motivation for capturing the boys. It was common for Apaches to take young captives to learn more about an area so that the Apaches could raid more efficiently and safely. They preferred younger individuals because they had looser tongues and were less likely to be dangerous. For this reason, the Apaches rarely took adult men as hostages, often killing them on the spot. They also killed younger captives who refused to provide information. Those who proved valuable might be released unharmed or even adopted into the tribe. Indeed, this is likely what happened with Rafael's father. Apaches captured him from a Hispanicized Indian settlement at a young age and took him in as their own.[40]

UNFORTUNATELY FOR THE APACHES, new captives lacked their captors' riding skills, did not have the same ability to disguise their tracks, and would therefore slow down escape after raids. Whether it was the presence of captives, the livestock they had captured, or the added weight of the loot taken in the past month, Corporal Juan Leal was able to pick up the Apaches' trail and follow it to their Sierra Cabeza del Oso hideout, where a fight broke out on March 25.[41]

Although Leal did not provide specifics of the battle when later reporting on the incident, it may have been the same offhand encounter described by a traveler who later passed through the region. As he relayed things, "in another instance a small smoke was discovered on the prairie; three poor savages were surrounded by 100 dragoons and ordered to lay down their arms; they smiled at the officer's demand, and asked him if he could suppose that men who had arms in their hands would ever consent to become slaves. The officer, being loath to kill them, held a conference for an hour; when, finding that his threats had as little effect as his entreaties, he ordered his men to attack them at a distance, keeping out of the reach of their arrows, and firing at them with their carabines, which they did, the Indians never ceasing to resist as long as life remained."[42]

As in this story, the Spanish soldiers fired at the Apaches for hours, at one point sending a bullet through Rafael's leg. The battle continued until three o'clock in the afternoon, at which point Rafael, José Antonio, and Chinche retreated, an impressive feat considering the forces mounted against them and Rafael's injury. Leal was able to recover two of the male captives, but the Apaches took José Salvador Bueno Laicano with them. The boy may even have voluntarily left with the Apaches, as this is what happened with Ultin's wife. During the battle Leal attempted to rescue the woman, but she rebutted the Spanish officer, mounted a red horse, and rode off with Rafael. In addition to the two captives who Leal was able to recover, the Apaches left behind nine animals, two firearms, and two lances.[43]

In the month following his March 25 battle with Leal at Cabeza de Oso, there would only be three sightings of Rafael. On April 23, Rafael and his companions attacked the Villela Ranch, where they killed a muchacho and took off with two horses. Shortly thereafter, a vaquero from the Hacienda de Salasces claimed to see an Apache with a boy, likely Laicano, riding behind him on the horse's haunches in the Sierra de Armoloya. Soldier Pedro Barraza also saw a small group being led by a man riding with a boy on his horse's haunches as he was traveling through a mountain pass on the outskirts of Aguaje de Terrazas. Barraza was off duty due to illness, but on recognizing Rafael, he quickly drew his firearm and trained it on the Apache. Rafael drew his own weapon and aimed it at Barraza. The two men faced off with each other until their horses passed and each went their own way. At some point in April, Rafael released Laicano or the boy made his escape and returned to the Hacienda del Canutillo.[44]

CHAPTER THREE

The Barbarian Enemy,
April 1805–January 1806

R AFAEL'S MULTIPLE ESCAPES from Spanish forces frustrated Commandant General Nemesio Salcedo. As commandant general, Salcedo was the preeminent authority in the Internal Provinces, an area made up of the provinces of Texas, Coahuila, New Mexico, and Nueva Vizcaya, the latter province further subdivided into the intendencies of Chihuahua, Durango, and Sonora. Spain had created the commandant general's office and politically separated the Internal Provinces from New Spain in 1776 as a measure to better deal with the Apaches and Comanches. The thinking was that by placing a local military commander in charge of maintaining presidios, organizing campaigns against hostile Indians, and overseeing missionary efforts, it would be much more efficient and cost effective than having a viceroy in distant Mexico City perform these duties.[1]

The implementation of the commandant general's office had met with mixed results, as there was frequent turnover of the position and policies could vary greatly from one individual to the next. One commandant general wanted "drunkenness, tobacco, and cards to be the gods of the Apaches" and plied the Indians with liquor, cigars, dice, and playing cards, thinking that if the Apaches gave into vice, it would both weaken their ability to make war and force them to become reliant on the Spanish to provide the substances they needed to get their fix. Instead, gambling and substance abuse became "the first milk they sucked from the Christians," and the policy undermined a subsequent commandant general's efforts to turn Apaches into sedentary, law-abiding Catholics. Another commandant general saw his efforts to settle Apaches at presidios damaged when the following commandant general ordered his soldiers to attack all Apaches, even those who were attempting to make peace with the Spanish. Thankfully for Salcedo, the commandant general who preceded him, Pedro de Nava, had served in the office for more than ten years, and had therefore brought some stability to the position.[2]

Still, lingering questions remained over the extent of a commandant general's power when Salcedo took over as commandant general in 1802. The commandant general had to obey edicts from the king, and he relied on the viceroy of New Spain for supplies and assistance, but it was unclear if viceroys could override a commandant general's orders. There were also jurisdictional issues. If an uprising happened in viceroy-controlled Zacatecas, Spanish law did not clarify if the commandant general was obligated to send soldiers from neighboring Nueva Vizcaya to put it down. Nor was it explained how

Map of the Internal Provinces by Zebulon Montgomery Pike. Nemesio Salcedo was the preeminent military authority over an area that included what is today Texas, Coahuila, Nuevo León, New Mexico, Chihuahua, Durango, Sonora, and Sinaloa. Library of Congress.

Salcedo was supposed to approach international matters. Wars in Europe and changes in North America meant that the commandant general had to watch for possible invasions from Britain, France, and the United States, but it was unclear if the commandant general could negotiate with these foreign powers or if he were just there to defend in case of war.[3]

The United States was a particular source of anxiety for Salcedo considering that in 1803, the nation had purchased the Louisiana Territory from France, who had acquired Louisiana from Spain only three years before. This placed the Internal Provinces against a burgeoning expansionist power with citizens who eyed the mineral wealth of New Spain with envy. Not only did the United States have a population that doubled roughly every twenty years, but its president, Thomas Jefferson, believed that the Louisiana Purchase included the province of Texas, and it appeared that he might go to war to uphold this claim. This forced Commandant General Salcedo to redeploy some six hundred soldiers to Texas, including men from the Segunda Compañía Volante of San Carlos de Parras who might otherwise have been searching for Rafael. In August 1804, Salcedo also had to send out soldiers to arrest a group of Americans under a "Captain Merry" who were traveling west on the Missouri River. The leaders of the expedition, Meriwether Lewis and his co-captain William Clark, claimed they were making the journey for science, but Salcedo suspected them to be spies or a vanguard for an American invasion.[4]

SALCEDO'S PROBLEMS went further, as he also had to suppress a Navajo uprising at the same time he was dealing with Lewis and Clark. In August 1804, some one thousand Navajos attacked the newly founded Spanish settlement of Cebolleta, New Mexico, killing or injuring half its residents. Tentatively, the Navajos took the action because Cebolleta was on land they considered to be theirs. The Navajos were ethnically, culturally, and linguistically related to the Apaches and like their Athabaskan cousins they remained largely independent of Spanish control. Unlike the Apaches, however, the Navajos usually remained at peace with Spain and had never settled at establecimientos. The Navajos also differed from the Apaches in that they derived most of their diet from animal and food sources that they raised themselves. The Navajos were upset with Spain and had attacked Cebolleta because the area around the settlement was one of the few locations they reserved for hunting.[5]

There may have been another reason for the Navajo raid on Cebolleta, but existing documents are inconclusive on the matter. In 1804, the Spanish began receiving reports that Apaches from the Carrizal establecimiento were inciting the Navajos to war, while a separate rumor held that a "José Antonio" had been meeting with the Navajos and Apaches de paz from other presidios to encourage a collective rebellion against the Spanish. Considering José Antonio's connections to the Carrizal Apaches, these rumors may have had something to do with the "providing intelligence to hostile Apaches" charge that led to Rafael's band's imprisonment. However, in spite of multiple historians describing Rafael's attack on the Spanish as a rebellion, there is not enough evidence to tie him or José Antonio to the Navajo revolt, especially considering there were multiple Apache José Antonios on the northern frontier.[6]

Regardless of whether Rafael was involved, the Navajo uprising would serve as a distraction in Spain's search for his band. Indeed, Commandant General Salcedo had to send Francisco Narbona and 215 Spanish and Ópata soldiers to the Canyon de Chelly, where the Navajos maintained extensive fields of corn and lived in stone dwellings along the canyon walls. This meant that when Narbona arrived in the Canyon de Chelly on January 17, 1805, to punish the attack on Cebolleta, the Navajos could not retreat without abandoning their homes. This hesitance allowed the Spanish to use their firearms and technological advantages to drive the Navajos into a cave. Unable to escape, the Spanish opened fire at the cave entrance, their ricocheting musket balls killing more than one hundred Navajos sheltered inside. This defeat led surviving Navajo leaders to meet with Commandant General Salcedo on May 12, 1805 and abandon their claim to Cebolleta.[7]

In addition to serving as a distraction, the Navajo rebellion provides an interesting counterpoint to the search for Rafael. Although the Navajos were much more numerous than Rafael's band, they were much less mobile, which allowed Narbona and his men to bring Spain's technological advantages to bear. Lucas Valenzuela on the other hand struggled to even find Rafael owing to the rapidity to which he moved, his knowledge of Spanish tactics, and his elaborate disguises. In the few instances when the Spanish located the Apaches, Rafael and his followers had proven so mobile that they were usually able to escape unharmed. Indeed, even when Juan Leal and his men had the Apaches surrounded, all they managed to do was wound Rafael and liberate some but not all captives.

IT WAS PERHAPS because he was busy dealing with the Navajos and the United States that Salcedo seems to have ignored Rafael before 1805, paying so little attention to the matter that he would later misidentify the year the band left Guajoquilla as 1803, not 1804. Indeed, the only correspondence from Salcedo that *may* have referred to Rafael prior to 1805 was a November 19, 1804 order telling the captains and commanders of Nueva Vizcaya to send "diaries and news of their campaigns to the governor intendent of Durango," not him. This implies that Salcedo saw dealing with the handful of rogue Apaches as a local matter, not something for a commandant general.[8]

After learning about Leal's battle with the Apaches in March and the number of dead attributed to Rafael, Salcedo changed his tune and determined that the matter was deserving of his attention. On April 5, 1805, he issued a proclamation denouncing the "the iniquity and perfidy with which the Apache Indians named Rafael, José Antonio, and Chinche" had committed "horrific crimes," which he ordered posted in towns throughout Nueva Vizcaya. The proclamation warned that Rafael's band had "robbed and killed defenseless people on roads, haciendas, and ranches" using devious methods to prey on the weak. Salcedo cautioned that Rafael used soldier uniforms and paisano clothing to trick potential targets and described the Apaches' "cunning and speed," which had thus far allowed them to escape into the mountains to avoid punishment. Salcedo concluded by giving "authority to anyone regardless of class or condition to apprehend or kill the stated three Indians."[9]

The order to kill was significant, considering that officials rarely authorized execution without a trial. According to Spanish law, governors could issue the death penalty, but only after they had conducted criminal proceedings and received permission from higher authorities, in this case the commandant general. Salcedo preferred not to use this power. When the king of Spain ordered him to execute two out of a group of ten Americans who had been caught trespassing on Spanish territory, Salcedo counted an American who had died of illness while in captivity as part of the king's quota, leaving him to execute only one person. At another time in his tenure, the commandant general commuted a death sentence for a group of his trusted advisers who he caught conspiring to overthrow and execute him. Apparently, Rafael's crimes went beyond what even the sympathetic Salcedo could tolerate.[10]

IT WAS PERHAPS because of Salcedo's proclamation and the additional attention it brought that there would be no sightings of Rafael from April 1805 to October 1805. The absence of activity may also have owed to Rafael needing to heal from the broken leg and gunshot wound he suffered in the battle with Leal's forces in March 1805. There are no records explaining how Rafael recovered from these injuries, but owing to the risk of bacterial infection, gunshot wounds were often fatal in the nineteenth century, especially without proper medical treatment. Fortunately for Rafael, he or a member of his band was likely familiar with traditional Apache treatments for wounds. Apaches had little understanding of the circulatory system, but they knew that the first order of business after someone had been shot was to seal the wound to prevent further blood loss. They often did this by wrapping an ash tree leaf around mescal root fibers and then jamming the resulting bung into the bullet hole. They then changed the plug as needed and sang songs and recited incantations to aid in the healing process. If possible, Apache surgeons, meaning anyone in the band skilled in using bladed weapons, would use hunting knifes or dirks to dig out the bullet.[11]

Once the danger of bleeding out subsided, Apaches removed the plug and applied a series of herbs to help the wound heal. Although imperfect, the herbal combination seems to have had anti-bacterial properties, and this type of treatment allowed many Apaches to survive wounds that would otherwise be fatal. The famous Apache chief Geronimo told a story about an Apache woman who was attacked by a grizzly bear and during the assault, "the grizzly struck her over the head, tearing off almost the whole scalp." The woman managed to stab the animal four times, forcing it to flee. After that "she replaced her torn scalp and bound it up as best she could" until her fellow Apaches found her and brought her back to camp. Using traditional Apache medical care, "all her wounds were healed." Whatever treatment Rafael received prevented him from dying, but he did not fully recover from his wound, as he would walk with a limp for the foreseeable future.[12]

BY OCTOBER 1805, Rafael appears to have been sufficiently healed to recommence raiding. Early in that month, he, José Antonio, Chinche, and Ultin's wife made their first appearance since April when they emerged from the wilderness north of what is today San Andrés, Chihuahua, and stopped a paisano and his sixteen-year-old son, José Rafael Antonio Mendoza, as they were traveling between towns. The Apaches killed the older man and took José Rafael captive. The reasons for the attack are unclear but having been out of the loop for eight months, Rafael may have wanted to press the sixteen-year-old for information on what had occurred while the Apaches were in hiding.[13]

Whatever their motivation, the band and their new captive then traveled in the direction of Santa Cruz de Valerio, where they stole four horses. They then moved downstream to Moradillas, where they killed two additional victims before proceeding to the Arvisu Plain and killing a paisano in front of Toro Rosillo. This brought the total number of dead in early October to four, indicating that the band may have killed the victims to use their clothes as disguises. The four stolen animals meant that each adult would now be mounted.[14]

Later in October, the band stole additional horses belonging to Lázaro and Jorge Mesa near what is today Nuevo Casas Grandes. The Mesa family was a short distance away at the Eusinillas House when the theft occurred, thereby escaping death. Others were not so lucky. Flores, Rosamancha, and Leocadio Acosta disappeared during this time, and locals feared that Rafael's band was responsible for their deaths. Although Spanish authorities could neither confirm nor deny the suspicions about the Acostas, burial records show "Indios," "Barbaros," and "Apaches" as having killed at least five people in the area on October 13. The reasons for the theft from the Mesas and these murders are unclear, but Rafael may have been acquiring horses in another attempt to trade with the Carrizal Apaches.[15]

INDEED, soon after the raids, Rafael's band passed through the Hacienda del Carmen, an extensive cattle ranch adjacent to the Carrizal Presidio and its establecimiento de paz. Likely recognizing that she was close to her husband and kin, Ultin's wife took the opportunity to flee her captors. It is unclear how she carried out the escape, but she successfully reached Carrizal on October 22 and informed Pedro Ruiz de Larramendi of what had happened, telling him that Rafael's band had killed eighteen people during her time in captivity. Ultin and other Apaches de paz at Carrizal offered to help track down and kill the band, and Larramendi sent their request and news of what had occurred to Commandant General Salcedo.[16]

Salcedo immediately ordered nearby presidio commanders to send troops to reconnoiter the countryside around Carrizal for any sign of Rafael, José Antonio, and Chinche. To prevent further "atrocities," soldiers should employ "all methods" of pursuit and capture or kill the fugitives if found. Recognizing that the Apaches' familiarity with the province would make them difficult to locate, Salcedo ordered soldiers to report any discoveries that might indicate the presence of Rafael's band to nearby military and civilian authorities so they could assist in the search. Salcedo also warned the various *justicias mayores* of Nueva Vizcaya that Rafael had been sighted, and he ordered royal officials in nearby towns to tell paisanos and those working on haciendas to be vigilant.

No one should leave population centers unless they were armed, and travelers should avoid mountainous areas.[17]

Salcedo also cautioned his men to watch out for the Apaches' captive, José Rafael Antonio Mendoza. The commandant general feared that Rafael and his band had won the young man over with "their perverse ideas" and that he was no longer a captive but a willing participant in their crimes.[18]

It seems that Salcedo believed that the same thing had happened with Ultin's wife, as he ordered her interrogated about her time with the band. The results of the interrogation and the woman's ultimate fate are unknown, but Salcedo would later report that he had "imprisoned" one of four members of Rafael's band. It is possible that the commandant general was referring to another captive, an unknown individual who assisted Rafael, or Rafael's young son, but it is more likely that he was referring to Ultin's wife, especially considering the various reports that she had been actively involved in some of the attacks. This meant that she faced imprisonment, deportation to Cuba, or worse for her participation.[19]

Salcedo also suspected that, despite their offers to assist in the search, the Carrizal Apaches had helped Rafael. For this reason, the commandant general began restricting the time they spent away from the establecimiento. On November 6, 1805, he denied Apache chief Jasquedegá's request to leave the Carrizal establecimiento with his seventy-four-member ranchería to go hunting at the El Carrizalillo watering hole. Salcedo suspected the true purpose of their trip was to conduct illegal trade, and so he informed the commander of the Carrizal Presidio that if Jasquedegá insisted on going, the commander should grant the request, but send soldiers to closely monitor the Apaches' activities. Salcedo then ordered that Spanish officers should only give out licenses for hunting and gathering in locations where the Apaches "would not be placed under suspicion."[20]

Salcedo took the additional policy measure of restricting future establecimientos to only presidios distant from major Spanish settlements. As he would later explain, "it was never advisable to allow Apaches de paz to live anywhere other than presidios on the advanced frontier. They should be prohibited from moving away from their preferred terrain." The commandant general believed that allowing Apaches to live in places like Guajoquilla familiarized them with the layout of the wealthier interior, thereby making it easier to conduct raids in these areas.[21]

SALCEDO'S LATEST PROCLAMATIONS and the renewed attention they brought sent Rafael and his band into hiding for the next month. During this time, Rafael, José Antonio, Chinche, and their captive José Rafael Antonio Mendoza made camp in or near the Sierra la Campana, a popular hiding spot for Apaches when raiding into Spanish territory in the eighteenth and nineteenth centuries. This owed, in part, to the numerous caves dotting the mountains that are only accessible by scaling precarious cliffs. These natural defenses allowed Apaches to raid nearby settlements and then flee to the caves, where they could hide without fear of reprisal. Indeed, the name Sierra la Campana, or Bell Mountains, is said to have come from an eighteenth-century incident wherein a group of Apaches stole a church bell from the Hacienda Encinillas chapel, took it to their mountain cave, and rang it incessantly, having no fear that the sound would reveal their location. As the story goes, whenever the bell rang, its clangs reverberated off the canyon's walls, terrifying villagers below.[22]

In addition to their natural defenses, the caves made a good hideout because they were adjacent to El Camino Real de Tierra Adentro, a roughly 1,600-mile road extending from Santa Fe, New Mexico, to the capital of New Spain, Mexico City. Hugging the eastern edge of the Sierra Madre Occidental, the Camino Real served as the primary means by which precious metals made their way south from mines of the Internal Provinces to Mexico City, where they were then minted into coinage or sent to Veracruz for shipment to Spain. Manufactured goods and materials that could not be produced in the Internal Provinces traveled in the opposite direction, making their way from Mexico City to markets in places like Chihuahua and Santa Fe.[23]

Those who conducted trade on the Camino Real were known as muleteers because they brought most of their goods on the back of mules or in mule-drawn two and four-wheeled wagons. During the early years of Spanish settlement, muleteers sometimes traveled alone with only a few mules or in small groups driving a few dozen mules. However, the increase in Apache raids into Nueva Vizcaya in the seventeenth and eighteenth centuries led more and more muleteers to join large caravans for protection. Although muleteers still occasionally traveled in small groups, by the nineteenth century, it was common to see caravans of five hundred muleteers escorting a mule train consisting of thousands of animals. Military escorts sometimes joined the muleteers to offer additional protection, especially when mule trains carried precious metals bound for the royal treasury.[24]

Traveling in large numbers deterred Apache attacks but the life of a muleteer was still difficult, as it required carters to spend much of the year on the road exposed to the elements and away from the comforts of civilization.

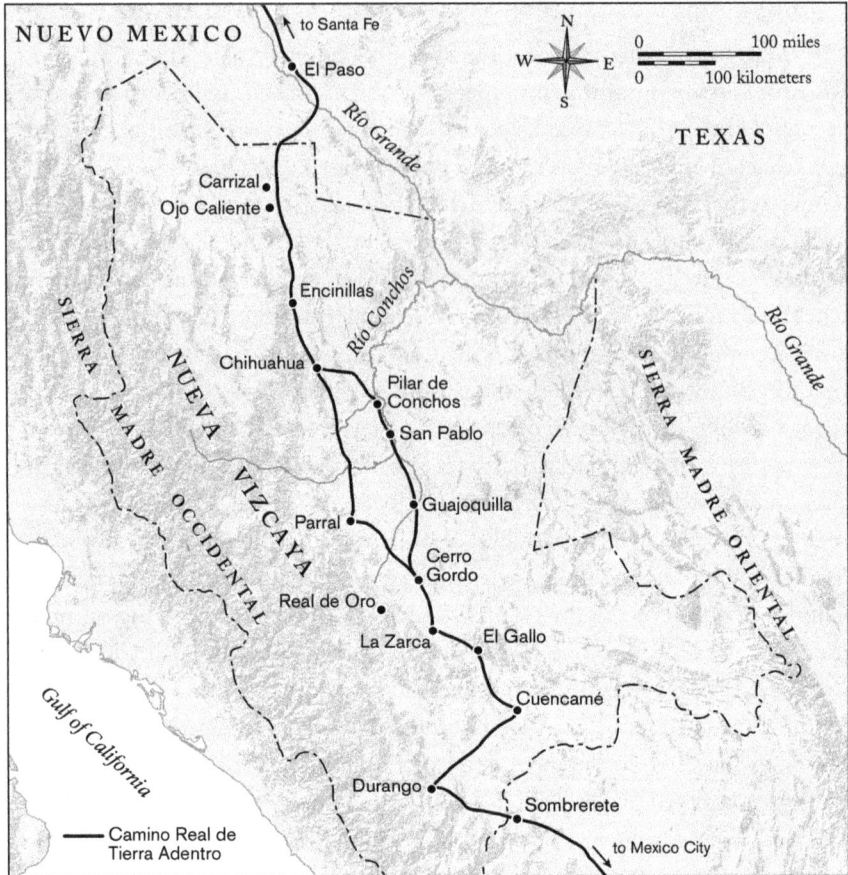

The Camino Real stretched from Mexico City to Taos, New Mexico. Owing to traffic and the density of settlements near the Camino Real, many of Rafael's attacks took place adjacent to the road. Map by Ben Pease, cartographer.

Things were especially challenging once mule trains reached the sparsely populated Internal Provinces, as travelers could go days without shelter, supplies, or water and pasturage for their animals. One ninety-mile stretch of desert had no sources of water of any kind. For these reasons, the few small settlements on the Camino Real, such as Hacienda Encinillas, served as islands of civilization where muleteers would frequent hacienda stores to obtain bread, meat, and other needed supplies for the road ahead. The owners of the haciendas generally ran these stores from their homes and used their geographical monopolies to overcharge the muleteers and hacienda workers who relied on them.[25]

In late October 1805, Rafael's band descended from their hiding places in the Sierra la Campana and killed two muleteers and their mules traveling in La Boquilla, just west of La Laguna. It is unclear why the men were traveling outside of a caravan, but whatever the case, Rafael realized that if he disguised himself and the members of his band as muleteers, they would not need to trade horses for supplies. Instead, they could dress like muleteers and use hard currency stolen from travelers to obtain what they needed from hacienda stores. Because stores generally only served those who worked on haciendas, if Rafael came dressed as a paisano, it would arouse suspicion, but there would be no reason to suspect unfamiliar muleteers, considering that they were transients by profession. In addition, the Camino Real would be particularly busy with itinerant traders in late 1805, as Commandant General Salcedo had established a duty-free trading fair in San Bartolomé to stimulate the local economy. The muleteer disguise would also help explain the fact that Rafael's band consisted of Indians. The difficulties associated with the muleteer trade and the additional opportunities Spanish society afforded those of European ancestry, saw few whites serve as muleteers, leaving mainly Indians and mestizos to perform the job.[26]

The only thing that might arouse suspicion in the settlements along the Camino Real would be that the band was traveling with just four men, not the dozens or hundreds that usually made up muleteer caravans. Likely with this in mind, Rafael concocted a story for whenever they visited a hacienda or other population center. He, José Antonio, Chinche, and any captives they had at the time would pretend that they were a part of a larger mule train but had been sent ahead to procure supplies. The rest of the muleteers would be arriving shortly. By the time the band had gotten what they wanted, and the hacienda store proprietor realized there was no mule train coming, the Apaches would be long gone.[27]

IT IS UNCLEAR how many times Rafael successfully used this ploy, as Spanish officials would not have received reports whenever the Apaches' disguises worked as planned. However, it appears that the first time the disguises aroused suspicions was November 23, 1805. That day Rafael, José Antonio, Chinche, and their sole captive, José Rafael Antonio Mendoza entered the Hacienda Encinillas store and told its proprietor that they were muleteers on their way from Carmen and explained that the remainder of the muleteers would be arriving shortly. The store owner saw no reason to suspect the men and sold them two reales worth of cigars and one real worth of tortillas. He then watched as the men departed in the direction of the Mulato Hills.[28]

Shortly thereafter, the *alférez* of Hacienda Encinillas, don Manuel Carrasco, learned about these visitors and, perhaps unaware of any caravans in the area and with Salcedo warning to be wary of outsiders, he grew suspicious and ordered a corporal, another soldier, and the hacienda foreman to join him in riding out to investigate the unknown individuals. The armed party soon caught up to the Apache's captive, José Rafael, and took him into custody. Rafael, José Antonio, and Chinche were able to evade Carrasco long enough to take refuge in the rugged Sierra de la Campana. Once there they ascended the sheer walls of Tascate Canyon and watched from above as their pursuers entered the mouth of the gorge below them.[29]

Instead of launching an ambush, Rafael called down and asked Carrasco to parlay. It is unclear why he made this request, especially considering that his band often ambushed soldiers in a similar situation, but the Apaches may not have had functional firearms at this point, and they almost certainly lacked the ammunition and gunpowder needed to carry out a long firefight. Rafael may also have spared Carrasco because he liked him. A story from the time said that Apaches in similar situation did not attack a young Spanish officer because in the past he "had treated them with great kindness," and instead they "sent him home safe and unhurt." Perhaps more likely, Rafael believed that if he spared Carrasco, the alférez might be able use his influence to assist him in getting his son back.[30]

Ignoring Salcedo's orders to kill or capture the Apaches if found, Carrasco accepted the request to parlay. He probably had little option but to do so. Rafael had almost certainly taken up a position just outside the range of Carrasco's firearms, which would have been of poor-quality owing to the lack of trade and manufacturing in the Internal Provinces. Indeed, Spanish guns were so bad, that one officer complained that the "weapons carried so short a distance that the Apaches were wont to get just out of range and make open jest of the Spaniards." Ascending the walls of the canyon was not an option either, as it would open Carrasco and his men to a flurry of arrows, musket balls, rocks, and anything else Rafael's band could rain down on them.[31]

Once both parties agreed to parlay, Rafael sat on the edge of the canyon rim while Carrasco called up to him and the two had "una larga conversación." The men discussed several subjects with Carrasco asking Rafael whether the

Carrizal Apaches had assisted him over the past year. Rafael answered in the affirmative and even provided Carrasco with a list of establecimiento Apaches who had "protected and assisted" his band. Although Rafael may have been using the discussion with Carrasco as an opportunity to levy unwarranted blame on Apaches he disliked, his specificity indicates that he was telling the truth, which begs the question: Why sell out the Carrizal Apaches if they had helped him?[32]

Fairly or unfairly, outsiders who interacted with the Apaches in eighteenth and nineteenth centuries have portrayed the Apaches as willing to turn against friends and loved ones if it served their short-term interests. Sources describe Apaches as having little regard for those who helped them in the past and little forethought as to how someone might provide for them in the future, an understandable attitude considering that the need for survival often confined Apaches to thinking only about the present. Even understanding this, those who served with the Apaches often found their disregard for others off-putting. As one soldier who worked with Apache auxiliaries described the situation, "the fiendish cruelties committed by them when on the warpath give one a creepy feeling while among them, and when a son brings in his father's head on which a reward had been placed, not because he had trouble with him, but because he happened to know where he was in hiding and wanted the reward, it makes one doubt whether they are human." Another soldier went so far as to claim that after providing an Apache with a fine gray horse as a bounty for bringing in the head of his cousin who had committed murders and robberies, the grateful Apache stated, "if the officer had another good gray horse, he had another cousin whose head he could bring in at any time."[33]

Whatever Rafael's motivation for providing information on the Carrizal Apaches, Carrasco turned the conversation to Rafael's plans for the future. At this point, Spanish forces had been pursuing Rafael's band for more than a year, and soldiers had come close to catching the Apaches on multiple occasions. Carrasco believed that it was only a matter of time before Rafael slipped up and when this happened, the soldiers who caught him were unlikely to be as merciful as he was. For this reason, Carrasco implored Rafael to come down from the canyon and give himself up. He even promised to personally escort the Apaches to Guajoquilla, implying that he would ensure that Rafael would be treated fairly and perhaps even be absolved for any crimes he had committed against the Spanish.[34]

Rafael refused the overture, responding that he, José Antonio, and Chinche did not want "to go down for peace, but instead walk the mountains." However, Rafael called down that if Carrasco brought his son to the villa of Picacho, in front of the old houses of de la Noria, in five days' time, they could speak about the prospective peace further. Rafael closed the conversation by asking Carrasco to leave him alone, promising that "if they did not hurt him, he would not hurt them." With that Rafael and his companions disappeared over the lip of the canyon, leaving Carrasco and his soldiers to contemplate what had just happened.[35]

IT IS UNCLEAR if the Apaches showed up to the meeting spot in Picacho or if Salcedo ever considered allowing his soldiers to bring Rafael's son to the designated area. By the time of the meeting with Carrasco, Rafael's son had spent at least a year with the Nevares family and depending on his father and mother's involvement in his life before this time, he may have spent most of his life in a Christian household. Owing to his young age, he likely spoke Spanish as his primary language and had adopted the basic tenets of Catholicism. Turning the boy over to Rafael would be tantamount to surrendering a Christian to the life of a pagan, something that Spanish officials were uncomfortable doing.[36]

Indeed, there had recently been a debate over whether such actions were even permissible as Christians. In 1792, an Apache chief agreed to make peace with Spain and settle at an establecimiento if then Commandant General Pedro de Nava returned his daughter, whom Spanish soldiers had captured while on campaign a few years earlier. Nava was hesitant to grant the request because the Apache girl had been living in the home of a Spanish family who had provided her with an education and had taught her the basics of the Christian faith. By 1792, she showed "signs of true devotion" and did not want to return to the life of an Apache. She broke into tears when informed of her birth father's request and joined her adopted parents in begging Nava to let her remain where she was. The commandant general, weighing the benefits the peace would provide, ignored these protests and forced the girl to live with her birth family at the establecimiento. Local Friar Diego Bringas criticized Nava's actions, lamenting that it "was a scandal to the whole province," and "caused injury to a Christian girl who was naturally repelled by union with a pagan." Although Nava often courted controversy for the sake of practicality, Salcedo was more reserved and less willing to upset influential families like the Nevareses, so it is unlikely that he ever considered Rafael's request.[37]

AT ELEVEN O'CLOCK on the night of December 30, Rafael, José Antonio, and Chinche watched from concealed positions as Ignacio Rodríguez and his nineteen-year-old son rode north on a desolate road carrying goods they planned to sell in Parral, a silver mining community of some five thousand people. It had been a full month since Rafael had carried on a conversation with Carrasco in Tescate Canyon, and since that time, the Apaches had put over 150 miles between themselves and their last known location. Because of this, no one would be looking for them near Parral. However, as Rafael surely knew, the situation would quickly change if the Apaches decided to attack Rodríguez and his son.[38]

Apparently, Rafael so valued the goods the Rodríguezes were carrying that he deemed the risk worth it, because he, José Antonio, and Chinche emerged from the darkness and attacked the two travelers. The younger Rodríguez somehow survived the ambush, escaped, and would later report what had happened to Spanish authorities. The elder Rodríguez was not so fortunate. Rafael's band killed him and took the goods that they had so endangered themselves to obtain: *marquesotes de rosa*, a sweet bread made with pink sugar.[39]

At first glance, the decision to attack the Rodríguezes made little sense. Although the motivations for all the bands' previous assaults cannot be determined with certainty, they seem to have all been conducted for personal defense, revenge, as a means of hiding their identity or location from authorities, to acquire information, to procure livestock or material goods for trade, or to steal horses for riding. The December 30 attack outside Parral fits none of these patterns, but instead seems to have been carried out exclusively to acquire calories. If this were indeed their only motivation, it helps validate the opinion of historian Jorge Chávez Chávez who argues that from late 1805 forward "the homicides that these Indians committed" became less about vengeance and obtaining material goods and were instead "probably done to defend their lives" and to "obtain items and livestock for survival."[40]

Some of Rafael's future actions call Chávez Chávez's hypothesis into question, but there is no doubt that beginning around late 1805, Rafael's band would conduct more attacks aimed primarily or exclusively at meeting their basic nutritional needs. While at Guajoquilla, the Spanish government provided rations to establecimiento Apaches and allowed them to hunt to supplement their diet, and as Rafael's caretaker, Father Nevares would have been expected to provide food for his protégé. After leaving Guajoquilla, however, Rafael's band had to use other methods to acquire calories. Hunting and gathering served as the main calorie source for non-establecimiento Apaches, and it is almost certain that Rafael's band hunted the plentiful wild game in Nueva Vizcaya and ate native plants like persimmons, berries, pinon nuts, acorns, and mescal. Raiding also provided the Apaches with sustenance. The band ate horses, mules, and cattle captured in raids, and they traded stolen livestock, goods, and currency for food, as they had done when acquiring tortillas from Encinillas.

At the time of the attack on the Rodríguezes, however, many of these food sources would have been in short supply. It had been over two months since the band's last recorded raid, leaving them with no livestock to eat or trade. More than a month had passed since they acquired tortillas from Hacienda Encinillas, and the onset of winter meant that natural sources of food were hard to come by. Edible plants and animals could be found in abundance around Parral during the summer, but by December the cool of winter had set in, shriveling flora and sending many animals into hibernation. Because of Parral's high elevation, it is also possible that snow had covered the surrounding area and buried other possible calorie sources under a layer of fine powder.[41]

Without food, and specifically carbohydrates, Rafael's band would suffer significant weight loss, a deficit of energy, and possibly other short and long-term health effects. Hunger could also affect mental status. Without carbohydrates, the human body breaks down fat and muscle for energy, leading the afflicted to experience "mood disturbance" and "anger hostility." Such persons will often take extreme measures to consume carbohydrates. Almost exactly one hundred years later in the same area, Pancho Villa, then a young bandit on the run from the law and having yet to make his name, grew extremely disturbed when traveling companion José Solís became so hungry that he demanded of a harmless old man carrying bread, "sell us the bread or I'll take it from you." When the man replied, "in my affairs only I command," the ravenous Solis grew enraged, shot the old man twice, and took the bread.[42]

Therefore, as Chávez Chávez might argue, it may have been exclusively starvation or starvation-induced anger that drove Rafael to kill the Rodríguez elder. Even if this were not the case, the band likely consumed the marquesotes de rosa immediately, as Apaches tended to binge whenever food was available. As one Spanish officer described this proclivity: "they are excessive gluttons when they can eat in abundances, for I have seen many times one Apache eat a rack of ribs, the lungs, both skirt steaks, the liver, and all of the intestines of a large beef; but they also admirably suffer hunger and thirst without becoming demoralized or losing their strength. They can go two, three, four, and eight days without eating or drinking."[43]

UNFORTUNATELY FOR CHÁVEZ CHÁVEZ'S Rafael-as-a-hungry-survivor interpretation, the band would attempt to steal more cattle than they could possibly consume themselves less than a week after the marquesotes de rosa theft. The attempted rustling occurred some fifty miles to the northwest at Zanja, an outpost on the Hacienda de Dolores only two leagues away from their former home of Guajoquilla. On January 4, 1806, Rafael, José Antonio, and Chinche encountered a cowboy named Ignacio Ontiveros and an unnamed twelve-year-old boy who were herding cattle at Zanja. Ontiveros "was killed by the Apaches," but they chose to take the twelve-year-old boy as a captive, likely to press him for information about the ranch and what had occurred since they were last near Guajoquilla. Rafael's band then tried to take Ontiveros's cattle as their own, but when they could not get the animals past an unwieldy fence, they left the herd behind. They kept their captive and then headed in the direction of Río Florido.[44]

Lucas Valenzuela was in Guajoquilla at the time of the raid on Zanja, and after learning of the attack later that day, he enlisted Maríano Varela Ramírez and a group of Spanish soldiers to investigate.[45] At this point, Valenzuela had been searching for Rafael for almost a year with no success, and so the prospect of finally catching his adversary must have been exciting to the seasoned veteran. After investigating Zanja, he recovered Ontiveros's body, but was unable to find any eyewitnesses to the murder. Despite this, Valenzuela determined that "the signs confirmed that the aggressors had been at that place and carried out the murder. I know it was the Indian Rafael and his companions." Armed with this knowledge, Valenzuela sent word to local officials and hacienda owners on January 4, informing them that it was "very important" that they "do not allow anyone to leave your jurisdiction unless they are carrying arms for their defense."[46]

In order to "prevent many atrocities," Valenzuela came up with a plan to capture Rafael and, not wanting to give his quarry time to escape, he decided to implement it even before Commandant General Salcedo could weigh in on the matter. He sent word that civilians needed to report anything out of the ordinary to local military and civil authorities "immediately." They should not only be able to describe what happened, but also when and where it happened.

Local leaders were then to send this information directly to Valenzuela, as well as to civilian and military authorities in neighboring districts so that they could be on the watch for Rafael. Valenzuela explained that he wanted to be "like a sponge for information." By recording so much data he hoped to "get a rough guess as to what mountain pass the barbarian enemies were using" so he could track down the band.[47]

SOON THEREAFTER, Salcedo issued a proclamation in which he essentially reiterated and approved of Valenzuela's orders. To stop Rafael, he required that civilians were to report unusual occurrences to local leaders, and the commandant general asked that these leaders then forward the information to neighboring districts, presidios, and other military posts. Salcedo's address went further than Valenzuela's in one regard: he added legal repercussions for employers and civic leaders who failed to provide weapons to their workers so that they could defend themselves. Believing such measures were necessary "in order to prevent the hostilities committed by the Indian Rafael," the commandant general stated that if employees did not receive weapons, the commandant general would hold employers responsible for "any misfortunes that may occur due to their omission."[48]

Salcedo knew when issuing this order that employers would have a hard time providing their workers with even hand-held weapons, and he understood that it would be impossible for every worker to carry a functional firearm, as the commandant general did not even have enough guns to arm his soldiers. Indeed, a recent census of presidios revealed that there were only 200 working long guns and 180 pistols for some 3,150 soldiers, and as Carrasco and other Spanish soldiers had learned, even the best of these weapons was ineffective at long range. The shortage led Salcedo to ask the Spanish Ministry of War and the viceroy of New Spain to send him new firearms, but they were unable to do so. War had broken out between Spain and Britain in 1805, and the firearms were needed in Europe and to defend the coast of New Spain.[49]

This convinced Salcedo to use his background in engineering to develop a prototype for a functional, easy-to-make smooth-bore musket that could be produced locally.[50] Unfortunately for the commandant general, he lacked the money, gunsmith, factory, tools, and iron to produce the weapons in bulk, leading him to complain that "these provinces are so unfortunate that they depend on Mexico for everything, the sending of iron, files, etc., without knowing if the quality is good or bad, or if they are of use or trash."[51]

Salcedo overcame these problems by borrowing from the veteran companies of Nueva Vizcaya and collecting donations from wealthy citizens in Nueva Vizcaya to purchase tools and rent out a building in Chihuahua for use as the firearms factory. He then had presidio commanders send in malfunctioning firearms and artillery to be melted down for iron and commissioned Martín Irigoyen of the Company of Cerro Gordo, purported to be an exceptional gunsmith, to run the factory. Salcedo wanted Irigoyen to produce fifty muskets a month to sell to both the military and civilians for a cost of thirty pesos per gun. Salcedo defrayed some of the startup cost by purchasing the first set of guns himself, and he allowed the rest to be sold at the annual trade fair in San Bartolomé tax free. The commandant general hoped that once his factory was up and running, the addition of hundreds of guns to the soldiers and subjects in Nueva Vizcaya would make things much more difficult for Rafael.[52]

CHAPTER FOUR

An Inhuman and Ferocious Man,
January 1806–December 1806

VALENZUELA'S PURSUIT and the increased scrutiny brought by Salcedo's proclamations forced Rafael and his band to flee the area of Guajoquilla for the more sparsely populated deserts of northeastern Nueva Vizcaya. Their new twelve-year-old captive would later remember "transiting to diverse places and crossing hills" on the way to the Plains of Hormigas, a flat, barren part of the Chihuahua Desert with few sources of water. Because it was outside of the rainy season, Januarys on the Plains of Hormigas could be especially dry, forcing travelers to navigate long distances to find pasturage and a place for their horses to drink. For this reason, it was not uncommon for multiple traveling parties to arrive at a known watering hole at the same time.[1]

Considering these circumstances, it may not have come as a surprise to Rafael, Chinche, José Antonio, and their captive when on January 23, 1806, they saw whom they judged to be Mescalero Apaches crossing the desert and approaching the same watering hole to which they were headed. The Mescaleros hailed from the region between the Pecos River and the Río Grande in what is today Far West Texas, and they differed from the Apaches of Carrizal in mannerism and dress, perhaps the biggest contrast being that the Mescaleros' home on the plains allowed them to hunt buffalo for use as food, clothing, and shelter. The Mescaleros were also more numerous than other Apache groups, although they had seen a population decline in recent years owing to war with the Comanches and the Spanish.[2]

The watering hole where Rafael encountered the Mescaleros was possibly the Agua del Cuervo, where only ten years before, a group of Mescaleros had ambushed and slaughtered some fifty Spanish soldiers. Things had changed since that time, as most Mescaleros in the area had accepted life on establecimientos. Indeed, the presence of women among the group suggested to Rafael that the Mescaleros were Apaches de paz who had received a pass to leave their establecimiento to go hunting.[3]

The twelve-year-old captive would later recall that Rafael initially considered attacking the Mescaleros and stealing their wives but reconsidered. Rafael may have noticed the Apaches were carrying firearms and would therefore be able to defend themselves better than most of the band's victims. Having upset the Carrizal Apaches de paz, Rafael might have seen the Mescaleros as prospective partners with whom he could trade stolen livestock and horses for firearms and other manufactured goods. It is also possible that Rafael recognized some of the Mescaleros as his kinsmen.[4]

CONTEMPORARY SOURCES are largely silent concerning Rafael's life before he came to live with Rafael Nevares at Guajoquilla. Rumors say only that an unspecified Apache group captured his father and adopted him into their tribe. His father then had a sexual relationship with an Apache woman, who would later give birth to Rafael and raise him with her ranchería for his first years of life. This lack of specifics, and the fact that Spanish sources are frustratingly silent concerning his childhood, has led historians to come up with different interpretations of Rafael's native tribal affiliation.[5]

Some of the more outlandish theories hold that Rafael was not an Apache at all. The Tepehuanes contend that Rafael was one of their own who grew upset with the Spanish and decided to adopt Apache war tactics as a means of resistance. Historian José de la Cruz Pacheco Rojas calls Rafael a "Comanche leader," but offers no evidence to support this contention. Others downplay or ignore Rafael's indigenous roots, insinuating that he was of European ancestry. These interpretations do not hold up as dozens of Spanish documents from multiple sources specifically refer to Rafael as an "Apache" in the same manner that they would an Athabaskan Apache, but none specify to which of the nine or so Apache predominant nations he belonged.[6]

The most prevalent theory holds that like José Antonio and Chinche, Rafael was born a Mimbres Apache, or another subgroup of the modern Chiricahua. For example, one Chihuahua legend says he was related to Chiricahua Chief Geronimo; another that he was an ancestor to Victorio, a Mimbres Apache. Unfortunately, there is little evidence to support or discredit these assertions. The only contemporary document to identify him as having been born to either a Chiricahua or Mimbreño mother is an 1808 newspaper article that claimed that Rafael "was born in the desert country occupied by his nation, between 30 to 38 degrees latitude and 264 to 267 of longitude, counted from the island of Tenerife." Adjusting these coordinates to a modern map, it would read between 30 and 38 degrees latitude and 104 to 107 degrees longitude, a wide swath of territory in New Mexico and Chihuahua that was home to the Chiricahuas and Mimbreños. Unfortunately, the author who cited the coordinates may not have had inside information about Rafael but was instead repeating information from a highly circulated report by officer Antonio Cordero about the general homeland of all Apaches, not Rafael's birthplace.[7]

The idea that Rafael was a Mescalero stems from an 1856 report out of Chihuahua that gives an alternative birthplace "in the Sierra of Cibolo, east of the state, situated in the eastern desert that is today part of the United States of the North." The only state in the United States directly east of Chihuahua in 1856 was Texas, and the only part of Texas that has geography that can both be described as sierra and a part of the Chihuahua Desert is Far West Texas. Unfortunately, no Sierra de Cívolo or, using the more modernized Spanish, Sierra del Cibolo, exists in West Texas today. Nor is there a "Cibolo Mountains" or using the English translation of Cibolo, "Buffalo Mountains"

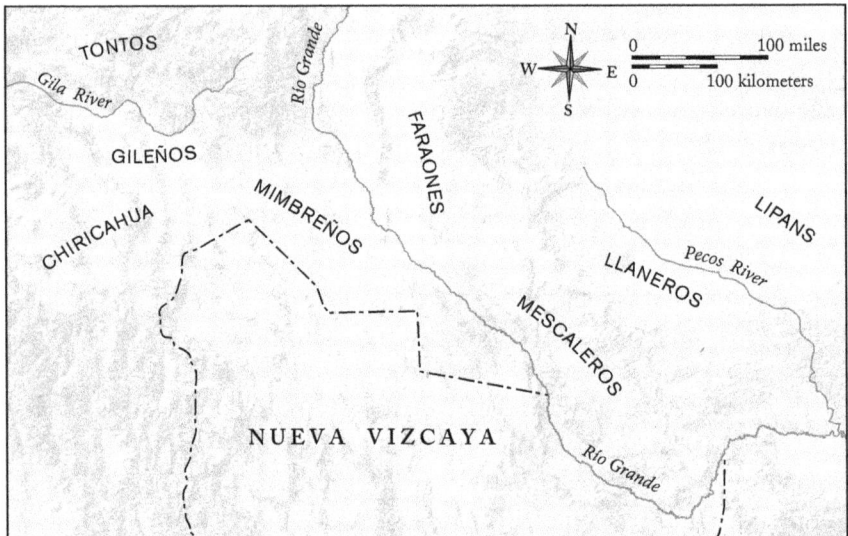

Apache homelands as identified by Juan de Pagazaurtundua in 1792. Apache identifiers vary across sources, and owing to war, raiding, and the establecimiento system, Apache groups could often be found outside of these regions.
Map by Ben Pease, cartographer.

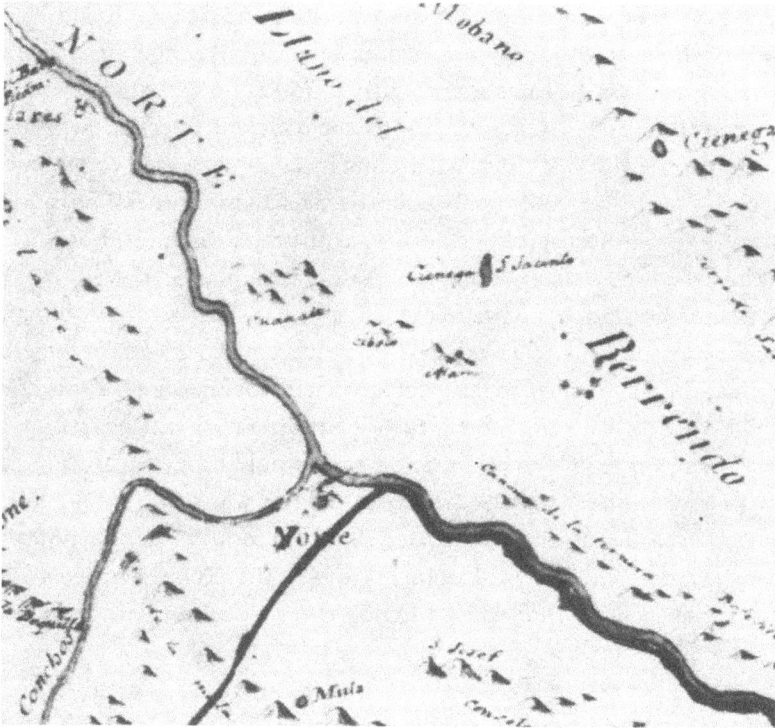

Section of an 1805 map by Juan Pedro Walker, an American who came to live in the Internal Provinces. Walker lists the mountains just northeast of Presidio Del Norte (today's Ojinaga, Chihuahua) as "Cibolo" while other maps of the time write it as "Diablo." Merino's description and Walker's map suggest Rafael's birthplace was somewhere near modern Cibolo Creek. Courtesy Special Collections, University of Texas at Arlington Libraries.

in the area. However, an 1805 map by Spanish officer Juan Pedro Walker lists the word "Cibolo" by a set of mountains east of the Rio Grande just south of what is today Marfa, Texas, that is home to a Cibolo Creek. This suggests that Rafael's birthplace was roughly on the spot of what is today the Cibolo Creek Ranch, which was in the center of Mescalero Apache territory. The fact that the Spanish conducted extensive campaigns into this region during the 1780s and 1790s in which they took numerous children captives further speaks to a Mescalero origin.[8]

Beyond the purported birthplace and circumstance, there is little to either confirm or invalidate a Mescalero origin, and it is possible that Rafael had been born into a lesser-known Apache group, perhaps one that eventually "faded away" or "whose remnants may have been absorbed by the conquering Apaches." One such group was the Faraones, who shared close cultural ties and lived in the same general area as the Mescaleros. The Faraones spoke a dialect that was similar to both Mescalero and Chiricahua, making it easy to trade and communicate with both groups, but would not be considered relatives of either. The Faraones ceased to exist as a distinct tribe in the nineteenth century around the time Rafael was active. Perhaps Rafael was one of the last of their numbers.[9]

In many ways, it does not matter whether Rafael's mother was Mimbreño, Mescalero, Faraone, or if he was born into a different Indian group altogether. His time with Father Nevares had almost certainly severed most connections with the Apaches of his childhood, and José Antonio and Chinche's acceptance meant that by the time he begun raiding, he would have identified himself more as a Mimbres Apache or whatever group it was that his companions belonged. Apache custom also dictated that men adopt the identity of tribes they marry into, and because documents suggest that Rafael married a Mimbreño woman at Guajoquilla, this would further render his childhood Apache affiliation irrelevant.

WHETHER OUT OF FAMILIAL TIES, a desire to trade, or some other motivation, Rafael called on the Mescaleros to parlay. The particulars of the ensuing meeting are lost to time, but on conferring with the Mescaleros, Rafael learned that they were indeed Apaches de paz from the El Príncipe Presidio in nearby Coyame. Unbeknownst to Rafael, the Mescaleros were aware of his band's fugitive status, as Lucas Valenzuela had sent word to all neighboring presidios to be on the watch for three Apaches and a twelve-year-old boy. They also likely knew about Salcedo's "dead or alive" order and that Spanish officials would be grateful to anyone who brought in Rafael's head. The Mescaleros might even receive extra rations, luxury goods, or possibly firearms as rewards for killing the fugitives. Even if the Mescaleros were somehow unaware that Spanish authorities wanted Rafael, they certainly would have noticed that they outnumbered Rafael's band, who were in possession of nice horses and other accoutrements.[10]

Whether motivated by financial gain, loyalty to the Spanish, anger over a disagreement or misunderstanding, or for some other unknown reason, the Mescaleros decided it was in their best interest to kill Rafael and his companions. With the three Apaches and their captive unaware of what was about to happen, the Mescaleros drew their firearms and began shooting.[11]

There is no detailed account of what happened next, but a story told by an Apache woman in the early 1900s might provide some insight into the encounter, as it involved someone with a derivation of Rafael's Apache name faced with very similar circumstances. At some point in the nineteenth century, Hashkeedasillaa, or One Who Is Angry All the Time, and some companions were traveling when a group of Mescaleros ambushed them. Their gunfire caused Hashkeedasillaa to fall off his horse and injure his arm. Hashkeedasillaa then "crawled behind a big rock. He fired his gun with one hand, resting it across his knee," and drove the Mescaleros back. Unable to push forward, the Mescaleros called out, "we know you," and "you are not going to live any longer." Fortunately for Hashkeedasilla, the latter statement proved untrue as the Apache would eventually escape and survive. One of his companions was not so lucky, as the Mescaleros shot and mortally wounded him.[12]

Although the story told by the woman almost certainly referred to a different encounter than the one that happened at the watering hole in January 1806, the results would be the same. Like his namesake, Rafael survived the Mescaleros initial barrage of gunfire, as did José Antonio and their captive. Chinche was not so lucky. He was at the water hole getting a drink when the fighting began and was caught by surprise when a Mescalero fired a musket ball into his chest. The bullet caused instant death and Chinche's body collapsed into the watering hole, his blood mixing with the bubbling spring water. Unable to assist their comrade, Rafael, José Antonio, and their captive mounted some of the Mescaleros' horses and escaped.[13]

AT SOME POINT in February 1806, three Mimbres Apaches de paz received permission from the commander of the Carrizal Presidio to go hunting. Perhaps traveling farther than their passport allowed, the three headed to the area around the Babícora Basin. Although still considered to be part of Nueva Vizcaya, the region bore little resemblance to the Plains of Hormigas and the deserts some 150 miles to the east where Rafael had last been seen. Whereas eastern Nueva Vizcaya is flat and dry, the Babícora Basin sits on the eastern edge of the Sierra Madre Occidental, and enough rain drains from the mountains to create Lake Babícora, one of the largest lakes in northern New Spain. Oak and juniper trees cover much of this area, and the forests serve as home to plentiful deer, antelope, jackrabbits, and turkeys.[14]

It was perhaps this abundance of wildlife that led the three Mimbres Apaches to travel almost 100 miles from Carrizal to hunt. Unfortunately for the two Mimbreños, Rafael, José Antonio, and their twelve-year-old captive had also chosen to travel to the Babícora Basin, but instead of hunting animals, they tried to kill the three Mimbreños. Once again sources provide little insight into the particulars of the attack, saying only that on February 18, there was a "skirmish" in which Rafael and José Antonio killed one of the establecimiento Apaches. They shot another named José Damián in the leg, but he and the third Mimbreño managed to escape and tell the *justicia* of Hacienda del Carmen, don Antonio Ponce de Léon about the attack.[15]

De Léon assembled a militia and set off in pursuit of Rafael's band. They were soon joined by establecimiento Mimbreños from Carrizal, likely angry about the attack on their three brethren, the kidnapping of Ultin's wife, and perhaps Rafael's accusation that they had been protecting and assisting him in his raids. Although the combined Mimbreño-Spanish force failed to catch Rafael and José Antonio or recover their captive, the pursuit put pressure on the fugitives and forced them to kill two of their horses and leave behind their saddles, bags, food, braces, and spurs. Considering that they had barely escaped from the Mescaleros a month before, this likely left Rafael, José Antonio, and their captive with no horses and few supplies.[16]

THE ATTACK ON THE CARRIZAL APACHES may have been a reaction to Chinche's death. When an Apache died, their close friends and relatives often entered a period of mourning, followed by a time of anger. The mourning period typically started with the Apaches coming to view the site of their loved one's death with "eternal horror" leading them to "immediately strike their ranchería, never to locate it there again, nor even its vicinity." This, along with the obvious need to put distance between themselves and prospective pursuers, may help explain why Rafael and José Antonio chose to relocate so far away from the site of Chinche's death.[17]

After a period of mourning, Apaches often sought revenge against those who they perceived had wronged them. This revenge extended not only to those who had participated in killing the loved one, but also anyone associated with them. For example, after Mexican soldiers killed Geronimo's father, Geronimo "vowed revenge upon the Mexican troopers who had wronged me, and whenever I came near his grave or saw anything to remind me of former happy days, my heart would ache for revenge upon Mexico." True to his word, Geronimo spent much of the rest of his life killing not just Mexican soldiers, but Mexican citizens, partially out of the hatred that came from his father's loss. Although there is no record of how Rafael and José Antonio felt after Chinche died, there is no question that their attacks on Spaniards and the Apaches who were allied with them would become much more violent and deadly beginning in 1806.[18]

THE MESCALERO ATTACK at the desert spring and the subsequent flight from the Carrizal Apaches left Rafael, José Antonio, and their captive bereft of horses and other supplies. They sought to remedy this situation on March 2 after encountering Domingo Quezada, María Manuela Ríos, and her son at a ranch near Potrero de los Domínguez. The Apaches used a firearm, perhaps one captured from the Mescaleros at the watering hole, or one taken from the three Mimbreño hunters, to shoot and kill Quezada. They also fired at the child but only managed to shoot him in the hand before he was able to flee. His mother was unable to escape, and Rafael took her as a captive. The raid did not net any mounts, meaning that María Manuela Ríos would have to walk with the band on foot as they traversed the Sierra de Santa Cruz for the next nineteen days.[19]

On March 21, the band reached a small village called Cantera, where Rafael wanted to buy cigars and liquor. Rafael likely worried that with the increased attention, he, José Antonio, and perhaps their male captive, who had been with them for almost three months at this point, would be recognized if they went into town. Any disguises they had were almost certainly so worn down that they would stand out. Therefore, Rafael ordered the newly captured María Manuela Ríos to purchase the liquor and cigars, possibly threatening to kill her if she betrayed him. The woman promised to comply with the request, but when she entered Cantera to purchase the goods, she instead reported the circumstances of her captivity to local authorities. They then sent word to Lucas Valenzuela, who once again set off in pursuit of Rafael's band.[20]

With Valenzuela closing in, Rafael and José Antonio needed to either leave the area or find a way to blend in with the local populace. Both options were difficult considering that the Apaches likely had no horses and a witness had just described their location and attire. The band may also have gone a month or longer without sufficient food. In spite of these circumstances, Rafael and José Antonio quickly recovered. On April 3, 1806, they killed a paisano named José Enriquez in the Sierra de Santa Bárbara and stripped him of his clothes. On Easter Sunday, April 6, they stripped, but did not kill, a group of shepherds and stole their clothes and sheep, likely wearing the former and eating the latter. A few days later they killed and robbed two cobblers near Santa Eulalia, possibly with the intent of adding shoes to complete their outfits. Shortly thereafter, they killed two cowboys from the Hacienda de la Ciénega and presumably took their horses.[21]

Rafael realized that disguises would not be helpful if he were seen by Valenzuela or another Spanish soldier who could recognize their faces. Therefore, in his newly assembled outfit, Rafael began asking locals in the San Bartolomé Valley if they had heard any news about fugitive Apaches or the soldiers who were pursuing them. A *vecino* in Santa Cruz named Marcos López told Rafael that soldiers were combing the valley looking for an Apache named Rafael and they planned "to take his life." López also told the disguised Rafael how the Spanish had locked up another Apache named Esquilnote at Conchos, who Rafael seemed to know. A second person in San Bartolomé confirmed López's story.[22]

To prevent López and others he spoke with from complying with Salcedo and Valenzuela's instructions for civilians to report encounters with suspicious individuals, Rafael told his informants, "do not tell anyone about us because we are deserters." As Rafael would have known from his time at Guajoquilla, it was common for the Spanish to impress the poor into military service and then expect these conscripts to meet the rigid expectations of a soldier's life on the frontier. Those who failed to conform to protocol often faced additional service time or imprisonment as punishment. This led many who were unsuited for military life to abandon their duties, desert, and attempt to live discreetly. Therefore, considering that there were many deserters among the populace of Nueva Vizcaya, Rafael was right to assume that poor residents would sympathize and be willing to keep his secret. The cover story was successful for a time, allowing Rafael to evade detection for most of April.[23]

IN SPITE OF THESE MEASURES, Lucas Valenzuela was able to track Rafael to the Sierra Ojito on April 25, 1806. As had happened when Carrasco followed him into the Sierra de la Campana, Rafael recognized that he was being pursued, and he, José Antonio, and their captive took up a position on a canyon ledge to await Valenzuela. When the Spanish officer arrived at the bottom of the canyon, Rafael called down from above that "he wanted to give himself up peacefully." Recognizing that he could not approach Rafael without subjecting himself and his men to Apache gunfire, Valenzuela called back to say that the two could mediate by means of Rafael's twelve-year-old captive, who could deliver messages back and forth. Soon thereafter, the captive arrived in Valenzuela's camp, and the Spanish officer told him to tell Rafael that if he turned himself in now, he would not be killed and could live in peace at Guajoquilla.[24]

After the captive delivered the message, Rafael sent him back to tell Valenzuela that he was too scared to surrender because he thought the Spanish officer was lying. He revealed that he had spoken to Marcos López and another vecino who had informed him of the commandant general's authorization to kill him. Valenzuela tried to reassure Rafael that his offer of peace was genuine, saying that "he wished that he and his companion would come down peacefully." As Valenzuela likely explained, the Spanish had forgiven other Apaches for their crimes and allowed them to live on establecimientos. Valenzuela could arrange for the same thing to happen to Rafael and José Antonio. Rafael retorted that he was just as likely to end up being chained, and he informed Valenzuela that he had learned that fellow Apache Esquilnote was at Conchos in shackles.[25]

Valenzuela recognized that he could not convince Rafael to come down, nor could he attack him on his outcropping, so he made Rafael a final offer that closely resembled the one Carrasco had given the Apaches five months before. If Rafael and José Antonio would meet him at Tulecillo, they would speak further and go to Guajoquilla together. Valenzuela did not need to say what would happen if Rafael did not comply with his offer of friendship. Apparently leaving their young captive, who had been with the Apaches for four months by this time, at the bottom of the canyon with Valenzuela, Rafael and José Antonio disappeared from the outcropping.[26]

The two Apaches did not go to Tulecillo, and Rafael did not accept Valenzuela's offer, severing any prospect of a peaceful resolution to the conflict. With their captive gone and Chinche dead, he and José Antonio were now alone in a world against them. They likely understood that they could no longer hope to negotiate and there was no returning to the way things had been. Indeed, for the coming months, their attacks would become more violent and less purposeful than they had ever been before.

FOLLOWING THEIR MEETING with Valenzuela, Rafael and José Antonio made their way some fifty miles to the west, where on May 19, 1806, they killed José María Vela and his son Francisco while the two were plowing their fields near Arroyo del Arco. Although the motivation behind this attack is unknown, the two Apaches may have been seeking food. The reason for their next attack is clearer. On May 20, they raided the Peña Ranch and stole all the firearms and ammunition they could find. Three days later, on May 23, they happened upon a group of Tarahumara Indians near the town of Santa Rosalia de Cuevas, José Manuel Sansaba, Francisco Soza, Soza's wife, the couple's fourteen-year-old daughter, Maríana, and another young boy, possibly Sansaba's son. After killing the two men and the woman, Rafael and José Antonio took Maríana and the young boy as captives.[27]

By the time Lucas Valenzuela arrived in the area to investigate the incident, Rafael and José Antonio were already making their way south along the Parral Road toward what is today northern Durango. On the way, they killed a servant of Hipólito Salas as he was cutting wood on May 31 on a hill about a league away from the wealthy gold-mining community of Real del Oro. A short time later they killed a paisano just south of Santa Bárbara, Chihuahua. They then set upon four muleteers, killing one and severely injuring three others.[28]

On June 21, they took twenty-three horses and two mules from the Ramos Ranch near Santa María del Oro. The following day, Rafael and José Antonio found two men who had become lost near the Hacienda de Santa Catalina. Rafael lanced one of the men twice, but the man survived, and he and his companion were able to escape with their lives. However, they left behind ammunition, a brooch, silver spurs, clothe, and a shotgun, which the Apaches took as their own. That same day, near the Hacienda de la Zarca, they attacked a shepherd and his wife, killing the man, stripping him of his clothes, and taking the woman as a captive.[29]

THIS NEW SERIES OF ATTACKS placed Rafael under the jurisdiction of the intendant governor of Durango, Bernardo Bonavía y Zapata. Headquartered in the city of Durango, Bonavía was subordinate to Commandant General Salcedo in all matters, but distance from Chihuahua meant that Salcedo usually handled politics in northern Nueva Vizcaya while Bonavía dealt with day-to-day civics and economics in the south. Indeed, the commandant general usually only intervened in affairs in the south to offer military assistance following Indian raids, but, owing to the relative peace Spain had made with the Apaches over previous years, such instances were increasingly rare. Indeed, in the past year, travelers in Durango had ceased to use escorts.[30]

Rafael's arrival in the interior of Durango in summer 1806 threatened this peace and led Bonavía to seek assistance from Salcedo. Unfortunately for the intendant governor, the commandant general was in no position to help as he had just learned of some disturbing news. On March 19, 1806, American President Thomas Jefferson went before the United States Congress and asked for an increased military presence on the border of Spanish territory, suggesting that he planned to invade the Internal Provinces. Rumors also said that a private army of "10,000 men, subjects of the United States, are being organized in Kentucky with the object of overpowering the uninhabited provinces of this kingdom." This diverted even more soldiers and resources, as well as the commandant general's attention, from Rafael and left Bonavía, Lucas Valenzuela, and the few men they commanded in Nueva Vizcaya to deal with him.[31]

With Salcedo busy and Rafael's latest attacks on the Hacienda de Santa Catalina and Hacienda de la Zarca being much closer to Durango than Salcedo's headquarters in Chihuahua City, the intendant governor developed a plan to encourage non-military personnel to seek out Rafael. On June 24, Bonavía issued a circular asking the people of Durango to dedicate themselves to apprehending Rafael and his companions, and he offered five hundred pesos to anyone, including Spanish soldiers, who could bring Rafael and José Antonio in "alive or dead."[32]

Bonavía did not specify how the reward was to be collected, but in the past, the Spanish had accepted the heads of wanted criminals if an entire body could not be brought in as proof. Indeed, in the early years of the establecimiento system, Spanish officials offered four pesos to Apaches de paz who would bring in the heads of relatives who refused to move on to establecimientos. Just how many Apaches accepted this offer and how many pesos were paid out is unknown, but the fact that Rafael and José Antonio commanded a price that was more than sixty-two times what the average Apache enemy brought in shows the degree to which the two men worried Spanish officials.[33]

BY THE TIME that Bonavía issued his announcement, Lucas Valenzuela and his cadre of soldiers had made their way south into Durango to investigate the recent spate of attacks. After consulting with survivors and speaking to witnesses, Valenzuela learned that Rafael, José Antonio, and their recently acquired captives were traveling north in the direction of Santa Bárbara, Chihuahua. One witness claimed to see Rafael two leagues from the town with two others, possibly José Antonio and the captive woman from La Zarca. They were carrying two muchachos on their laps in front of them. This could have been the fourteen-year-old Tarahumara girl Maríana and the boy captured with her.[34]

Valenzuela's investigation, and perhaps Bonavía's offer of five hundred pesos, helped Manuel Sáenz, Antonio Soto, and a third Spanish soldier track Rafael, José Antonio, and their captives to a hill just outside of Santa Bárbara on July 3, near the local cathedral. A firefight ensued, during which Soto received a bullet in his right arm. Although this battle appears to have been on relatively level ground, Sáenz's men still found it difficult to shoot the Apaches. This may have owed to the way Apaches do battle. As one person who fought them noted, "Apaches zigzag and shoot fast, for they can move and shoot very quickly. If he was going forward toward the enemy he goes sideways and he stands sideways so that he isn't so big a target like the edge of my hand." Whether or not the Apaches employed this method is uncertain, but Spanish forces failed to hit either Rafael or José Antonio during the battle. In spite of this, Sáenz's soldiers eventually forced the Apaches to flee, leaving behind one of their captives, a shotgun, three hats, and a bridle.[35]

The Apaches would remain in flight from the Spanish for the rest of July. On July 29, Corporal Lorenzo Minjares located the body of a paisano, which led him in the direction of Rafael's camp. Although the Apaches were able to escape before Minjares could surround them, they left behind a lance and nine mules. At some point in July, their two remaining captives escaped.[36]

WHEN MANUEL SÁENZ SPOKE with the captives, he found them to have been "very mistreated." Although Saénz leaves out details as to what he meant by this, it can be assumed that the captives were victims of torture. The way in which Apaches treated captives varied greatly based on the needs of the band, the attitude and adaptability of the captive, the temperament of the Apache captors, and a multitude of other factors. In some cases, captives essentially became a part of band and were treated the same as those born into the tribe, but at other times, Apaches treated captives as slaves and objects which they could torture whenever they saw fit.[37]

As one observer later noted of the Apaches, "they were cruel to everything that came within their power. If the young Apache could capture a bird or a mouse or any living thing, he took the keenest delight in torturing it, and this species of cruelty did not disappear even when they were stalwart men. They took pleasure in tormenting any living creature from a bird to a horse. Their atrocities are simply too horrible and shocking to write out in words."

Cultural observers and historians have attempted to explain this attitude only to arrive at vastly different conclusions. Some historians believe that torture was as an act of revenge. Even though the captive might not have caused harm to an Apache, their cultural kinsmen had, and so Apaches used violence as a means of getting back at the original offender. Others argue that torture was "a psychological message to their enemies showing that their presence was unwelcome." If someone knew that if they fought Apaches and lost, torture awaited them, they might be less inclined to fight in the first place.[38]

Whatever their reasoning, Rafael and José Antonio's most recent captives were still able to communicate despite their wounds. In a deposition given to Sáenz, one of the female captives reported that Rafael was feeling the pressure of the Spanish dragnet, and because of this, he planned to go further into Durango and the foothills of the Sierra Madres "with the intention of living more peacefully."[39]

THIS DECLARATION PROVED TRUE in the short term, as there would only be three outbreaks of violence involving the Apaches for the remainder of 1806. Unfortunately for those involved, these incidents would be very violent and deadly. The first series of attacks occurred over the course of three days in late August, and it seems that Rafael and José Antonio carried them out to acquire food and supplies. On August 21, they injured two shepherds near Parida in northern Durango, took their saddles, and five of their flock. Two days later, August 23, they raided nearby Hacienda del Táscate, where they killed four and wounded two others. They then took a young boy captive from the town of San Gregorio.[40]

The motivations behind the remaining attacks in 1806 are less clear. On the night of September 17, a local priest from the villa of Santa Bárbara, don José Rafael de Miranda had just performed nightly prayers at the Rancho de la Aguazarca and was preparing to offer confession to parishioners Perfecto Madrid and María Ignacia Gutiérrez, when Rafael and José Antonio rode up, drew their lances, and stabbed Madrid seven times. They then began lancing Gutiérrez. Both victims would survive the incident, as would a young man named Pedro José Villalobos, whom the Apaches left alone. Rafael and José Antonio, however, took two girls as captives, twelve-year-old María Guadalupe Montes and fourteen-year-old Margarita Florentín. A different report said that one of the girls was named Josefa.[41]

Considering they had taken similarly aged girls in previous attacks, the motivation behind the raid on Rancho de la Aguazarca attack was likely sexual in nature. What makes the raid illustrative, however, is Rafael and José Antonio's disregard for Catholic institutions. When Rafael was a youth, Buenaventura, Petra, and Rafael Nevares had taught him that he must accept the divinity of Jesus Christ and adhere to the edicts of the pope and the Catholic Church hierarchy. The Nevareses emphasized that piety, monogamy, abstinence from earthly pleasures, good deeds toward others, and delayed gratification would lead to salvation in the afterlife. Those who failed to conform to church edicts, committed adultery, spoke heresy, practiced idolatry, and otherwise violated religious instruction were sinners and were destined for eternal damnation. At least some of these lessons had taken hold, as even after leaving Guajoquilla, Rafael continued to pray, make the sign of the cross, and carry a rosary. Rumor also held that he sometimes attended mass in disguise.[42]

However, the attack on Father Madrid, the multiple women Rafael would take as wives, and the multitude of thefts and murders his band committed illustrate that these were likely superficial overtures or selective choices meant to gain power from the Christian god, not true signs of devotion. Like many Indians raised in Spanish homes, Rafael probably adopted elements of Catholicism because doing so brought tangible and intangible benefits. Spanish priests often rewarded attending mass and compliance with Catholic instruction with material goods, and one could avoid punishment or ostracization by at least pretending to adopt Catholicism. Catholicism also promised magical benefits to Indians. Not only would you enter the afterlife if you were faithful, but you also would have a vengeful god and his saints on your side in a fight. For this reason, some historians have credited what little success the Spanish had with converting Apaches to Apaches seeking divine assistance in battle.[43]

It seems that by 1806, Rafael had largely rejected Catholicism and instead his religious beliefs fell more in line with that of most Apaches. Apache religion was fluid and could vary greatly from one group to the next, but most Apaches believed in multiple supernatural beings, each responsible for aspects of nature and daily life. They shared the Catholic view that a Supreme Being created all things, but unlike the Christian god, the Apache "captain of the sky" Yastaritanne did not cast divine judgement on sinners and remained largely detached from human affairs. He had no say in whether someone passed into the afterlife, nor did someone's actions on earth determine their post-corporeal status.[44]

Instead, the Apaches saw little reason to abstain from earthly pleasures. They frequently ate to excess, took as many sexual partners as they could, stole, and lied when it would bring immediate benefit. Anthropologists have speculated that this was a cultural reaction to "the short duration of their existence," wherein a swipe from a bear, a bite from a rattlesnake, a scratch from a poisonous plant, or a bullet or arrow fired from an enemy might end someone's life at a moment's notice; many Apaches in the nineteenth century only ever saw their relatives die of violence and some did not even recognize that death from old age was a possibility. As one observer noted, this meant that Apaches "forget about the past and they live without worry because they never think about the future: they are interested in the present." Having already alienated Catholic society and with death an ever-present reality, it is understandable that Rafael had little compunction rejecting his adopted father's teachings in favor of those of his birth culture.[45]

RAFAEL AND JOSÉ ANTONIO would conduct a second assault on a Catholic institution and make their final appearance in 1806 soon after the attack on Father Madrid. In late September, Rafael and José Antonio encountered a Tarahumara woman from the small village of Baquirrachi as she was traveling with her three infants to San Pablo. The woman was making the journey because a Spanish priest had come to San Pablo to baptize local Tarahumara children. Once a year or so, priests would travel to larger Tarahumara settlements, ring a bell announcing that they were giving baptisms, and send Tarahumara runners to inform locals in more remote villages to assemble in the town with their children. Whether wanting to ensure their children's salvation or simply to partake in the fiesta that accompanied the baptism ceremony, Tarahumaras, such as the woman traveling to San Pablo with her three children, made the trip.[46]

Unfortunately, the woman and her infants would not complete the journey, as Rafael and José Antonio killed them before they reached their destination. Soon thereafter the Apache band attacked two Tarahumara men and two women from Tecorichi who were on their way to San Pablo to witness the baptism, killing the men and taking the two women hostage. They then attacked and killed a Tarahumara man and woman near Baquirrachi before moving on to Reventón, where they killed three muleteers before escaping in the direction of Batopilas. In total they killed eleven people over the course of a few hours.[47]

The death total may have been even higher had one of the two captive Tarahumara women not escaped and alerted Spanish authorities about what had happened. She described her kidnapping and reported that "in addition to her companion [Juana María], the enemies had two captives, one bigger and one smaller." This implies that Rafael had killed one of the two young girls he had captured in September at the San Mateo Chapel, possibly the twelve-year-old María Guadalupe. This appears to have left the other girl Josefa, the Tarahumara Juana María, and the boy they had captured from San Gregorio as their sole captives.[48]

THE WOMAN'S TESTIMONY and news of the attacks horrified Spanish officials, but they continued to struggle to locate Rafael's band. On October 27, Alberto Maynez reported to Bernardo Bonavía that he had not heard "any news whatsoever of the unceasing hostilities and lamentations committed by the Indian Rafael. Several parties of troops are in pursuit of him and I will inform you of their operations and results." Lucas Valenzuela combed the area of the recent attacks with no luck.[49]

Making matters worse, Commandant General Salcedo was in no position to offer military aid. At approximately the same time that word arrived in Chihuahua concerning Rafael's latest series of murders, Salcedo received news that American General James Wilkinson planned to march an army into Texas to claim the province as part of the Louisiana Purchase. Recognizing that the precarious situation required his personal attention, Salcedo set off for Texas, bringing even more troops from Nueva Vizcaya to accompany him.[50]

With government forces occupied and considering the religious nature of the recent attacks, the bishop of Durango, don Francisco Gabriel de Olivares y Benito, hoped to enlist an even higher power to stop Rafael. Although Olivares y Benito had been bishop of the Durango Archdiocese since 1796, he had little experience dealing with Apaches. He had never traveled to New Mexico or the northern half of Nueva Vizcaya even though they were part of his diocese because he feared that Apaches would attack him if he made the journey. Now with Rafael raiding deep into Durango, it appeared that Apaches would be coming to the bishop if nothing was done.[51]

Addressing the people of his archdiocese on October 28, Olivares y Benito said that he had just received news that "the barbarous Indian Rafael with his companion had cruelly assassinated two men, three women, and three children that in their company they lead of the Towns of Baquirachic, Todarichic and

Guasarachic to be baptized in the parishes of San Pablo or Guejoquita." The bishop claimed that "this event has distressed his heart" and that he was "dismayed at the horror of so much death and havoc caused by this inhuman and ferocious man." Because the government's efforts to track Rafael down had to this point been ineffective, Olivares y Benito hoped to "implore the mercy of God" by asking his parishioners to "attend a Mass on the first holiday that would be celebrated with the greatest solemnity." In doing so, he asked "Lord free us from him, and succor in such grave need."[52]

Others believed that the Spanish would need luck more than God's help. In late 1806, presidio commander Alberto Maynez sent a letter to the Intendent Governor Bonavía informing him that "the vague news that runs in this villa is that the Indio Rafael is reduced and has returned to the interior of the Province between the Ciénega de los Olivos and El Parral and confirms the acknowledgments that have been made of my order by different Border points. Lieutenant Don Lucas Valenzuela persecutes him with perseverance, but I consider that only luck can free us from this enemy who possesses our language, who uses our own costumes, who knows how we operate, who has practical knowledge of all the lands of this Province." Unfortunately for Maynez and Bonavía, luck would not be on their side, and neither would Lucas Valenzuela, as he disappears from the historical record for a time. It is unclear what happened to him, but he may have been among the hundreds of soldiers joining Salcedo on the border with the United States.[53]

CHAPTER FIVE

A Well-Armed and Mounted Man,
January 1807–June 1807

O N JANUARY 10, 1807, the senior military intendent of Durango,
Lieutenant Félix Colomo, learned that a week earlier, Rafael and
José Antonio had killed three men at Jicorica. This was some three
months after and 125 miles away from the last reported sighting of Rafael at
Batopilas. The Apaches had then taken the road to Guanaceví, where they
captured a sixteen-year-old boy named Agustin Nájera on January 5, increasing
their total number of captives to four. Witnesses last reported seeing the group
near Tizonazo, Santa Cruz, and El Zape.[1]

The situation infuriated Colomo, who seems to have taken over for Valenzuela as the primary Spanish officer in charge of finding Rafael. Colomo was a
good choice for this duty. He had more than a decade of experience dealing
with rebellious establecimiento Apaches, and at one point he had been stationed in Guajoquilla as part of the Primera Compañía Volante and had
therefore likely served with Rafael and José Antonio. As Colomo saw things,
the location of the new attacks was problematic. Rafael's previous raids had
occurred mostly in central Nueva Vizcaya, where soldiers from the Guajoquilla
and San Pablo presidios could respond to attacks within a few days' time. The
area around Guanaceví, on the other hand, was located in the heart of the
Sierra Madres, far from the frontier. Few Apaches had ever raided so deep into
Spanish territory; therefore, there were no presidios nearby.[2]

Making matters more difficult for Colomo was the region's rugged geography. The Sierra Madre surrounding Guanaceví stood at elevations from nine
to ten thousand feet, making traveling to the area a time-consuming process.
Heavy snowfalls were common in winter, and during the wet season, roads
turned to mud, threatening to toss travelers off cliffs. Animal life in the region
was hostile as well, with bears and mountain lions occasionally attacking

Presidio
Flying Companies
(Compañías Volantes)
City, Town, or Hacienda
Mountains or Peak

Carrizal ↑ to El Paso

Ojo
Caliente

Rio Grande

Namiquipa

Coyome
Llano de
Hormigas

Encinillas

Norte

Río Conchos

Camino Real de Tierra Adentro

Matachit

Aldama

San Carlos

Chihuahua

Basnuchi
San Andrés

Pilar de
Conchos

Papigochi

San Estevan

Santa Roslia
de Cuevas

San Pablo

Valerio

Río Conchos

NUEVA VIZCAYA

Río Florido

Batopilas

Guajoquilla

El Reventon
Parral
San
Bartolomé

Santa Bárbara

SIERRA

Bolsón de
Mapimi

MADRE

La Parida

Cerro Cabeza
del Oso

Canutillo

Cerro Gordo

Sierra Ojito

Real de Oro
Tizonazo

Mapimí

Guanacevi

Indé

OCCIDENTAL

Zape

Zarca

El Gallo

Río

Jicorica

Nazas

Santiago
Papasquiaro
Ulana
San
Andrés
△Mountains

Amoles

San Gregorio
Soyupa
San Hipólito

Cuencamé

Guatinape

N
W　E
S

0　25 miles
0　25 kilometers

Acatita

Marquezotes

Otatitlán

to Zacatecas

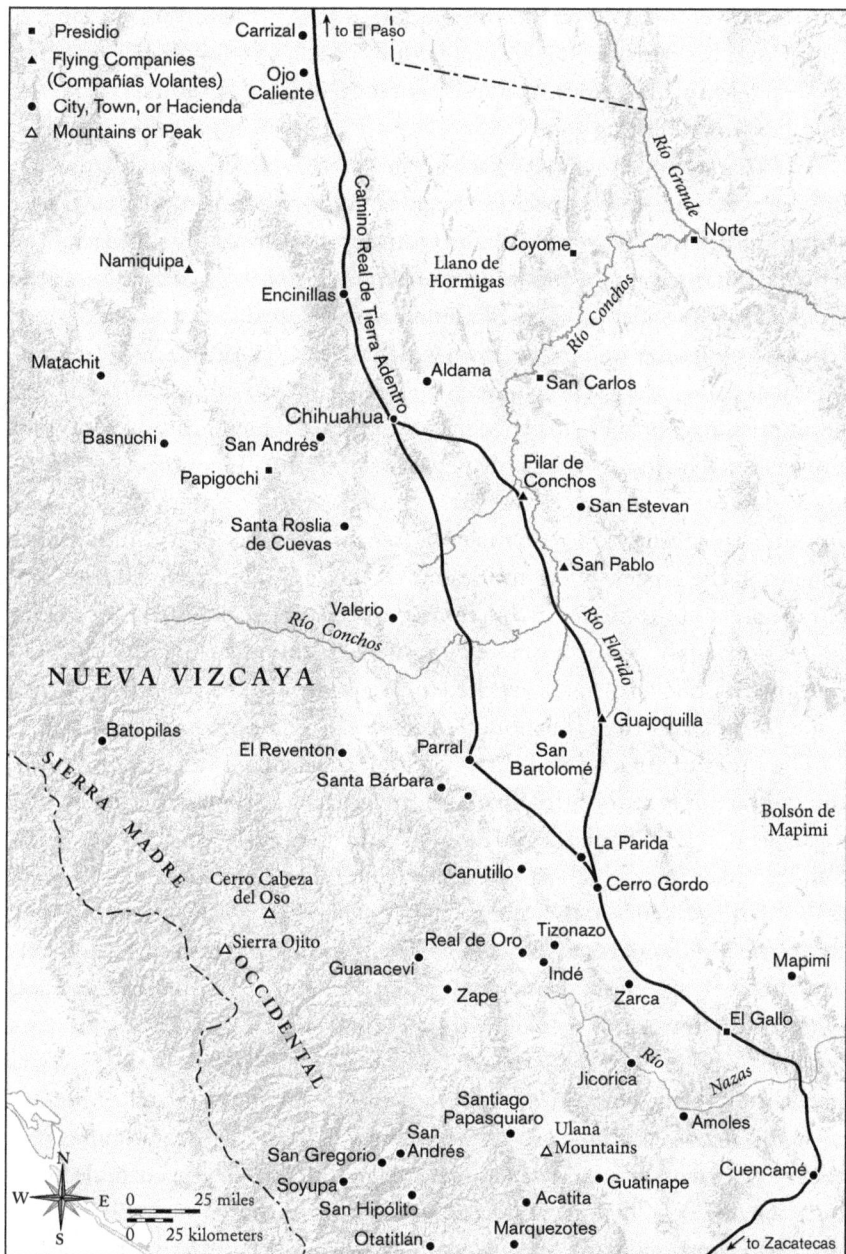

Western Nueva Vizcaya. Spanish officials suspected that Apaches assisted Rafael in his raids in the north, and blamed disaffected Tarahumaras, Tepehuanes, and other Hispanicized Indians for his success in the Sierra Madre Occidental.
Map by Ben Pease, cartographer.

those who ventured down remote mountain paths. These various dangers meant that by the time Rafael's band committed an assault, locals reported the incident to authorities, and soldiers reached the area to investigate, the Apaches would be long gone.[3]

The area around Guanacevi was also home to Tarahumara and Tepehuan Indians who had little respect for Spanish authority. When Spaniards first arrived in the region in the sixteenth century, they forcefully displaced the sedentary agriculturalist Tarahumaras from their homes in the valleys of the Sierra Madre Occidental. The Tarahumaras responded by settling in distant, remote mountain communities, from which they would launch raids on Spanish towns. When the Spanish military failed to halt these raids, Spain deployed Jesuit missionaries to Hispanicize the remote Tarahumaras through religious conversion. The Jesuits were only partially successful. Tarahumara groups at lower elevation and nearer to the Spanish, such as those whom Rafael and José Antonio had recently killed on their way to baptism, accepted the missionaries and began the process of acculturation. Others, especially those in the more remote areas of the Sierra Madre, refused the Jesuit overtures and continued to live outside the Spanish sphere of influence. Still others initially accepted missionaries, but when Spain expelled the Jesuits from its colonies in 1767, they joined their kinsmen in the mountains in rejecting the Spanish way of life.[4]

The onset of Apache raids into Tarahumara lands in the last decades of the eighteenth century further complicated matters. In spite of the fact that Apaches attacked Spaniard, Christian Tarahumara, and non-Christian Tarahumara alike, Spanish officials came to believe that many Tarahumaras were assisting the Apaches in their raids, and, for this reason, they began referring to hostile Tarahumaras as "Apaches." This meant that Spanish settlements were beset by the more traditional "external enemy" Athabaskan Apaches who raided from lands to the north, and the "internal enemy" Tarahumara Apaches, who assisted the "external enemy" Apaches in their raids. This was in addition to the abiego rustler "Apaches" who might be Apache, Tarahumara, or any other ethnic group. The degree to which the Tarahumara and the Apaches worked with one another to fight the Spanish is debatable, but a questionable 1771 Spanish investigation concluded that some 1,700 Tarahumara had conspired with Apaches during one particularly destructive raid.[5]

COLOMO WAS AMONG THOSE who felt there was significant collusion between the Tarahumara and the Apaches. Soon after learning that Rafael had begun to raid in the Tarahumara homeland, Colomo remarked, "having been infidels, it would not be long before the people of this region have friendly and hospitable relationship with the Indian Rafael and provide him with warnings about troop movements." Indeed, Colomo believed that Rafael had already received aid from the Tarahumara, as he suspected that Rafael's new sixteen-year-old captive, Agustin Nájera, was not a captive at all but had willingly joined the Apache band. Even if Nájera or the rest of the Sierra Madre Tarahumara were not actively supporting Rafael, Colomo felt that they would be less likely to assist soldiers in searching for Rafael than those in more-Hispanicized areas of Nueva Vizcaya.[6]

The Tepehuanes also fell under suspicion of providing Rafael with aid. Like the Tarahumara, the Tepehuanes called the Sierra Madre Occidental home, with the northernmost branch of Tepehuanes, the Odamí living near Santiago Papasquiaro, just south of Tarahumara territory. Like their northern neighbors, the Tepehuanes maintained many aspects of their native culture, and some almost entirely rejected Spanish language and lifestyle. However, the passage of time and pressure from the Spanish had led many Tepehuanes to intermarry with Tarahumaras, blending the cultural line between the two Indian groups. This multiculturalism inspired distrust among the Spanish, and for this reason, officials would suspect collusion when in January 1807, Rafael also conducted a series of raids near the Tepehuanes.[7]

The January 1807 raids in Tarahumara and Tepehuan territory were different than many of the band's previous raids in that Rafael seems to have conducted them without José Antonio. On January 21, Rafael went to the region around Marquezote and Piedras Azules, where he killed Juan José Nores on the San Juan del Río Hacienda. Two others fell to the Apache near Santiago Papasquiaro around the same time. On January 25, Rafael killed two paisanos near Pachón. Later, he killed two vintners on the Salto de Lúeas stream and severely injured another who was transporting wine to Santiago Papasquiaro. On January 27, Rafael killed Mateo Marrufo in the Sierra de Armoloya.[8]

When a frustrated Colomo arrived to investigate, he was able to track the Apaches across the plains of Guatimapé, and he even managed to locate one of their former camps where he found the remains of a bonfire and a half-eaten horse. Unfortunately for the Spanish officer, the area was covered in horse tracks, and it was unclear which direction the Apaches had gone, leading Colomo to remark in frustration, "it was not possible for their punishment to be achieved."[9]

Based on Colomo's description, Rafael and José Antonio had become aware
of Colomo and had departed camp at the last second. As one Spanish officer
described this process, "it is impossible to measure the speed with which they
break camp when they have perceived hostile superior forces in their vicinity.
If they have animals, in a moment they are laden with their belongings . . .
the men armed and mounted on their best horses; and everything in order to
start out for country which they judge properly safe."[10]

Rafael and José Antonio had also likely put in place traditional Apaches measures meant to fool those looking for them. Apaches sometimes threw young
branches and leaves on bonfires to produce smoke and blind pursuers. They also
often set out from camp in different directions to create multiple tracks so those
coming after them would not know which to follow, and they disguised those
tracks which might lead to their true destination. As one Apache explained this
process, "a small group goes this way and another goes that way. They run on
rocks as much as possible so that their tracks will not be seen. They say, 'Go on
rocks so your tracks will not be fresh. Keep off soft ground.' A person hides his
tracks by jumping from rock to rock and from bunch of grass to bunch of grass
to get away from those who are following. Another thing he does sometimes is
to take grass and rub out his tracks with it so they won't be noticed." Once safely
away, Apaches would meet at a predetermined location, or use smoke signals or
stone and wood markings to find the rest of their band.[11]

IT WAS PERHAPS AFTER READING Colomo's report that Commandant
General Salcedo realized that he needed to take additional measures if he
hoped to stop Rafael. In February 1807, the commandant general sent out
a missive to be taken as a precaution for "the repeated hostilities that have
been executed by the Apache Indian named Rafael." In it, he required that
all local officials in Nueva Vizcaya were to hold a meeting of residents on the
morning of February 28 to discuss what needed to be done to bring Rafael
and José Antonio to justice. Salcedo had grown increasingly frustrated that
his warnings not to leave population centers unless armed had been ignored,
and he blamed ignorance of the rules as part of the reason for Rafael's success.
Those who did not attend the meeting or provide a sufficient excuse would
be "reprimanded for their absence." Local leaders posted announcements
throughout their towns to inform residents of the requirement.[12]

The timing of the announcement was significant in that Salcedo delivered
it while on his way back from Texas, where the commandant general and

his advisers had narrowly averted war with the United States by approving a plan to establish an unoccupied neutral zone between Spanish Texas and American Louisiana where neither nation would settle or maintain soldiers. The compromise allowed Salcedo to withdraw many soldiers from the border and return them to duty in Nueva Vizcaya, a welcome outcome because the commandant general had noticed an increase in Indian attacks in their absence. Perhaps recognizing that the returning soldiers would perform better with an incentive, it was around this time that Salcedo matched the five hundred pesos put up by Bonavía with the same amount of his own, bringing the reward for Rafael's capture or execution to one thousand pesos.[13]

ON FEBRUARY 9, Rafael killed two shepherds and captured a boy near Por, which was near the town of Atotonilco. The addition of the boy from Por brought the total number of captives in Rafael's band to five, which may help explain why José Antonio was absent from Spanish reports from January 3 to February 9. When they first began raiding, Rafael's band brought their captives with them on raids, but this method had proved to be impractical. Whereas older captives, those who had been with the band a long time, and Apaches, such as Ultin's wife could keep up with the band, children and non-Apache women often found it difficult to maintain the pace of their captors.[14]

This led Rafael and José Antonio to occasionally leave captives in camp during raids. To prevent detainees from escaping and warning local officials about the band's whereabouts, Apaches sometimes tied captives to trees and placed bags over their heads. This made breaking out of ropes more difficult, and it prevented the captives from seeing which direction the Apaches were headed. Therefore, even if the captives escaped before the Apaches returned, they could not direct pursuers to the raiding location. It also put fear in the captives that they might escape only to run into the Apaches as they were returning from their raid.[15]

Indeed, fear would prove to be the most efficient way to prevent captives from fleeing. Captives knew that if Rafael or José Antonio caught them while they were escaping, it might mean death, and considering that some of Rafael's captives go unaccounted for in Spanish records, including one of the six they held in early 1807, it is likely that some met their end during a failed escape attempt. Apaches understood that when there were multiple captives, as was the case with Rafael's band in January and February 1807, fear and ropes might not be enough, so they often left a trusted member of the band behind to prevent escapes. Although this role usually fell to Apache women in larger bands, José Antonio's absence from the records in January and February 1807 may mean that he took on the task during this time.[16]

Captives sometimes escaped in spite of these precautions. Indeed, soon after the boy from Por arrived, he and two other captives—the boy captured near San Gregorio the previous year and Nájera, the sixteen-year-old Tarahumara taken in early January—fled the Apache camp. Spanish documents suggest that they left together on or around February 10. Perhaps the boy from Por knew the area and encouraged the others to escape, or perhaps Rafael and José Antonio partook in too much wine stolen from the vintners near Pachón and passed out.[17]

It is also possible that Rafael and José Antonio, after extracting as much information about the surrounding area from the boys as they could, simply realized that their captives' value had come to an end and allowed them to leave. This was a fairly common practice whenever Apaches felt that captives had been cooperative but had outlived their usefulness. For example, after one Apache chief captured a boy and killed his father and brother, he "gave him liberty, and brought him back in safety to the settlements in the neighborhood of the city, and when he left him, gave him friendly advice how to avoid the danger of again falling in with his tribe." Whatever the case, after leaving the Apaches' camp, the boys split up—perhaps to prevent Rafael from tracking them—and each found their way to Spanish authorities.[18]

Interestingly, the two female captives, Juana María and Josefa, were not among the escapees. This may have simply been a matter of opportunity. Apache men would often take captive women as concubines and tie them to themselves at night to prevent their escape. Additional evidence, however, points to the possibility that the women remained with the Apaches voluntarily. It was common for captive Hispanicized women to adapt to the lifestyle of Indian captors, and Spanish officials feared that young women, even more so than young men, could yield to "the sensuous liberties afforded them in Indian society."[19]

LIKELY UNDERSTANDING that the escaped captives might reveal the location of their camp, Rafael's band disappeared for the next month, only to reemerge in Tarahumara lands southwest of Chihuahua City. On March 11, Rafael snuck up on two Tarahumara boys who were fishing in the San Ignacio River. Rafael lanced one of them in the chest, and it passed all the way through him. The other Tarahumara boy ran and was not only able to escape death, but he also managed to warn the *subdelgado* of Satevó in time for Spanish forces to return to the scene of the attack and save his friend's life.[20]

Much has been said about the Tarahumaras' ability to run long distances without rest. Without treading too heavily on this proverbially well-worn ground, it is sufficient to say that an important aspect of Tarahumara culture was a kick ball race, during which a team of men kick a wooden ball long distances, sometimes for days on end, with little rest. The game may have had its origins in pre-Columbian times, but it might also have developed as a cultural response to the incursions of the Spanish or the Apaches. Whatever the case, the long-distance running required to compete in the game increased endurance, meaning that those who played were more likely to survive Apache attacks. Whether it was this running ability that allowed the boy fishing in the San Ignacio to escape or something else entirely is unknown.[21]

After receiving the boy's warning, the subdelgado of Satevó sent a message to Corporal Juan Mendoza, stationed nearby at the Río de las Quintanas. Mendoza received the missive on March 16 and dispatched groups of soldiers to track down the Apache band. Corporal Francisco Espinosa led one of these parties, consisting of himself, José Manuel Quiros, and three other mounted cavalrymen of the Primera Compañía Volante into the Sierra del Carmen or Camarones. Because no roads existed in this area and traveling at elevation taxed horses and required regular stops whenever ravines bisected paths, the soldiers moved slowly, spending days traveling alongside and within canyons carved out by the San Ignacio River and its tributaries. Unfortunately for Espinosa's party, as previous searchers had learned, this methodical and deliberate pace allowed Rafael to not only detect the soldiers but also to plan an elaborate ambush.[22]

A soldier who would later conduct numerous campaigns against Apaches noted that the Indians "will watch for days, scanning your every movement, observing your every act; taking exact note of your party and all its belongings. Let no one suppose that these assaults are made upon the spur of the moment by bands accidentally encountered. Far from it; they are almost invariably the results of long watching-patient-waiting-careful and rigorous observation, and anxious council." As one historian put it, "these factors all combined to produce in the Apache warrior a truly deadly adversary. Their ambush tactics epitomized their principles of war." Another who campaigned against the Apaches said simply of his adversaries, they are "the tiger of the human species."[23]

The tiger leapt on March 26 when a hail of rocks and arrows began raining down on Espinosa and his soldiers as they passed through a narrow mountain canyon in the Sierra de la Piedra Lumbre. Espinosa would later recall that Rafael and his "compañeros" had taken a position on the cliff far above. His use of the plural "compañeros," indicates that Rafael was joined not only by José Antonio, but also the female captives, Juana María and Josefa. With projectiles incoming, the soldiers either dismounted or fell off their horses and attempted to return fire on their assailants. They soon discovered that they were unable to hit the targets above them.[24]

Before long it became apparent that they were on the losing end of what Quiros would later call a "battle of arms against El Indio Rafael." As the soldiers learned, "the Apaches are incomparable archers, and seldom miss; their arrows, when let fly by a strong arm, have more power and effectiveness than a bullet from the best musket." It was also difficult for the soldiers to find an opening to return fire. As one priest described the Indian nations proficiency with the bow, "in battle they often aim at a man as though preparing to let fly an arrow at him instantly. Then, when the person threatened covers himself with his shield, they turn with the greatest dexterity and shoot the arrow at another who least suspects it." One such arrow hit Espinosa and another his fellow soldier, severely injuring them both. Two other soldiers were pelted by rocks.[25]

Espinosa and his men soon discovered that in spite of their injuries, they were not the primary targets of the Apache ambush. Instead, Rafael was employing a tactic that served as a mainstay of Apache combat: the main objective when confronting an enemy was to cripple their ability to pursue you further. In general, whoever was looking for the Apaches did not know the land as well as the Apaches and would have little hope of catching them on foot. This fact made horses especially important for the Apaches' pursuers. With the Spanish soldiers taking cover from the stones and arrows, Rafael focused his attack on their horses and mules, forcing the animals to flee. Unable to recover the horses without further subjecting themselves to rocks and arrows, Espinosa ordered his men to escape the scene on foot, leaving behind their mounts as well as the bags, papers, uniforms, and orders they carried. Espinosa and his men then stumbled into the nearby Hacienda de Guadalupe to report on the incident.[26]

VICTORY OVER THE SPANISH SOLDIERS left Rafael and his band in possession of new mounts, firearms, and uniforms, which they would use on April 10 to conduct a series of attacks. This included an assault near Gavilán on a muleteer, who would later report that "four well-armed and mounted men" robbed him of his "money, clothes, and jewelry." Interestingly, the muleteer was able to determine that it was Rafael's band who attacked him, but he was unable to tell that two of the "men" were the women Juana María and Josefa.[27]

Shortly thereafter, the Apaches traveled in the direction of Guanaceví, executing three at a place called Las Lacenas on the way. They then killed a father, mother, and two small children who were servants on the Cerro Prieto Rancho on their way back home after having received confession in Guanaceví. Two Indians traveling from Nabogame to Guanaceví also fell to Rafael and José Antonio's lances. At some point, likely between April 10 and 19, Rafael killed a mozo servant of the priest of Real del Oro as he was traveling on the Las Cruces Road. This may have been fourteen-year-old Juan Francisco Martinez, whose burial record says, "was killed in the countryside by the barbarous Indian Rafael, according to all available indications."[28]

In what was perhaps the most disturbing of the mid-April attacks, Rafael stole some horses from the Cerro Prieto Ranch and captured a mozo and his thirteen-year-old son from Estolano. The mozo and the boy did not last long. A short distance away, the Indians killed the mozo by "a substantial number of arrow and lance wounds." On April 11, Rafael or a member of his band stripped the child of his clothes, hung him from a pine tree by his hair, and lanced him eight times. Shortly thereafter, locals discovered a third victim whom "the barbarous enemy Rafael had violently killed" and dismembered. Those recovering the body could only bring back a single bone to be interred because "animals had eaten most of the rest of the corpse."[29]

Spanish sources are largely quiet on what state Rafael's band left the bodies of most of their victims, but the manner in which the Apaches killed the mozo and his child from the Cerro Prieto Ranch indicates that they mutilated at least some before and after death. Although historians argue about how often Apaches performed mutilations, there is no question that as a people, Apaches would at least occasionally perform elaborate, sadistic rituals to end the lives of their enemies. Indeed, stories of Apaches mutilating their enemies are legion in Spanish, Mexican, and United States sources.[30]

For example, more than one traveler reported hearing that Apaches would cut off the soles of victims and force them to run across hot sand. Supposedly, Apaches once captured a man, rubbed him with sweet cooked mescal, and "buried him, all but his head, in close proximity to a large black ant hill." They buried another man up to his neck, sliced his eyelids off, and forced him to stare at the sun until his eyeballs burned out. In a less destructive but equally cruel affair, Apaches buried another prisoner up to his neck and placed water just out of his reach. Geronimo, in an instance that mirrored what Rafael had done to the boy from Estolano, once left a still-alive young girl hanging from a meat hook that he had jammed under her skull.[31]

While those who fought the Apaches might exaggerate the degree of cruelty and the commonness of such incidents, there is no question that mutilations occurred. There are several possible cultural and psychological explanations for the practice. Many Spaniards felt that it owed to an inherent bloodlust. One priest said of Apaches, "in the fury of the onslaught, they kill everyone in sight, and their cruelty is so great that they will inflict wound after wound, just as though their lust for blood were insatiable. I have buried victims whose bodies were unrecognizable, so gashed were they from head to foot by lances."[32]

Others believed that mutilation was a response to the violence the Apaches themselves had received at the hands of enemy Indians, the Spanish, and later Mexicans and Americans. The Spanish and their Comanche allies had killed thousands of Apaches during the past century and sent hundreds of others to Cuba never to see their families again. Mexicans and Americans sometimes killed Apache women and children and imprisoned countless others. To an Apache, torture and mutilation offered an outlet for those angry over the loss of a loved one, especially considering their belief that those with mutilated bodies maintained this condition in the afterlife. Some historians believe that the Apaches never mutilated before the arrival of Europeans and only began to do so after witnessing soldiers cut off Apache ears and scalps to serve as prizes and proof of kills.[33]

Whatever the motivation, Rafael and José Antonio were likely not the ones to mutilate the mozo and the thirteen-year-old. Instead, they probably forced Juana María and Josefa to carry out the deed as a rite of passage. When they took Ultin's wife on raids with them, they had forced her to stab a woman multiple times, and a different captive would later describe José Antonio as forcing him to execute a young boy. By requiring captives to engage in such activities, it would further distance them from Spanish society. After all, someone would be less likely to escape if they believed that they would face punishment for murder or if their loved ones knew they had participated in such horrific mutilations.[34]

ON APRIL 22, "el Indio barbaro Rafael" killed two of Felipe Rosi's muleteers as they were traveling two leagues away from Guanaceví. Another rancher, Diego Nuñez, reported that two servants from his San Estevan Ranch had gone missing. Spanish soldiers investigating the incident suspected Rafael's band was responsible but did not pronounce the servants dead because they could not locate their bodies.[35]

On April 30, Rafael, José Antonio, and "another" dressed in soldier uniforms approached a group of servants at the Perrero de Ronsesvalles as they were gathering wood. At least one of the servants carried a gun. Although Salcedo's firearms factory was now producing dozens of weapons a month, firearms were still costly in the Internal Provinces, indicating that whoever oversaw the servants had taken the commandant general's decree requiring arms seriously. Considering Salcedo's frequent warnings about Rafael and the number of attacks by the band in the Santa Bárbara jurisdiction prior to this time, there is little question that the servants knew about Rafael and his propensity to wear a soldier's uniform as a disguise. In spite of this, Rafael's band was able to wound one of the servants, Juan Ignacio Barrozo, steal a horse, and take off with all of the servants' supplies, including their firearm. Shortly thereafter, Rafael's band killed Ramón Sandoval near the Paraje del Sitio in the San Bartolomé Valley.[36]

Although the way Rafael was able to get the jump on the armed servant is unknown, the soldiers' uniforms almost certainly played a part, as they created a "Catch 22" for Spanish subjects of the Internal Provinces, with lower class Indians facing an especially difficult situation. Commandant General Salcedo had issued orders for locals to watch out for Apaches posing as soldiers, but at the same time he had tasked his soldiers with finding Indians who might disguise themselves as peasants. Therefore, Hispanicized Indians might be hesitant to cooperate with soldiers, fearing that they were Rafael's band in disguise, but the soldiers might have viewed this hesitancy as evidence that the Indians were Rafael or working with him. Soldiers might be especially fearful of a civilian with a firearm.

Even if they did not believe that they were Rafael, soldiers might view a civilian's reluctance to comply with their orders as disrespect for their authority,

and on the northern frontier, soldiers often responded to perceived disobedi-
ence with violence. For example, in March 1807, Spanish soldiers in Santa Fe
demanded that a group of Indians provide them with information about two
of their neighbors, whom the soldiers suspected of criminal activity. When the
Indians hesitated, "several were knocked down from their horses by the Spanish
dragoons with the butt of their lances," leaving the Indians with "blood streaming
down their visages." The mistreated had little hope of seeing the Spanish soldiers
punished for such slights because the Spanish military was not subject to the
same judicial system as civilians. Soldiers received *fuero* privileges, meaning that
whenever they were accused of a crime, they stood trial under a jury of fellow
military members, who rarely convicted their comrades in arms.[37]

In light of these circumstances, it is understandable that, in spite of Salcedo's warnings, some settlers simply complied with anyone wearing a soldier's
uniform. On May 3, for example, two cowboys near Salgado willingly gave
Rafael and José Antonio the strongest horses in their herd. This cooperation
might have saved their lives, as the Apaches spared the two men, although
they did tie them up, strip them of their clothes, and wound one. The Apaches
also robbed but spared a shepherd they encountered near Basquillo peak at
noon after he provided them with news. A cowboy who the men encountered
near Aguaje de Guajolotes was not so lucky and lost his life. Rafael and José
Antonio also killed two cowboys, a shepherd, and a traveler on May 4 and 5.[38]

IT IS AT THIS POINT that Spanish records concerning Rafael's crimes become
especially clinical. Most Spanish documents from the colonial period are
bureaucratic in nature and contain only enough information to the meet the
document's intended purpose. There are cultural and practical explanations
for this, but perhaps the biggest reason was that paper and ink were expensive in colonial Spanish America, especially in remote areas like the Internal
Provinces that lacked the means to produce stationary. To save paper, the
lurid, emotional, and attention-grabbing details that one might find in a late
nineteenth-century American newspaper about Apaches are rare in Spanish
documents. Instead, reports contain dates the message was sent, the name of
the person reporting the information, the origin of the message, the intended
recipient of the report, and their location. Letters concerning crimes often
give the location of the act, the suspects involved, how the crime was carried
out, the state of the victims, and the actions the sender employed to rectify
the situation, but only occasionally are motivations assigned to criminals.[39]

The early documents assembled by Bustamante in his report on Rafael's crimes generally follow this informative yet unexciting pattern. Bustamante was especially good about recording the names of victims, the purpose of the crime, and how Rafael carried out the act. By 1807, however, Bustamante's report skips details, and his entries often contain little more than the number of victims, the name of the responding officer, and the location from where the responding officer reported his information. For example, when describing two of the murders committed on May 4 and 5, Bustamante wrote only, on May 4 "the Indian Rafael killed a cowboy on the road to Basnuchil Valley at a place named San Diego; on the fifth, he killed another outside of the same Basnuchil." Neither of the victims was named, and in both cases, the taking of a human life did not even receive its own independent sentence.[40]

The trend continues throughout May and into June 1807. On May 10, "Rafael killed two vecinos in the Sierra de Santa Bárbara." Later that day, the "same Indians killed another two Christians in the Arroyo de los Gentiles." On May 14, "Rafael killed one at the Padre Velázquez Ranch and he took seven horses from the Hacienda de Santa Bárbara." On May 17, a company of Spanish soldiers under Rafael Urías found "two bodies dead two or three days." On May 17, Captain Francisco Gerónimo del Valle "found two bodies that had just been killed by Rafael." Shortly thereafter, Valle "also found the body of a servant the same Indian had killed near the Charcos Ranch." He then "found three bodies the same Indian had killed in El Puerto de Santa Gertudis." There are similar, almost disinterested, descriptions for three other murders committed over the next three days.[41]

It is unclear if this decline in detail is present in the original reports or if the fault lies with Bustamante. Perhaps Bustamante, or the Spanish officers making the original report, saw little reason in continuing to try to explain or assign motivation to Rafael's crimes. By 1807, the Apaches' methodology was clearly laid out, and the band had killed so many people that the Spanish may only have been interested in stopping them and no longer cared why they did what they did. Perhaps Spanish officials were wracked with a sense of hopelessness, and this despair manifested itself in their reports. However, the simplest explanation for the brevity in later reports may be that as time went on, Rafael left fewer and fewer people alive to report what had occurred, so soldiers had no details to write down in their reports.

The lack of detail may also owe to the location of the crimes and the types of people being attacked. Whereas most prior crimes had occurred in areas populated by Spaniards and Hispanicized individuals, many of those that took place in summer 1807 were committed in Tarahumara or Tepehuan areas distant from cities most Spanish authorities called home. Some were carried out on unacculturated Tarahumara Indians, who the Spanish regarded as internal enemies. Not only were crimes against these Tarahumaras less likely to be reported to Spanish authorities, disinterest and a language barrier might leave reporting officers with fewer details to write down.

IT SEEMS THAT THESE RECENT ATTACKS, and perhaps the lack of attention from Spanish authorities, led some Tarahumaras to take matters into their own hands and attempt to stop Rafael themselves. As one nineteenth-century traveler said, "one who has ever seen a group of the wild Tarahumaris, would never credit them with anything warlike or aggressive, or even with much of the defensive combativeness that is necessary to fight for one's country. However when 'equally armed-which they seldom were—were more than a match for these Bedouins'" and for this reason "the Apaches, so dreaded by all others, gave the mountainous country of the Tarahumaris a wide berth."[42]

The Tarahumara ability to make war is evident in a June 8, 1807, report concerning an "action of war" fought between Rafael's band and a group of Tarahumara Indians at the remote village of San Joseph de Temaichi. Temaichi had previously been home to a Jesuit mission, but following the expulsion of the Jesuits in 1767, its Tarahumara villagers revolted against the Spanish and refused to accept replacement Franciscan missionaries. This left the people of Temaichi largely autonomous and allowed them to maintain their language and cultural practices free from Spanish influence. However, the autonomy also meant that Spanish soldiers were not there to protect the people of Temaichi from Apaches, and the villagers would have to provide for their own defense.[43]

It seems that after learning that Rafael's band had captured a child on June 4 on the Santa Inés Ranch and then killed a Tarahumara in the nearby Sierra de Papigochi on June 6, the people of Temaichi formed a militia to defend their settlement, conscripting warriors from nearby Pichachichi to join them. When Rafael's band then tried to raid their town on June 8, the Tarahumaras fought back, firing arrows at the Apache invaders. Tarahumara woman may also have participated in defending the settlement. Local legend holds that the women of Temaichi were highly effective fighters in their own right, with one popular Mexican corrido containing the lines, "the women in the tower, what good shots they are/ The blood that runs in them is the blood of liberty."[44]

During the attack on Temaichi, two arrows hit either Rafael or José Antonio, injuring and possibly poisoning whichever of the two was hit. The Tarahumaras often rubbed arrow points in a pulp made from local poisonous leaves and smashed up venomous spiders in the hopes of debilitating opponents. The injuries allowed the Tarahumara to press forward against Rafael and José Antonio and capture their horses and all their equipment. The Tarahumaras also briefly liberated the two female captives, Juana María and Josefa, before Rafael and José Antonio recovered enough to push the Tarahumaras back and retrieve the women and their horses. Eventually, Rafael's band escaped, but they abandoned a horse, a shield, two sabers, and a sarape in the scuffle. They also left behind the bodies of six dead Tarahumaras who had died defending Temaichi.[45]

Although there is almost no information available about this event, the success of the people of Temaichi fits with other depictions of the town and a general understanding about Tarahumara warriors. One observer remarked of the Spanish military's ability to defend settlements in the Sierra Madre and thereby prevent Apaches from invading Sonora to the west, "they are not the caliber of men from which Sonora can expect its salvation. Their neglect of duty makes the Spanish military increasingly contemptible, and the Apaches, on the other hand, increasingly bold, since their wicked deeds go for the most part unpunished. The Christian Indians at times still administer a defeat to the Apaches. This is the only thing which to some extent restrains them and has kept them from destroying Sonora completely."[46]

CHAPTER SIX

An Apache Assassin,
June 1807–December 1807

O N APRIL 2, 1807, Spanish soldiers escorted American Zebulon Montgomery Pike into Chihuahua City to speak with Commandant General Salcedo. As Pike would explain in his meeting with Salcedo, he was a scientist who had been sent west by United States General James Wilkinson to conduct a geographic survey of the recently purchased Louisiana Territory. His mission was to navigate the Arkansas River to its source and document any interesting plant and animal life he found along the way. Unfortunately, while carrying out his duties, Pike and his men had become lost and, in their confusion, had accidentally crossed into Spanish New Mexico when a patrol from Santa Fe located and arrested them. The Americans had not meant to trespass, and if the commandant general permitted Pike and his men to return to the United States, he would have their eternal gratitude.[1]

Salcedo did not buy Pike's story. Only weeks before, the commandant general had been in Texas, where he had narrowly averted an all-out war between Spain and the United States. Since that time, Salcedo continued to hear rumors of a planned American invasion, with one suggesting that former American Vice President Aaron Burr was assembling a private army to march into the Internal Provinces. Perhaps Pike was a vanguard for this invasion. Even if Pike was telling the truth about his mission, the United States government had surely given him the additional tasks of gathering intelligence about Spanish defenses and plying the unincorporated Indians of the Internal Provinces with gifts in the hopes of turning them against Spain.[2]

Despite these suspicions, Salcedo knew that detaining Pike and his men would upset the fragile peace he had recently established with the United States, and possibly provide the Americans with an excuse to invade.

Therefore, Salcedo told Pike that he was free to move about Chihuahua until the commandant general could provide him with an escort to the Louisiana border.[3]

Pike and his men spent the next month in Chihuahua before undertaking a two-month journey to the United States. Although Salcedo did his best to monitor the Americans and limit what they learned during this time, the commandant general could not keep Pike from making the acquaintance of several prominent officials and soldiers who were eager to inform their new friend about the situation on the northern frontier. One of the biggest topics of discussion was the Apaches, and Spain's approach to dealing with them. According to Pike's informants, travelers in the Internal Provinces, "must either be so strong as to defy the Appaches *(sic)*, or calculate to escape them by swiftness, for they fill those mountains, whence they continually carry on a predatory war against the Spanish settlements and caravans."[4]

Surprisingly, Pike's informants told him that it was not the Apaches beyond the frontier who made the most trouble for Spain, but those who had agreed to make peace and settle at establecimientos de paz. They noted that, "those savages who have been for some time about the forts and villages become by far the most dangerous enemies the Spaniards have, when hostile, as they have acquired the Spanish language, manners, habits, pass through the populated parts under the disguise of civilized and friendly Indians, commit murders and robberies, and are not suspected."[5]

An "Apache Assassin" named "Ralph" was particularly problematic in this regard. Pike would later recall that,

> there is in the province of Cogquilla *(sic)* a partisan by the name of Ralph, who, they calculate, has killed more than 300 persons. He comes into the towns under the disguise of a peasant, buys provisions, goes to the gambling-tables and to mass, and before he leaves the village is sure to kill some person or carry off a woman, which he has frequently done. Sometimes he joins people traveling on the road, insinuates himself into their confidence, and takes his opportunity to assassinate them. He has only six followers, and from their knowledge of the country, activity, and cunning, he keeps 300 Spanish dragoons continually employed. The government has offered $1,000 for his head.[6]

Upon returning to the United States, Pike would include this biographical sketch of "Ralph" in a memoir of his journey called *An Account of Expeditions*

Zebulon Montgomery Pike (1779–1813) by Charles
Wilson Peale, from life, c. 1808. Courtesy of
Independence National Historical Park. Pike likely
heard stories about Rafael from the Spanish soldiers
who escorted him from Chihuahua to the border of the
United States.

to the Source of the Mississippi and through the Western Parts of Louisiana, which
he published in 1810. In addition to being the first written description of Rafael in a language other than Spanish, Pike's account was, for the most part,
accurate, and it included information that cannot be found elsewhere, such
as Rafael's propensity to gamble. Indeed, the only things that Pike reported
incorrectly were no fault of his own. His refers to Rafael as "Ralph" and wrote
either Coahuila or Guajoquilla as "Cogquilla," but these are understandable
misnomers considering that Pike could not speak Spanish and was writing
from memory. Pike was also likely incorrect in reporting that Rafael had
killed three hundred people by the time the Americans had returned to the
United States in July 1807. The death count was probably a third of that total.

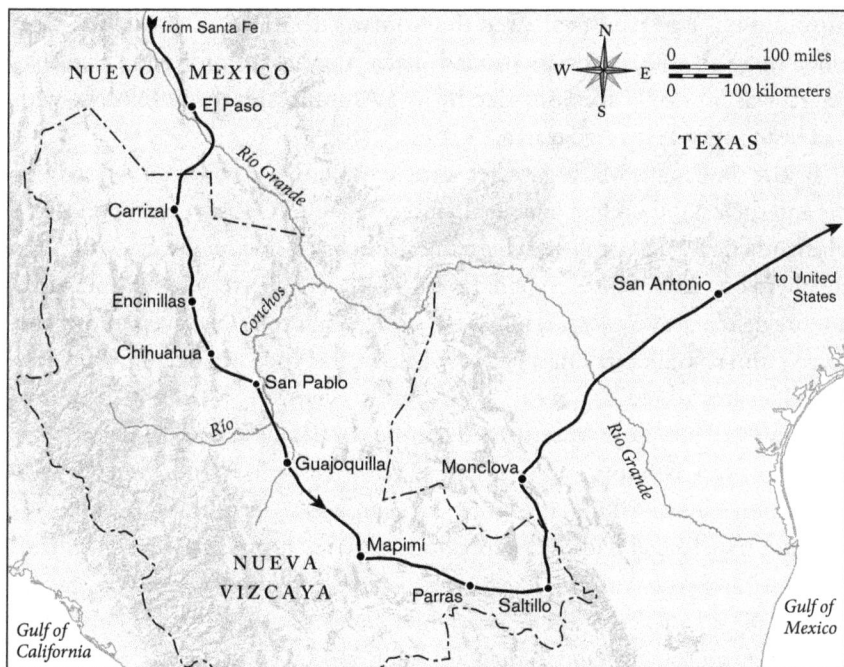

Route of Zebulon Pike through the Internal Provinces.
Map by Ben Pease, cartographer.

However, the exaggeration likely came from Pike's informants involuntarily inflating the number of dead out of fear and misinformation.[7]

PIKE'S INFORMANTS were also incorrect about the number of members of Rafael's band, as it had fallen to four by the time they provided the information to their American friend. The child the band had captured shortly before the incident at Temaichi does not appear in records following the battle, indicating that he or she escaped or that that Rafael or another member of the band executed the child. An additional captive would leave the band on or around August 8, when the older of the two remaining captive women, Juana María, escaped from camp and made her way to the town of San Pablo. Having been captured in September 1806, she had spent almost a year with Rafael and José Antonio and had joined them in several of their crimes, so it is unclear why she decided to escape at this time. However, considering that the band was passing near the same area where they had captured her, recognition of familiar surroundings may have prompted the woman's decision. Whatever the case, when Spanish authorities questioned Juana María, she informed them that Rafael was now only accompanied by José Antonio and the girl, Josefa, who had been taken from Aguazarca.[8]

By the time Juana María gave her statement, the band had returned to raiding and their numbers had once again increased. On August 11, they raided the Hacienda de Santa Catalina, where they killed two shepherds. They found a shepherd boy named Nevares and the ranch's *baciero*, or overseer, herding cattle a short distance away. Rafael killed the baciero but took Nevares captive and forced him to walk carrying a heavy saddle as they rode beside him. Two days later, Nevares joined Rafael and José Antonio when they killed three vecinos, one man and two boys working in a cornfield on the Rancho del Cristo near the towns of Las Bocas and Guadalupe. Although it is unknown if Nevares participated in the killing, it would be reasonable to assume that he did, considering that Rafael had forced previous captives to join in their murders.[9]

Rafael and José Antonio likely never analyzed their own behavior, but in forcing Nevares to carry the heavy saddle and participate in their raids, they were essentially putting him through the same operant conditioning, resocialization, and reward and punishment behaviors used in prisoner-of-war camps and military boot camps. Apaches often applied constant stressors to their captives in the form of starvation, work to the point of physical exhaustion, and fear that they could be killed if they did not conform. As one Apache would later explain about boy captives, "at first they have to act as servants. They have to eat as servants." This sometimes involved creating work. One Apache captive said, "[they] seemed to create necessities of labor, that they might gratify themselves by taxing us to the utmost, and even took unwarranted delight in whipping us beyond our strength." This, along with the general hardships of Apaches life, broke down the captive's ability to not only physically resist, but it also removed their ability to question the torture to which they were being subjected.[10]

In prisoner-of-war camps, military boot camps, and other cultural reorientation scenarios, physical and mental hardships are accompanied by lifestyle changes. Recruits and prisoners must make their beds in a certain way, conform to uniform standards, and perform rituals in the manner deemed best by those in charge. Similarly, Apaches taught captives their preferred methods of riding horses and killing. By requiring captives to participate in the latter activity, Apaches also made their captives into criminals, alienating them from the society of their birth and creating dependence on the band, a psychological method used by cults. Also like cults, who often reward those who cut ties with outside society, Apaches eventually eased the workload of captives and eventually adopted them as full members of their band. Although Nevares would never achieve this latter status, Rafael did allow the boy to ride on his red horse instead of walking.[11]

Two additional captives would soon join Nevares and Josefa in the Apache camp. On August 27, Rafael found three Tarahumara Indians, a husband, wife, and their daughter picking corn outside the Pueblo de Tecorichi, near where the Apaches had executed the mother and her three children on their way to a baptism a year before. They took the girl captive, killed the woman, and wounded the husband. The man would later die of his injuries. They captured an additional woman just over a week later on September 5 when Nevares joined them in raiding Las Cuevas. They killed two men there, ripped the entrails out of a third, and kidnapped a woman. Spanish authorities later found the man with his "intestines outside" but still alive. He informed them what had happened and died shortly thereafter. Rafael and José Antonio brought their new captives to their camp, which was on a neighboring mountain peak.[12]

Apparently, Rafael and José Antonio trusted Josefa and Nevares to watch the two new captives, because they left them at camp while they conducted a series of raids near the small town of Cerro Prieto. The residents, perhaps having heard what happened in nearby Las Cuevas, barricaded themselves in their homes as Rafael and José Antonio approached. Rafael and José Antonio broke down the door to one of the homes, injured two who were inside, and raided the home for corn, salt, soap, and cigars before retreating to the Sierra de Barajas. On September 9, Rafael arrived at the home of don Santiago Terrazas near Tule. Like the people of Cerro Prieto, Terrazas tried to hide inside a jacale building, but the Apaches broke in, killed him, and took his possessions and horses. Around the same time, they killed an Indian woman on the Aborcachi Ranch near the Norogachi mission.[13]

On September 21, they injured a young cow herder in San Cristóbal de Chávez. Four days later, on September 25, they killed José María Ochoa at the Corral de Palos near the Hacienda de Santa Cruz. Ochoa "did not receive the sacrament because he died at the hands of the Indians." They also injured a mozo and ran after another, but he escaped unharmed. On October 11, near Santiaguillo, they killed two shepherds, left another wounded, and escaped with the wife of one of the men, although the woman escaped from the band shortly thereafter. On October 14, they captured two paisanos at the Hacienda de la Mimbrera, but later killed them. They also killed another paisano at the Corral de Piedras and conducted a raid on the Hacienda de Iturraldi.[14]

While Rafael and José Antonio were gone on these raids, all four captives, Josefa, the boy Nevares, the Tarahumara girl, and the women from Las Cuevas, escaped. Josefa's decision to leave was especially interesting considering that she had been with the band for well over a year. Although it is unclear what transpired, the introduction of the unconditioned older woman from Las Cuevas may have been the impetus for the exodus. Those indoctrinated into a belief system often forget that there is an alternative way of life until someone with an outside perspective reminds them. It is for this reason that cults often refuse to allow their members to see their families or socialize with those outside the cult. Whatever prompted the escape, the captives soon made their way to Spanish authorities who took testimonies from each about what they had experienced while in captivity.[15]

JOSEFA AND THE REST of the captives' departure and the increased scrutiny of Spanish soldiers appear to have changed Rafael, with sources describing him as becoming increasingly "distrustful" and "suspicious" around this time. Whereas before, Rafael would occasionally enter towns or speak with peasants while in disguise, he seems to have become much more hesitant to confer with anyone except José Antonio and whoever the band had as a captive. Recognizing that Spanish soldiers were likely to look for the fire of their camp at night, Rafael and José Antonio began finding even more secluded spots to make camp, and they started sleeping only during the day. According to a contemporary observer, Rafael "always spends the middle of the day in the forests or inaccessible mountains, and it is during this time only that he lights a fire to season his tough food, because its brightness cannot be seen with that of the sun."[16]

With more people carrying weapons while they traveled, Rafael and José Antonio also started relying less and less on their disguises and began carrying out more raids at night. This was a common strategy for Apaches, with one Spanish priest noting, "usually they set out on their plundering expeditions at night, and by moonlight." Full moons were preferential for these raids, as the night would disguise the Apaches' approach and retreat, while the light of the moon could serve as a guide to and from intended targets. However, Rafael does not seem to have followed this model, favoring nights with less moonlight. Of eleven instances where Bustamante specifically recorded Rafael as having conducted an attack in the late evening or night, only two were carried out during a full moon, and four took place during a one-third moon. Although inconsistent reporting of dates may explain this pattern, it might mean that Rafael did not raid during full moons to avoid being spotted.[17]

Rafael and José Antonio also responded to the increased pressure by attacking more private residences. Although Apaches often attacked en masse when raiding settlements or larger haciendas, they would occasionally employ stealth to carry out precision raids. For example, in the early morning hours of December 29, 1789, six Lipan Apaches snuck into the middle of downtown San Antonio, then a relatively bustling town of more than two thousand residents, broke into the home of Texas governor Martínez Pacheco, and entered the Spanish official's sleeping quarters, hoping to settle a recent dispute between the Apaches and the Spanish. After awakening to find the invaders standing around his bed, Pacheco displayed uncanny composure and spoke calmly to the Apaches as he stood up and slowly made his way to a window, where he was able to clandestinely signal nearby soldiers for help. The soldiers then burst into the room, killing the Apaches and saving Pacheco.[18]

Rafael Castillo was not so fortunate when Rafael and José Antonio snuck into his home on the evening of October 18 and killed him as he slept. The Apaches conducted a second evening attack on a private residence two nights later when they assaulted brothers Perfecto and Pedro Hernández as they were outside their home chopping wood. Perfecto died immediately, but Pedro held on to life for another twenty-four hours. This allowed him to report that Rafael and José Antonio had carried out the attack, but he noted that they were joined by "a white-faced woman dressed in the clothing of an Indian woman."[19]

THE "WHITE-FACED WOMAN" was María Martina López, a thirteen-year-old girl of Spanish ancestry from the Estancia de Toro whom Rafael and José Antonio had captured sometime at the beginning of October. Unfortunately for posterity, the records collected by Bustamante do not explain how her capture took place, an especially glaring omission considering that López would remain with Rafael's band for longer than any other captive, and it seems that she would do so, at least for much of the time, voluntarily.[20]

Although the particulars of María Martina's relationship with Rafael and José Antonio go largely undiscussed in historical documents, it is apparent that she would earn the trust of the Apaches more than any other individual since the death of Chinche. Indeed, it seems that she took on the role of a wife to one of the men and would perform duties normally reserved for Apache women.

Sometimes she remained behind at camp to ensure that no captives escaped when the men went away on raids, while other times, she joined Rafael and José Antonio on their excursions. Owing to the patriarchal and racist nature of Spanish society, officials found the idea of a woman of European ancestry committing violence at the behest of an Indian husband to be shocking, and they assumed that María Martina was participating only under threat of violence. Over time, however, Salcedo would come to regard María Martina as a voluntary member of the band.[21]

Another interesting captive joined the group during a raid on the Hacienda del Canutillo on or around November 5. This was the third time in just over three years that the band had raided the ranch. The hacienda had been the site of Rafael's first recorded raid in October 1804, and the band had returned a year later, taking Ignacio Mata and thirteen-year-old José Salvador Bueno Laicano as captives. Mata escaped within a few days, while Laicano remained with Rafael and José Antonio for twenty-two days. In the November 1807 raid, the band encountered a cowboy who was feeding his cattle, shot him with their muskets, and robbed him of twenty horses. They recognized a different cowboy to be the former captive Laicano and kidnapped him a second time.[22]

It is possible that Laicano was simply the unfortunate victim of coincidence, but Spanish officials believed that Laicano had intentionally rejoined Rafael. This was not unusual for former captives. As one resident of northern New Spain described the situation,

it is known, nevertheless, in spite of the foregoing, that different persons, not only Indians but also Spaniards who were carried off by the Apaches, have become so accustomed to the free and unrestrained life of these barbarians that they no longer desired to return to their former life. It sometimes happens that when children have lived among the Apaches for some years and are finally ransomed, they will go back to these Indians at the first opportunity. I myself knew a Spanish girl who was nine or ten years old when she was abducted by the Apaches. She remained with them for four years before being ransomed and returned to her parents in the way described above. But she had almost become a savage, and all efforts of her family to imbue her with other ways were in vain. After two months she crept out of the house of her parents at night and returned to the Apaches, where in all probability she will remain for the rest of her life, for those who deliver themselves up to the Apaches voluntarily and those whom the Apaches believe to be loyal are looked upon by them not as strangers, but as countrymen.[23]

Rafael and José Antonio would test Laicano when they captured an unnamed woman and a young boy named José Bernardo Abad Léon shortly thereafter. In what was likely a measure to determine Laicano's loyalty, José Antonio demanded that Laicano kill Abad Léon. When Laicano refused, José Antonio threatened and taunted him. When Laicano still resisted, José Antonio stabbed him. Fearing that he would lose his life, Laicano killed the boy. Laicano may also have participated in the theft of two horses from the padre of Guanaceví and the November 9 killing of two shepherds at El Pandito. The band may have killed the two shepherds for their clothes, as two days after the El Pandito attack, sources say that Rafael and José Antonio carried out an attack at the Turuachi Ranch wearing disguises.[24]

AS HAD HAPPENED DURING THEIR PREVIOUS FORAYS into the remote Tarahumara and Tepehuan lands in the Sierra Madre, sources are vague concerning what transpired in this instance and those immediately following. This lack of information is evident during a raid, or series of raids, on the Tarahumaras of Navogame on or around November 12. The exact date of the attack is unknown because Spanish soldiers would not learn about it for at least a week, and the information they received came from three different reports, each with its own details on what took place. From what can be gathered, it seems that Rafael and José Antonio entered the town of Navogame wearing muleteer disguises. Either something compromised their disguises, or the Apaches determined that deception was unnecessary, because they began to openly assault the town's inhabitants.[25]

One report had Rafael and José Antonio shooting the Spanish-appointed governor of Navogame with a gun, while another said the governor was from nearby Chinatú, perhaps having come to Navogame to visit or trade. It is also possible that the Apaches shot both the governor of Navogame and Chinatú in the same or separate attacks. Two similar reports said the Apaches killed three children, while a third, that may be referring to a different instance altogether, added two men and three women to the governor and children, bringing the total number of dead to nine. Bustamante read the reports as three separate instances and counted thirteen dead. Adding to the confusion, additional victims may have gone unidentified after Rafael and José Antonio lit four jacales on fire and burned their inhabitants alive inside. They did this even though some of the huts contained firearms and lances. Making matters both more confusing and more deadly, Rafael and José Antonio returned to the area of Navogame a few days later and killed at least two additional women, but possibly as many as four.[26]

The Apaches were able to operate with such impunity because the Tarahumara either did not report the incident to Spanish authorities or the news took so long to reach them that it proved too late for soldiers to pursue Rafael. As one traveler through the region stated, "the law here is merely a shadow, the only laws that can be said to be in force being the military and the exxlesiastical (sic)." Indeed, it took the closest priest, who would occasionally travel to Navogame to minister to its people, to learn about the attack and report it to the subdelegate of Zape, who then informed Corporal Juan Leal of what had happened. By the time Leal could react to the information, Rafael, José Antonio, María Martina, Laicano, and an unnamed female captive were already making their way south where the Spanish would not be looking for them.[27]

ON NOVEMBER 29, just over two weeks after their attack on Navogame, Rafael, José Antonio, and the members of their band came across don Vicente Herrera in the area that is today La Joya, Durango and unseated the men off the mules they were riding. A few years after this event, a traveler passing through this region described a method that Rafael may have used to carry out the attack: "I was overtaken by a man, who entered into conversation with me. I suspected no mischief, but directing my attention to a particular object on the road before us, he suddenly checked the reins of his animal, whereby he placed himself a little in my rear, caught hold of my collar, and as, nearly as possible unhorsed me." Whether or not this was the technique used, Rafael's band killed Herrera, wounded his son, and took one of the mules and its saddle. Although the survivor reported what happened to local authorities, they did not make the connection that Rafael's band had committed the crime. Not only was La Joya some 350 miles southeast of Navogame across incredibly rough terrain, but it was also so far from the frontier that Apaches had never raided this far south before.[28]

Considering this distance, it would take subsequent attacks at the beginning of December before Spanish authorities recognized that it was Rafael committing the crimes. On December 4, the Apaches killed two shepherds in San Gerónimo. On December 6, they killed a shepherd in a place named Mesquitalillo, and the following night, they killed another at Amóles. The next morning, they attacked two men near the Las Ayuntes ranch, killing one. They stripped the other of his clothes, tied him to the back of their horse, and dragged him to the ranch. This treatment was not unique to Rafael, as other Apaches dragged lassoed victims behind horses, often through cactuses, as a form of torture. Although such treatment often resulted in death, the man from Las Ayuntes survived and was found by Corporal José Reyes. Reyes nursed the man back to health and after hearing his account of the attack determined that Rafael had been the one to carry it out.[29]

Reyes was a fifty-two-year-old, grey-eyed, brown-haired veteran of the Primera Compañía Volante who had been on several campaigns against Apaches. Unfortunately for him, none of his previous targets had been as elusive as Rafael, and considering the long distance from the presidio line, Reyes and his men may have been the only military personnel in the region. For the next week, the soldiers followed Rafael's path of destruction, with Reyes reporting to Colomo that he heard that the Indians had killed two men on December 8 and another two men at Alto de las Cruces on December 9. That same day, witnesses told Reyes that they had seen Rafael, two other men, a woman, and two children near the Hacienda de San Sebastián, and not long after they stole nine horses from Juan Pérez. Reports also came in that Rafael's band killed two cowboys at the Hacienda del Toro, before executing four peasants and injuring a fifth in the vicinity of San Salvador, near the modern border of Durango and Zacatecas.[30]

While investigating these crimes, Reyes found a saddled dead horse that he determined to be either Rafael or José Antonio's. Reyes noticed that instead of the horse's shoes being made of iron, bronze, or steel, as was typical, the animal had rawhide horseshoes. Curious, Reyes removed the shoe and showed them to a local official who remarked, "it is the same as one made of iron with the only difference being that it is made of a thick and strong rawhide." Indeed, the shoe was in the traditional horseshoe shape, and it had been nailed to the horse's hoofs with iron nails in the same manner as an iron horseshoes, but it was made of specially fashioned leather.[31]

The soldiers marveled that "it does not break, no noise is made, no beast slips, and with the nails renewing every time they need it, it will last a long time." A quieter horse allowed Rafael to sneak up on victims, and it meant nearby Spanish patrols, night watchmen, and militia were less likely to hear him galloping away. A horse in rawhide shoes was also more surefooted and could traverse difficult mountain paths. Reyes concluded that it could be fashioned much cheaper than one made of metal, and at least one person who inspected the shoe determined that it was superior to those used by the Spanish, remarking, "let us spread this invention to all who have horses to shoe."[32]

Soon after Reyes made his discovery, a debate sprang up among local Spanish officers over whether Rafael had designed and constructed the shoes himself or if he had acquired the idea or the shoes from someone else. It is certainly possible that Rafael used a traditional Apache design. Apaches lacked the iron working necessary to construct metal shoes, and as one Spanish priest who visited nearby Sonora in the mid-eighteenth century observed, "for the want of horseshoes, they cover their horses' hoofs with thick horse or oxhide to protect them." The problem with this interpretation is that Apaches fashioned these shoes, which could also be made of deer, buffalo, or cow hides, into a pouch that they tied together over the horse's hooves with a leather string. The horseshoe Reyes found was not a pouch, and if the shoe had been a traditional Apache design, Reyes or another soldier who had served with establecimiento Apaches would have recognized it as such.[33]

It is also unlikely that Rafael acquired the shoes or the design for the shoes from someone else. Spaniards and Hispanicized Indians generally used copper and iron alloys to make their horseshoes, and although leather horseshoes were common among European cultures in Roman times, their use had fallen out of favor long before the colonization of the Americas.[34]

Therefore, the most likely conclusion is that Rafael was responsible for both the design and manufacturing of the rawhide horseshoes. The Spanish may have been reluctant to credit him with the invention owing to long-held racial biases originating from the Reconquista, a nearly eight-century-long conflict from AD 711 to AD 1492 in which generally whiter-skinned Christians fought and defeated generally darker-skinned Muslim Moors for control of Iberia. The Christian victors took their victory as a sign of racial superiority and over time came to view those with dark skin as *sin razón*, or "without reason."[35]

The Spanish applied this logic to the darker skinned Indian people of the New World, even developing an entire "cognitive and legal system of hierarchically arranged socioracial statuses" to classify Old and New World people. In this *sistema de castas*, Europeans occupied the top of the intellectual and social hierarchy and Indians, Africans, and mixed-race people the lower tiers. Groups like the Apaches who refused to accept Spain's version of civilization occupied an even lower rung or were left outside of the sistema de castas entirely. To many Spaniards, the Apaches would not accept the Spanish way of life not because they chose not to accept it, but because they were intellectually incapable of accepting it.[36]

What the Spanish failed to understand was that the Apaches, as well as the other "sin razón" groups, were reasoning human beings, but they often devoted their mental effort to different things than the Europeans. In 1973, scientists conducted a series of tests on hunter-gatherer bushmen to determine whether they were able to "reason at the formal level." The bushmen did not meet the scientists' standards for reasoning except when it came to tracking and hunting prey. The logic behind this was obvious: hunting and tracking was what was important to them, and therefore that was where they devoted their mental energy. They cared little about the other aspects of the scientists' tests. Therefore, while it may have seemed to the Spanish that Rafael and other Apaches were sin razón, instead, they were capable of complex thought when it concerned the things most important to them. For Rafael, this was raiding, evading the Spanish, and staying alive, things rawhide horseshoes accomplished better than iron horseshoes.[37]

FOR SOMEONE SO ADAPTIVE AND INTELLIGENT, Rafael was also capable of repeating stupid mistakes. On the night of December 9, Rafael's band arrived at the estancia of Mateo Gómez, a sizeable hacienda just outside of Sombrerete. Wanting cigars and other provisions from the hacienda store but likely worried that the estancia housed Spanish soldiers or militia, Rafael decided to send the two-time captive José Salvador Bueno Laicano to buy the desired items. Although evidence indicates that Laicano had become a trusted part of the band by this point, the decision to send the sixteen-year-old was still questionable, considering that in March 1806, they had sent a different captive to make purchases in Cantera, only to have the woman alert authorities to Rafael's presence.[38]

Making Rafael's decision even more confusing was the fact that Laicano's clothing was "soaked in blood" from the multiple murders the band had committed during his month in captivity. As could be expected, when Laicano went to make the purchases, the proprietor of the store noticed the blood and alerted local authorities, who then took Laicano into custody and questioned him. After Laciano told them who he was, who he had been with, and what he had seen, the residents of the estancia sheltered the boy and informed the local subdelegate of what he had said.[39]

Fortunately for Rafael, the estancia of Mateo Gómez was located in Zacatecas, an intendancy not considered part of the Internal Provinces. When establishing the borders of the Internal Provinces, Spanish authorities had tried to include all areas of New Spain that might come under attack by hostile unincorporated Indians. Zacatecas did not fit this bill because prior to this time, Apaches had never raided that far south. For this reason, the intendancy and the region south of it remained under the jurisdiction of the viceroy of New Spain in Mexico City, meaning that for a short time Salcedo was no longer the preeminent authority in charge of apprehending Rafael. Spanish law was even unclear on whether the commandant general could send troops into Zacatecas to assist in searching for the Apaches. Indeed, Salcedo would later come under criticism when the viceroy of New Spain asked him to send troops to Zacatecas to assist in putting down an uprising, only for the commandant general to refuse because he did not believe he had the authority to do so.[40]

In addition, the nearest settlement of size to the estancia, Sombrerete, had no professional infantry or cavalry stationed in the town, only a lieutenant captain and a handful of militiamen. Considering that the area had never faced an Indian raid, it is doubtful that the members of the militia had much experience fighting Apaches. These circumstances allowed Rafael and his band to continue raiding with little fear of retribution for the following week. On December 10, the band encountered Francisco Chávez escorting a twelve-year-old girl from the Hacienda de San Marcos to Las Bocas. Rafael lanced Chávez repeatedly and took the girl captive. Two days later, December 12, witnesses testified that Rafael and José Antonio, two women, and a child killed four people at the Peñol-Blanco al Cerro-Blanco. They then killed three men at the ranch of Mateo Gómez and three in Tapia and La Escondida near Corrales. They left one of their captives at Escondida.[41]

On December 14, the band crossed back into Nueva Vizcaya proper and found a shepherd named Luciano González, a cowboy, and a fourteen-year-old male traveling near the Hacienda de Sauceda. They took the fourteen-year-old captive and lanced and killed the shepherd. They also lanced the cowboy and stripped him of his clothes, but he survived. Around December 16, witnesses reported seeing Rafael, José Antonio, three women, and a captive child near the junction of the Nazas and Del Peñol rivers.[42]

They then attacked three men near Guichapa, killing two and severely injuring the third. Rafael and José Antonio mounted the injured man on a mule and tied his feet below the animal's body. This was a method of torture wherein the victim, unable to shield his body and face from the sun, would eventually die of exposure and dehydration. Fortunately for this particular victim, Santos

Palmares found him before the elements could take their toll. Palmares then formed a search party and set off in pursuit of the Indians, tracking them to a ranch near Peñol-Blanco, where they found another gravely injured victim of Rafael and José Antonio named Leuterio Reino who would die six days later.[43]

Palmares and Corporal Reyes's dogged pursuit led Rafael, José Antonio, and their captives to retreat northward along the eastern edge of the Sierra Madre Occidental into Nueva Vizcaya, committing many murders and injuries in their flight. Exactly how many died and were injured is unclear, as Salcedo received multiple reports that may refer to the same incident. On December 24, 1807, Rafael and José Antonio killed a shepherd near the Hacienda de San Sebastián, and two days later, a cowboy on the Hacienda de Guatinapé found a former female captive of Rafael "wounded with her intestines hanging out." On December 31, don Leandro Sánchez reported from Santiago Papasquiaro on the cowboy finding the injured girl at Guatinapé on December 26. The following day, don Maríano Díaz related from the Hacienda de San José de Gracia that someone found "a young woman between twelve and thirteen years of age who had been lanced in her breasts" near Guatinapé. Although this is almost certainly the same girl, Bustamante records it as two separate instances. On December 30, Rafael injured two peasants at Ciénega de los Suárez in the El Oro district.[44]

However many died, Reyes finally caught up to Rafael on or around January 10 after he, five soldiers, and a paisano from the Álamos Ranch tracked Rafael and his companions into the Ulana Mountain Range bordering Chinacates. A fight ensued, but details are lacking with Reyes reporting only that "he had attacked Rafael and his companion." They managed to liberate a captive and a horse, which they brought to the mayor of Santiago Papasquiaro.[45]

Over the next week, Rafael's band fled northwest pursued by Reyes and other Spanish forces. On January 14 they killed a shepherd, wounded another, and took a teenager from the massive Gogojito Ranch as a captive. The boy did not last long, as searchers would locate his body the following day. They also discovered that the band had killed a female herder, stole her cattle on January 15, and took forty horses from the area of Arroyo de la Pitarilla. They killed many of the animals before retreating into the remote Sierra de la Iglesia near Guanacevi.[46]

While Rafael was committing these crimes, Spanish officials in Sombrerete were grilling José Salvador Bueno Laicano about the month he had spent with the band. He testified that during his time, they had killed nineteen people, and tried to kill at least one more, but that person may have survived. They had also kidnapped five, including himself. José Salvador even admitted to participating in the crimes and confessed that he had been the one to execute José Bernardo Abad Léon. However, he said that he had only done it after José Antonio threatened and stabbed him. Spanish authorities brought Laicano up on charges, but Commandant General Salcedo, believing the young man's story, pardoned him on February 8, 1808.[47]

RAFAEL WOULD NEVER RETURN to Zacatecas, but neither would any other Apaches, at least for forty years. When the next Apache raid happened in 1847, it sent shockwaves throughout the region. An Englishman who was present during the mid-nineteenth century event described the feat thusly: "to give general notion of the import of this fact, without sending the reader to a map, we may say that it is about the same as if it were announced in the Annual Register of 1847 that the Picts and Scots had been at Worcester." This was an apt comparison, considering that the northern Scotland homeland of the Picts was some five hundred miles from Worcester, and the closest Apaches to Zacatecas were the Mescaleros of West Texas, some five hundred miles to the north.[48]

The wide swath through which Rafael's band operated might have been a matter of opportunity, but it was also almost certainly a tactic meant to confuse Spanish soldiers. As one observer noted of Apaches,

> often, having scarcely hidden their spoil, they appear, striking terror and confusion around, at some place in a direction diametrically opposite to that of their first foray. This gives rise to erroneous calculations as to their numbers; the two distinct actions being attributed to two different parties, whereas, in reality, one and the same party performed both. They can well afford to move rapidly, as horses killed in a day's galloping are replaced without cost, from the great number that accompany them from the nearest cattle estate. They are said to accomplish, easily, a hundred miles in a day, if hard pressed, and not too much encumbered by spoil.

As one author later would later describe Rafael's ability to travel long distances in short amounts of time, "the Spaniards were unable to rest, el 'indio Rafael' ruthlessly attacked Santiago Papasquiaro and then afterwards appeared in Guanacevi, Alayá, El Salto, Guatimapé and other settlements and places."[49]

CHAPTER SEVEN

The Subject of All Conversations,
January 1808–December 1808

THE APACHES' BRIEF FORAY into Zacatecas stirred emotions throughout New Spain and would lead to the first time that Rafael's name appeared in type. On December 26, 1807, the *Diario de México*, one of only two regularly published newspapers in New Spain, printed a letter from a Juan Josef Flores Alatorre of Sombrererte claiming that "in the interior territory, or internal provinces, exists an Apache Indian named Rafael, who is the discussion of all daily conversations in this place. They say that he has killed 300: the commandant general has dispatched troops from various places to capture him, but with a thousand disguises and strategies, he escapes. He [Salcedo] has offered a thousand pesos to whoever can bring him in alive or dead."[1]

The letter elicited so much attention that the *Diario de México* printed a second letter from Alatorre four days later. As Alatorre described things, fear permeated the border of Nueva Vizcaya and Zacatecas and locals prepared "as if they were going to war, with everyone carrying lances and firearms." According to Alatorre, Rafael and his band were "the subject of all conversations and disturbances in this place . . . here there is no other news than that of the Indian Rafael." Alatorre reported that "his vice is not to steal, but to treacherously kill with a lance," and warned, "although they say he has killed more than 200, I believe this only a quarter of the actual number."[2]

Considering that it is almost nine hundred miles from Mexico City to Chihuahua, it likely took two or more weeks before copies of the *Diario* reached subscribers in Nueva Vizcaya. When it did, one person in the province, known only by the pseudonym "Mr. Arezi," concluded that Alatorre had not provided enough background information about Rafael, and so he took it upon himself to clarify matters by sending a third letter to the *Diario*, which appeared on the front page of the February 1, 1808, edition of the periodical. After informing readers that, "I have very reliable news about this bloodthirsty Apache, that I am going to tell you," Mr. Arezi summarized Rafael's upbringing with Rafael Nevares, his trial in Guajoquilla, and ultimately his decision to turn against the Spanish.[3]

Arezi's letter and the Apaches' retreat from Zacatecas proved to be the end of the news cycle concerning Rafael, as events in Spain soon dominated headlines. In October 1807, the king of Spain, Charles IV, allowed his ally Napoleon Bonaparte to send a French army across Spain to invade Portugal, who was allied with Britain in a war against France and Spain. However, once French forces entered Iberia, Napoleon determined that he could make better use of Spain's resources if he removed Charles IV and placed his own brother Joseph Bonaparte on the Spanish throne, and so in February 1808, he ordered his armies to march on the Spanish capital of Madrid. In a last-ditch effort to save the monarchy, Charles IV abdicated the crown in favor of his son Ferdinand VII, but Napoleon took both men into custody, allowing Joseph to ascend to the throne of Spain. Most readers of the *Diario* dismissed Joseph's claim and were eager to hear about the revolution arising in Spain against his rule, and so any additional letters concerning a troublesome, but localized, Apache band apparently fell to the cutting-room floor.[4]

THE REMARK IN ALATORRE'S LETTER about the locals in Nueva Vizcaya preparing "as if they were going to war, with everyone carrying lances and fire-arms" indicates that recent orders from Salcedo were being followed. Salcedo had spent much of 1807 implementing a strategy that he hoped would "hinder any aggression on the part of the enemy." Instead of devoting additional professional soldiers to actively seek Rafael, it seems that Salcedo determined that the best way to stop the gang was a well-armed and attentive populace.[5]

On June 16, 1807, the commandant general sent out a proclamation to towns throughout Nueva Vizcaya making it a crime to travel unarmed. He ordered that

> any person who goes into the country must carry a musket, pistol, or lance, according to his means. Even the poor must be armed and familiar with the usage of weapons. Tame Indians may choose a bow and arrow or a lance. Judges are to fine offenders one peso for the first offense; those short of means are to be fined 4 to 8 reales; those who are absolutely poor

are to be given 3 to 6 days on the public works; Indians are to receive 8 to 16 lashes. Those taking well-loaded mules into the countryside must be accompanied by three servants, at least one of whom will have a musket and the others lances. For breaking this regulation, the delinquent is to be halted until armed as ordered and the owner or mayordomo levied a three peso fine.[6]

Fortunately for those needing to meet these requirements, Salcedo's weapons factory had reached its production goal of fifty guns per month. This increased turnout dropped the cost of manufacturing new weapons to twenty pesos each and allowed for the sale of the weapons to the general public, not just soldiers. The quality of the firearms also improved, with Salcedo soon bragging that "they now turn out to be excellent, the best of the best."[7]

Salcedo's June 1807 proclamation also dictated that villagers were to form neighborhood watches to alert residences in case of attack. He ordered "every village and hacienda to constantly maintain in the field a party of vecinos with the mission of patrolling only their particular district." Salcedo did not explain the particulars of how his "neighborhood watch" system was to work, and because there was little uniformity across Nueva Vizcaya concerning militias, what took place in one town might vary greatly from a different town.[8]

However, the way in which area villages would watch for Apaches later in the nineteenth century might offer a general clue to the procedure. Towns would set guards at strategic outposts on the outskirts of town to watch for telltale signs of incoming Apaches, such as a cloud of dust on the horizon indicating approaching horses. Upon receiving visual confirmation, watchmen would fire their weapons in the air or shout "los indios" to warn the people of the village. Women and children would hide under floorboards, in caves, or in well-defended buildings in the center of town. Men reported to the hacienda store or militia captain's home to receive weapons. Some of the more trusted men obtained guns, while lowly hacienda employees would have to fight with handheld weapons or farming equipment. Local government officials and militia leaders would then either prepare the town for defense or gather horses for a pursuit. At the same time, messengers ran or rode to nearby towns to warn them to assemble their own militias.[9]

Salcedo's new plans also called for stationing small groups of soldiers in haciendas and smaller villages throughout Nueva Vizcaya to assist militias in their searches. This arrangement would make it much more difficult for Rafael to avoid areas with soldiers, and it would allow for more effective dragnets. Whenever anyone learned of an attack, they would send word to soldiers in surrounding outposts, who would then use a grid search to close in on the Apaches' location. Local militia and the newly created neighborhood watches would join in the search. Any soldiers who retreated from the brothers were to be arrested.[10]

Again, Salcedo provides only a rough outline of how he wanted this plan carried out, but it appears to have been remarkably similar to the one United States soldiers would use a century later to capture Geronimo and his followers. Recognizing that it was "impossible to run them down and capture them," the American officer in charge of bringing Geronimo to justice, General Nelson A. Miles, directed his engineers to "establish a network of points of observation and communication . . . over the country most frequented by the Apaches." Each post would be home to a small contingent of American soldiers, as well as a handful of friendly Apache scouts. Whenever word arrived that Geronimo had been spotted, the soldiers and scouts from all nearby posts would "move against the hostile Apaches, striking and hunting them down from five or six different points at nearly the same time, thereby keeping the Indians constantly on the alert to prevent themselves from being surprised, and subjecting them to such a continued, apprehension of death and disaster that he hoped the continued mental strain might, in the course of time, break down their defiant spirit and induce them to finally sue for peace."[11]

SALCEDO'S PLAN differed from the Americans in that instead of relying exclusively on Apache auxiliaries, it called for "transferring 60 men from Sonora from infantry companies of Ópata and Pima Indians and dividing them into six parties to be distributed with total knowledge of the terrain." The Ópatas were fearsome warriors who had initially driven the Spanish out of Sonora in the sixteenth century but had later accepted Hispanicization at the behest of Jesuit missionaries. From that time forward, the Ópatas had joined the Spanish in fighting the Apaches, with the Spanish making use of the Ópatas' excellent tracking and archery skills on long campaigns into Apache territory. Indeed, the Ópatas had proven such valuable allies in combating Apaches that in 1784, Spanish officials went against their long-held prohibition against providing Indians with guns, and created two companies of Ópata soldiers, even allowing the Ópatas to hold military rank and wear the same uniforms as the regular army. Salcedo believed that "the agility and perseverance of these troops in their infantry service would allow them to ensure the proper persecution by leading the rest of the men."[12]

The addition of the Ópatas to the search for Rafael was especially interesting because all indications are that Rafael was half Ópata, and it is possible that his father was among those sent to search for him. What little we know of Rafael's father comes from an addendum to the copy of Juan José Ruiz de Bustamante's 1810 report published in José Merino's documentary history of Chihuahua, *Apuntes históricos*. According to Merino, Rafael's father was not an Apache, but an Ópata Indian who was captured by the Apaches when he was "very young" and incorporated himself into his captors' tribe. While among the Apaches, he had a sexual relationship with an Apache woman, and the product of this relationship was Rafael. At some point in "advanced adolescence," Rafael's father was liberated and returned to living among the Spanish and Ópatas. Merino does not say how or when this happened, but he does mention that in 1856, Rafael's father was still alive at more than one hundred years old, and living in Santa Cruz de Rosales, Chihuahua.[13]

As someone who had lived with the Apaches and spoke their language, it would make sense that after returning to the Spanish, Rafael's father joined the military as a translator and scout. Indeed, former captives were highly valued as soldiers. The contention that Rafael's father was still alive in 1856 would also mean that he would have been young enough to campaign in 1808, so it is plausible that he was among the Ópatas deployed to capture his son. Unfortunately, there is no evidence that this exciting, Star-Wars-esque scenario occurred, and even if Rafael's father were among the Ópatas sent to Nueva Vizcaya, the effectiveness of the other aspects of Salcedo's plan would see few chances for a dramatic showdown between father and son.

SALCEDO'S NEW PLANS would be tested in early February 1808 when the subdelgado of Cuecamé, José María Durán, learned that Rafael had been spotted near the Nazas River in the area that is today eastern Durango. On February 6, his band killed three people at the estancia de Acatita and the following day they killed two more at the Puesto de Tetillas near Fernández. On hearing of the attacks, Durán, "immediately dispatched twenty men to pursue them," as well as "three other strike force parties" made up of local miltia.[14]

The rapid response allowed the various groups to track Rafael's band to Animas Canyon where the militiamen "tried to cut off the path of the Indians." Trapped, Rafael and José Antonio had to fight one of the parties to escape.

Militia forces managed to wound three members of the band, presumably Rafael, José Antonio, and María Martina, but the Apaches got the better of them in the end, killing three and forcing the rest to flee. In the scuffle, the Apaches had to leave behind thirteen horses and five saddles.[15]

One of the remaining responding party leaders, don Francisco de la Riva located the bodies of the three men who died in battle. It fell on the local priest of Santa María del Oro to inter the victims, as well as some of those killed on February 6 and 7. In what was apparently an effort to save ink, paper, or time, he combined four burial records into only two entries in his ledger. Unable to identify two victims, the priest listed their names under the single heading of "two whose life was ended by the Indian Rafael."[16]

With Spanish forces in pursuit, Rafael, José Antonio, and their captives fled west and then north along the Nazas River, moving some thirty miles west and fifty miles north in a matter of days. Sometime between February 7 and 12, a witness saw Rafael's band near the Hacienda de Ramos and the Sierra de Ticorica (likely Jicorica). They killed a vaquero in this area, as well as two Mescalero Apaches—perhaps establecimiento Apaches serving as scouts for the Spanish army. The band then passed through the Hacienda El Gigante, and shortly thereafter on February 12, Rafael and José Antonio killed two travelers at the Encino de la Paz. On or around this time they encountered a group of muleteers under don Fernando Jurado who were leading thirty mules bringing corn to miners in the Sierra Tierra Caliente. They killed two of the muleteers and injured a third, but the rest escaped unharmed. Rafael and José Antonio confiscated the mules and presumably consumed the corn. At some point during this time, they also stole some twenty-one horses.[17]

News of the recent attacks reached Spanish authorities in El Oro, who sent word to all nearby soldiers and local officials to assemble militia for the pursuit. Pedro Pérez moved south with militia from Parral, while soldiers under Second Lieutenant Agustín Ceballos and another six men commanded by Carbinero Fabián Juárez moved in from different directions. With the three groups closing in, Rafael killed his mules and attempted to "move with great speed to reach the sierra to the west," but once again Spanish forces cut him off. On or about February 13, Juárez's group tracked Rafael to Encino de la Paz and a battle took place. Rafael, José Antonio, and María Martina were able to escape the confrontation, but they left behind twenty-one horses, three lances, and three recently acquired captives.[18]

The soldiers and militia continued to pursue the Apaches over the following days and weeks, and they were soon joined in the manhunt by additional soldiers, as well as local vecinos from Santiago Papasquiro and nearby municipalities who had "armed themselves with whatever they could find." Farmers showed up with hoes, threshers, and pitchforks. Some vecinos came with slingshots. On February 28, Vicente Gómez del Campillo and a group of miners from San Andrés arrived carrying pickaxes and shovels.[19]

The search continued over the next month, but outside of an unconfirmed report that the Apaches had injured one person and kidnapped another, there would be no additional sightings. With farmers needing to plant their crops for the spring, Salcedo suspended the manhunt. However, he warned that Rafael and his companions might still be in the area, and locals needed to report any suspicious activity to Spanish authorities and be prepared to form new search parties at a moment's notice.[20]

THE ONLY NEARBY TOWNS that did not participate in the search were the remote, predominantly mixed-race communities of San Javier, San Gregorio, and Soyupa. Only a few families called these villages home, and they scraped together a hardscrabble existence raising cattle and goats and growing corn and wheat to sell to nearby miners. Owing in part to the economic unimportance of these towns, Spanish officials paid them little attention. The governor appointed an Indian alcalde as a go-between for each community and the provincial government, but there was little legal oversight unless the towns caused problems for more lucrative settlements. This arrangement left the Indian alcaldes in a difficult situation. They had to enforce enough Spanish laws to be left alone, but not enough to displease the people of their towns, who might react violently if there were too many restrictions. No matter the level of effort these alcaldes put in, the Spanish generally regarded them as corrupt, inefficient, and sometimes criminal.[21]

When Spanish officials questioned the leaders of San Javier, San Gregorio, and Soyupa and asked why they did not join in the manhunt for Rafael, the alcaldes claimed that they did not have any weapons. This was certainly a valid reason, considering that many poor remote towns lacked proper farming implements, let alone expensive guns. However, Intendant Governor Bernardo Bonavía did not buy the excuse. Like most other Spaniards of the time, Bonavía likely held racist assumptions about the people of the towns because their inhabitants were of mixed Indian, African, and European ancestry, and the

Spanish often regarded such persons as having the negative qualities of each race and none of the positives.[22]

Bonavía grew even angrier when residents of the towns tried to claim some of the horses recovered from Rafael, saying that they had been stolen from their herds. Bonavía responded by saying that he would "only reward those who risked their own horses and lives, not those who had provided saddles to Rafael through their carelessness." Instead of returning the animals to San Javier, San Gregorio, and Soyupa, he thanked Gómez del Campillo and the miners from Vicente for responding so quickly and rewarded them with the recovered horses.[23]

Soon thereafter, word reached Bonavía that not only had the people of San Gregorio not participated in the search for Rafael, but they also may have actively helped him "to commit as many atrocities as possible" and escape punishment. The specific nature of the charges was that after "the barbarous Indian known as Rafael" committed two murders in the area, the residents of San Gregorio "secluded him in a secure and hidden location where he could hide with his mounts without risk of being found by the troops and people [militia] who were following him." There was even a rumor that residents of San Gregorio had killed a cow and enjoyed a barbecue with Rafael. Spanish officials also suspected that residents had helped Rafael kill someone near the Arroyo de Macos, and that certain individuals may have escorted his band out of the area to escape the militias and soldiers looking for him.[24]

Bonavía ordered an investigation of the town to determine the validity of these charges. His investigators learned that San Gregorio had been the site of a former Jesuit mission, but it had been secularized in 1753 after missionaries determined that local inhabitants had successfully converted to Christianity. From that time forward, church officials rarely visited, and the only legal authority was the government-appointed alcalde. With little legal oversight, the small village became home to deserters, escaped African slaves, and fugitives from the law, with locals even publicly proclaiming that "they live like the moor, without a lord." Residents regularly assisted rogue Tarahumaras in their raids on Spanish settlements, and not long before, a gang from San Gregorio had robbed corn and cattle from a nearby town. This led Bonavía's investigators to characterize the people of San Gregorio as a "bunch of thieves," who did not sow corn and instead stole to survive.[25]

To determine if the town was complicit in assisting Rafael, Spanish officials took testimonials from a number of witnesses, asking them each ten questions to determine whether anyone had assisted Rafael or committed other crimes. Although some of these witnesses feigned ignorance, others pointed to specific residents who had provided aid to the Apaches. One eyewitness suggested that Rafael had also paid residents to lead his band to nearby ranches that they could raid. Unfortunately, the testimonials do not make clear whether those committing these acts understood Rafael's level of notoriety, or if they saw him as one of the many common criminals who regularly passed through their town.[26]

After reading the ninety-eight-page investigation, Bonavía ordered that several of San Gregorio's residents were to be "punished for their collaboration with Rafael." He had his men take those arrested to a prison in Durango where they were forced to break rocks. After a time, some of the prisoners escaped. To prevent another escape, Spanish officials forced those remaining to wear hand and footcuffs while they worked.[27]

The testimonials suggest that at least some residents of the Internal Provinces knowingly supported Rafael, lending credence to those who see the Apache leader as a revolutionary figure who mobilized the lower classes against Spain. While this scenario is possible, it is more likely that the people of San Gregorio supported Rafael without knowing much about him. News about the extent of Rafael's activities would not have been as prevalent in remote locations like San Gregorio, and the people of the town likely saw Rafael as one of the many abiegos or fugitives who came to trade. Even if they were aware of the extent of Rafael's activities, they may not have known the person they were trading with was Rafael considering his use of elaborate disguises and cover stories. It is perhaps for this reason that one Spanish official would later conclude that he "did not have even the slightest suspicion that the two aforementioned Indians had any connection, dealings, help, or communication concerning their atrocities with any class of people."[28]

ON MAY 22, 1808, Pedro Burciaga, José Rodríguez, Antonio Quiroz, and two additional Spanish soldiers were escorting some six mules from Real de Oro to Guanaceví. The duty was difficult because the road between Real de Oro and Guanaceví was hard to traverse. The remote path was rocky, and it narrowed when snaking across ravines, making it difficult for multiple travelers to walk abreast. In places, even steadfast mules struggled to maintain their footing. Making matters more difficult for the pack animals was the fact that they carried bags loaded down with heavy silver specie, ammunition, the soldiers' extra equipment, uniforms, clothing, and papers bearing Salcedo's latest orders.[29]

As the soldiers were making their way through a particularly treacherous stretch of road near the peaks of the remote Sierra del Carmen, they came under attack by Rafael and José Antonio. Sources do not explain the exact method the Apaches used to ambush the soldiers, but it would be reasonable to assume that, as they had done in the past, Rafael and José Antonio operated from an elevated position and used their height advantage to fire rocks, arrows, and other projectiles on targets below. The attack almost certainly came quickly and without warning, considering, as famed Spaniard Bernardo de Gálvez once said of the Apaches, "no description is possible of the speed with which they attack, or the noise they make while fighting, how the terror spreads among our own, and the promptness with which it all ends." Whatever the methodology, the assault frightened two of the soldier's mules, sending them, as well as the silver and supplies they carried, tumbling down a ravine.[30]

The Spanish soldiers responded to the attack in different ways. Antonio Rodríguez did as he had been trained, grabbed his gun, and returned fire at the Apaches. Rifleman Pedro Burciaga, on the other hand, fled almost immediately. Three other soldiers initially joined with Rodríguez in attempting to combat the Apaches, but when it became apparent that they could not hit their targets, they flung themselves down steep ditches to escape the Apache trap. With his comrades gone, Rodríguez too had to flee, leaving behind at least three of the soldiers' mules and the cargo they were carrying.[31]

Rafael and José Antonio took stock of what they had found. In addition to the silver, the mules carried a lance, three saddles, saddlebags, papers, clothing, and perhaps most important, sixty cartridges of ammunition, something the Apaches sorely needed after having been on the run for the past three months. Although Rafael and José Antonio likely picked up some of the clothing to use as disguises, they left many articles scattered on the ground. Rafael and José Antonio then decided to press their luck. Moving south in the direction of Zape, they came across a group of muleteers, killed them, and took their cargo. They also robbed a group of paisanos and took two of their mules.[32]

While Rafael and José Antonio were headed south, Burciaga and three of his soldiers regrouped and returned to the sight of the ambush in the hopes of recovering their mules, cargo, and, perhaps, their dignity. The fifth soldier did not join them because he got lost while running away, and it would take him time to return to civilization. Burciaga and his men found that the Apaches had left some clothes strewn about, but everything else was gone. The soldiers then stumbled into the nearest settlement to report what had happened.[33]

Salcedo was livid upon learning about the loss of the silver shipment, as the soldiers had clearly violated his order to engage Rafael and not run away. The commandant general was especially upset with Pedro Burciaga's cowardice and had him arrested for desertion. As Salcedo would learn, Burciaga was experienced, and he had even been in the Tarahumara area of the Sierra Madre since at least 1807 working with Félix Colomo in his search for Rafael. Considering his failure in spite of these qualifications, it is likely that Burciaga faced imprisonment in a presidio jail.[34]

FOLLOWING THE ATTACK on the silver shipment, Rafael and José Antonio went into hiding, disappearing for two months before killing two vecinos at sunset at a ranch near Julimes on July 30, some 170 miles to the north of their last known location. The next day, they moved on the Jatero Ranch, also near Julimes, where they injured two boys and stole clothes from a third. Unfortunately for Rafael and José Antonio, the Spanish military and local militia once again responded quickly to the news. After investigating the attacks and learning from the injured boys that Rafael and José Antonio had been the perpetrators, Corporal Cornelio Durán sent word to neighboring locales to be on watch.[35]

Durán and his men soon tracked Rafael's band to the Sierra del Maguey, where they fell into an ambush. Rafael and José Antonio opened fire on the soldiers as they attempted to reach the Apaches' location, immediately killing soldier Juan Cisneros and pinning down Durán and the rest of his men. Fortunately for the soldiers, Sergeant Ignacio Noriega arrived on the scene with reinforcements and local militia, leading Rafael and José Antonio to fall back to the peak of the Sierra del Maguey. At this point, Noriega had the Apaches surrounded but two of his soldiers, Miguel Alarcón and Pedro Gardea broke ranks and fled the scene, allowing Rafael, José Antonio, and María Martina to escape once again. Although unable to bring the Apaches to justice, the rapid response of the Spanish soldiers and the quick deployment of local militia had almost led to Rafael's death or capture twice in 1808, and Salcedo's reliance on an attentive militia would continue to be an effective countermeasure in the coming months.[36]

As had happened the last time a manhunt was mounted to find him, Rafael's band disappeared, laid low, and moved locations, this time traveling south to northern Durango and waiting a month before striking. On September 5, they attacked and killed three vecinos on the San Salvador Ranch at six o'clock in the afternoon and took a boy, José Castillo, as a captive. They then severely injured two others north of the Rancho de los Peinados.[37]

The survivors apparently took little time informing local officials of what had happened, because by ten o'clock that evening workers from San Salvador and Indians from nearby Tizonazo had arrived in the area with torches and weapons to search for the Apaches and the missing boy. The search was difficult enough in the dark, but soon after it commenced, it began to rain heavily, covering the tracks left by Rafael, José Antonio, and their captives, allowing them to escape into the night.[38]

Rafael's band briefly emerged from hiding on September 25, when they attacked the houses of la Hacienda de la Concepción during evening prayer and took a teenage girl captive. It seems that this girl was able to escape the following evening when the Apaches killed a woman a quarter league away from the hacienda. That same day or the next, they killed four people who were traveling to the nearby village of Santa Catalina, after which, perhaps fearing a quick response from local militia, the band returned to hiding.[39]

OVER THE NEXT TWO MONTHS, Spanish officials suspected that Rafael committed a series of murders, but they were unable to confirm his involvement. For example, on October 16, don Narciso Díaz de Bustamante reported that someone had killed Hilario Chávez near the Hacienda de la Ramada, "but he could not say who did it." When Spanish officials later recorded the incident, they credited Rafael with the crime in spite of Bustamante's uncertainty. The same thing happened on November 26 when rumors swirled that Rafael and José Antonio had killed Patricio Vargas and José Acosta in the Cañon de Majalea, but with no survivors and no other crimes committed in the immediate area, Spanish officials determined "there is no evidence that the Indian Rafael and his companion killed" the two men. Burial records say only that Vargas "died at the hands of the Apaches" while Acosta was "killed by the Indians." Eight days later the young grandson of Lorenzo Herrera, the foreman of Torreon, claimed that Rafael had injured him and killed his grandfather, but Herrera's burial records are inconclusive, stating only that the foreman "had been killed by the Apaches."[40]

It is possible and perhaps likely that Rafael committed these crimes, but the uncertainty suggests that over the years at least some of the crimes that the Spanish blamed on Rafael were committed by others. If someone committed a crime at the same time and in the same area where Rafael was known to be operating and there were no witnesses, the Spanish would logically conclude that Rafael was responsible, allowing the true perpetrators to go unpunished. Indeed, there were likely multiple bandits, robbers, and hostile Apaches who escaped prosecution because officials attributed their crimes to Rafael.

Witnesses may even have invoked Rafael's name knowing that it would lead to a desired reaction from Spanish authorities. Shortly before Rafael began his rebellion, a group of Christian Indians in Nueva Vizcaya grew upset at the Spanish government for a perceived slight and so they concocted a story that a small group of Apaches had attacked them while traveling. They then directed Spanish soldiers to a location where other angry Hispanicized Indians lay in wait to ambush the soldiers. Establecimiento Apaches were perhaps the biggest beneficiaries of Rafael's criminal activities. As has been noted, these groups often violated the conditions set forth in their peace agreements with the Spanish, raided settlements, and then blamed unincorporated Indians like Rafael for their crimes.[41]

UNFORTUNATELY FOR ESTABLECIMIENTO APACHES, they were also targets of Rafael. At the beginning of December, six Apaches from the establecimiento de paz at Carrizal received a license to leave the area of the presidio to go hunting. On December 8, while hunting in the Valle de Santa Clara, Rafael and José Antonio attacked this group. They killed one Apache man and captured an Apache woman and a five to seven-year-old child named Francisca. They also took a horse and the Apaches' equipment.[42]

This would mark the second time that Rafael took an establecimiento Apache woman as a captive, and he had also considered taking Mescalero women during the encounter at the watering hole. There may have been an intimate reason for seeking out these Apache women, but it might also have been a matter of revenge or a power fulfillment fantasy. This seems to have been the case with the Apache Kid, who, like Rafael, was an Apache who turned from being a scout for military authorities to using his knowledge of military protocol to conduct raids and attack Apaches who continued to work with soldiers. One observer described the Apache Kid's attacks on cooperative Apaches thusly: "Apache Kid would come sneaking into their camp and paralyze the lot of them more than a whole regiment of soldiers would. The Kid would eat his fill, catch the best horses of the tribe, grab anything else he wanted, and then, cutting out the best-looking squaw in the camp, ride off with the lot, leaving every Indian too scared to lift a hand."[43]

Revenge may have been a motivator for attacking the Carrizal Apaches, but it is likely that Rafael and José Antonio targeted Apache women because they needed skills that only plains Indian women possessed. At this point, their captive María Martina had been with the band since October 1807 and all indications are that she had accepted her role as a wife and had taken to life as an Apache. Indeed, one story about Rafael that may refer to María Martina says that she knew how to fight "like a true Indian squaw." However, María Martina seems to have lacked certain skills that only come from being raised as an Apache from birth, and because she was not a captive at the same time as their first female Apache captive, she had no time to learn certain things like how to treat wounds and clean and dress in the traditional Apache manner. The new Apache woman could fill these roles and teach other captives.[44]

Like María Martina, the unnamed Apache woman soon became a willing member of Rafael's band, and it seems that she also took on the role of a wife to Rafael. The idea of Rafael having multiple wives, especially with one being white and another Indian, became a point of emphasis in contemporary sources and later legends. Possibly owing to the patriarchal and racist nature of Spanish society, the way in which contemporary writers discuss female captives varies. Sometimes, the Spanish portrayed the women as unwilling members of a "harem" who Rafael had forced into submission. Other times, sources refer to them as members of the band or as Rafael's wives, implying that they had agency in their decisions, and willingly participated in the brutality. However, even in these instances, the women are seen more as pawns in Rafael's story, and little attention is afforded to their background history and motivations.[45]

Likewise, little can be learned about the various women of Rafael's band from legends because stories about European and Indian women either fighting alongside or submitting to an Apache male are so pervasive in northern Mexico that it is often impossible to tell if a legend refers to female captives of Rafael, a different Apache, or if the legend is entirely fictional. For example, while traveling through Coahuila during the United States invasion of Mexico in 1847, American soldier Samuel Chamberlain learned a story about a "Great Chief" from decades in the past whose "desire to drive all Spaniards from our land" had led the Indian to kill hundreds across northern Mexico. According to Chamberlain "romors (sic) tell of two Amazons who ride with the Great Chief in all his raids, one white and one Indian, of the fearful cruelties inflicted on such unfortunate Priests as fall in to their hands, torn to pieces by wild horses, lashed to the great cactus, the petahaya [saguaro], and kept alive by careful nursing while the thorns grow into the flesh and take root in the bodies of the victims." Chamberlain even sketched a mural he saw depicting the chief and his wives. Although the image and the stories match what is known about Rafael, there is not enough to definitively tie him to the legend, and even if there was, it would be impossible to know to which of Rafael's multiple wives the story refers.[46]

This lack of clarity and the sexualization of female captives continues in modern histories. For example, when Victor Orozco reprinted Bustamante's report on Rafael in his book *Las guerras indias en la historia de Chihuahua* in 1992, he included a drawing of an Apache, presumably Rafael, grabbing a woman by the wrists. Rafael peers into the woman's eyes while wearing an expression that can either be interpreted as a smirk or a loving gaze. The woman looks back with what can only be described as a cross between longing and fright. An article in a modern magazine contains a picture of Rafael riding side-by-side with a woman who seems to be more his equal than a captive. Understandably considering the lack of sources and the confusion surrounding Rafael's legend, neither Orozco nor the magazine article name the women in the images, nor do they conjecture about their role in the band.[47]

DECEMBER 8 may have given birth to a different legend about Rafael. Shortly after capturing the Apache woman, Rafael's band encountered and killed two vecinos traveling on the Cosiguiriachi Road near a place named Charco del Burro. Rafael and José Antonio then attacked an Indian from the village of Matachit who had left town in search of a cow that had wandered off. Fortunately for the man, he had heeded Salcedo's orders to arm oneself whenever traveling, and he was able to injure one of the two Apaches and force them both to flee. This story fits with a local legend that a poor farmer was somehow able to fight off a particularly brutal Apache chief in one-on-one combat.[48]

Whether or not this legend refers to Rafael, by the end of 1808, it was apparent that Salcedo's system of requiring the citizens of Nueva Vizcaya to carry weapons, form neighborhood watches, and establish local militias was working. Indeed, Bustamante records only thirty-three deaths for the year of 1808, compared to nearly two hundred in 1807.[49]

CHAPTER EIGHT

A Good Person from Laguna,
January 1809–April 1810

IN EARLY JANUARY 1809, José Castillo, whom Rafael and José Antonio had captured at the Rancho de los Peinados the previous September, escaped while the band was in the Sierra de Nonolata. When he later explained where and how he had gotten away, Spanish officials may have been confused. The Sierra de Nonolato was near the Laguna de Jaco in the Bolsón de Mapimí. This was in the province of Coahuila, farther east than Rafael's band had traveled up to this point.[1]

Indeed, Castillo's report put the band in eastern Comarca de la Laguna, an area of low elevation where the drainages of the Sierra Madre Occidental and the Sierra Madre Oriental meet to form a number of shallow lakes like the Laguna de Jaco. This access to water and the relative fertility of the soil owing to the minerals brought in by drainage made La Laguna well suited for commercial agriculture. However, long dry spells sometimes leave the region without water, while periods of heavy rains lead to flooding, a consequence of evaporation being the only natural way water leaves the Laguna basin. Lack of access to the sea also means that it is difficult to bring any crops produced in the area to market, making raising and driving cattle one of the few profitable ventures in the region.[2]

The biggest producer of cattle in La Laguna was the Hacienda Márquez de Aguayo, an opulent and massive estate that served as perhaps the clearest example of the disparity in wealth between the haves and have-nots in the Internal Provinces. The estate was the property of the descendants of the Marquis de San Miguel Aguayo, a high-ranking Spanish official who received title to much of the lands in the Internal Provinces as a reward for helping Spain drive the French out of Texas in the early eighteenth century. At the beginning of the nineteenth century, the Aguayo family lived in Mexico

City and used their landholdings in the north as a source of revenue and as a summer estate. The luxury of the property amazed Zebulon Pike when he passed through it on his way back to the United States in 1807. He described the buildings of the Hacienda de Pattos, where the Aguayo family stayed during their visits, as being, "elegantly furnished" and centered on a "Jet d'eau, which cast forth water from eight spouts, extended from a colosean female form."[3]

Most who lived on the estate were the Aguayo family's employees, and they did not share in this luxury. Indeed, Hacienda Márquez de Aguayo had a population that numbered in the thousands, with employees and their families living in scattered, smaller haciendas within the larger estate. Some of these

Southeastern Nueva Vizcaya, western Coahuila, and northern Nueva Galicia. Rafael's raids took him outside of Nueva Vizcaya on multiple occasions. A 1785 order transferred political jurisdiction of Parras and Saltillo to the governor of Coahuila, but the border between Nueva Vizcaya and Coahuila remained largely undefined by the nineteenth century. Map by Ben Pease, cartographer.

employees were well armed, with Pike estimating that the Aguayo family used some 1,500 guards to protect their property from "the savages." Although soldiers in regular Spanish service regarded such private armies as inferior, the guards were often better equipped than the military, and certainly better armed than most civilians in the Internal Provinces. However, most employees on the hacienda were not guards but poor ranch hands, and like the hacienda workers who had previously fallen victim to Rafael and José Antonio in Nueva Vizcaya, many went about their duties unarmed.[4]

Considering that Rafael's band had yet to attack in the region, and that many of Salcedo's previous decrees regarding Rafael had been for Nueva Vizcaya specifically, it is unclear if the average subject in Coahuila even knew anything about Rafael, much less that they were supposed to carry weapons when traveling or that they needed to form neighborhood watches. This made the Aguayo Hacienda, neighboring ranches, and Coahuila as a whole, fertile ground for Rafael's raids. Unfortunately, the absence of a substantial military presence also makes it difficult to track Rafael historically, as many of his activities may have gone unrecorded. Bustamante readily admits in his report that he is uncertain about the extent of Rafael's crimes in Coahuila.[5]

RAFAEL, JOSÉ ANTONIO, MARÍA MARTINA, and the recently captured Apache woman and child entered Coahuila at the beginning of January 1809 and would spend much of the following two months preying on the people of the province. On January 14, they killed five servants of the Márquez de Aguayo as they were traveling through the Marrufo Meadow on their way to Sombreretillo. They then proceeded to the Mesa de San Juan Bautista on the Hacienda San Juan de Castro, where they killed Juan Antonio Cerda, a servant of don Juan Zambrano. They also killed four more people near the Hacienda los Hornos.[6]

These latter deaths were mentioned in an article by historian Atanasio Sarabia, but Bustamante did not record them in his tally of those killed by Rafael and José Antonio, likely one of many incidents of which Bustamante was unaware that took place in Coahuila from January to March 1809. Indeed, Bustamante mentions that during this time the duo killed seven people, but also says, "that the number of killed may have been as high as twelve." He chose not to add the additional deaths because without military records and lacking access to documents from Coahuila, he could not confirm their validity.[7]

Historian Gildardo Contreras would later investigate parochial records to determine if Rafael and José Antonio were responsible for the rumored deaths. His investigation confirmed that they were accountable for at least four murders outside of the seven recorded by Bustamante. Parochial records indicate that in mid-January, Rafael's band killed Victoriano Padilla, a servant of the Laguna Ranch; José Praxedis Martínez, a servant on the Marqués de Aguayo's estate; Josef Antonio Parra, a servant from Hornos; and Josef Inocente Perales of the Alamo Ranch. Contreras seems to believe that these were different than the those suggested by Bustamante, meaning Rafael's band was responsible for some fourteen deaths on or around January 14 and possibly as many as twenty-two. Contreras's research also revealed the human cost to these deaths. The wife of Padilla was unable to recover her husband's remains from the church and have them properly interred because she could not afford the three pesos to cover funeral costs.[8]

Whatever the number of people the band killed, the deaths sent locals scrambling to form militias. Laborers and guards from the Hacienda de Aguayo assembled with their weapons and created search parties. Groups of men from Hornos, Jimulco, La Cueva, and Toledo joined them and looked for the Apaches throughout the remainder of January. By the time the search parties set out, Rafael and José Antonio were making their way back west along the Río Nazas through the Cañon de Fernández in the direction of Cuencamé.[9]

A party of eleven men picked up Rafael's trail and tracked him through the canyon, eventually catching sight of the Apaches and three women, presumably María Martina and the recently captured Apache woman and Apache child, as they were ascending the Sierra del Rosario, a rugged, jagged mountain in eastern Nueva Vizcaya. The party got so close to the band that they were able to discern that "Rafael was wearing blue shorts and a suede jacket with a red back, while Antonio was dressed all in suede, both carrying rifles, lances, and well-stocked quivers." The female members of the band especially impressed the pursuers who would later remark that one of the women, "due to the lightness with which she climbed the mountain, showed signs of being Apache, and that all went with hats and mounted on horseback like men."[10]

By the time the party caught up to the band, Rafael and José Antonio had already taken a position above them in an area that served as a natural fortification. When the party leader yelled up and asked them to surrender, Rafael initially feigned ignorance, claiming that "he and his companions were good people from La Laguna who had no weapons. They had not killed anyone." When the pursuers refused to believe this, Rafael pointed to María Martina and the Apache woman and said it was they who had done all the killing, not them. Rafael may have been truthful in this statement, as captives had voluntarily or involuntarily participated in the band's bloodshed in the past. However, because the idea of a woman committing such violent acts would be scandalous in patriarchal Spanish society, the statement may also have been intended as a joke or a means to emasculate the men below.[11]

Whether because of Rafael's reputation, the advantageous position the Apaches held, or the natural fortifications surrounding them, the party was hesitant to press the attack. As one observer noted of such situations, "nor can the Spaniards do much damage to the Indians when these are near a mountain. The Spaniard cannot follow, over steep brush-covered rocks, the speedy enemy who is as practiced as a deer in climbing around the hills, and who, protected by rocks, trees, and brush defies the Spaniard, sending many an arrow after him with impunity." This failure to act led Rafael to call down to his pursuers and dare them to come up the mountain. If they were too frightened to do so, Rafael wanted the men to leave because he and José Antonio "had things to do." Dejected, the patrol broke off their pursuit and began descending the mountain. As they did, Rafael called out, warning that "he would see them soon in La Laguna."[12]

The party reported what had happened to the governor of the Mapimí intendancy, Manuel Cubillas, who could do nothing but relay what had occurred to Commandant General Salcedo and tell the people of La Laguna to be mindful. Spanish forces continued to comb the region until March 7, when José Joaquín Ugarte, son of former commandant general Jacobo Ugarte, concluded that "the enemy has retired from the borders of this province." Ugarte then sent word to Nueva Vizcaya, Texas, and Nuevo Léon to be on alert for Rafael, cautioning Spanish officials to "watch with the greatest caution the land which they might invade, so with quick notice of them, we will be able to apprehend or capture them." He let them know that he and his soldiers were standing by to assist their militias should word arrive that Rafael was in the area.[13]

THE INABILITY OF SPANISH FORCES to fire on Apaches when they were at elevation frustrated Commandant General Salcedo, who was struggling to deal with not only Rafael, but also other formerly peaceful Apaches groups. The war in Europe had syphoned supplies earmarked for the Internal Provinces, forcing Salcedo to reduce rations to the establecimientos de paz. This upset resident Chiricahua and Mescalero Apaches and led many to leave their establecimientos and recommence raiding. By the end of 1808, Spanish travelers in New Mexico were coming under frequent assault by former Apaches de paz.[14]

Indeed, only a few months before Rafael's entry into Coahuila, the commandant general had to read about Spanish officer Francisco Amangual suspending his attempt to scout a road between Santa Fe and San Antonio to pursue a group of Apaches who had stolen horses from his supply train. When Amangual finally located the Apaches in the Sacramento Mountains of what is now southern New Mexico, he found them standing on a cliff above him, mocking him and his men because their firearms were ineffective at such heights. The unfortunate thing for Amangual was that he had brought cannons on his trip, but he had left them in camp because they were too cumbersome and difficult to move in mountainous terrain.[15]

After reading about instances like this and the various times Rafael had taken up position just out of the range of Spanish firearms, Salcedo designed a small-caliber, lightweight swivel cannon (less than six arrobas or 152.22 pounds), with a one *vara* length barrel (approximately thirty-three inches) that could be carried and fired from the back of a mule. The commandant general believed that such a weapon was "indispensable for using smooth ball to dislocate the enemy that has occupied or is found in a dominant location." To minimize weight and save iron, which was in short supply in the Internal Provinces, only those parts susceptible to cracking when firing would receive iron reinforcement. The chamber was cylindrical and aligned in a way to lessen recoil and decrease noise to prevent the mule from fleeing when the cannon was fired. Salcedo even designed a carrier for the device that would not rub the mule's haunches.[16]

Salcedo finished his prototype by 1809, but he did not deploy it for use against Rafael, possibly because outside of a single instance in April, his band is absent from the historical record from March to September 1809. On April 18, don Nicolás Tarín reported from Guajoquilla that "Rafael and his companion had just killed four people on the San Pedro Ranch" and advised local leaders to be on alert. The dead were José Guadalupe Rodríguez, Miguel Portillo, Juan Antonio Fiero, and José María Peña, each of whom burial records describe as "having died at the hands of the barbarous Indians." A priest in Guajoquilla reported two additional dead around this time owing to "barbarian Indians," José Antonio Cárdenas and José Manuel Calletana de los Relles, but because Bustamante does not credit Rafael with killing them, it is possible that other rebellious Apaches were responsible for their deaths. Whatever the case, neither of the two men received the sacrament, as Calletana "died in the country" and Cárdenas because of "the violence of his death."[17]

Interestingly, Rafael Nevares was not the one to conduct the funeral services for the two men killed near Guajoquilla. In 1808, feeling sick and overwhelmed by his workload, the priest decided that he could no longer meet the religious needs of the people of Guajoquilla and handed over the marriage, baptism, and internment duties and logs to Juan José de Sida. For the foreseeable future, Nevares would focus exclusively on providing religious services for soldiers of the presidio and overseeing construction of a new church for Guajoquilla, El Templo Santo Cristo de Burgos. It is unclear if the news about his former protégé's activities played into his illness and his decision to scale back his ecclesiastical duties.[18]

With Rafael spending the summer of 1809 in hiding and with Apaches in other areas in revolt, Salcedo decided to send the cannon to Captain Juan Francisco Granados who was on campaign against Apaches in New Mexico. Granadas reported that he "took a small cannon that was fired from the mule that carried it, and the test proved to be advantageous," and that his men captured a number of Apaches on the campaign. The positive test led Salcedo to determine that "nothing prevents the animals from following the troops at all times and over all terrain," and he dispatched a letter to the marshall of the Royal Corps of Engineers of New Spain requesting assistance so that more of the cannons could be made.[19]

THE INCREASE IN APACHE ATTACKS in 1809 would cause confusion when Rafael returned to raiding in September of that year. On September 15, don Jacinto Rivera of the Hacienda de Río Florido dispatched a mozo to the Aguaje de Barraza to fetch some oxen. When the mozo did not return, Rivera and four vecinos went to look for him, only to find his dead body at the nearby watering hole. Apparently, Rivera did not think the deed to have been committed by Rafael, and he did not report the crime immediately. There had not been a dependable sighting of Rafael's band for six months, and Rivera may have assumed that an abiego gang or a different band of Apaches carried out the attack.[20]

The following evening, September 16, two soldiers approached a group of four men who had stopped at a stream on their way from Río Florido to the Pastores Ranch to say their nightly prayers. The soldiers, actually Rafael and José Antonio, interrupted the prayer and either demanded the men hand over their possessions or simply started stabbing. Whatever the case, two of the men ran across the stream, only to be cut down and killed before they reached the other side. The Apaches injured the two other men, don Juan de Urquidi and don Manuel Taguada, but they survived their wounds and reported what had happened to local officials.[21]

Urquidi and Taguada's stories differed. One said that it had only been Rafael and José Antonio who had assaulted them. The other claimed that the attackers had been accompanied by twenty other Apaches. Although Spanish officials later determined that this was untrue, an Indian woman had come along on the raid, likely the unnamed female Apache who had dazzled the men of La Laguna with her riding skills six months before. It is unclear why the second man reported that there were nineteen other Apaches present, but the fact that both men had the title "don" preceding their names indicates that they were nobles and came from prominent families. Perhaps the embellishment was to avoid accusations of cowardice.[22]

That same night, Rafael's band attacked and killed a farmhand three quarters of a league away from don Marcos Váguez y Marco's hacienda near the Río Florido. After learning about the attack, don Marcos assembled a party to search the area and discovered that the Indians had also killed a nearby man, woman, and boy. Váguez y Marco also found another woman barely clinging on to life. When questioned about what happened, she told don Marcos that the attackers had taken a boy, José Dionisio Gómez, and then "she declared that it had been the Indian woman in the company of Rafael who had injured her."[23]

THE APACHE WOMAN would join Rafael and José Antonio again a little over a week later, when on the morning of September 23, they killed a man and a woman and injured the woman's sister in the town of San Felipe. Rafael's band then took the wounded woman and "fell upon the Galeras Ranch" some three leagues from Ciénega de los Olivos. Although they killed no one at Galeras, they likely took cattle and horses before making their way to the nearby Vallecilio Ranch, a lush plot of land owned by the wealthy and prestigious Loya family. The ranch's location in a fertile valley surrounded by small hills made it excellent for raising cattle, but its isolation meant that it would take a long time for help to arrive after the Apaches launched their attack.[24]

Someone either saw the Apaches approaching or word had reached Vallecilio of the earlier raids, because residents of the ranch were able to barricade themselves within the Loya homestead before Rafael's band arrived. Considering that Apaches generally preferred to rely on stealth rather than brute force, sheltering oneself in a fortified structure was often an effective strategy that had saved many lives over the past decades. Those living in stone and adobe homes, which was likely the case with the wealthy Loya family, were especially protected considering that Apaches could not break through walls as they could jacale and wooden homes. Unfortunately for the three men, five women, and thirteen-year-old Doña María Jesús Loya sheltered inside, they were only protected by a wooden door, and someone had left an ax outside.[25]

In what must have been a frightening scene, Rafael took the ax and proceeded to chop down the Loya family's door. Once it had been cleared, Rafael, José Antonio, and the Apache woman entered the home and killed all eight adults sheltered inside. They then took doña María Jesús Loya captive. They left the woman whom they had captured in San Felipe bleeding but still alive on the cabin floor. A search of the ranch home discovered clothes, three silver bars, a holster, a jar of gunpowder, a spear, a saddle, and other jewels, which the Apaches took with them before departing.[26]

THE BAND BROUGHT their new captive to a mountain peak adjacent to the abandoned Chorreras Presidio, some fifty miles east of Chihuahua City, where they would remain for the next three months. At this point, the band now consisted of Rafael, José Antonio, long-time member María Martina, the Apache woman, the Apache child, María Jesús, the boy they had captured on September 16, José Dionisio, and a woman named Dolores about whom little is known. The group consisted of a wide variety of ethnic and social backgrounds, and the addition of María Jesús Loya added economic diversity. The "doña" preceding her name indicated that she was upper class, of noble lineage and *limpieza de sangre,* or "of clean blood," a designator the Spanish gave to those who could prove exclusive ancestral links to Iberia.[27]

As had happened with María Martina and the Apache woman, María Jesús would soon become a trusted member of the band and a wife to Rafael. Although this transformation may have come about out of fear or a form of

Stockholm syndrome, Rafael may have gained the girl's loyalty during an instance that occurred sometime between September 1809 and January 1810 when Rafael, José Antonio, and José Dionisio left María Jesús and the other female captives at camp to trade with a passing ranchería of Apaches. Sources do not make clear whether the Apaches were on leave from an establecimiento, were among those who were in rebellion against the Spanish, or were members of a group who had remained consistently at war with Spain. Whatever the case, when Rafael approached two of the Apaches and offered to trade a gun for some arrows they were carrying, the Apaches seemed receptive.[28]

After carrying out the exchange, Rafael, José Antonio, and José Dionisio returned to find that while they were gone, other Apaches from the ranchería had attacked their camp, killing the female captive Dolores and wounding María de Jesús Loya. After discovering the treachery, Rafael "angrily moved on the Apaches and fought them," shooting one of the Apaches with a musket ball. "Realizing the danger they were in" after what he had done, Rafael grabbed the surviving captives and fled, relocating his band to the Sierra de Tinaja y Sal si Puedeas.[29]

ON OR AROUND JANUARY 11, Rafael, José Antonio, and captive José Dionisio Gómez once again left the women in camp to conduct their first series of raids in months. They began by attacking two Tarahumaras near the town of San Lorenzo. They injured one and "dispatched the other." At around the same time, they attacked a group of shepherds at a place named Cuevillas near the town of Babonoyaba on January 11. Rafael and José Antonio killed two of the shepherds and ordered José Dionisio to execute the third, threatening to kill him if he refused. Dionisio complied. The Apaches spared a fourth shepherd, a young man named José Tomás Matías Ochoa, whom they brought back to camp with them.[30]

On January 17, don Felipe González of the Hacienda de Mala-Noche reported that the previous evening four muleteers were leading a mule train through a place called Los Adobes when "the Indian Rafael and five of his companions killed all of the drivers." They also killed one of the mules and took the saddlebags off the rest. It is unclear how González knew that Rafael had carried out the attack or how many companions he had considering that, according to his story, all witnesses had been killed. Some two weeks later, on January 31, Rafael and José Antonio attacked two vecinos from San Gerónimo,

Manuel Jáquez and Policarpo Vázquez, as they were traveling along the Río Conchos. In the skirmish Policarpo was killed, but Manuel, once a corporal in the military, sustained only injuries.[31]

At dawn on February 12, Rafael and José Antonio took a woman from Guajoquilla at the Cañada de Santa Ana. Little more is known about the woman, so perhaps she escaped, the Apaches killed her, or Spanish officials confused her in the records with another captive. At or around this time, they also stole eight mules from Carrizo. Word of the attack immediately went out, sending multiple patrols of the Tercera Compañía Volante in search of Rafael. One was under Second Lieutenant Francisco Minjares, who had been among those devoted to searching for Rafael for the past three years. Corporal Juan Fraire led another.[32]

On February 13, Minjares and Fraire's patrols tracked Rafael to the band's camp in the peaks of the Sierra de Tinaja y Sal si Puedeas. The Apaches became alerted to the incoming soldiers and as they had done in preparation for previous battles, took up a position above them. A gunfight broke out. During the battle, Rafael and José Antonio fired down on the soldiers while José Dionisio Gómez brought them arrows, ammunition, and whatever else could be thrown or fired at the soldiers. At one point, the Apaches pushed eight of the recently captured mules off the mountain hoping to crush the men below. Two Spanish soldiers, Urbano Domínguez and Roberto Visuaño, fell victim to the assault.[33]

Instead of retreating, Minjares and Fraire's remaining men continued to fire back at the Apaches expending 519 musket balls in the process. While the battle raged, the Spanish officers implored the various captives to run to their protection, but even though the captives "had plenty of time to leave if they had wanted, the calls were ignored." Despite this, the Spanish soldiers eventually either captured or liberated the Apache woman taken from Santa Clara on December 8, 1808, who had been with the band for more than a year. With their ammunition running out, the soldiers could not press the attack any further and brought the Apache woman to the nearest settlement for interrogation. As with the first Apache "La India," the fate of this woman is unknown.[34]

ON THE MORNING OF FEBRUARY 19, two soldiers of the Segunda Compañia Volante Juan Parada and Ramón Márquez were on their way to deliver mail to Hacienda del Carmen. They were accompanied by a vecino from

El Paso who had likely joined the two soldiers for safety. The Spanish had created a royal mail service for New Spain in 1768, but it was not until over a decade later that it extended to include the northern provinces. Customarily, only two or three soldiers served as mail carriers. Riding in smaller numbers allowed them to more quickly traverse the long distances between towns in the Internal Provinces, but it also made them more susceptible to ambush from Apaches and bandits. For this reason, mail carriers generally traveled at night to avoid being seen.[35]

The fact that Parada and Márquez were traveling in the morning indicated that they had fallen behind schedule, perhaps because they had allowed the traveler to join them when they left El Paso. Whatever the case, it was during their journey to Hacienda del Carmen that, according to Márquez, the two soldiers and their traveling companion came under attack by "a large group of Apaches." The Apaches killed Parada and the vecino and took a saddled red horse, a saddled mare, a shotgun, ammunition, suede pants, cowboy boots, another pair of boots, a brown sarape, mail, and jewels. Faced with such overwhelming opposition, Márquez turned his horse, fled the scene, and reported what had occurred to Spanish authorities in the Hacienda de Encinillas. Considering the recent rebellion of establecimiento Apaches, leadership believed Márquez, and he faced no punishment for running away.[36]

Unfortunately for Márquez, shortly after he made his declaration, the two male captives of Rafael and José Antonio, José Dionisio Gómez and José Tomás Matías Ochoa, escaped and made their way to Encinillas the following morning, February 20. When Spanish authorities asked about the attack on the mail carriers, the captives gave an accurate description of what had been taken and claimed that Rafael and José Antonio had conducted the attack alone after leaving camp that morning to "look for cows to eat." The captive's testimony meant that Márquez had fled the scene in violation of the commandant general's orders to stand and fight if attacked by Rafael, leading military authorities put Márquez on trial for dereliction of duty. The results of this trial are unknown.[37]

Dionisio and Ochoa faced their own trials shortly thereafter. They were asked about what had happened during their captivity. Dionisio admitted that he had killed a shepherd but insisted that he had done so only under threat of death. Spanish officials noted that his account mirrored that of former captive José Salvador Bueno Laicano, who had killed only after José Antonio threatened to murder him if he did not. Ultimately, Salcedo determined that

Dionisio and Ochoa had taken it upon themselves to escape, and "their escape showed the disgust at the oppressiveness that they were facing." For this reason, the commandant general ordered the two to be freed.[38]

THE ROBBING OF THE MAIL CARRIERS left Rafael and José Antonio with ammunition and a new uniform, and they would use these tools in a series of attacks over the following months that covered a wide swath of territory in what is today Chihuahua, Durango, and Coahuila. On March 8, José Antonio, Rafael, and "a woman behind him with a spear and colored skirt," probably María Martina, attacked Vicente Antillón as he was delivering goods in his cart near the town of Adobes. The Apaches shot Antillón, hitting him in the hand but not killing him. They then burned his cart.[39]

Later that day, the Apaches attacked two people, Gregorio García and Nepomuceno Parraleño, at a creek near the town of San Andrés. García was armed with a musket, but he apparently missed, or the gun was defective because Spanish authorities would later find the weapon lying next to his dead body. The fact that Rafael and José Antonio left the gun behind may imply inferior quality to the ones they already possessed, or it may simply be an indication that they lacked the gunpowder necessary to use the weapon.[40]

At some point between March 17 and March 20, Rafael and José Antonio left the other members of their band behind in the Sierra de Vitorino and set out on another series of raids, attacking and killing someone in Sinecio Vargas. Two guards of the Hacienda del Torreón, Juan Núñez and his son Manuel Núñez, "were killed at the hands of Rafaelillo" while they were cooking dinner near Sendradita. As one priest said of such attacks, "if the guards are vigilant and wide awake, the Apaches seldom accomplish anything, but if they are careless they must pay for their negligence with the loss of their horses and sometimes with their lives." Rafael and José Antonio took the guards' firearms, as well as a number of mules from the Hacienda of Torreón. Spanish authorities also reported that during this time Rafael's band killed two paisanos in the Sierra de Huerachi Canyon, but this might have been another reference to the Núñezes. Rafael and José Antonio then returned to camp in the Sierra de Vitorino.[41]

After learning of the attacks, the hacienda owner informed Corporal José Medrano of what had occurred and formed a search party to assist the soldiers in looking for Rafael. Medrano and his men followed their trail back to the

Sierra de Vitorino. On April 2, they located the band's camp, and Rafael and José Antonio and their captives had to make such a hasty retreat that they left behind twelve animals, as well as the firearms they had taken from the guards at Torreón. However, just as it seemed the soldiers and militia were closing in on the Apaches, it hailed, and the falling ice covered the band's tracks, allowing Rafael to escape capture once again.[42]

CHAPTER NINE

The Apostate Apache,
April 1810–September 1810

A N ADDITIONAL APACHE WOMAN joined the band on April 19, 1810, when Rafael, José Antonio, María Martina, and María Jesús Loya encountered four families of Apaches from the Carrizal esta-blecimiento who had received permission to hunt upstream from the com-mander of the San Buenaventura presidio. In recent months, Spanish and Ópata soldiers had joined forces with their Comanche allies in campaigning against the various Mescalero and Chiricahua Apache groups who had left their establecimientos in rebellion in 1808 and 1809. Armed with Salcedo's newly designed muskets and cannon and led by officers like Félix Colomo, who had previously been assigned to track down Rafael, Spain's forces marched into the mountain homelands of the Mescaleros and Chiricahuas and engaged the Apaches in a series of battles. Faced with this opposition, the Mescaleros and Chiricahuas petitioned Salcedo for peace. The commandant general agreed and promised that if the Apaches returned to the establecimientos, he would provide them with additional rations and continue allowing presidio com-manders to give temporary leave for hunting.[1]

The four Apache families upstream of the San Buenaventura presidio had received one such pass. As Rafael's band noticed upon approaching this group, the men of the camp had left to go hunting, leaving behind their women and children. This allowed Rafael and José Antonio to kill two Indian women and take another two as captives. They also took four mules. Those who escaped being killed or taken captive reported to the commander of Carrizal that it was Rafael and José Antonio who assaulted them, but there were "two people that did not join in on the attack on the ranchería. They were carrying weapons and appeared to be women." This was almost certainly María Martina and María Jesús.[2]

Little is known about the new Apache captives, but one disappears from the historical record, indicating that she died or escaped. The other Apache woman, however, was named María, and like the previous two female captives from the Carrizal establecimiento she appears to have quickly accepted her role in the band and, unlike María Martina, and María Jesús, who went along on raids but generally avoided combat, this third Apache "La India" would fight alongside Rafael and José Antonio.[3]

On April 29, Bartolo Zubia and Cecilio Tarango left San Gerónimo to sell bread at the Hacienda de Encinillas. While crossing the Llano de los Asituches, Rafael and José Antonio attacked and killed the pair and made off with the food they were carrying. With no witnesses, Spanish authorities may not have connected the crime to the Apache duo, had they not made an attack on the Dolores mine the following day. At approximately four o'clock in the afternoon, Rafael and José Antonio fired an arrow at Polonio Arias, who was outside the mine in the area where the deposits were collected. The arrow injured but did not kill Arias. Another miner, Julián Hernández, witnessed what had happened and tried to flee into the mine. The Apaches followed him, eventually tracking him down and killing him. They then left the mine, stealing several mules they found outside.[4]

The fact that the duo used arrows indicates that they had run out of ammunition or lost their firearms when fleeing José Medrano's forces on April 2. If so, they would not be without guns for long. On May 7, they attacked the Hacienda de Corral de Piedras, killing a shepherd. Shortly thereafter they encountered a group of men bringing fresh horses to a Corporal Granillo. Perhaps Granillo was searching for the Apaches, and Rafael and José Antonio, wanting to slow his pursuit, intentionally sought out the men bringing him new horses. They may have encountered the group by chance. Whatever the case, the Apaches surely noticed that soldiers Luis Vargas and Isidro Alarcon were serving as escorts for the four men driving the herd. This apparently did not deter the Apaches, as they attacked and killed all six men. They took three saddled horses, fifteen other horses, and a shotgun.[5]

AFTER COMMITTING THIS AUDACIOUS ROBBERY, the Apaches disappeared for the next two months. On or around July 1, in the area of Cuesta del Ratón, Rafael lanced and killed a paisano from Noyar and slaughtered his mule. This was only seven leagues from the Conchos Presidio, so the commandant of the presidio sent soldiers to investigate. They determined that the act had been committed by Rafael, and the discovery of three additional corpses downstream confirmed their suspicions.[6]

By the time the soldiers made their discovery, the Apaches were already moving on to their next target. On July 5, Rafael and José Antonio killed two of José Antonio Loya's cowboys in an arroyo some seven leagues distant from Ciénega and some 120 miles away from their previous attack. They took a fifteen-year-old male captive. They then traveled along a stream near San Felipe where they executed another. By July 10, they were fifty miles away at Parral, where at four o'clock in the afternoon, they wounded a cowboy in the Real de Minas Nuevas. That night they killed a muleteer and took a boy captive. The child and the new fifteen-year-old captive do not appear in subsequent records, so it can be assumed that Rafael killed them. Perhaps they tried to force the teenager to execute the child as they had done with Dionisio and Laicano, but he refused, leading the Apaches to kill them both.[7]

Unfortunately for Rafael and his band, a group of Ópata and Pima soldiers was in the area. This would mark the first, and ultimately, only recorded instance where the Ópatas and Pimas would confront Rafael. This is surprising considering that in addition to their tracking skills, the Ópatas were much more mobile than regular Spanish soldiers and militia. They did not wear the heavy leather *cueras*, finding the armor to be cumbersome and immobile, and they forwent Spanish horses and instead rode mules, because although slower, the more sure-footed mules could better traverse the type of precarious mountain terrain where Apaches often made their camps.[8]

On July 13, Corporal Martín Peña and the Ópata soldiers under his command tracked Rafael and his captives to Cañada de Ronsesvalles in the Sierra de Santa Bárbara. As the Ópatas approached the Apaches, Rafael and José Antonio would have noticed that their faces were painted. As one observer described the practice, "they take special pains to appear as horrible as possible to their enemies, hoping thus to excite in them fear and trembling. With this idea in view they smear their faces with black and blood-red paints, which make them unrecognizable, like hideous masks. They also paint their bodies all over with different colors and embellish them with figures of all kinds of snakes, toads and other horrible animals. Above all, they never fail to don their fearsome war bonnets."[9]

Rafael and José Antonio may also have been intimidated by the Ópatas' reputation. Owing to their tenacity and tracking abilities, the Apaches came to fear the Ópata presidio companies more than Spanish ones, and it was even said that the Apaches "acknowledge the superiority of the Ópatas." It is unlikely that Rafael and José Antonio shared this sentiment, but they certainly understood that they could expect no mercy from the Ópatas if captured. Spanish soldiers never left the Ópatas alone with Apache prisoners because they knew they would kill them.[10]

Like many of the battles featuring Rafael, details surrounding the July 13 encounter with the Ópatas are sparse. However, it is likely that the Ópatas subjected Rafael and José Antonio to more consistent fire than they had experienced before as the Ópatas continued to use bows and arrows in addition to firearms, because they could fire many more arrows in the time it took to reload a gun. Ultimately, however, this would not prove to be a decisive factor. During the battle, Rafael and José Antonio killed an Ópata named Mauricio Enríquez, and their barrage of arrows forced the remaining Ópatas and Pimas to flee. The soldiers later reported that Rafael and José Antonio, "left with their captives without experiencing any damage at all."[11]

FOLLOWING THE ENCOUNTER WITH THE ÓPATAS, Rafael's band fled some 250 miles to the east, returning to Coahuila just east of the modern Durango-Coahuila border and north of the modern Zacatecas-Coahuila border. The journey took them once again to the massive Hacienda de Aguayo, near the area known as the Acatita de Baján.[12]

On July 26, Rafael, José Antonio, and their captives confronted two young men, Cecilio Martínez and his brother Magdaleno Carrulo near the Vega Redonda on the Hacienda de San Antonio de la Laguna and "began to run after them and harass them." Because it is unlikely the two brothers were carrying anything of value, it appears that they may have been worried the boys recognized them. Whatever the case, Rafael and José Antonio went after Magdaleno, stabbing him with their lances. This allowed Cecilio to escape and make his way to the hacienda where he let the senior administrator, don José Manuel de Cárdenas know what had happened.[13]

Cárdenas immediately ordered the mayordomo Victoriano Waldo Rubio to call together as many men as he could and pursue the fleeing Apaches. Rubio complied, forming a small militia of fourteen men made up of three guards and other shepherds and ranchers, some of whom worked on the Aguayo Ranch and others on neighboring haciendas. In addition to Rubio, the assembled group included a guard named Inocente Perales and a rancher known only as Longinos. The militiamen then gathered lances and other weapons, and following Rubio's lead, departed in search of Rafael. One report suggested that the group was joined by a cadre of Comanches who were returning from a trading trip to Durango and volunteered to assist the search effort.[14]

Soon after departing, three of the men broke off to look for Magdaleno Carrulo, whom they found injured but alive. The remaining eleven set off after Rafael and José Antonio. Tracking the Apache band must have been much easier for this group than it had been for soldiers in Nueva Vizcaya, as the geography of Coahuila was much more open than the terrain to the west. There were fewer trees than the areas of Nueva Vizcaya through which Rafael's band normally passed, the mountains were smaller and more spread out, and the canyons shallower. Because the pursuers were traveling from the west at sunset, the Apaches may not have even noticed that anyone was coming after them. Whether it was this advantageous geography, assistance from the Comanches, or some other unknown factor, Rubio, and his men eventually tracked the Apaches to a location some five leagues from a place called the Cerros de Acatita.[15]

HAVING ONLY A LIMITED KNOWLEDGE of this region, Rafael made the mistake of bringing his band into the open end of a basin that was surrounded by steep hills with no easy means of escape. Making matters worse for the Apaches, the ground within the basin was very sandy, almost like quicksand, limiting the speed with which the Apaches could maneuver. Also restricting movement were mesquite trees. They filled the basin and their dense, wiry branches made it difficult to move while on horseback. Unfortunately for Rafael, by the time he recognized the problematic circumstances in which he had placed his band, Rubio's forces had entered the opening of the basin. This left Rafael with no easy means of escape, and so he and José Antonio determined that they would have to fight their way out. It seems that the newly captive Apache woman stayed to fight alongside them while María Martina, María Jesús, and the Apache child did their best to climb out of the basin.[16]

Unlike most times they had been forced to fight, Rafael and José Antonio lacked the element of surprise, and, if anything, the pursuers were the ones who surprised the Apaches. Rafael also did not have an elevation advantage over his opponents, with the fight taking place on level ground. Rubio and his men also outnumbered Rafael and José Antonio more than five to one, and they had superior firearms to the Apaches. Indeed, it seems that Rafael and José Antonio had run out of either gunpowder or ammunition at this point, meaning their lances would have to serve as their primary weapons.[17]

Although Apaches did their best to avoid such circumstances, they understood that if they acted aggressively and employed shock and awe tactics, it often scared opponents into fleeing and opened a path to escape. As one observer phrased it, when an Apache "is cornered and desperate and thinks the end has come, he tears off his shirt and headband. He tears off all his clothes but his loincloth, and he goes right into the thick of it. Sometimes he fights so hard that he gets away." Hacienda guard Inocente Perales found out about this behavior the hard way. Possibly envisioning the one thousand-peso reward he would receive for killing Rafael, Perales attempted to rush the Apaches, but his horse got stuck in a mesquite tree. This allowed Rafael to thrust his lance into the attacker's leg, likely severing the femoral artery as the end of the lance passed in one side of the thigh and out the other. Perales would die of the wound shortly thereafter.[18]

The rest of Rubio's forces were more cautious. Although details of what took place next are lacking, sources imply that the remaining Spaniards approached José Antonio with their lances at the ready, while a second group led by the rancher named Longinos moved on Rafael. The circumstances were somewhat ironic, considering that the most famous "Longinos" in history was the Roman soldier who earned his fame by piercing Christ's side with a spear at the Crucifixion.[19]

What happened next is conjecture, but it seems that Longinos was able to drive his lance into Rafael before then dropping his weapon. The two men then began to fight each other "in man-to-man combat." At this point Longinos surely discovered what others who had engaged Apaches in combat well knew, "a badly wounded Indian is much more dangerous than one who is not. Feeling that he cannot escape, his first object is to kill as many of his foes as possible." In spite of this ferocity and Rafael's extensive combat experience, Longinos started to get the better of his Apache opponent, eventually immobilizing him. One or more of Longinos's companions were able to do the same with José Antonio.[20]

Once this happened, the remaining men set upon the two Apaches with their weapons, stabbing Rafael and José Antonio until they "were devoid of blood" and their bodies "destroyed." Although such violence might seem excessive, with the level of superstition surrounding Rafael and the stories of his miraculous escapes having spread throughout northern New Spain by this time, it made sense for Rubio's men to take extra precautions to ensure that their opponents were dead. Once the bodies had no hope of returning to life, the victorious militiamen cut off Rafael and José Antonio's heads, as well as "some other members of their destroyed corpses." The rest of the remains were left for carrion.[21]

THE DESTINATION OF RAFAEL AND JOSÉ ANTONIO'S severed "members" is unknown, but it is likely that the victors took ears, hands, and feet as trophies, as it was common for Spanish soldiers and militiamen to cut off Apache extremities for display as evidence of manhood and military prowess. Rafael and José Antonio's heads were almost certainly destined for Chihuahua to serve as proof of their deaths to collect the one thousand-peso reward from Salcedo. To prevent the hot July weather from rotting the two Apaches' faces and rendering them unidentifiable, Rubio likely had his men pack the heads in salt.[22]

There is no record of the arrival of Rafael and José Antonio's heads in Chihuahua. This is understandable considering that Spanish official documents often leave out details that might make them look as barbaric as those they call savages. However, the scene likely played out like a similar instance witnessed by a traveler passing through Chihuahua a few years later. As he described,

> one morning, a lusty sound of trumpets called me to the balcony before my windows; and, from an opposite street, I saw issuing a troop of lancers, defiling slowly towards the Government House. In the centre of this troop rode two corporals, bearing two Indians' heads on the point of their lances, and various officers, with drawn swords, surrounded, pompously, this centre of attraction. The multitude, in exuberant joy at the defeat of their arch-enemies, pressed round the horses of the warriors, who, conscious of their merit, rode slowly and with stately bearing through the crowd of their admirers.[23]

There is also no description of how Salcedo reacted upon seeing the heads or learning about the death of his long-time nemesis. Based on similar circumstances, Salcedo likely had witnesses confirm Rafael and José Antonio's identities before paying out the promised bounties. He probably then ordered his men to put the two Apaches' heads in cages to be affixed atop poles and placed in Chihuahua's city square. As one observer described a similar scene, "in Chihuahua City itself the windows of the Governor's Palace were festooned with strings of dried Apache scalps and the plaza in front of the Cathedral was ornamented with Apache heads on the top of poles."[24]

WHILE THE MEN OF RUBIO'S MILITIA were disassembling Rafael and José Antonio, María Martina López and María Jesús Loya fled, carrying the Apache child Francisca with them. The recently captured Apache woman, who stayed with Rafael and José Antonio, seems to have escaped in a different direction. Young María Martina and María Jesús, having been indoctrinated by Rafael and having been complicit in his crimes, believed that if Spanish forces caught them, they would be tortured or killed.[25]

Eventually a party of guards under don Antonio Sufrido located the girls, but there is some discrepancy concerning what happened when they did. According to historian Hubert Howe Bancroft, one of the women, either María Martina or María de Jesús, took up arms and resisted capture. As he described it, "when [Rafael's] band was ultimately exterminated by a part of Mexican troops, and he himself was killed, she refused to surrender to her own countrymen, and fell, fighting like a true Indian squaw, after her arrows had pierced the bodies of several soldiers."[26]

Although it is possible that one or both young women violently resisted Sufrido and his men, there is no indication that they "pierced the bodies of several soldiers" or otherwise caused any serious harm to their pursuers. Likewise, neither did Sufrido nor his men kill María Martina, María Jesús, or the Apache child. Bancroft likely confused the story with another involving a female captive, or the legend had become exaggerated by the time he reported what had happened.[27]

Instead, Sufrido seems to have taken the three into custody without violence. He then asked María Martina and María Jesús to show him where they had last seen Rafael and José Antonio in order to confirm their deaths. The two women guided the guards to site of the battle in the Cerros de Acatita where they saw "their cadavers were missing their heads and some other limbs were gone from their destroyed corpses." Sufrido then escorted the women to Juan Zambrano's Hacienda de San Juan de Castro where Spanish officials questioned them about their time in captivity. A different group of soldiers placed the Apache woman María in custody and took her to an *obraje*, meaning either workhouse or mine, in nearby Alamo de Parras.[28]

NEWS OF RAFAEL'S DEATH and the rescue of the captives eventually made its way to Mexico City, where a short article describing the last days of the Apache band appeared in the August 17, 1810 issue of the *Gaceta del Gobierno de México*. The author stated that news had arrived from Chihuahua:

> the apostate Apache Rafaelillo and his companion Antonio, also a hea-
> then Apache, had died at the hands of the servants of the Sr. Marqués
> de S. Miguel de Aguayo. [He had been] as terrible to that province as
> Napoleon was to Europe, with the difference being that one destroyed
> with his infernal armies and the other with only two men. They have
> sacrificed more than 1300 victims in a matter of 6 to 8 years, and the
> departures of veteran troops of Ópatas and paisanos have been unable
> to stop him owing to his cunning and unique strategy for his attacks
> and retreats. By his death they have saved four captives that they had in
> his harem, among them a young Spanish woman from Cienega de los
> Olivos, from 18 to 20 years old, called Loya.[29]

The story of Rafael's death even made its way across the Atlantic to Spain, where it was described in essentially the same manner in the *Gaceta de la Regencia de España é Indias*. The newspaper elevated the number of killed by Rafael to "no less than 1,800 homicides had been committed" by "los dos Apaches Rafaelillo y Antonio." The story ended by calling Rafael "a horrible example of the maliciousness of the human species." The fact that the *Gaceta de la Regencia de España é Indias* even devoted space to Rafael is telling considering that at the time of publication, the Spanish were still waging an all-out war to expel Napoleon's forces from Iberia. The story may also have elicited so much attention because, although the war in Spain was bloody, no single soldier in the Napoleonic Wars had killed nearly as many people as Rafael or José Antonio.[30]

The death count also intrigued Commandant General Salcedo. When writing about Rafael around 1808, Salcedo had estimated that he and José Antonio had killed some eight hundred people in their attacks. Various news-papers had claimed anywhere from 200 to the 1,800 given by the *Gaceta de la Regencia de España é Indias*. The commandant general wanted to know which was most accurate.[31]

To satisfy his curiosity, on September 5, 1810, Salcedo ordered Juan José Ruiz de Bustamante to assemble an account of Rafael's actions from 1804 to 1810. Bustamante was one of the best educated individuals on the northern frontier of New Spain. He was from a wealthy family, meaning he was one of the few on the frontier to have received a formal education and knew how to read and write. He also understood government documents, having served as a prosecutor at numerous regional trials, including, famously, the one that convicted the American adventurers who trespassed into New Spain under Philip Nolan. Bustamante was also the head of the Hacienda de Dolores, a massive estate that the government had taken over from the Jesuits after their expulsion from the Americas. This duty required Bustamante to maintain extensive records concerning the livestock and crop output of the estate. Because the Hacienda de Dolores was located only three miles south of Guajoquilla, it meant that Bustamante had also been privy to many rumors about Rafael's activities over the past six years.[32]

In addition to a death count, Salcedo wanted Bustamante to calculate the number of people that Rafael's band had injured and taken captive and to determine whether Rafael and José Antonio had received help from hostile Apaches, establecimiento Apaches, or other Indians. The commandant general also asked Bustamante to interview the band's various captives to see if they should be punished for their participation, and he wanted an appraisal of the items recovered from the Apaches at the time of their death. To complete these tasks, Salcedo authorized Bustamante to consult any "official documents, campaign diaries, other papers relative to the hostilities."[33]

Bustamante set to work, spending the following four months pouring over various government documents for any references to Rafael. Some of what Bustamante discovered was not particularly insightful. For example, his appraisal of Rafael's personal items revealed that the Apaches were carrying little of value when they died. Two officers sent twenty-six pesos that they recovered from the bodies, as well as ninety-eight pesos worth of sellable items. This included the saddle of mail-carrying soldier Luis Vargas, whom the Apaches had killed in May. Other than that, Rafael and José Antonio had only three socks, two small bags, and a metal horse bit. Bustamante described these items as "all useless and therefore nobody wants to buy them."[34]

Bustamante also had to determine the fate of María Martina, María Jesús, and the Apache child Francisca, as well as the Apache woman María who had been captured after fighting with Rafael and José Antonio. Although Salcedo had pardoned some of the band's previous captives, others had faced punishment. As part of his research, Bustamante attempted to take testimony from each of the adult captives. He was unable to fulfill this duty with the Apache woman María, as she remained in the obraje in distant Alamo de Parras, so a local administrator don Juan de Dios Cárdenas took her testimony instead.[35]

Unfortunately for the woman, the fact that she had initially remained to fight with Rafael and José Antonio did not work in her favor, nor did the fact that she was an Apache in a legal system that she did not understand and one that treated Apaches differently from Hispanicized Indians and people of European ancestry. For these reasons and possibly others, Bustamante, Salcedo, or local leaders eventually determined that, in spite of the fact that the Apache woman had been a captive and had only been with the band for a few months, she was responsible for the crimes she committed and should face deportation.[36]

The punishment could not be carried immediately owing to a lack of funds, so the Apache woman continued to work in the obraje until passage could be secured. Eventually, the Apache child Francisca was also placed in the obraje under María's care. During this time, regidor don Joaquín Marichalar used his own money to pay for the two female Apaches' upkeep, a fact that Marichalar would later complain about to Spanish officials. On December 8, Marichalar's burden increased when María gave birth to Rafael's child. She did not want it, and so the child was given over to Juan de Dios Calderón. Calderón "gave his word that he would raise and care for the child without prejudice and in the best manner possible." Whether or not Calderón carried through with this promise is unknown, as is the ultimate fate of María and Francisca.[37]

María Martina and María Jesús were not Apaches, but if Bustamante determined that they were complicit in Rafael's crimes, they might also face imprisonment. In some circumstances, Spanish women who had been with Indians for a long time before liberation received the same treatment as captured Indian women. For example, Spanish officials considered selling one European woman redeemed from Taovaya Indians into slavery before ultimately rejecting the proposition.[38]

Fortunately for María Martina and María Jesús, when Bustamante took their testimony, he determined that the two young women had "told the truth about the circumstances of their captivity" and had been very helpful in his investigation. They confirmed José Dionisio Gómez and José Salvador Bueno Laicano's story that Dionisio had killed a shepherd only after José Antonio threatened to kill him if he did not. As far as their own crimes, Bustamante determined that the two women had only gone along with Rafael because they had been "under his power" and "had suffered an intolerable oppression." Their assistance in his investigation convinced Bustamante that the two women were remorseful and should not be blamed for their crimes. Salcedo would eventually agree with this assessment and pardon both women.[39]

Although they were absolved of legal responsibility and would not face the same punishment as the Apache woman, María Martina and María Jesús would find it difficult to return to the lives they had lived before being captured. Spanish patriarchal society placed a burden on women to remain chaste until marriage and to have sexual partners that belonged to one's own race; this was although Spanish men often maintained multiple sexual partners, many of whom were of Indian or African ancestry. This double standard applied even in matters where the woman did not consent to a sexual relationship, as authorities understood was the case for both María Martina and María Jesús. Spanish society often regarded such women as impure and subjected them to the same treatment faced by women who voluntarily chose to engage in promiscuous and interracial sexual activity. For example, when one Spanish officer was asked about two white women who had been captives among Indians for an extended time, he suggested that they should not return to Spanish society, "because, having had union with the Indians, from which have issued children, whom their fathers would not give up, they would remain, not alone because of their natural mother love, but also through the well-merited shame which they would suffer among Christians for their infamous unchastity."[40]

As for Salcedo's question concerning whether Rafael and José Antonio had received help from hostile Apaches, Apaches de paz, or another group, Bustamante concluded that he "did not have even the slightest suspicion that the two aforementioned Indians had any connection, dealings, help, or communication concerning their atrocities with any class of people; on the contrary, it appears they were staunch enemies of their own kind." Bustamante did not offer an opinion on whether the people of San Gregorio had supported Rafael, but the fact that some residents of the town would remain in prison even after he issued his report suggests that he did not investigate the question.[41]

Bustamante's conclusion about the complicity of outside Apache groups is problematic. He seems to have based his assessment on the testimony of María Martina López and María de Jesús Loya, as well as reports received from establecimiento Apaches about their interactions with Rafael. Although there is little question that Rafael had multiple negative interactions with various establecimiento Apache groups, many of these encounters occurred while the groups were conducting illegal trade with the fugitives, and Rafael himself suggested that he had a long-time trading relationship with the Apaches at Carrizal. Apaches de paz would be unlikely to report any trade with Rafael that happened without incident.[42]

Also problematic is Bustamante's reliance on María Martina and María Jesús. Although the two women were likely truthful in saying that they knew of no complicity with outside Indians, they had not joined Rafael until October 1807 and September 1809, respectively. This meant that they had no direct knowledge of Rafael's activities with groups like the Carrizal Apaches prior to 1807. Likewise, they would have been unaware of any interactions that Rafael and José Antonio might have had whenever they left the women in camp.[43]

THE MOST EXTENSIVE PART of Bustamante's report concerned the deaths, kidnappings, and injuries inflicted by Rafael and his band. To this end, Bustamante collected as much official correspondence as he could from 1804 to 1810 concerning Rafael. He then summarized the documents and provided a running tally of each statistic alongside every entry, with the numbers increasing from four dead and one injured from the first entry, incident 1, on October 16 and 17, 1804, to the final entry, incident 137, made shortly after Rafael and José Antonio's deaths. The increase in numbers is sobering reminder of the destruction that the two Apaches caused.[44]

In the end, Bustamante estimated that Rafael, José Antonio, and Chinche had taken some forty-five captives and injured fifty-three from 1804 to 1810. The Apaches had either killed or ordered their captives to kill some 298 during this time. Although this is obviously an incredible number of deaths to be attributed to a small group of individuals, it was much less than the estimates featured in the various newspaper articles about Rafael. Bustamante recognized this discrepancy and offered some caveats that left open the possibility that the death total was higher than the one he provided. For example, he noted that there "was a difference of six persons" between those whom the Apaches had captured and those who Spanish officials knew had either escaped or been killed. This led Bustamante to conclude that because "the two Indians very often killed [their captives] it seems that this number should be higher than the 298 reported here." He also noted that his death count did not include the injured who died after speaking with Spanish authorities. Surely some of the fifty-three injured had succumbed to their wounds.[45]

Still, Bustamante felt that while the number of reported deaths was almost certainly higher than 298, the final count would not be significantly higher. When speaking of this, he noted that "although these Indians Rafael and José Antonio may have committed more murders and injuries than appear in the reports, considering that parties of troops and neighborhood militias conducted multiple and repeated searches for them, as well as the commandant general's strict orders for justices to send any news of their ravages, it can be judged on solid grounds that the number of [additional deaths, injuries, and captives] is small."[46]

Still, historians have uncovered additional deaths that Bustamante missed, and there are other issues with Bustamante's methodology. Most glaringly, the report gives no estimates of deaths attributed to Rafael and his band before October 15, 1804. Considering the regular state of war between the Comanches and Apaches, Spanish and Apaches, and Apaches and Apaches, José Antonio and Chinche, and perhaps Rafael, almost certainly had combat experience prior to arriving at Guajoquilla. In addition, the men had likely served as auxiliaries for the Spanish during their time at Guajoquilla and such military campaigns often resulted in the deaths of unincorporated Apaches.[47]

The figure of 298 deaths also fails to account for any clandestine raids that Rafael might have conducted while still at Guajoquilla or deaths that were never reported to Spanish officials. For example, death records from Guajoquilla indicate that "enemy Apaches" killed a Juaquin Velarano on or around August 23, 1804, and on October 4, a "José Ricardo Silva "died at the hands of the enemies." Although there is nothing to directly tie Rafael and José Antonio to these deaths, it was around this time Spanish officials began to suspect they were providing information to enemy Apaches. Perhaps these deaths were the first of many. Finally, as Bustamante himself admitted, he did not have an accurate account of deaths outside Nueva Vizcaya. Historian Gildardo Contreras used parochial records to determine that Rafael and José Antonio were responsible for at least four deaths in Coahuila not mentioned by Bustamante.[48]

Although Bustamante missed several deaths, he also likely overcounted in some instances. For example, Bustamante cites three official documents that reported that Rafael committed a murder on January 7, 1806. One, written by Maríano Varela, says that Rafael killed a cowboy and kidnapped a boy at a place called Zanja. The other two were written by Lucas Valenzuela. The first says that Rafael killed a cowboy at Zanja but makes no mention of a kidnapping. The second Valenzuela document mentions a murder of a cowboy and the kidnapping of a child but does not give a location. Bustamante concluded that the Varela report and the second Valenzuela report were discussing the same murder, but the first Valenzuela report was a second, separate murder, and recorded Rafael as having been responsible for two deaths.[49]

Instead, what likely occurred was that Valenzuela made his initial report after discovering the cowboy's body, but before anyone realized that the child was gone. On learning of the kidnapping, he then made a supplementary report that included the additional information. Varela either arrived later or heard the news secondhand and made his own report, meaning Rafael likely only killed one person on this date. Parish records from Guajoquilla and records from the Parral archives seem to confirm this was the case because they list only a single murder.[50]

There are other possible instances of overcounting in Bustamante's report, but they are almost certainly countered by the deaths for which Bustamante was unable to account, meaning that 298 serves a good baseline for the number of people killed by Rafael. Surviving church records from Nueva Vizcaya support a death count in this range. Many burial records from Nueva Vizcaya from August 1804 to August 1810 have been lost or destroyed, and of those that survive, only some 35 percent list a cause of death for those being interred, meaning we have a cause of death for perhaps a quarter of those who died during these years. Of these, some twenty-three burial records specifically name Rafael as the reason the dead was unable to receive the sacrament, and seventy others list victims as having fallen to "Apaches," barbaros," "enemigos," and "infieles." Considering that the vast majority of the deaths correspond with instances listed by Bustamante, and that priests used these terms interchangeably with Rafael—calling him "enemigo Rafael," "Bárbaro Rafael," and in one instance attributing two deaths in the same location on the same day to "los Indios" and "el Indio Rafael, respectively"—it is safe to assume that Rafael's band were the "Apaches" or "enemigos" in question for at least fifty of the seventy more ambiguous causes of death. Therefore, if a quarter of the records survive with a cause of death, and of these some seventy to ninety seem to point to Rafael, it provides a range between 280 and 360. Although the value of this range is limited by the number of variables involved and is of little value by itself, it lends credence to Bustamante's conclusion of 298.[51]

Bustamante completed his assessment on January 21, 1811 and presented his findings to Salcedo. The final report consisted of ninety-six handwritten pages as well as additional boxes containing the original reports, captive testimonies, campaign diaries, and other primary source material relating to Rafael. There are no records of how Salcedo responded to the report. However, considering that at the time, the commandant general was having to fend off an insurrection, he may not have even looked at it.[52]

CHAPTER TEN

A Legendary Marauder,
September 1810–1900

O N OCTOBER 1, 1810, Commandant General Salcedo received news that some seven hundred miles to the south, the people of Guanajuato had risen in rebellion against the colonial government of New Spain. As Salcedo would learn over the coming days, the rebellion was led by Father Miguel Hidalgo y Costillo, a charismatic *criollo* (a person of European descent born in Mexico) priest who had come to believe that New Spain's social and political system benefited the mother country at the expense of the colony's criollo, mestizo, and Indian inhabitants. Inspired by Enlightenment literature, Hidalgo saw the racist policies that had oppressed Indians and mestizos since the Spanish conquest as evil, and he decried Spain's exclusionary practice of denying criollos positions in the higher echelons of New Spain's government. He believed that everyone, including, as he phrased it, "brute tribes like the Apaches" deserved self-representation and thought the only way to bring about such change was through revolution. As the parish priest of the predominantly Indian and mestizo community of Dolores, Hidalgo hoped to use his influence to unite the town's lower classes with dissatisfied middle-class criollos to create an army and march it against the colonial government in Mexico City.[1]

Hidalgo carried his plan into effect on September 16, 1810, when he addressed the people of Dolores from atop his church. Claiming allegiance to the deposed King Ferdinand, Hidalgo called on his parishioners to expel the *peninsulares* (Spaniards) and overthrow the illegitimate government in Mexico City, which he portrayed to be nothing more than a puppet of Joseph Bonaparte, who continued to sit on the Spanish throne. Hidalgo then reportedly cried, "Viva Nuestra Señora de Guadalupe, viva la independencia," and finished with the call, "Viva México." Oppressed for centuries, Indians and mestizos from Dolores and nearby villages rallied to Hidalgo's call and within weeks, the priest stood at the head of an army that numbered in the tens of thousands. Criollo leaders in towns and provinces throughout New Spain joined in the rebellion and unseated peninsular officials. Criollo army personnel also seized control of military installations, arrested European-born officers, and declared in favor of the revolution. By the last months of 1810, it appeared that Mexico City, and the government of New Spain, would soon fall to Hidalgo's army.[2]

WHEN NEWS OF THE REBELLION eventually made its way north, it left Salcedo with the difficult task of maintaining royalist control of the Internal Provinces without support from the viceroy or the Spanish government. This proved difficult. In Texas, criollo officer Juan Bautista de las Casas overthrew and imprisoned Salcedo's nephew Manuel Salcedo, who was serving as that province's governor. Criollo soldiers did the same to the governor of Nuevo Santander. The governor of Nuevo León did not wait to be overthrown, and instead defected to the insurgency.[3]

Revolutionaries were not as successful in the areas that Rafael had threatened from 1804 to 1810. In Durango, for example, José Jerónimo Hernández gathered an army of four hundred men to support Hidalgo, but a royalist militia quickly assembled and suppressed the uprising. When José María González de Hermosillo attempted to take control of southwestern Nueva Vizcaya, Bernardo Bonavía dispatched an army that defeated the insurgents in little over a month's time. In January 1811, a group of conspirators, which included Mariano Herrera, the auditor in command; Salvador Porras, the alderman of the Chihuahua ayuntamiento; and Juan Pedro Walker, the former head of the cadet academy; attempted to stage a coup and overthrow Salcedo, but the commandant general discovered the plot before it could be carried into effect and arrested those involved.[4]

Although there is no way to definitively tie this quick response to the preparedness brought on by years of being vigilant for Rafael, it would not be unreasonable to assume that regular militia drills and the near constant state of alertness played at least some part in maintaining royalist control of Nueva Vizcaya. The lack of support for Hidalgo in the province may also have owed to recognition that Spanish authority was the one thing that stood between themselves and hostile Apaches or the next Rafael. As historian Jorge Chávez Chávez phrased the situation, "it is not surprising that in 1810, after the insurgent outbreak in in El Bajío, the inhabitants of Nueva Vizcaya were more concerned with an Apache attack than the insurrection of Hidalgo."[5]

Fortunately for those in favor of peninsular rule, the coming months would see royalists retake most areas that had fallen to the revolutionaries. The dissolution of Hidalgo's plan began when many criollos withdrew their support after the priest's primarily Indian and mestizo army killed several criollos while taking the city of Guanajuato. Problems continued when Hidalgo delayed his attack on Mexico City, giving the royalists time to muster their forces under Spanish general Félix María Calleja. Calleja took the offensive against Hidalgo, handing the revolutionary a major defeat at the Calderón Bridge and sending the priest and what remained of his army fleeing northward in the hopes of finding refuge in the United States.[6]

On March 21, 1811, Hidalgo's flight took him within a few miles of where local ranchers and hacienda guards had killed Rafael and José Antonio, and it would be on almost the exact same spot that the priest's rebellion would meet its end. By March 1811, the revolutionary army had fallen from more than fifty thousand at its peak to a little more than one thousand men, with only the most loyal soldiers and advisors remaining by Hidalgo's side. Hoping to increase these numbers, Hidalgo made plans to rendezvous at the Wells of Baján in southern Coahuila to unite his forces with those of Ignacio Elizondo, a criollo military leader who had declared for the revolution at the end of 1810. Unbeknownst to Hidalgo, Elizondo had since changed his mind, returned to the royalist fold, and had enlisted the help of loyalist locals to capture the revolutionary leader and his followers when they arrived at Baján. As reported in the *Gazeta del Gobierno de México*, among those who answered the royalist call were "soldiers of the traitor governor Santa María and others from Cordero's camp; Longinos was among them, he who killed Rafael."[7]

With Longinos's assistance, Elizondo arrested Hidalgo and what remained of his followers and sent them to Salcedo in Chihuahua. Salcedo spent the following four months overseeing Hidalgo's trial and eventual execution. As part of this procedure, he employed Juan José Ruiz de Bustamante to interview Hidalgo and his co-conspirators. Using this testimony, a tribunal found Hidalgo guilty of treason, after which Salcedo ordered a firing squad to end the rebel leader's life. To show what would happen to those who opposed Spanish rule, Salcedo had his men behead Hidalgo and his closest advisors. He then dispatched the heads to various locations throughout New Spain so they could be displayed as a sign of what happened to those who opposed royalist rule. It is likely that at least some of the craniums of the would-be revolutionaries ended up on spikes in Chihuahua City alongside those of Rafael and José Antonio.[8]

Salcedo continued to serve as commandant general for the next two years, but with his health failing—at one point he was too sick to even hold a pen— he regularly asked for permission to retire. In May 1813, officials in Spain finally granted his request and ordered Salcedo to turn over command of the western Internal Provinces to Bernardo Bonavía. Simón de Herrera would take over as commandant general of the eastern Internal Provinces. As part of the turnover, Salcedo provided Bonavía and Herrera with the lengthy document he had written when he first thought he was going to retire in 1808. The commandant general had failed to update it in the past five years, so the document explained Salcedo's plan to kill Rafael, but did not mention that the Apache was already dead, an omission that convinced multiple historians that Rafael survived well into the nineteenth century. After turning over the document to Bonavía in Cuencamé on July 18, 1813, Salcedo left the Internal Provinces for Mexico City and Veracruz where he received transport back to Spain.[9]

By the time Salcedo crossed the Atlantic, coalition forces in Europe had defeated Napoleon Bonaparte, and Ferdinand VII had retaken the throne of Spain. In 1815, the restored king thanked Salcedo for his loyalty and his years of service by naming him an inaugural member of the Order of the Knights of Isabel the Catholic, a special order created to honor service in Spain's wars in the Americas. Salcedo spent his final years on the Basque Coast overseeing reconstruction of a family home that had been destroyed during the French occupation of Spain.[10]

THE COMMANDANT GENERALS who succeeded Salcedo soon discovered the difficulties their predecessor had faced in retaining royalist control of the Internal Provinces. Indeed, just as Salcedo was preparing to vacate his position as commandant general, a private American army invaded Texas and joined with a group of revolutionaries who sought to make New Spain independent of the mother country. Although Spanish forces eventually defeated the invaders, revolutionary sentiment and hostility toward peninsulares continued to fester throughout New Spain until 1821, when a criollo officer in the Spanish army named Agustin de Iturbide defected to the insurgency and brought a significant portion of New Spain's military with him. Iturbide's army then marched on Mexico City, drove the Spanish military out of New Spain, and forced the sitting viceroy to recognize Mexican independence from Spain.[11]

The fight for independence and the first years of Mexican rule would prove disastrous to the peace Spain had established between the frontier settlers of Nueva Vizcaya and the Apaches. Beginning with Hidalgo's revolt, funds normally designated to provide rations to establecimiento Apaches went to combating insurgents, leading many Apaches de paz to abandon establecimientos and return to raiding. Because Spain's soldiers were either fighting revolutionaries or joining them, there was no one there to stop them.[12]

Things continued to deteriorate following Mexican independence. In January 1823, Iturbide invited a group of Apache chiefs to travel to Mexico City to witness his coronation as Emperor Agustin I of Mexico and to sign a formal peace treaty with the new nation. Several Apaches made the trip, agreed to peace terms, and received promises from the Mexican government that they would collect gifts and rations as they had under Spain. Unfortunately for Iturbide and the prospect of long-term peace between Mexico and the Apaches, the new emperor would not remain in his position for long. Federalist politicians, believing authority in Mexico to be too centralized, overthrew Iturbide and installed a form of government where local leaders held most of the power. Political infighting continued to plague the new Mexican government over the ensuing decades. The resulting conflicts syphoned promised supplies meant for the Apaches, effectively neutering any chance at a long-term peace. By 1824, the Apaches had recommenced raiding.[13]

THE SITUATION ON THE FRONTIER proved to be even more difficult for frontier Mexican officials than it had been for their Spanish predecessors. When the Spanish first came into conflict with the Apaches, they were a dangerous, but identifiable threat. It was clear who was and who was not an Apache. From its birth as a new nation, Mexico had to contend with hundreds and perhaps thousands of Apaches who had spent years in establecimientos in close proximity to the Hispanicized population of the frontier. This meant that, like Rafael, many Apaches knew how to speak Spanish, dress like pasainos, and imitate Hispanic social customs. Considering that Mexico's military had adopted Spanish martial traditions, they also knew how Mexican soldiers operated and they were more likely to raid because they "could undertake them with more confidence because they had learned well from the ideas, maxims, and movements of their enemies."[14]

Indeed, several Apaches with similar backgrounds to Rafael would take over as leaders of Apache bands. For example, an Apache with the Hispanic name

Gómez would "dress something like a Mexican and [speak] excellent Spanish" and use these talents to become "the most terrible chief of these savages" before Mexican soldiers eventually captured and killed him. Another Apache, Juan José Compá received an education while a child at the Janos establecimiento de paz, even learning to read and write Spanish. After independence, he served as a translator for presidio soldiers until the Mexican government could no longer afford to provide rations for the Apaches at Janos, at which point Compá led his people in revolt. The Mexicans struggled to apprehend him because he often captured mail shipments, read their plans to stop him, and was able to avoid entrapment.[15]

The Comanches, who had been Spain's stalwart allies during Salcedo's time as commandant general, also saw opportunity in the chaos and began to raid Mexican settlements. And, like the Apaches, some of the most successful Comanche leaders were those who knew the mannerisms of their opponents. In the mid-nineteenth century, Mexico impressed a young Comanche named Antonio who had been captured as a youth and raised among the Spanish into military service near Durango. While stationed at a hacienda, the residents "abused him grievously" owing to his Comanche ancestry. This included one old woman who refused to sell the Indian tortillas at a reasonable price, leaving Antonio "half starved." This led the young Comanche to escape the hacienda and return to his people, and from that time, "the knowledge which Antonio had acquired while a soldier stood him in good stead among his new friends. He became a chief among the Comanches, and eluded every attempt made to capture him." Eventually Antonio burned the hacienda to the ground and scalped the woman who had overcharged him for tortillas.[16]

As the Apaches and Comanches used their knowledge of the enemy to expand into areas where few had raided outside of Rafael's band, wealthier Mexicans fled for the relative safety of Central Mexico. For example, the population of the city of Durango dropped from some thirty thousand residents to just eight thousand after a particularly brutal decade of Indian attack. Unable to mount an effective defense against the Indians, many smaller settlements disappeared, their residents dead, captured in raids, or having fled to population centers that offered protection in numbers. As one observer described it, "only very few villages are not still half in ruins, and the trails are dotted with mementos of Bloody tragedies." Historian Brian DeLay even went so far as to define this unique period of warfare between the settlers of Mexico and Plains Indians as the "War of a Thousand Deserts" because residents left behind "deserts" when they fled to safer areas.[17]

AS ONE OF THE LARGER POPULATION CENTERS in the north, Guajoquilla would survive the War of a Thousand Deserts, and it even saw its population increase from the influx of those abandoning smaller settlements. Unfortunately for new and old residents, this did not mean that Apaches and Comanches sidestepped Guajoquilla during their raids as those working on the outskirts of town or traveling between towns frequently came under attack. Rafael's surrogate father, Chaplain Rafael Nevares, might have been the victim of one such assault in 1824. Although the cause of death goes unrecorded in official documents, a newspaper from around the time reported that "the body of Rafael Nevares was found with fifty lance wounds." Whether this was the same man who tried to convert Rafael is unclear, but Nevares's death marked the end of forty years of service as the chaplain for the local presidio company.[18]

With national politicians too busy dealing with matters in Mexico City, local leaders lacked the funds and political coordination to do anything about the Indian threat. As one observer noted, "the Apaches had committed robberies and murders in the province of Chihuahua, the well concerted measures of the public authorities there have proved [insufficient] to put a stop to these evils." Another went so far as to lament that the oppressive Spanish government was no longer in charge, saying, "no commandant general since 1817 has been successful, the presidio companies have decayed and they have failed to reestablish order."[19]

The situation led some local authorities to take extreme measures, including using residents of the United States, which still sought to incorporate Mexican lands, as a means by which to deal with the Apaches and Comanches. For example, one Chihuahuan governor contracted a band of Americans under James Kirker to kill Apaches, offering the Americans specie in exchange for Apache scalps. The deal turned sour when Kirker realized that friendly, Hispanicized Indians like the lower Tarahumara had similar hair to Apaches but were much easier to kill. In another famous measure to bring a halt to Apache and Comanche raids, Mexico approved American settlement of Texas. Like with Kirker, this plan backfired when the American settlers revolted against Mexico in 1836 and formed their own independent government.[20]

In a way, Rafael's raids, the increase in Apache attacks in post-independence Mexico, and the loss of Texas were connected in that they all resulted from failed attempts to convert traditional enemies into military allies. Spain and then Mexico tried to Hispanicize Apaches like Rafael, Gómez, and Juan José Compá to better indoctrinate or subdue hostile Apaches, only to see these Apaches use the knowledge gained through interaction with Hispanic people to turn on their teachers. The Texan victory at the Battle of San Jacinto came about, in part, due to the American settlers in Texas having learned Mexican military techniques from years spent living under Mexico's flag. The American knowledge of Mexican culture and military measures would also serve the United States during the U.S.-Mexico War from 1846 to 1848, wherein the northern country invaded Mexico and forced its politicians to sign over New Mexico and California. The addition of the new international border in 1848 only served to embolden the Apaches and Comanches, as they could now make their home in the United States, raid Mexico, and then return north where Mexican soldiers could no longer pursue them.[21]

Fortunately for Mexico, they had at least one soldier who seemed up to the challenges presented by the new, partially Hispanicized Apaches: Rafael's son. In the addendum to *Apuntes historicos*, José Merino mentions that the child recovered by soldiers in 1804, and presumably raised by the Nevares family, joined the Mexican military upon reaching adulthood. He then became a member of a presidio company and would serve in this capacity for most of his adult life. As a soldier, he "had the same warrior qualities as his famous father, though not to such an eminent degree as he."[22]

Unfortunately for the Mexican government, if rumors and legends are to be believed, Rafael had other children and, unlike their sibling, they had no interest in defending the citizens of Mexico but instead took after their father in raiding them. Indeed, multiple authors credit Rafael with being a direct relation to a variety of famous Apache chiefs. One called him the ancestor of Victorio, a Mimbres Apache who would terrorize the people of northern Mexico during the mid-nineteenth century. Another claims that Geronimo descended from Rafael.[23]

Considering that both Victorio and Geronimo would lead small bands of raiders that successfully evaded not just the United States but also Mexico for many years, there is certainly tangential evidence of familial relations. In addition, because Rafael kidnapped, and likely had sexual relations with at least three Apache women, it is not beyond the realm of possibility that one of these women had a child who would then go on to lead a tribe. Unfortunately, none of the authors who make these claims provide sources, indicating that any link between Rafael and Victorio, Geronimo, or any other famous Apache leader is based on hearsay.[24]

WHEREAS SOME IN NORTHERN MEXICO speculated that Rafael fathered the next generation of Apache raiders, others believed that Rafael himself continued to raid. As one historian explained, "for many years an uneasiness existed in all of the lands of the sierra. The name of 'indio Rafael' held the conscience of the colonizers, who feared that he would reappear." A widespread belief in the supernatural throughout northern Mexico and the thought that one might return from the dead to exact revenge may explain such fears, but it is possible that a number of people had heard of Rafael but never learned of his death. Indeed, although Bustamante's report detailing Rafael's death appeared in multiple books in the nineteenth century, even some modern historians are unaware of how Rafael died. For example, Gildardo Contreras Palacios wrote in his 1992 history of Torreón, "we do not know what end the dreaded Rafael faced, but due to his calamitous life, it is certain that he did not die quietly in a rocking chair."[25]

At least one set of industrious bandits determined to use this lack of aware-ness to their advantage. According to Chihauhua resident José de la Luz Reyes, in 1860, someone spread rumors that Rafael was alive and was planning to attack the towns of El Refugio, La Loma, and nearby haciendas. Having ei-ther personally experienced Rafael's reign of terror or having been raised on horror stories about the legendary Apache, the rumors made the people of these locations nervous. Therefore, when a group of men later approached the towns and haciendas dressed like Rafael and his band, "the inhabitants of those places at the mere announcement of their proximity fled in terror, and the assailants calmly took away the cattle and provisions."[26]

The manager of Hacienda de Refugio, don Doroteo Meraz, was not so easily intimidated and so he devised a plan to capture the resurrected Indian chief. Although De la Luz Reyes did not describe what happened, Meraz's trap worked, allowing the *hacendero* to capture the zombie Rafael and strip him of his disguise, revealing the culprit to be local well-known bandit Antonio Pina. As it turned out, Pina and his band were the source of the ru-mors concerning Rafael's return, and the bandits had "disguised themselves, taking advantage of the terror that [Rafael's] memory still caused." Pina was hanged shortly thereafter, and his companions jailed, returning the region to relative tranquility.[27]

ALTHOUGH RUMORS OF RAFAEL'S RESURRECTION proved to be greatly exaggerated, Pina's story illustrates the changing nature of banditry in northern Mexico, a change that Rafael helped foresee and bring about. Whereas definable "outside" groups like the Comanches, Apaches, and American invaders were the main threat to frontier security for much of the nineteenth century, by the end of the 1800s, bandits, born and raised in Hispanicized settlements in northern Mexico, had replaced them. In the final decades of the nineteenth century, a period of relative political peace coupled with technological advancements such as automatic weapons allowed the Mexican and United States militaries to chase down and capture or kill most of those who they identified as Apaches. They confined almost all who retained Apache cultural traits and spoke the Apache language to reservations in the United States or chased them to remote regions of the Sierra Madre where they could cause little harm.

However, the military could not round up Hispanicized citizens who conducted Apache-like robberies and raids but spoke Spanish and otherwise looked and lived like most settlers on the northern frontier. As Rafael had demonstrated, those who had a working knowledge of local customs could better blend in with frontier settlements and escape reprisal from government forces. Indeed, although almost all Apaches had either been killed or forced on to reservations, banditry abounded in northern Mexico at the end of the nineteenth century. Men like Francisco "Pancho" Villa made a living by robbing travelers and then escaping into the Sierra Madre or moving to a new settlement and blending in with its populace.

IT WAS AT THE END of the nineteenth century that another rumor spread about Rafael. In the late 1800s, residents of Torreón became obsessed with finding "the treasure cave of the Indian Raphael," where supposedly, the "legendary marauder had hidden in a cave in the nearby sierra the fruit of his very abundant robberies, noting the amount of the treasure in thousands and thousands of pesos."[28]

Whereas rumors of bandits and Apaches hiding treasure are common, they usually fade over time. This proved not to be the case with the story of Rafael's treasure. The reasons for this longevity are many, but the supposed location of the treasure in the Sierra Madre Occidental surely contributed to its persistence. As one historian noted of fictional treasures, "the best place in Mexico to hide gold is in the trackless spaces of the Sierra Madre." Indeed, the Sierra Madre has come to be known as the "fabled treasure land of Mexico," owing to its small population, craggy peaks, and stark canyons dotted with caves that might all hold secrets waiting to be found. Sharp mesquite and cactus impede investigation, while wild animals including bears, mountain lions, and biting insects serve as sentinels protecting potential treasure stores.[29]

The legend of the treasure cave has also endured because of its feasibility. Records clearly show that from 1804 to 1810, Rafael and José Antonio acquired a significant amount of mineral wealth, and extant sources cannot account for what happened to it. For example, when raiding the Loya Ranch, the Apaches stole three silver bars and other jewels, and in a robbery near Santa María del Oro, they took a brooch and silver spurs. They also stole silver from a mule train and captured jewels from multiple travelers. This is in addition to what was almost certainly a substantial amount of specie and precious metals taken from robberies that went unrecorded. Although sources mention that soldiers periodically recovered some of what Rafael had taken, salvaged goods were not equal to what had been stolen, and Rafael carried almost nothing on him when he died, only some socks and a few "useless" trinkets.[30]

Residents of Torreón determined that if Rafael stole things of value and they were not recovered on his death, these valuables must be somewhere. Why not a treasure cave? Apaches occasionally used "storage caves" in the Sierra Madre to protect their goods from the elements and as "a hedge against the future." To this end, during the late nineteenth and early twentieth centuries, treasure hunters from Torreón spent countless hours exploring the mountains outside their city searching for Rafael's lost loot. The most searched location was a cave known as "La Cueva del Indio" on the Cerro de las Noas outside Torreón, near the site of where today sits a 580-ton statue of Jesus. Others said the cave was closer to Topia.[31]

According to Torreón resident, José de la Luz Reyes, "so much was said about it and such an aspect of possible truth was given to the matter," that the Treasury of Mexico even commissioned a group of professional explorers to search for the cave. Reyes was able to recall the event so clearly because he received a job as a bookkeeper for the explorers. After an extensive search, the explorers determined that the cave, and therefore the treasure, did not exist.[32]

Their conclusion was almost certainly correct. Although Rafael and José Antonio used caves as hideouts, what the legend failed to consider was that in multiple instances, Rafael's disguises and knowledge of Spanish customs allowed him to spend money and gamble in Spanish settlements. Such transactions would have gone unrecorded. In addition, time restraints meant that soldiers did not always record what they recovered from the Apaches, and, considering the poor pay and working conditions for the military on the frontier, it can be assumed that soldiers pocketed at least some of what they were able to recover. Therefore, the story of Rafael's treasure cave is likely untrue, but as an author said of rumors of another treasure in the Sierra Madre, "the partial basis in fact upon which the story of his hidden loot rests is too firm for the legend ever to die."[33]

CONCLUSION

ALTHOUGH THE LEGEND OF RAFAEL has survived into modern times, many of the specific details of his crimes have faded in the historical memory of northern Mexico, and fallacies about the six years he spent as a fugitive have replaced reality. Why is this the case? Why has Rafael's legend endured, but in a distorted form? Why was he not forgotten altogether like whoever or whatever was behind the Primer Montezuma and Juan Tigre legends? At the same time, why has the history and the mythology of Rafael sat on the periphery and not become as pervasive or as ingrained in the character of northern Mexico as mythological figures like La Llorona or real-life personalities like Pancho Villa? Perhaps a more important question is, is Rafael worth remembering?

Part of the reason that Rafael has survived in historical memory is that at the end of the nineteenth century, the image of Indians, and Plains Indians in particular, received a reformation in the public consciousness of Mexico and the world as a whole. This coincided with the Mexican and United States governments' forced relocation of Apaches and Comanches on to reservations, ending the threat they posed to the average citizen of Mexico's north. In the absence of fear, the masses began to view Indians as noble savages, and time healed wounds of the past. Apaches ceased to be those who destroyed towns on the frontier and instead became strong, complex, and even sympathetic figures who struggled to maintain their culture in the face of the unrelenting advancement of civilization.[1]

Mexican historians and artists also began embracing their nation's multi-racial and multiethnic heritage and started placing greater importance on the historical contributions of Indians. Although the predominant discourse in Central Mexico involved honoring the Aztecs, Mayans, and other technolog-ically advanced sedentary groups, in the north, semi-autonomous groups like the Tarahumara began to receive praise, as did groups like the Apaches and Seris who had largely ceased to exist as independent cultures in Mexico by the twentieth century. Instead of destroying the frontier, Apaches had helped create the frontier identity and the independent spirit of the north.[2]

By the end of the twentieth century, this cultural shift had become so pervasive that Lucha Libre fighters honored Apaches by wearing headdresses when they entered the ring, and festivals dedicated to the Apaches popped up in towns throughout Mexico. The city of Chihuahua even erected a statue of Chief Victorio whose band was responsible for hundreds of deaths only a century before. The Apaches became so synonymous with Chihuahua that when a player draws the "El Apache" card in the popular Mexican Lotería card game, they have to say the phrase "Ah Chihuahua! So many Apaches with pants and sandals."[3]

THIS CULTURAL REAPPRAISAL and the renewed interest in Apaches certainly played a role in keeping Rafael's memory alive, although it has led to misrepresentation. For example, journalist Enrique Vega Galindo referred to Rafael as "the picturesque Apache" and "the immortal Apache Indian," comparing his life to that of Chief Victorio. The author noted that Rafael's legend is still discussed among the people of northern Mexico, who recognize him as the prototype of "the warrior apache and prowler, a terror to their region. His memory has persisted in the memory of a people who consider him a legendary hero, despite the passing years, his image is still present in the memory of the region as much as the mystical figure Pancho Villa."[4]

As this work makes clear, Rafael was far from the "picturesque Apache" most would envision when thinking of a Plains Indian. He was something different. Like many in Mexico, he was the product of both Spanish and Indian culture. He had an Apache mother, a Hispanicized Ópata father, and a surrogate Spanish father in Chaplain Rafael Nevares. Although the role each of these individuals played in Rafael's upbringing is unclear, each undoubtably had a part in creating the cultural chameleon that Rafael would eventually become. Unlike Chief Victorio, who was born to Apache parents and spent his early life with an Apache family, Rafael was a Spanish-speaking, European-clothes wearing, Catholic-baptized Apache who raided like an Apache but was also the enemy of Apaches. To be fair to Vega Galindo, as well as anyone else who viewed Rafael as a prototypical Apache, many other famous Apaches were not exclusively "Indian" as the general public would understand the term. For example, Apache chief Mangas Coloradas was known by a Spanish name, may have had European ancestry, dressed in the manner of Europeans, and used European firearms.[5]

THE DICHOTOMY OF RAFAEL'S LIFE, someone with one foot in the Apache world and another in that of the Spanish, may provide another explanation for his cultural persistence. In 1959, sociologist Eric Hobsbawn published a study in which he asked why bandits, an individual "who methodically acquires human capital for the purpose of robbing others" are the subjects of songs and stories, often sung and told by the same people upon whom the bandit preyed. Labeling such individuals "social bandits," Hobsbawn offered a Marxist conclusion for their cultural endurance: they were popular because they fought with the lower classes against an oppressive elite. Peasants saw an ally in their class struggle and forgave the bandit's crimes against them because they shared a common cause. They then told their children tales about the daring deeds of their class allies, and, over time, these bandits became legends.[6]

There is little doubt that many authors have portrayed Rafael using this Marxist lens, turning him into a revolutionary who fought against a tyrannical Spanish monarchy. In a way, this transformation is logical. During the colonial period, Spain exploited the people of the Internal Provinces for the benefit of the home country by instituting racist and abusive policies that marginalized Hispanicized Indian groups such as the Tarahumaras and the Tepehuanes. Since independence, historians and the Mexican government have continued to reinforce this narrative of the colonial era, and in the process, they have transformed many Spanish officials, even reasonable and largely benign ones like Nemesio Salcedo, into villains to be reviled. In many interpretations, anyone who fought Spain was a hero, even those who were morally questionable.[7]

Hobsbawm's interpretation deserves consideration as an explanation for Rafael's popularity, as subsequent generations have indeed come to view Rafael as a "social bandit." For example, Victor Campa Mendoza, in his history of the background to the Chiapas Rebellion of 1994, contended that the six years Rafael spent fighting the Spanish should be considered a part of the Mexican War of Independence and a predecessor to later indigenous conflicts fought against Mexico. To Mendoza, the entirety of the Apache war on Spain was a rebellion. In 1999, a journalist claimed that "the Indian Rafael [was] a kind of Robin Hood Duranguense of the last century, who assaulted the caravans and distributed the booty to the needy." Another author concluded of Rafael's legacy, "his name continues among all of the campesinos of the region, he is still revered. They say that his mounted frame on a painted horse can still be seen on the plains, in the forests, and in the mountains, and that one day he will return to rescue them from dictatorship and violence." Yet another author compared Rafael to Ernesto "Che" Guevara, the Argentinian who aided Fidel Castro in bringing revolution to Cuba.[8]

Although there is no doubt that some have come to view Rafael as a social bandit, there is little to suggest that he thought of himself as a political reformer and almost no evidence that the lower classes of his time viewed him as an ally in a class struggle against Spain. As an Apache raised in Spanish society, Rafael certainly dealt with adversity and in 1804, he faced trial and imprisonment for crimes that he may or may not have committed. Rafael was angry about the treatment he had to endure, and his anger fueled multiple attacks on Spanish soldiers and wealthy elites. However, his feud was a personal one, and there is nothing to suggest that he was concerned with the interests of anyone outside of himself and the members of his band. As historians Vicente García Torres and Jorge Chávez Chávez concluded of Rafael, he committed "crimes that any adventurer or delinquent would have committed."[9]

Nor is there any reason to believe that the Tepehuan, Tarahumara, or any marginalized group viewed Rafael as anything other than a threat, or, perhaps, a source of contraband. The Spanish suspected that certain Tarahumaras and the people of San Gregorio traded with Rafael, but even if they did, there is nothing to suggest that they did so for social reasons, a shared resentment of the Spanish, or any other reason than to acquire material goods. Instead, most Hispanicized Indians of the time viewed Apaches as an equal or greater threat to their livelihoods than the Spanish, and available sources show that these groups feared Rafael. Even his fellow Apaches were wary of him, not something that would happen if he were a Robin Hood-like figure.[10]

Making the Rafael-as-a-social-reformer narrative even more problematic is the likelihood that Rafael actually hurt local efforts to combat Spain, and, in some ways, his band may have been responsible for Spain maintaining its hold on Mexico longer than it would have had he not been around. The effect that Rafael had on military preparedness in Nueva Vizcaya cannot be measured with certainty, but there is little question that the people of the province were quicker to form militias and support the Spanish government than most areas of New Spain when Miguel Hidalgo's rebellion broke out in 1810. In addition, it could be said that by attacking peasants as they traveled outside of towns, Rafael discouraged support for revolution. One historian concluded that because of fear of Rafael and Apache raids, the people of Nueva Vizcaya "did not participate in the independence process, because it did not affect their interests. They were more concerned with the weakening of the presidio line than with Mexican independence." A different historian summed up the situation thusly, "peons might have chosen virtual imprisonment on the hacienda rather than death on the open plains."[11]

PERHAPS THE ASSESSMENT OF RAFAEL as a "picturesque Apache" or a "Robin Hood Duranguense" is not the reason for his endurance, but a product of it. Instead, the people of northern Mexico may remember Rafael for the ingeniousness of his crimes and his consistent ability to escape punishment: the long distances he covered between raids, the length of time he spent as a fugitive, and the resourceful ways he outwitted the Spanish. Whereas Australians have held on to the memory of Ned Kelly for creating an armored suit to fight police, Mexicans may remember Rafael for his leather horseshoes, his "1000 disguises," and his innovative ambushes.[12]

Although the other explanations of Rafael's cultural endurance do not hold up to historical scrutiny, there is little doubt that Rafael displayed an uncanny ability to consistently carry out crimes, defeat technologically superior forces, and escape punishment using only his intellect and the most basic of tools. This is evident by the consistent, begrudging praise his adversaries levied upon him in Spanish documents, with even Commandant General Salcedo referring to Rafael and José Antonio as "the most inexorable, elusive, fierce, and cunning men imaginable."[13]

Of course, what many of those who praise the daringness of Rafael's feats leave out is historical context. Rafael was aided, in part, by the time in which he committed his crimes, a time when Spain was mired in local and international conflict. From 1803 to 1807, Commandant General Salcedo had to face the possibility of invasion from the United States, forcing him to station hundreds of men in Texas and New Mexico that might otherwise have been used to search for Rafael. The situation in Europe, with Spain at war with either Britain or France for almost the entirety of the time Rafael was active, also robbed Salcedo of money and manpower that could have been devoted to a manhunt. As soon as the Internal Provinces entered a period of relative peace beginning around the start of 1808, Salcedo was able to carry out a plan that greatly reduced the severity of Rafael's attacks.

Perhaps Rafael's legend has endured because of the scale of his crimes. Indeed, some of those who have written about Rafael have portrayed him not as a revolutionary or a Ned Kelly-esque anti-hero, but as a quintessential villain. For example, in his 1901 psychological study of crime in Mexico, author Julio Guerrero unfavorably compared Rafael to infamous Spanish generals Felix María Calleja and José de la Cruz, two men who executed hundreds during Mexico's War of Independence to maintain Spain's rule of Mexico. Guerrero even put Rafael in the same sentence as perhaps the most notorious figure in Mexican history, Antonio Lopez de Santa Anna. As stated by the author, Rafael "that by his own hand and with the delight of a jackal, he killed more than a thousand victims in the haciendas and missions of Coahuila."[14]

Rafael's supposedly villainous exploits even became the subject of stories outside of Mexico. In 1919, United States-based *Adventure* magazine featured a fictional story written by Hugh Pendexter called "The Gate through the Mountain," wherein a character named for Rafael served as the antagonist to a group of gunslingers in California. The story, which calls Rafael "Ralph" and appears to be based entirely off what Zebulon Pike had heard about Rafael, portrays Rafael as a wealth-seeking bandit who traveled to California at the end of the 1840s to take advantage of those hoping to profit from the gold rush. He manages to acquire a small fortune by donning a variety of disguises to infiltrate mining camps and commanding a loyal gang to steal whatever he discovers. When American gunslingers chase Rafael into a canyon after learning that he kidnapped a local woman, they find the bandit accompanied by "more of Ralph's devils made up as soldiers" and a showdown ensues. Thankfully for the Americans, a group of their Indian allies shows up at the scene and helps put an end to Rafael's reign of terror.[15]

The thing that contributes most to Rafael's legacy as a villain is the sheer number of people he killed. Although it is morbid to consider that death may make someone the subject of legend, there is no denying that popular culture is fascinated with killers. Setting aside men whose job it was to kill, such as Finnish sniper Simo Hayha who killed some five hundred Soviets during the Winter War of 1939, and Soviet executioner Vasily Blokhin who served as an executioner for some 6,800 Polish prisoners at roughly the same time, there are few who can claim to have taken more human lives than Rafael and José Antonio. Indeed, depending on the definition one uses and what number one chooses to accept as accurate, Rafael and José Antonio may be the most prolific serial killers in the history of North America. They were almost certainly the most successful serial annihilators, a subdivision of serial killer wherein attackers commit mass murder on multiple occasions.[16]

For example, some of the most often-cited prolific serial killers in the history of North America are Americans Henry Lee Lucas and Samuel Little. Little likely murdered more than fifty and possibly as many as one hundred, but this does not come close to equaling Rafael and José Antonio. And although Henry Lee Lucas claimed to have killed some six hundred people, he likely made the assertion to receive benefits while in prison, with some suspecting that he was only responsible for the murder of his mother. Somewhat ironically, one of the only true challengers to Rafael in the serial annihilator category is James Kirker, the American hired by the Mexican government to kill Apaches. Kirker's biographer estimates that he was responsible for killing some 322 Apaches from 1840 to 1846, although he did so with a gang of twenty-five armed men, not the two to three that usually made up Rafael's band.[17]

IT IS ALSO POSSIBLE that Rafael has endured not for his heroics or his villainy but instead his story's ability to harmonize with many preexisting myths and superstitions from northern Mexico. As discussed in the introduction, one of the most cited boogeymen in Spanish America is El Cuco, a shapeshifting creature who would take the form of someone trusted and then kidnap children who misbehaved. The legend of El Cuco originated in Europe and was around well before Rafael, but his mythical antics are very similar to Rafael's real crimes, so it is easy to imagine that parents in Mexico wanting their children to behave would choose to replace El Cuco with a real-world example.

Rafael's use of disguises also makes him a good stand-in for a devil myth that is persistent in northern Mexico. According to legend, a handsome devil would show up in small towns and attend a local fiesta. He would then set about wooing a Mexican girl, eventually asking her to dance with him. At this point in the story, a child notices that the handsome stranger has hooves, but before he can warn anyone, the devil whisks the girl away to an unknown fate. In a similar vein, Rafael pairs well with indigenous myths like that of Coyote, a demi-god that can be found in Apache and Navajo folklore who used deception to fool unsuspecting victims into giving him what he wants.

The comparison between Rafael and other Mexican myths can be seen in a nursery rhyme that children began to tell about Rafael at some point in the twentieth century. It describes a child talking to a raven who tells him that Rafael has murdered his grandmother:

Cuervo, cuervo que have tu nana?	Crow, crow what does your nana say?
Croac croac (ya se murió)	Caw caw (she has passed away)
Quién la MATÓ	Who made her this way?
Croac croac (el indio Rafael)	Caw caw (the Indian Rafael)
Malaya pa' el[18]	May he go to hell

These jingles often involve children speaking to animals, typically birds, and asking them about a horrific incident or a terrible mythical being or evil person. The children chant the lines of the jingle rapidly and once complete, someone shouts "tell it again" and the lines are repeated at a more rapid pace. This version of Rafael as an almost supernatural threat for children to fear seems to have been so prevalent in northern Mexico popular culture that it led one author to conclude, "when the children of the north are preparing to sleep, a troop of Apaches appears on top of a barren hill above their bed, and they rush down screaming and firing. In front of everyone rides El Indio Rafael."[19]

ALTHOUGH MANY HISTORIANS have written snippets about Rafael, and his story is well known enough to elicit a nursery rhyme, the collective memory of the once-deadly Apache has faded over time to the point where it seems that only older generations or those well versed in history are familiar with aspects of his story. There are no well-known corridos about Rafael, and no recent collection of northern Mexico folktales tell his tale. Rafael is not remembered as much as the mythical El Cuco or La Llorona, and he is certainly not as popular as real-life historical figures such as Pancho Villa. Whereas Villa received a significant amount of press while active, he dictated his memoirs for publication, and a Hollywood film crew even made a movie about him while he was fighting in the Mexican Revolution, no one has made an El Indio Rafael movie.[20]

There are several possible reasons for this. Perhaps the fading of Rafael's legend can easily be explained by the time in which Rafael was active and the passage of two centuries. Nineteenth-century Apaches such as Victorio were photographed and were the subject of hundreds of newspaper articles, but at the time that Rafael committed his crimes, the camera had yet to exist and there were only two newspapers in the entire colony of New Spain. In addition, these newspapers were more interested in issues close to

Mexico City or those that related to the empire as a whole, so Rafael had to compete for headlines with the likes of Napoleon, Miguel Hidalgo, and Thomas Jefferson.

Rafael's legacy may also have suffered from an inundation of people with similar, albeit not as exceptional, stories that may have diluted or distorted his historical image. Indeed, just a year after Rafael's death, the future president of Mexico, Santa Anna, then serving in the Spanish military, fought a battle against an "Indio Rafael" in Tula in what was then the Eastern Internal Provinces. Although Spanish forces quickly defeated this Rafael, the confusion may have put off some who wanted to chronicle the Apache Rafael's story. In addition, at around the same time as Rafael, a famous Comanche named "El Cautivo Rafael" became known for having been captured but ultimately rejected by the Comanches. There was also an Apache Rafael who the Spanish deported to Cuba in 1803, only to see him flee and start a rebellion in the Cuban countryside. Although these individuals bear no direct relationship to Rafael, it is easy to understand how someone might conflate the various figures.[21]

Further complicating matters, Rafael was certainly not the first or last Hispanicized Apache to "break bad," and use their knowledge of the Spanish language and Spanish culture to better raid frontier settlements. Captured Apache José Reyes Pozo led his own rebellion years before Rafael. Decades after Rafael, Spanish educated Apaches Gómez and Juan José Compá used their knowledge of the Spanish language and Hispanic culture to better raid. Although Rafael was more destructive than those who came before and after him, it is easy to imagine that these Apaches confused the memory of him. The sheer degree to which the Apaches laid waste to northern Mexico following his time, and the success of other Hispanicized Apaches may also have diluted his story. During the later years of the nineteenth century, many Mexican mothers turned to frightening their children with names like Geronimo rather than the temporally distant Rafael.

Indeed, it is likely that the story of one particular Apache, the Apache Kid, took the Rafael narrative and placed it in more familiar and understandable surroundings, at least in the United States. The Apache Kid served as a scout for the United States Army only to run afoul of the law and lead a murderous rampage out of the Sierra Madre. Making the parallels even more compelling, the Apache Kid's spent roughly the same amount of time on the run as Rafael, and a rancher was the one to kill him, not the United States Army. Entire paragraphs from articles reporting on the Apache Kid in the 1890s could be swapped with those on Rafael in the first years of the 1800s:

> Every day repeats the story of his crimes. At unexpected times the Kid appears in many different guises, but he is usually dressed as a Mexican, with a drooping sombrero, flannel shirt, belt, trousers, and top-boots or shoes. In this attire, with his square, swarthy face, com pact figure, and careless grace, he looks more like a Mexican than an Indian, and this effect is heightened by his perfect Spanish speech. He rides in advance of his band, solitary on a wild mustang, scanning the horizon and planning his raids, often making his attacks entirely alone.[22]

IN SPITE OF THE SIMILARITIES to other Spanish-speaking Apaches and the existence of multiple people named "Indio Rafael," Rafael's story was unique, and it is worth remembering because it is representative of larger trends. Throughout the history of northern New Spain and then Mexico, Indians adopted Spanish cultural norms only to then realize that the system they bought into was not what was promised. Recognizing the inconsistencies in how they were treated, these Indians pushed back against the ruling class using violence and ingenuity.

In this way, Rafael may also serve as a lesson. Spain, and later Mexico and the United States, used enemies as military allies. As the Spanish learned with Rafael, and the United States with the Apache Kid, such measures often met with significant short-term success. Apache scouts helped these nations capture and subdue Apaches who made war against them and were unwilling to accept any form of accommodation. However, as Rafael makes clear, by using your enemies in this manner, you teach them your habits and make them more effective at fighting you. This is especially problematic in societies like the Spanish at the beginning of the nineteenth century and the United States at the end of it, where Apaches, no matter their service, would never be accepted as equals because of their ethnicity and background. When such persons become ingratiated in their new culture enough to recognize this inequality, the realization can lead to negative consequences.

Rafael also provides insight into a largely unexplored and unknown period and region of time. Although historians are writing exciting scholarship on

Spanish-Apache relations in New Spain at the end of the eighteenth century and the beginning of the nineteenth, there are few personal stories coming out of this time, especially from the perspective of Indians. Of course, Rafael is not representative of other Apaches, and certainly not demonstrative of Hispanicized Indian groups, but his story serves as a reminder that in a time where Napoleon, Miguel Hidalgo, and Thomas Jefferson dominated headlines, the lower classes continued to face regional problems, and in the case of Rafael, these matters were often more important to their lives than battles taking place half a world away.

Finally, Rafael is worth studying because many aspects of his life remain a mystery, and these mysteries can only be solved with increased attention. Although Bustamante, Salcedo, Pike, Alatorre, and many of their contemporaries wrote extensively about Rafael, they each wrote from a highly biased perspective, and they left out details that Rafael and those hoping to learn more about him would find important. For example, estimates of Rafael's age are questionable, and little is known about his early life, other than he spent much of his youth with Rafael Nevares. To what Apache group did he and his mother belong? Did he learn to read as some suspect? Was he guilty of the charges that led him to revolt, and what was the specific nature of the accusations levied against him? What else led Rafael to begin his spree, and what emotional experiences did he have while conducting these killings? Was he aware of his fame and how did he feel about it? Did he see himself as a revolutionary? Were his surviving victims able to overcome the emotional ordeals they faced in captivity and after returning home?

Searches of archives have uncovered numerous letters and official documents concerning Rafael and his band's actions, but there are doubtlessly more to be found in regional collections in Mexico, the United States, and Spain. Because the Spanish often made multiple copies of official documents, the various letters, campaign diaries, and captive testimonials that Bustamante used to compose his appraisal of Rafael that all seemingly burned in the 1941 fire may survive in some other location. Perhaps the documents are hidden away in someone's private collection. Stories that children learned from their grandmothers about an El Indio Rafael who once terrorized northern Mexico might also provide valuable insights.

Of course, these hypothetical sources of additional information may not exist and time may have distorted any passed-down stories so that they offer nothing of historical value. Questions about Rafael's past may no longer have answers, and most of what there is to know about Rafael is already known. Even if this is the case, it should not detract from his importance, and it may even contribute to his legend. After all, for someone who was so influential and destructive to somehow remain so mysterious is itself an achievement worthy of consideration.

Reports Concerning Rafael,
October 1804–July 1810

T HE FOLLOWING TABLE lists the reporting locations and dates of all documents Juan José Ruiz Bustamante consulted when assembling his report on Rafael's activities to Commandant General Nemesio Salcedo in 1810. Also included is Bustamante's estimate of the number of people Rafael's band killed, injured, or captured in the incidents described in each report, as well as the number of captives recovered.*

Reporting Date	Reporting Location	Killed	Injured	Captured	Escaped
October 18, 1804	Guajoquilla	4	1		
November 1, 1804	San Pablo	3	3		
November 28, 1804	Guajoquilla		2		
November 28, 1804	Guajoquilla	2		1	1
January 1, 1805	Carrizal			1	
February 5, 1805	Santa Catalina	1			
February 19, 1805	Santiaguillo	2			
February 19, 1805	Durango	8	1		
February 26, 1805	Hacienda de Guatimape				
March 18, 1805	Sardinas			1	
April 1, 1805	Sestin			2	2
April 3, 1805	Guajoquilla			2	3
April 10, 1805	Guajoquilla				
April 25, 1805	Guajoquilla	1		1	
October 22, 1805	Carrizal				
October 29, 1805	San José	4		1	

(*continued*)

Reporting Date	Reporting Location	Killed	Injured	Captured	Escaped
October 29, 1805	Curinillas	2			
November 23, 1805	Encinillas	2			1
November 26, 1805	Encinillas				
January 3, 1806	Valle de San Bartolomé	1			
January 7, 1806	Guajoquilla	1			
January 9, 1806	Guajoquilla	1		1	
January 23, 1806	Guajoquilla				
January 25, 1806	Coyame				
February 27, 1806	Hacienda de Carmen	1	1		
March 23, 1806	San Pablo	1	1	1	1
April 30, 1806	Sierra del Ojito	5			
May 21, 1806	Arroyo del Arco	2			
May 26, 1806	Pilar de Conchos	3			
May 27, 1806	San Lorenzo			1	
June 2, 1806	Real del Oro	1			
June 8, 1806	Sitio	1			
June 9, 1806	Guanaceví	1	3		
June 22, 1806	Santa Catalina		1		
June 24, 1806	Durango				
June 27, 1806	Hacienda de Ramos	1		1	
July 9, 1806	Hacienda de Santiago		1		1
July 31, 1806	Julimes	1			
August 8, 1806	Guajoquilla				2
August 22, 1806	Río Florido	4	4	4	
September 18, 1806	Santa Bárbara		1	2	2
September 30, 1806	Cienega de los Olivos	11		2	1
January 10, 1807	Durango	3		1	
January 21, 1807	Durango	3			
February 1, 1807	Durango	4	1		
February 13, 1807	Valle de San Bartolomé				1
February 23, 1807	Guajoquilla	1			1
February 28, 1807	Santa Cruz	2		1	1
March 14, 1807	Satevó		1		

Reporting Date	Reporting Location	Killed	Injured	Captured	Escaped
March 29, 1807	Río de los Quintanas		1		
April 11, 1807	Guanaceví	9			
April 13, 1807	Mezquital				
April 19, 1807	Guanaceví	3			
April 27, 1807	Guanaceví	2			
April 30, 1807	Guajoquilla		2		
May 1, 1807	Valle de San Bartolomé		1		
May 6, 1807	Santa Bárbara	1			
May 21, 1807	Hacienda de los Fresnos	6			
May 26, 1807	Rancho-viejo	3			
June 1, 1807	San Antonio del Tule	3			
June 1, 1807	Guajoquilla	4	2		
June 11, 1807	San Borja	2			
June 12, 1807	Santo Tomás	9		1	
August 27, 1807	Tanquegrande	3			
September 1, 1807	Santa Isabel	2			
September 9, 1807	San Estéban	4			1
September 9, 1807	Cienega de los Olivos				2
September 10, 1807	Corral de Piedras	2	3	1	2
September 10, 1807	San José	2		1	1
September 15, 1807	Cienega de los Olivos	2			
September 30, 1807	San Julián	2			1
October 9, 1807	Valle de San Bartolomé	1	2		
October 21, 1807	Gallo	2	1	1	
October 23, 1807	Valle de San Bartolomé	3			1
November 1, 1807	Hacienda del Sancillo	3			
November 25, 1807	Cerro Prieto	3		2	
November 27, 1807	Zape	4			
November 29, 1807	Batopilas				
November 30, 1807	Cienega de los Olivos	11			
November 30, 1807	San José		1		
December 12, 1807	Sombrerete	1		1	1
December 15, 1807	Durango	8			1

(*continued*)

Reporting Date	Reporting Location	Killed	Injured	Captured	Escaped
December 16, 1807	Cuencamé	3	1		
December 16, 1807	Canatlán	1	1	1	
December 19, 1807	Pilar de Conchos				
December 20, 1807	Cienega de los Olivos	2			
December 27, 1807	Sestin	6	1		
December 28, 1807	Santa Cruz de los Francos	2			
December 29, 1807	San Miguel de las Bocas				
December 31, 1807	Santiago Papasquearo				1
December 31, 1807	Cuencamé	1			
December 31, 1807	Oligados	2			
December 31, 1807	San José	7	4	1	
January 1, 1808	San José de Gracia	1	1		1
January 2, 1808	Santiago				1
January 16, 1808	San Francisco del Toro	1			
January ND, 1808	Barranca Colorada				
January ND, 1808	Durango				
February 13, 1808	Encino de la Paz	2			2
February ND, 1808	No Location	7		1	
March ND, 1808	No Location		1	1	
May ND, 1808	Guanacevi	2			
May 27, 1808	Nopal	2			
June 11, 1808	Cienega de los Olivos				
July 31, 1808	San Pablo	2			
August 12, 1808	San Carlos	1	2		
August 13, 1808	Sestin				
September 22, 1808	Sestin	3	2	1	
September 30, 1808	Valle de San Bartolomé	5			
October 20, 1808	Ancon del Gallo	1			
November 1808	Cañón de Majalea	3	1		
December 15, 1808	Hacienda del Carmen	1		2	
December 22, 1808	Basuchil	2			
January 16, 1809	Guajoquilla				1
January 26, 1809	Mapimí	10			

Reporting Date	Reporting Location	Killed	Injured	Captured	Escaped
April 18, 1809	Guajoquilla	4			
September 17, 1809	Guajoquilla	2	2		
September 20, 1809	Guajoquilla	1			
September 21, 1809	Río Florido	5		1	
September 29, 1809	Cienega de los Olivos	10	1	1	
January 14, 1810	Pilar de Conchos	3	1	1	
January 18, 1810	Hacienda de Mala-Noche	4			
January 31, 1810	Río de Conchos	1	1		1
February 14, 1810	San Pablo	2			1
February 20, 1810	Encinillas	4			2
February 22, 1810	Guajoquilla			1	
March 10, 1810	Santa Isabel	2	1		
March 25, 1810	Sierra de Huerachi	3			
April 13, 1810	Sierra de Vitorino				
April 20, 1810	Carrizal	1		2	
April 30, 1810	Santa Eulalia				
May 8, 1810	Santa Rosalia-	7			
July 7, 1810	Pilar de Conchos	4			
July 10, 1810	Cienega de los Olivos	3		1	
July 13, 1810	Parral	1	1	1	
July 13, 1810	Sierra de Santa Bárbara	1			
July 26, 1810	San Antonio de la Laguna	1			
	Total	298	53	45	37

*Because it took time for news to travel, Spanish officials usually wrote their reports days and sometimes weeks after incidents occurred, and they generally sent letters from population centers. They also often sent news about multiple incidents. Therefore, the locations and dates here do not reflect the precise dates and locations of Rafael's attacks, but because the reporting location was usually near where incidents occurred, they do give a general time frame and area. Specific locations are discussed in the main text.

Deaths Attributed to Rafael and Apaches
in Nueva Vizcaya, August 1804–August 1810

The following table includes burial records from Nueva Vizcaya that report a cause of death as either "Apaches," "Indios," "Enemigos," "Infieles," or Rafael specifically. Although those records that do not mention Rafael may refer to a different hostile group, most of the deaths took place in an area in which Rafael was known to be operating shortly before the interments. Because the majority of death records do not list a cause of death, and many death records from the time have been lost or are unreadable, this is not as comprehensive of a list as Bustamante's, and it likely shows only a small percentage of those killed by Rafael's band.

Name	Location Interred	Date Interred	Quote
Joaquín Befarano	Guajoquilla	August 23, 1804	"fue muerto por los Enemigos Apaches"
Juan José Losoya	Satevó	August 23, 1804	"que murió a manos de los Indios"
José Francisco Losoya	Satevó	August 23, 1804	"por haber muerta a manos de los Indios"
Hipolito García	San Pablo	September 23, 1804	"que los mataron los apaches"
José Ricardo Silva	Guajoquilla	October 4, 1804	"murió a manos a los Enemigos"
José Ciriaco Guerca	Mapimí	March 13, 1805	"falleció a doce de decho en el camino de la cueva a Mapimí en manos de los Indio Apaches"
Bernardo Mendoza	Satevó	October 2, 1805	"por causa de haberlo matado los Apaches"
Ramón Mendoza	Satevó	October 2, 1805	"por haberlo matado los Apaches"
Prudencio Baca	San Pedro	October 13, 1805	"por que lo mataron los Indios"
"Adulto no conocido"	San Pedro	October 13, 1805	"que mataron en el campo los Apaches"
Salvador de los Santos	Cerro Gordo	October 14, 1805	"los que murieron el día trece "a manos de los indios Barbaros"
Antonio Delgado	Cerro Gordo	October 14, 1805	"los que murieron el día trece "a manos de los indios Barbaros"
Albino Trejo	Cerro Gordo	October 14, 1805	"los que murieron el día trece "a manos de los indios Barbaros"
Ignacio Rodriguez	San Bartolomé	December 31, 1805	"por haberle muerto los Indios enemigos"
Ignacio Ontiveros	Guajoquilla	January 9, 1806	"muerto a los Apaches"
Manuel Minas	Canatlán	May 12, 1806	"que murieron sin confesión a manos de los Indios Barbaros"

María Rita Espanola Doncella	San Bartolomé	June 22, 1806	"a causa de haber muerto violentamente"
María Viviana López	San Bartolomé	July 16, 1806	"por la violencia con que murió"
Juan Morales	Cerro Gordo	August 24, 1806	"murieron al día de ayer a manos de los indios Barbaros"
Bernabe Cardosa	Cerro Gordo	August 24, 1806	"murieron al día de ayer a manos de los indios Barbaros"
Juan Olayo Sisneros	Cerro Gordo	August 24, 1806	"murieron al día de ayer a manos de los indios Barbaros"
Juan Primo	Mapimí	December 28, 1806	"por haber sido muerto de los Indios Barbaros"
Mariano Nores	San Juan del Río	January 17, 1807	"fue muerto por el Indio Rafael"
Pedro Rodriguez Casado	Santiago Papasquiaro	January 17, 1807	"porque lo mataron los Indios"
Venancio Rodriguez	Santiago Papasquiaro	January 17, 1807	"porque lo mato el Indio Rafael"
Juan José Manuel Rodriguez Casado	Santiago Papasquiaro	January 26, 1807	"porque lo mato el Indio Rafael"
José Ilario Olvera	Santiago Papasquiaro	January 26, 1807	"porque lo mato el Indio Rafael"
Juan Francisco Martinez	Guanaceví	April 12, 1807	"por haberlo muerto en el campo el Indio Bárbaro Rafael"
Ventura Flores	Guanaceví	April 22, 1807	"por haberlo muerto en el campo el Indio Bárbaro Rafael"
José Carrera	Guanaceví	April 22, 1807	"por haberlo muerto en el campo el Indio Bárbaro Rafael"
José Miguel Callenos	Santa María del Oro	June 9, 1807	"el bárbaro Enemigo Rafael le dio muerte violentes"
José Cobos	Santa María del Oro	June 14, 1807	"murió en manos del Bárbaro Rafael"
Francisco de Aro	Mapimí	June 22, 1807	"falleció . . . en manos de los Indios Barbaros"
Christoval Rodriguez	Indé	August 20, 1807	"por murió a manos de los enemigos"
José María Ochoa	San Bartolomé	September 26, 1807	"por haber muerto en manos de los Indios"
Francisco Vázquez	Santa María del Oro	October 6, 1807	"habiendo muerto en el campo en manos del enemigo Rafael"

(continued)

Name	Location Interred	Date Interred	Quote
Felipe Morales	Santa María del Oro	October 6, 1807	"habiendo muerto en el campo en manos del enemigo Rafael"
Hilarion Amaro	Coneto de Comonfort	October 8, 1807	"por haberlo muerte los Indios"
Francisco Amaro	Coneto de Comonfort	October 8, 1807	"falleció en manos de los Indios"
Rafael Morales	Indé	October 10, 1807	"por haber muerto por mano de infieles"
Silberio Reyes	San Pedro	October 11, 1807	"por que lo mataron los Indios"
Atanacio Baldes	San Pedro	October 11, 1807	"por que lo mataron los Apaches"
María Rodriguez	San Pedro	October 13, 1807	"por que murio violenta"
José Perfecto Hernandez	San Bartolomé	October 20, 1807	"por haberlo matado los Indios"
Pedro José Hernandez	San Bartolomé	October 21, 1807	"también los mataron los Indios"
Anastacio Pulido	Cuencamé	December 7, 1807	"por haberlo matado los Indios"
Luciano Gonzalez	Canatlán	December 15, 1807	"muerto por el Indio Rafael"
"Una mujer"	Canatlán	January 6, 1808	"muerta por el Indio Rafael"
José Antonio Campos	San Juan del Río	January 14, 1808	"por que mato el Indio Rafael"
José Aguallo	Santa María del Oro	February 14, 1808	"habiendo muerto en manos del Bárbaro Indio Rafael"
José María García	Santa María del Oro	February 14, 1808	"habiendo muerto en manos del Bárbaro Indio Rafael"
Unknown	Santa María del Oro	February 18, 1808	"habiendo muerto en manos del Indio Rafael"
Unknown	Santa María del Oro	February 18, 1808	"habiendo muerto en manos del Indio Rafael"
José Domingo Espino	Mapimí	October 31, 1808	"por haber muerto en manos de Indios Barbaros"
José Acosta	Encinillas	November 28, 1808	"por haber matado los Indios"
Patricia Bargas	Encinillas	November 28, 1808	"por haber muerto a manos de los Apaches"

Name	Location	Date	Description
Lorenzo Mendoza	Encinillas	December 5, 1808	"por haberlo matado los Apaches"
José Marcos Talamantes	Parral	January 30, 1809	"falleció a manos de Indios Barbaros"
Ramón Castro	Parral	January 30, 1809	"falleció a manos de Indios Barbaros"
Juan Antonio de la Serda	Mapimí	February 18, 1809	"por haber muerto en manos de los Indios"
Pedro Gayardo	Coneto de Comonfort	February 25, 1809	"por haber muerto en manos del Indio Rafael"
Juan de Avitia	Coneto de Comonfort	February 25, 1809	"falleció en manos del Indio Rafael"
María Tores	Cerro Gordo	March 10, 1809	"que falleció en manos de los enemigos"
José Guadalupe Rodríguez	San Bartolomé	April 18, 1809	"por haber muerto en manos de los Indios barbaros"
Miguel Portillo	San Bartolomé	April 18, 1809	"por haber muerto en manos de los Indios barbaros"
Juan Antonio Fiero	San Bartolomé	April 18, 1809	"por haber muerto en manos de los Indios barbaros"
José María Peña	San Bartolomé	April 18, 1809	"por haber muerto en manos de los Indios barbaros"
María Valencia Merrno Valencia Bojorgdes	Conchos	June 28, 1809	"muerto de—de mano de enemigo"
José Saturnino Sambrano Hernandez	Conchos	June 28, 1809	"muerto de—de mano de enemigo"
Elanacio Moreno	Mapimí	June 30, 1809	"por haber muerto en manos de los Enemigos Barbaros"
José Antonio Cárdenas	Guajoquilla	September 14, 1809	"no recibió los santos sacramentos por la violencia de su muerte"
José Manuel Calletana de los Relles	Guajoquilla	September 20, 1809	"por haber muerto en el campo a manos de Indios barbaros"
Urbano Domíngues	San Pablo	February 14, 1810	"fue muerto por el Indio Rafael en la Sierra del Carriso"
Roberto Visuano	San Pablo	February 14, 1810	"fue muerto por el Indio Rafael en la Sierra del Carriso"

(continued)

Name	Location Interred	Date Interred	Quote
Juan Parada	Encinillas	February 20, 1810	"muerto por los Apaches"
Juan Nuñez	Encinillas	April 3, 1810	"que murió a manos a Rafaelillo"
Manuel Nuñez	Encinillas	April 3, 1810	"que falleció en manos del Indio Rafaelillo"
Francisco Granado	San Bartolomé	April 21, 1810	"por haber sido su muerte violenta"
Maríano Gongora	Guajoquilla	June 19, 1810	"no recibió los santos sacramentos por su violenta muerta"
José de Jesus Montreal	Indé	August 12, 1810	"murió en el campo (y no recibió sacramento) a manos de los enemigos"
Julian Rojas	Indé	August 12, 1810	"por haber muerto a manos de los enemigos"
Thranquelino Lopes	Indé	August 12, 1810	"por haber muerto de los enemigos"
María Secundina Rodriguez	Indé	August 12, 1810	"murió sin recibir los stos. Sacramentos a manos de los Apaches"

Source: The two collections used were "México, Chihuahua, registros parroquiales y diocesanos, 1632–1958." Database with images. *FamilySearch.* http://FamilySearch.org: 8 September 2021. Parroquias Católicas, Chihuahua (Catholic Church parishes, Chihuahua) and "México, Durango, registros parroquiales y diocesanos, 1604–1985." Database with images. *FamilySearch.* http://FamilySearch.org: 27 August 2021. Parroquias Católicas, Durango (Catholic Church parishes, Durango). Original spellings and grammar were used except in instances where the author's intent was obvious, such as changing "trese" to "trece." In a random sample of twenty Nueva Vizcaya death records during this time, only seven listed a cause of death. To maintain uniformity, the list does not include death records where a victim of Rafael is named in other sources, but no reason for death is given on death records. For example, Bustamante mentions Rafael as having killed a Policarpo Vázquez in February 1810, and a burial record from the location and time for a Policarpo Vázquez is clearly referring to the same person, but the priest did not list a cause of death. See, "Sucinta relación que manifesta las muertes, cautiverios, robos y demás atrocidades causadas por los indios apaches Rafael y sus compañeros," Incident 122, 124 (quotation in Incident 122); Policarpo Vázquez Burial Record, February 9, 1810, Aldama San Gerónimo Chihuahua, Defunciones, FHL.

Introduction

1. Ronald L. Ives, "The Sonoran 'Primer Montezuma' Legends," *Western Folklore* 9, no. 4 (1950): 321–25; Robert A. Barakat, "Juan Tigre: A Mexican Folktale," *Journal of Popular Culture* 4, no. 1 (1970): 230; Thomas A. Green, *Latino American Folktales* (Westport, Conn.: Greenwood Press, 2009), 34–38.

2. Robert A. Barakat, "Wailing Women of Folklore," *Journal of American Folklore*, 82, no. 325 (1969): 270–72; Rafaela Castro, *Chicano Folklore: A Guide to the Folktales, Traditions, Rituals, and Religious Practices of Mexican Americans* (New York: Oxford University Press, 2001), 57–58. For other versions of the La Llorona tale, see Domino R. Perez, *There Was a Woman: La Llorona from Folklore to Popular Culture* (Austin: University of Texas Press, 2008) and Wilson M. Hudson, *The Healer of Los Olmos and Other Mexican Lore* (Dallas: Southern Methodist University Press, 1951), 72–76. There are numerous variants of El Cuco's name in Spanish and Latin American history including "Coco," "Coca," and "Cucuy."

3. "Historia" *Diario de Colima*, October 24, 1993 (first quotation); Atanasio G. Sarabia, "El Indio Rafael," *Investigaciones históricas* I (October 1938): 56 (second quotation); Juan Josef Flores, "Juan Josef Flores escribe á su apoderado desde Sombrerete, en carta de 1 de Diciembre, entre otras cosas el párrafo siguiente," *Diario de México*, December 26, 1807 (third quotation). For examples of Rafael's story as a legend in Chihuahua, see Gildardo Contreras Palacios, *Antecedentes históricos a la fundación de el Torreón* (Torreón, Coah.: Ayuntamiento de Torreón, 1992), 136.

4. Enrique Vega Galindo, "El Indio Rafael," *Primera Plana* (Hermosillo), Edición 11, December 17, 2015; Sarabia, "El Indio Rafael," 56 (first quotation); Contreras Palacios, *Antecedentes históricos a la fundación de el Torreón*, 136 (second quotation); "Historia" *Diario de Colima*, October 24, 1993.

5. Jesús Ángel Ochoa Zazueta, *Apostillas de los Tepehuanes* (Mexico D. F.: Nueva Hispanidad, 1967), 68–69; Ángel Trejo, "Las rebeliones previas al Grito de Independencia," *Buzos: Revista de análisis político*, no. 474, September 26, 2011; Jesús G. Sotomayor Garza, *Anales Laguneros* (Torreón: Ayuntamiento de Torreón, 1992), 42 (quotation).

6. Victor Campa Mendoza, *Las insurrecciones de los pueblos Indios en México* (Durango: Ediciones Fondo Internacional de Becas para Estudiantes Indígenas, 2001),

60 (first quotation); Contreras Palacios, *Antecedentes históricos a la fundación de el Torreón,* 140 (second quotation).

7. José de la Cruz Pacheco Rojas, *El Proceso de Independencia en Durango: Periodo de la insurgencia, 1808–1812* (Durango: Universidad Juárez del Estado de Durango, 2010), 45; Ochoa Zazueta, *Apostillas de los Tepehuanes,* 69 (first quotation); Contreras Palacios, *Antecedentes históricos a la fundación de el Torreón,* 140 (second quotation); Sarabia, "El Indio Rafael," 56.

8. Hubert H. Bancroft, *The Works of Hubert Howe Bancroft: History of the North Mexican States and Texas* (San Francisco: Bancroft, 1886), 595; Nemesio Salcedo and Canales I. Vizcaya, *Instrucción reservada de don Nemesio Salcedo y Salcedo comandante general de provincias internas a su sucesor* (Chihuahua, Chih., México: Centro de Información del Estado de Chihuahua, 1991), 40–41; "España" *Gaceta de la Regencia de España é Indias,* February 7, 1811; Vicente Riva Palacio, *Mexico a través de los siglos,* v. 4 (Mexico: D. F.: J. Ballescá y Compañía, 1888), 778. At least one historian mistook the number of people Rafael's band had killed for the total number that *all* Apaches had killed during a five-year period. See, Keith Wayne Algier, "Feudalism on New Spain's Northern Frontier: Valle de San Bartolomé, A Case Study" (PhD diss., University of New Mexico, Albuquerque, 1966), 33, 42.

9. The population of the Internal Provinces of New Spain in 1800 is unknown, but most contemporary observers believe it to be somewhere from 200,000 to 400,000. For example, José Cortés gives the number as less than 300,000, Miguel Ramos de Arizpe 348,500, and Alexander von Humboldt some 400,000. See José Cortés, *Views from the Apache Frontier: Report on the Northern Provinces of New Spain* (Norman: University of Oklahoma Press, 1989), 24; Miguel Ramos de Arizpe, *Report That Dr. Miguel Ramos De Arizpe Presents to the August Congress on the Natural, Political, and Civil Condition of the Provinces of Coahuila, Nuevo León, Nuevo Santander, and Texas* (New York: Greenwood Press, 1969), 8, 12, 14; Alexander von Humboldt, *Political Essay on the Kingdom of New Spain* (London: Longman, Hurst, Rees, Orme and Brown, and H. Colburn, 1811), 425. For additional estimates see Peter Gerhard, *The North Frontier of New Spain* (Norman: University of Oklahoma Press, 1993), 24. I was unable to locate a comprehensive list of casualties caused by Geronimo, Victorio, and Mangas Colorado. However, based on estimates of deaths provided in Gregory Michno's *Encyclopedia of Indian Wars,* the number of killed by individual Apaches in the mid-to-late 1800s was not comparable to Rafael and José Antonio. Michno lists all Apaches combined as having caused some 566 deaths, although this number does not include deaths in Mexico and its count of civilian dead in the United States is incomplete. In his book *War of a Thousand Deserts,* Brian DeLay counted some two thousand killed by all Apaches and Comanches in Mexico from approximately 1830 to 1850, but, as he notes, this is likely a low estimate. See Gregory Michno, *Encyclopedia of Indian Wars: Western Battles and Skirmishes, 1850–1890* (Missoula, Mont.: Mountain Press Publishing, 2003), 363–70;

Brian DeLay, *War of a Thousand Deserts: Indian Raids and the U.S.-Mexican War* (New Haven, Conn.: Yale University Press, 2008), 136, 320–40, 394.

10. "Continuación de los donativos para zapatos y otros socorros en beneficio de los soldados del ejército de la península," *Gaceta del Gobierno de México*, August 17, 1810.

11. For a summary of the difficulties facing Spain from 1803 to 1810, see David Weber, *The Spanish Frontier in North America* (New Haven, Conn.: Yale University Press, 1992), 291–301.

12. Salcedo, *Instrucción reservada de don Nemesio Salcedo y Salcedo comandante general de provincias internas a su sucesor,* 40–42 (quotation on 40).

13. The only article about Rafael to be featured in a scholarly journal was Atanasio G. Sarabia's "El Indio Rafael" in *Investigaciones históricas* I. Sarabia's work provides insight into Rafael that cannot be found elsewhere. However, his article contains several inaccuracies and omissions. Although some of these are understandable considering the time in which he wrote the article, Sarabia does not seem to have had access to the collection of documents concerning Rafael that was assembled by Juan José Ruiz de Bustamante in 1810 and published in multiple works prior to Sarabia's article. For examples of works that discuss Rafael but only devote a few pages to discussing his activities, see Contreras Palacios, *Antecedentes históricos a la fundación de el Torreón,* 140; Ochoa Zazueta, *Apostillas de los Tepehuanes,* 69.

14. For an example of an Apache memoir, see Stephen Melvil Barrett, *Geronimo's Story of His Life* (New York: Duffield & Co., 1906); Jason Betzinez, *I Fought with Geronimo* (Harrisburg, Penn.: Stackpole, 1959). Betzinez not only wrote his experiences with Geronimo for publication, but he also appeared on the television program *I've Got a Secret* to tell his story.

15. Edwin R. Sweeney, *Mangas Coloradas: Chief of the Chiricahua Apaches* (Norman: University of Oklahoma Press, 2011), 32 (quotation); Charles R. Cutter, *The Legal Culture of Northern New Spain, 1700–1810* (Albuquerque: University of New Mexico Press, 2001), 9.

16. Affidavit of Sam Bean, *In the Matter of the Claim of Certain Mexican Citizens to Lands on the Rio Grande Known by the Name of District of "El Chamizal"* (Mexico D. F.: Secretary of Foreign Relations, 1905), 67 (quotation). For example, there are no documents in the microfilms of the Ciudad Juárez Municipal Archives at the University of Texas, El Paso from 1810 to 1821 and very few from 1807 to 1809. See Ciudad Juárez Municipal Archives Microfilm Collection, University of Texas at El Paso (hereafter cited as JMA), Microfilm Roll 15; Claudia Rivers, "JUAREZ ARCHIVES," *Handbook of Texas Online,* http://www.tshaonline.org/handbook/online/articles/lcj04 (accessed June 05, 2020). Some documents concerning Rafael are located in private collections and unavailable to the public. For example, in Sarabia's "El Indio Rafael," Sarabia mentions owning a diary of a Spanish soldier who went on campaign looking for Rafael.

17. Victor Orozco, *Las Guerra indias en la historia de Chihuahua* (Ciudad Juárez: Universidad Autónoma de Ciudad Juárez, 1992), 153–54, 194 (quotation on 194); Cutter, *The Legal Culture of Northern New Spain*, 9. The "nota editorial" section in *Las Guerra indias en la historia de Chihuahua* implies that José Merino was the one who put together the calendar and the list of deaths, injured, and killed, not Bustamante. I believe this assertion is an error. The calendar ends with Bustamante's signature, indicating that he was the one who both gathered the documents and did the math. For an example of a document referencing missing documents concerning Rafael, see Andrés Mattios to Bernardo Bonavía, Nov. 1, 1804, Archivo Histórico del Gobierno del Estado de Durango Microfilm Collection, University of Texas at El Paso (hereafter cited as AHED), MF492, R58. This microfilm contains multiple references to campaign diaries concerning Rafael but not the diaries themselves. It is possible that the archivists stored the diaries in a different location, the person photographing the microfilm did not photograph the diaries, or the archivists put the diaries on a different microfilm that I was unable to locate, but it seems more plausible that they ended up in Bustamante's collection.

18. Orozco discusses the creation and eventual publishing of the *Apuntes historicos* collection in Orozco, *Las Guerra indias en la historia de Chihuahua*, 153–54. In 1857, Vicente García Torres made a printed copy of Merino's summary and included it in *Documentos para la historia eclesiástica y civil de la Nueva Vizcaya*, a catalog of important documents concerning Chihuahua and Durango history that he included in his larger series about Mexican history. In 1909, Silvestre Terrazas came across a copy of Torres's work in the Instituto Nacional de Antropología library and decided to include Bustamante's summary in his collection of unusual stories about Chihuahua called *Curiosidades históricas* published in 1909. The most recent book to include the calendar was Orozco, *Las Guerra indias en la historia de Chihuahua* published in 1992. The validity of the supplemental information added in the various editions of the report will be discussed in later chapters. Although introductory information and page numbers differ from one version of the report to the next, the calendar itself appears to be identical in all four books. For this reason, and in order to make looking up information easy no matter which version of the report is on hand, I use "Sucinta relación que manifiesta las muertes, cautiverios, robos y demás atrocidades causadas por los indios apaches Rafael y sus compañeros," to refer to the report. Instead of page numbers, I use "Incident" to indicate which of the 137 sections of the report contains the relevant information. Information written by Bustamante and Merino before and after the numerical incident reports will be labeled "Introduction" and "Conclusion" respectively. Supplemental information exclusive to specific editions will use traditional citations. See also Vicente García Torres, *Documentos para la historia eclesiástica y civil de la Nueva Vizcaya* (Mexico, D. F.: Imprenta de Vicente García Torres, 1857); Silvestre Terrazas, *Curiosidades históricas* (Chihuahua: El Correo de Chihuahua, 1909).

It is unclear what motivated Merino to look up Bustamante's work, but at the time he was a military commander in Chihuahua and was amid peace negotiations with a group of Carrizálenos Apaches. It is possible that he was looking through the archives for prior peace agreements between the Apaches and found Bustamante's collection and decided it was worth publishing. He may also have remembered Rafael from his childhood and once he became commandant general and gained access to the archives, he looked through them to learn more. See Edwin R. Sweeney, *Cochise: Chiricahua Apache Chief* (Norman: University of Oklahoma Press, 1995), 102.

19. For example, Bustamante describes Rafael and his companions as having killed a man named Ignacio Ontiveros near what is today Jiménez, Mexico in January 1806. Parish burial records from Jiménez list a "Ignacio Ontio" as having been "killed by Apaches" that month, but they say nothing about Rafael. Someone unfamiliar with Rafael might assume that random Apaches had carried out the attack, while someone conducting a digital archival search would not find the entry because Ontiveros's name is spelled incorrectly. See "Sucinta relación que manifiesta las muertes, cautiverios, robos y demás atrocidades causadas por los indios apaches Rafael y sus compañeros," Incident 21, 22, 23, 24; Lucas Valenzuela to Nemesio Salcedo, January 4, 1806, Archivo de Hidalgo del Parral Microfilm Collection, Southern Methodist University (hereafter cited as AHP), R1791a; Ygnacio Ontio Burial Record, January 1806, Archivo de la parroquia de Santo Cristo de Burgos, Defunciones, Family History Library of the Church of Jesus Christ of Latter-Day Saints digitized at *Familysearch.org* (hereafter cited as FHL). For examples of service records where soldiers went on campaign against unspecified "enemigos" that may have been Rafael's band, see Rafael Provo Service Record, 1817, Archivo General de la Nación Microfilm Collection, Provincias Internas, University of New Mexico at Albuquerque (hereafter cited as AGN-PI), L254, R248; Julian Hidalgo Service Record, 1817, AGN-PI, L254, R248; Report of Captain of the Primera Compania Volante November 6, 1804, AHED, MF492, R58.

20. "Sucinta relación que manifiesta las muertes, cautiverios, robos y demás atrocid- ades causadas por los indios apaches Rafael y sus compañeros," Introduction. Merino's decision to leave in "provincialisms and antiquated" phrases and locations contributes to the confusion over place names. In general, I use place names as they appear in Spanish sources, changing them only if the spelling is very similar to the modern spelling and there is little chance of incorrectly misassigning locations.

21. For examples of historians regarding the late 1700s and early 1800s as a time of peace in which little of consequence occurred, see Robert Watt, *Apache Tactics 1830– 1886* (London: Osprey 2014); Edwin R. Sweeney, "One of Heaven's Heroes: A Mexican General Pays Tribute to the Honor and Courage of a Chiricahua Apache," *Journal of Arizona History* 36, no. 3 (1995): 209–10; Sweeney, *Mangas Coloradas*, 17; Frank C. Lockwood, *The Apache Indians* (Lincoln: University of Nebraska Press, 1987), 28; Jessica D. Palmer, *The Apache Peoples: A History of All Bands and Tribes Through*

the 1800s (Jefferson, NC: McFarland, 2013), 236–37; Stuart F. Voss, *On the Periphery of Nineteenth-Century Mexico: Sonora and Sinaloa* (Tucson: University of Arizona Press, 1982), 87–91; Miguel Ángel González Quiroga, *War and Peace of the Rio Grande, 1830–1880* (Norman: University of Oklahoma Press, 2020), 14–16; Ignacio Zuñiga, *Rápida ojeada al estado de Sonora: dirigida y dedicada al supremo gobierno de la nación* (Mexico City: Impreso por Juan Ojeda, 1835), 27–28; José Agustín de Escudero, *Observaciones sobre el estado actual del departamento de Chihuahua* (Mexico City: Juan Ojeda, 1839), 16–17.

22. William B. Griffen, *Apaches at War and Peace: The Janos Presidio, 1750–1858* (Norman: University of Oklahoma Press, 1988); William B. Griffen, *Utmost Good Faith: Patterns of Apache-Mexican Hostilities in Northern Chihuahua Border Warfare, 1821–1848* (Albuquerque: University of New Mexico Press, 1988); Paul T. Conrad, "Captive Fates: Displaced American Indians in the Southwest Borderlands, Mexico, and Cuba, 1500–1800" (PhD diss., University of Texas, Austin, 2011); Mathew Babcock, *Apache Adaptation to Hispanic* Rule (Cambridge: Cambridge University Press, 2016); Mark Santiago, *A Bad Peace and a Good War: Spain and the Mescalero Apache Uprising of 1795–1799* (Norman: University of Oklahoma Press, 2018); Mark Santiago, *Jar of Severed Hands: Spanish Deportation of Apache Prisoners of War, 1770–1810* (Norman: University of Oklahoma Press, 2011); Lance Blyth, *Chiricahua and Janos: Communities of Violence in the Southwestern Borderlands, 1680–1880* (Lincoln: University of Nebraska Press, 2012).

23. "Noticias ulteriores del Apache," *Diario de México*, February 1, 1808. "Hijos" can be translated into both "children" and "sons." Considering the patronizing nature of the comment, "children" may be more appropriate in the plural, but I used "sons" to make the use of the singular male "son" in the book title easier to understand.

24. "Noticias ulteriores del Apache," *Diario de México*, February 1, 1808. In order to overcome gaps in the historical records and provide insight when documents lack detail, this book will often make comparisons to what are believed to be similar, but better documented events. Supposition and bias recognition will be used to interpret impartial accounts and provide counternarratives when needed.

Chapter 1

1. Hal Jackson, *Following the Royal Road: A Guide to the Historic Camino Real de Tierra Adentro* (Albuquerque: University of New Mexico Press, 2006), 195; Bernardo Bonavía, "Lista o noticia de las jurisdicciones o partidos de la comprensión de la provincial de Nueva Vizcaya," in Enrique Florescano and Isabel Gil Sánchez (eds.), *Descripciones económicas regionales de Nueva España: Provincias del Norte, 1790–1814* (Mexico City: Instituto Nacional de Antropología e Historia, 1976), 87; George F.

Ruxton, *Adventures in Mexico and the Rocky Mountains* (London: J. Murray, 1849), 136–37; "Noticias ulteriores del Apache," *Diario de México*, February 1, 1808 (first quotation); Joaquín Befarano Burial Record, August 23, 1804, Archivo de la parroquia de Santo Cristo de Burgos, Defunciones, FHL (second quotation); José Ricardo Silva Burial Record, October 4, 1804, Archivo de la parroquia de Santo Cristo de Burgos, Defunciones, FHL (third quotation); Peter Stern, "Social Marginality and Acculturation on the Northern Frontier of New Spain" (PhD diss., University of California, Berkeley, 1984), 285–86.

2. Voss, *On the Periphery of Nineteenth Century Mexico*, 2–3; Gerhard, *The North Frontier of New Spain*, 161, 164–69; Algier, "Feudalism on New Spain's Northern Frontier," 26–27; Oakah L. Jones Jr., *Los Paisanos: Spanish Settlers on the Northern Frontier of New Spain* (Norman: University of Oklahoma Press, 1996), Susan M. Deeds, *Defiance and Deference in Mexico's Colonial North: Indians under Spanish Rule in Nueva Vizcaya* (Austin: University of Texas Press, 2003), 39–40.

3. Santiago, *A Good War and a Bad Peace*, 178–80. Apaches escaping their bonds and returning to the frontier became such a problem that in July 1788 the Crown had to issue a decree "requiring the viceroy to insure that prisoners arriving in Mexico City in the future could never return to their homeland and renew their depredations." H. Henrietta Stockel, *Salvation through Slavery: Chiricahua Apaches and Priests on the Spanish Colonial Frontier* (Albuquerque: University of New Mexico Press, 2008). Explorer Zebulon Pike noted the effect of the deportation policy: "the Spaniards used to take them prisoners and make slaves of them; but finding that their unconquerable attachment to liberty made them surmount every difficulty and danger in returning to their mountains, they adopted the mode of sending them to Cuba." Zebulon Pike, *The Expeditions of Zebulon Montgomery Pike: To Headwaters of the Mississippi River, Through Louisiana Territory, and in New Spain, During the Years 1805–1807* (New York: Francis P. Harper, 1895), vol. 2, 748–49. See also H. Henrietta Stockel, *On the Bloody Road to Jesus: Christianity and the Chiricahua Apaches* (Albuquerque: University of New Mexico Press, 2004), 77–95.

4. Frederick Albion Ober, *Travels in Mexico and Life Among the Mexicans* (Boston: Estes & Lauriat, 1887), 627 (first quotation); Stern, "Social Marginality and Acculturation," 260 (second quotation); Contreras Palacios, *Antecedentes históricos a la fundación de el Torreón*, 140 (third quotation).

5. Pike, *The Expeditions of Zebulon Montgomery Pike*, vol. 2, 752; "Sucinta relación que manifiesta las muertes, cautiverios, robos y demás atrocidades causadas por los indios apaches Rafael y sus compañeros," Incident 1, 2, 3, 94; Salcedo, *Instrucción reservada de don Nemesio Salcedo y Salcedo comandante general de provincias internas a su sucesor*, 20; Bancroft, *History of the North Mexican States and Texas*, 595.

6. Jesús A. Ramos-Kittrell, *Playing in the Cathedral: Music, Race, and Status in New Spain* (New York: Oxford University Press, 2016), 75–77, 170; William B. Taylor,

Theater of a Thousand Wonders: A History of Miraculous Images and Shrines in New Spain (New York: Cambridge University Press, 2016), 296; Héctor M. Bernal Vázquez, *Jiménez: 250 Años en lucha contra la adversidad* (n.p., 2003), 81 (quotation). Nevares was born in Spain in 1753, came to the New World at some point prior to 1776, and arrived in Guajoquilla in 1785. For more on the duties of chaplains, see Pedro de Rivera, Thomas H. Naylor, and Charles W. Polzer, *Pedro De Rivera and the Military Regulations for Northern New Spain, 1724–1729: A Documentary History of His Frontier Inspection and the Reglamento De 1729* (Tucson: University of Arizona Press, 1988), 120.

7. Robert H. Jackson, *Frontiers of Evangelization: Indians in the Sierra Gorda and Chiquitos Missions* (Norman: University of Oklahoma Press, 2017), 83–84; Gerhard, *The North Frontier of New Spain*, 164–67. Deeds, *Defiance and Deference in Mexico's Colonial North*, 25–27, 40.

8. Max L. Moorhead, *The Apache Frontier: Jacobo Ugarte and Spanish-Indian Relations in Northern New Spain, 1769–1791* (Norman: University of Oklahoma Press, 1968), 4, 6–7, 11; G. F. von Tempsky, *Mitla: A Narrative of Incidents and Personal Adventures on a Journey in Mexico, Guatemala, and Salvador in the Years of 1853 to 1855*, ed. J. S. Bell (London: Longman, Brown, Green, Longmans, & Roberts, 1858), 83. For a dramatic assessment of the Apache-Spanish conflict, see Escudero, *Observaciones sobre el estado actual del departamento de Chihuahua*, 12–14.

9. Babcock, *Apache Adaption to Hispanic Rule*, 19, 45–46, 66–69, 71–73; Robert S. Weddle, *The San Sabá Mission* (College Station: Texas A&M University Press, 1999), 23, 55–57.

10. Moorhead, *The Apache Frontier*, 11–15; Weber, *The Spanish Frontier in North America*, 187–88. Paul Conrad, "Empire through Kinship: Rethinking Spanish-Apache Relations in Southwestern North America in the Late Eighteenth and Early Nineteenth Centuries," *Early American Studies* 14, no. 4 (2016): 636–38; Von Tempsky, *Mitla*, 83 (quotation). For examples of Spanish soldiers failing to retaliate after an Apache raid, see James M. Daniel and Pedro José de la Fuenta, "Diary of Pedro José de la Fuente, Captain of the Presidio of El Paso del Norte, August–December, 1765," *Southwestern Historical Quarterly* 83, no. 3 (January 1980): 268–69.

11. "Noticias ulteriores del Apache," *Diario de México*, February 1, 1808 (first quotation); Santiago, *Jar of Severed Hands*, 71, 75–80, 90 (second quotation on page 90; third quotation on page 71); Babcock, *Apache Adaptation to Hispanic Rule*, 144; Max L. Moorhead, *The Presidio: Bastion of the Spanish Borderlands* (Norman: University of Oklahoma Press, 1991), 252–54; Conrad, "Captive Fates," 232, 251–52; James F. Brooks, *Captives and Cousins: Slavery, Kinship, and Community in the Southwest Borderlands* (Chapel Hill: University of North Carolina Press, 2011), 50–51, 134–38, 236–37. Santiago indicates that at least some of the Apaches who passed through Guajoquilla in 1789 died, while soldiers likely distributed the rest to Spanish families. For a comparable scenario, see the fate of José Antonio Montes in Conrad, "Empire

through Kinship," 655–56. Spanish soldiers captured José Antonio as a young boy in a raid on an Apache camp, brought him to a small town, and sold him to Mariano Montes, who raised him.

12. Brooks, *Captives and Cousins*, 127–28, 133–34; Conrad, "Empire through Kinship," 655–56. For an interesting comparison between Apache slavery and African slavery in the colonies, see Conrad, "Captive Fates," 60–62. For an example of a woman willing her belongings to an Apache she had raised instead of her natural born child, see Laura M. Shelton, *For Tranquility and Order: Family and Community on Mexico's Northern Frontier, 1800–1850* (Tucson: University of Arizona Press, 2010), 130, 144–45. For an overview of Indian slavery in Spanish America, see Andrés Reséndez, *The Uncovered Story of Indian Enslavement in America* (Boston: Houghton Mifflin Harcourt, 2016).

13. "Noticias ulteriores del Apache," *Diario de México*, February 1, 1808 (quotation); Stockel, *On the Bloody Road to Jesus*, 82, 98–99; Edwin R. Sweeney, "Mangas Coloradas and Apache Diplomacy: Treaty-Making with Chihuahua and Sonora, 1842–1843," *The Journal of Arizona History* 39, no. 1 (1998): 1–22; Sarabia, "El Indio Rafael," 53–57; Francisco R. Almada, *Resumen geográfico del municipio de Jiménez* (Ciudad Juárez: Editorial el Labrador, 1961), 35; Bernal Vázquez, *Jiménez: 250 Años en lucha contra la adversidad*, 195–96. It was common for children who shared their parent's or adopted parent's name to add a diminutive "illo" to differentiate between themselves and their namesake. It was also common for Indians to adopt a diminutive version of a prominent Spaniard. The Navajo leader Manuelito is an example of this phenomenon. One Apache who was baptized by Francisco Hermenegildo Garces gained the unwieldy name Francisco Hermenegildo Herran. For another instance of an Apache adopting the name of the priest who taught them religion, see José Luis Mirafuentes Galván, "Los dos mundos de José Reyes Pozo," *Estudios de Historia Novohispana* 21 (2009): 71. For an Apache with a similar upbringing to Rafael, see José Francisco Zozaya to Nemesio Salcedo, August 4, 1805, Janos Presidio Collection, Benson Latin American Collection, University of Texas at Austin (hereafter cited as Janos Collection), Folder 17, Section 2. Zozaya was the previous commander of the Primera Compañia Volante. In this letter he requests that Commandant General Salcedo employ his Apache servant Francisco Nevares as a soldier. Zozaya says that Nevares had lived with the Spanish since he was five and he was a faithful Christian, except for occasionally playing cards. Rafael and Nevares's backgrounds are so similar, that if not for the name differences and the 1805 date on the promotion request, it would be reasonable to assume that they were one and the same. Roberto Martínez García supposes that Rafael arrived at Guajoquilla alongside his father and they both served as scouts for the presidio soldiers. See Roberto Martínez García, *Indios, mineros, peones y maestros: ensayos y breves relatos* (Torreón, Coahuila: Universidad Iberoamericana, 2001), 24.

14. José Francisco Rafael Baptismal Record, October 24, 1800, Archivo de la parroquia de Santo Cristo de Burgos, Bautismos, FHL (quotations); Buenaventura Nevares and Petra Urguiro Marriage Record, February 17, 1798, Archivo de la parroquia de Santo Cristo de Burgos, Matrimonios, FHL.

15. Bernal Vázquez, *Jiménez: 250 Años en lucha contra la adversidad*, 83. Bernal Vázquez cited parish records for San Bartolome when giving a birthdate in 1781. I looked at digital copies of these parish records for that year but was unable to find the referenced document. Guajoquilla would later be renamed Jiménez.

16. Sarabia, "El Indio Rafael," 60. Considering that society often elevates the social stature of beautiful people, Rafael's attractiveness might be one of the reasons for the pervasiveness of his legend. For example, it is unlikely that famed robbers Bonnie and Clyde would have achieved their level of notoriety had they not been physically fit and possessed symmetrical faces.

17. Daniel S. Matson and Bernard L. Fontana, eds., *Friar Bringas Reports to the King: Methods of Indoctrination on the Frontier of New Spain, 1796–1797* (Tucson: University of Arizona Press, 2017), 118; Babcock, *Apache Adaption to Spanish Rule*, 129–30. Babcock lists some 929 Apaches killed by the Spanish and 1,254 captured from 1778 to 1795. Five years are missing from this table, and the number of deaths in captivity and deaths at the hands of Comanches are unrecorded, so it is reasonable to assume more than two thousand Apaches died in combat during this time.

18. José Refugio De la Torre Curiel, *Twilight of the Mission Frontier: Shifting Interethnic Alliances and Social Organization in Sonora, 1768–1855* (Stanford, Calif.: Stanford University Press, 2012), 124. For example, on November 7, 1786, Ópata captive turned Apache chief José María González led his ranchería of Apaches to the Bacoachi presidio in what is now Sonora where he promised that his people would no longer attack the Spanish if they ceased their campaigns. The distance that Apaches lived away from establecimientos varied with time and level of trust the Spanish held to the Apache group, with some groups forced to live within eyesight of presidios and others at a greater distance. In 1794, Pedro de Nava implemented a thirty-mile perimeter requirement. See also Cortés, *Views from the Apache Frontier*, 28–29; José Francisco Velasco, *Noticias estadísticas del estado de Sonora* (Hermosillo: Gobierno del Estado de Sonora, 1985), 240; Griffen, *Apaches at War and Peace*, 54–57; Babcock, *Apache Adaptation to Hispanic Rule*, 177–79. Babcock is the most comprehensive treatment of the establecimientos. For an excellent summary of the establecimiento policy, see Santiago, *Jar of Severed Hands*, 58–59.

19. Moorhead, *The Presidio*, 261; Rick Hendricks and W. H. Timmons, *San Elizario: Spanish Presidio to Texas County Seat* (El Paso: Texas Western Press, 1998), 102–103.

20. Pedro de Nava, "Instructions for Dealing with Apaches at War and Peace," in Hendricks and Timmons, *San Elizario: Spanish Presidio to Texas County Seat*,

102–103. The commandant general who issued this quote is Pedro de Nava. Nava is an interesting historical character deserving of his own full-length study. The most in depth looks at his administration are Santiago, *A Bad Peace and a Good War,* and Leandro Martínez Peñas and Manuela Fernández Rodríguez, "La guerra contra los Apaches bajo el mando de Ramón de Castro y Pedro de Nava en las Provincias Interiores," *Revista de Historia Militar* III (July 2012): 119–58.

21. Comprobantes de gastos de apaches establecidos de paz de la primera compañía volante, 1800, Indiferente Virreinal, Carceles y Presidios, Archivo General de la Nación, México, digitized at http://www.gob.mex/agn/guiageneral (hereafter cited as AGN), C0583 (first quotation); Babcock, *Apache Adaptation to Hispanic Rule,* 262; Daniel S. Matson and Albert H. Schroeder, eds., "Cordero's Description of the Apaches, 1769," *New Mexico Historical Review* 32, no. 4 (1957): 341, 353 (second quotation on 353). This conclusion is based on Cordero's contention that Mimbreños settled at Carrizal and the 1800 census of Carrizal, which indicates that some of its Apaches were away at Guajoquilla. Rafael's Apache name containing a "Jasquie" also indicates that those who gave him the name were of Mimbreño origin. There are many arguments over what to call certain Apache groups, with some using "Southern Apache," "Chihene," the more modern "Chiricahua," traditional Apache names, and the Spanish names for specific bands. Considering that the identity of many of the Apaches discussed in this work are unknown and that there are still questions over Rafael's Apache affiliation, I use the generic "Apache" in most instances. When clarity is needed, I use "Mimbreños" or "Mimbres Apaches" to refer to Apaches from Carrizal.

22. Victor Orozco, *El estado de Chihuahua en el parto de la nación, 1810–1831* (Mexico City: Plaza y Valdés, 2007), 305; Babcock, *Apache Adaptation to Hispanic Rule,* 149–51; Elizabeth A. H. John and John Wheat, eds., "Views from a Desk in Chihuahua: Manuel Merino's Report on Apaches and Neighboring Nations, ca. 1804," *Southwestern Historical Quarterly* 95, no. 2 (1991): 166; Griffen, *Apaches at War and Peace,* 63. The numbers of Apaches de paz at the various establecimientos changed regularly due to many factors. The numbers given for the Janos, Carrizal, and El Paso establecimientos are for 1793. Apaches sometimes moved to different establecimientos to be closer to family members and considering how little we know about his early life, it is also possible that a relative wanted to be closer to Rafael.

23. De la Torre, *Twilight of the Mission Frontier,* 136.

24. Ibid., 135–38.

25. Ibid., 136.

26. Sarabia, "El Indio Rafael," 60 (quotation); José Antonio Baptismal Record, January 1802, Archivo de la parroquia de Santo Cristo de Burgos, Bautismos, FHL. Baptismal records show José Antonio's godfather to be José Antonio Lujan, "who he informed had obligation and parentage." It is possible that this Apache was not the same José Antonio, and the one who would later ride with Rafael never received a

baptism, as two contemporary newspapers reported that he was a gentile. I suspect that this is an error due to José Antonio never having adopted Catholicism to the level of Rafael. See "Continuacion de los donativos para zapatos y otros socorros en beneficio de los soldados del exército de la península," *Gaceta del Gobierno de México*, August 17, 1810 and "España," *Gaceta de la Regencia de España é Indias*, February 7, 1811.

27. Jesús María Rafael Baptismal Record, January 2, 1802, Archivo de la parroquia de Santo Cristo de Burgos, Bautismos, FHL; María Jesús Josefa Jiménez Baptismal Record, December 25, 1801, Archivo de la parroquia de Santo Cristo de Burgos, Bautismos, FHL (quotation); "Sucinta relación que manifiesta las muertes, cautiverios, robos y demás atrocidades causadas por los indios apaches Rafael y sus compañeros," Incident 2. Spanish soldiers would later say that Rafael's child was three to four in October 1804. Although a late 1801 or early 1802 birthday would mean Jesús María was a few months shy of this age, it would be reasonable to assume a soldier might make a wrong guess about a child's age. Baptismal records show no Apache child baptisms at Guajoquilla in 1800, however, a Spanish census of the Guajoquilla Apaches indicates that the number of criaturas or infants at the presidio increased by one from September to October 1800, but it has no indication of who parented the newborn. See Comprobantes de gastos de apaches establecidos de paz de la primera compañía volante, 1800, Indiferente Virreinal, Carceles y Presidios, AGN, C0583. I was unable to find a study of maternal death rates during childbirth in New Spain at this time, but it was high in neighboring United States. It is likely that the death rates were similar, and perhaps greater, among establecimiento Apaches. See Nancy Schrom Dye and Daniel Blake Smith, "Mother Love and Infant Death, 1750–1920," *Journal of American History* 73 (September 1986): 329–53. The final words in Jesús María's baptism entry are unclear but appear to contain the word "confte." This is not a shorthand with which I am familiar. J. Villasana Haggard lists "confirma" as one possible longform of "conf," but nothing for "confte." See J. Villasana Haggard, *Handbook for Translators of Spanish Historical Documents* (Austin: University of Texas Archives Collection, 1941), 51. Whether María Jesús Josefa died in childbirth, chose to sell the child out of a need for money or necessity, or Rafael encouraged her to allow the child to be raised by the Nevares family is unclear with extant evidence. For a discussion of Apaches selling children to be raised by Spaniards, see Babcock, *Apache Adaptation to Hispanic Rule*, 148.

28. "Noticias ulteriores del Apache," *Diario de México*, February 1, 1808 (quotation); Magnus Mörner, *Race Mixture in the History of Latin America* (Boston: Little, Brown, 1975), 22–23, 53–55, 58–62, 41–42; Martínez García, *Indios, mineros, peones y maestros*, 24.

29. Martínez García, *Indios, mineros, peones y maestros*, 23–24.

30. "Noticias ulteriores del Apache," *Diario de México*, February 1, 1808; Willem De Reuse to Bradley Folsom January 16, 2020 (email) (first quotation); Ignaz Pfefferkorn,

Sonora: A Description of the Province, Theodore E. Treutlein, trans. (Albuquerque: University of New Mexico Press, 1949), 145 (second quotation). De Ruese suggested the "datsil" modifier would mean "one who stands above" initially, but also thought the name to be similar to a White Mountain Apache whose name meant "One Who Is Angry All the Time." For a use of "datsil" as meaning an elevated position, see Chip Colwell Chanthaphonh, *Massacre at Camp Grant* (Tucson: University of Arizona Press, 2007), 67. For a comparable name meaning "One Who Is Angry All the Time," see Allan Radbourne, "Great Chief: Hashkeedasillaa of the White Mountain Apaches," *The Journal of Arizona History* 50 (Spring 2009): 7–8.

31. De la Torre, *Twilight of the Mission Frontier*, 135–38.

32. "Noticias ulteriores del Apache," *Diario de México*, February 1, 1808; "Sucinta relación que manifiesta las muertes, cautiverios, robos y demás atrocidades causadas por los indios apaches Rafael y sus compañeros," Incident 4, 19; Frederick Adolph Wislizenus, *Memoir of a Tour to Northern Mexico: Connected with Col. Doniphan's Expedition, in 1846 and 1847* (Washington, DC: Tippin & Streeper, 1848), 46; William L. Merrill, "La economía política de las correrías: Nueva Vizcaya al final de la época colonial" in Marie-Areti Hers, José Luis Mirafuentes, María de los Dolores Soto, and Miguel Vallebueno, eds., *Nómadas y sedentarios en el norte de México: Homenaje a Beatriz Braniff* (México: Universidad Nacional Autónoma de México, 2000): 644–45; Hendricks and Timmons, *San Elizario*, 33. Daniel D. Arreola argues that trade between establicimiento Apaches and unincorporated Apaches was "a black market unofficially sanctioned by Spanish authorities." See Daniel D. Arreola, "Chiricahua Apache Homeland in the Borderland Southwest," *Geographical Review* 102, no. 1 (2012): 121–22; Moorhead, *The Presidio*, 261–64.

33. Willem De Reuse to Bradley Folsom January 16, 2020 (email) (first quotation); "Noticias ulteriores del Apache," *Diario de México*, February 1, 1808; Salcedo and Vizcaya, *Instrucción reservada de don Nemesio Salcedo y Salcedo comandante general de provincias internas a su sucesor,* 40–41; Palmer, *The Apache Peoples*, 93–94; Sarabia, "El Indio Rafael," 60 (second quotation). Peter Ellis Bean refers to "chinces" as biting insects, but he does not use the term when referring to flies. See Ellis P. Bean, "Memoir of Ellis P. Bean" in Henderson K. Yoakum, *History of Texas: From Its First Settlement in 1685 to Its Annexation to the United States in 1846* (New York: Redfield, 1855), vol. 1, 419–21. It is also possible "Chinche" was a Spanish attempt to write an Apache name.

34. "Noticias ulteriores del Apache," *Diario de México*, February 1, 1808 (quotations); A Spanish report said that "Rafael, José Antonio and [Side] were those who were at peace at Guajoquilla," indicating that Chinche was a member of the band of Apaches de paz. "Sucinta relación que manifiesta las muertes, cautiverios, robos y demás atrocidades causadas por los indios apaches Rafael y sus compañeros," Incident 3. One author believed Chinche to be a woman, stating "El Indio Rafael was an Apache who started a band made up of himself, José Antonio, and a brave woman

with a pale face known as *La Chinche*." The author almost certainly confused Chinche with one of the various Indian women who would later join Rafael's band. See José Manuel Valenzuela Arce, *Entre la magica y la historia* (Tijuana: Programa Cultural de las Fronteras, El Colegio de la Frontera Norte, 1992), 44; Griffen, *Apaches at War and Peace*, 91. Chinche may have been the same "Chinchisé" who escaped a collera traveling from the Internal Provinces to Cuba and returned back to the north. The viceroy feared that they "once escaped, they would return to their countries of origin." See Noriega to Commandant General, January 13, 1806, AGN-PI, L200, R210. It is also possible that "Side" was actually "Sída," as he could have adopted the last name of local priest Juan José Sída. For more on Sída, see Almada, *Resumen Geográfico del municipio de Jiménez*, 39; Rosa María Fuantos Rebolloso, "El Santo Cristo de Burgos," *Sobre todo la fe: revista mensual de la diócesis de Parral* 1, no. 7 (August 2013), 12. See also, Merrill, "La Economía Política de las Correrías," 644–45.

35. Hendricks and Timmons, *San Elizario*, 103; "Noticias ulteriores del Apache," *Diario de México*, February 1, 1808; Santiago, *A Bad Peace and a Good War*, 161 (quotation). Although it is true that the Spanish overlooked minor theft and some trade with unincorporated Apaches, they tried to prevent trade with hostile Apaches when possible, especially when their raids resulted in the deaths of Spanish civilians. See Arreola, "Chiricahua Apache Homeland in the Borderland Southwest," 120–22.

36. Griffen, *Apaches at War and Peace*, 91–92; Pike, *Expeditions of Zebulon Montgomery Pike*, vol. 2, 752 (quotation).

37. Babcock, *Apache Adaptation to Hispanic Rule*, 149–50, 198–201; Hendrick and Timmons, *San Elizario*, 103; "Noticias ulteriores del Apache," *Diario de México*, February 1, 1808; Santiago, *The Jar of Severed Hands*, 51, 54; Pike, *The Expeditions of Zebulon Montgomery Pike*, vol. 2, 749. Per the orders of previous Commandant General Pedro de Nava, presidio commanders were to arrest establecimiento Apaches who participated in the murder of a Spaniard and put them on trial in a local court. The sitting commandant general ordered two Apaches shackled for rustling earlier in 1804. See Nemesio Salcedo to Janos Commander, May 3, 1804, Janos Collection, Folder 17, Section 1.

38. Clare V. McKanna Jr., *White Justice in Arizona: Apache Murder Trials in the Nineteenth Century* (Lubbock: Texas Tech University Press, 2005), 23–25; John Carey Cremony, *Life Among the Apaches: The Classic History of Native American Life on the Plains* (San Francisco: A. Roman, 1868), 170.

39. McKanna, *White Justice in Arizona*, 23–25.

40. Cutter, *Legal Culture in Northern New Spain*, 74–75, 109–31. As made clear in Cutter's work, the Spanish legal system was much more complicated than it is portrayed here. For perhaps the most concise and understandable synopsis of tribunals in New Spain, see Mílada Bazant, *Bestiality: The Nefarious Crime in Mexico, 1800–1856* (Oakland: University of California Press, 2016), 196, 198.

41. Stern, "Social Marginality and Acculturation," 260.

42. Ibid.

43. "Noticias ulteriores del Apache," *Diario de México*, February 1, 1808.

44. Ibid.

45. Ibid (first quotation); Blyth, *Chiricahua and Janos*, 20 (second and third quotations); Helge Ingstad, *The Apache Indians: In Search of the Missing Tribe* (Lincoln: University of Nebraska Press, 2004), 35, 72, 126 (fourth quotation on 35). The idea of an Apache brave dead set on vengeance for a perceived slight is one that would find a home in twentieth century fiction. Leah Candolin Cook, "The Last Apache 'Broncho': The Apache Outlaw in the Popular Imagination, 1886–2013," MA thesis, University of New Mexico, Albuquerque, 2014, 23–24.

46. Cortés, *Views from the Apache Frontier*, 28–29. This quote is from 1799, but the Spanish had recently passed new restrictions on Spanish subjects trading with the Apaches and rations had fallen by a quarter from 1803 to 1804. See Babcock, *Apache Adaptation to Hispanic Rule*, 184–85, 190.

47. Ernest Bouldin Harper, "Personality Types: A Note on Sociological Classification," *Social Science* 1, no. 1 (1925): 26–29. Rafael also may have been what sociologists refer to as "maladjusted" and no matter what treatment he received, he would not be able to adapt to social norms.

48. Julius Froebel, *Seven Years' Travel in Central America, Northern Mexico, and the Far West of the United States* (London: Richard Bentley, 1859), 354 (first quotation); Ober, *Travels in Mexico and Life Among the Mexicans*, 627 (second quotation). For a similar quotation, see J. R. Flippin, *Sketches from the Mountains of Mexico* (Cincinnati: Standard Publishing, 1889), 115–16. Flippin believed that "sooner will the Ethiopian change his kin, and the leopard his spots than gentle blood flow through such veins. Such bad blood can only be washed out after the lapse of generations. Text-books, tracts, and sermons won't do it, when he has murder in his heart, the torch, knife and rifle in his hand."

49. Contreras Palacios, *Antecedentes históricos a la fundación de el Torreón*, 140 (quotation); Martínez García, *Indios, mineros, peones y maestros*, 24; "Sucinta relación que manifiesta las muertes, cautiverios, robos y demás atrocidades causadas por los indios apaches Rafael y sus compañeros," Incident 2.

Chapter 2

1. Report of Captain of the Primera Compañía Volante, November 6, 1804, AHED, MF 492, R58 (quotations); "Sucinta relación que manifiesta las muertes, cautiverios, robos y demás atrocidades causadas por los indios apaches Rafael y sus compañeros," Incident 1; Guadalupe Villa "La vida con Villa en la Hacienda del Canutillo," *Bicentario*,

el ayer y hoy de México, no. 7. The November 6, 1804, report originated with the commander of the Primera Compañía Volante José María de la Riva, but Riva says he received the information from Teniente Miguel de Mesa. Mesa was attached to Namiquipa at the time, which was home to the Segunda Compañía Volante. It makes sense the soldiers would be from this company, as they would have recognized Rafael had they been stationed in Guajoquilla.

2. Report of Captain of the Primera Compañía Volante, November 6, 1804, AHED, MF492, R58.

3. Jones, *Los Paisanos*, 4; "Sucinta relación que manifiesta las muertes, cautiverios, robos y demás atrocidades causadas por los indios apaches Rafael y sus compañeros," Incident 1–3; Pike, *The Expeditions of Zebulon Montgomery Pike*, vol. 2, 752; Report of Captain of the Primera Compañía Volante, November 6, 1804, AHED, MF492, R58 (quotation).

4. "Sucinta relación que manifiesta las muertes, cautiverios, robos y demás atrocidades causadas por los indios apaches Rafael y sus compañeros," Incident 1; Donald Emmet Worcester, *The Apaches: Eagles of the Southwest* (Norman: University of Oklahoma Press, 1992), 8–9; Von Tempsky, *Mitla*, 80; Stockel, *On the Bloody Road to Jesus*, 89 (quotation); Santiago, *A Bad Peace and a Good War*, 94; Reuben Gold Thwaites, *Early Western Travels, 1748–1846*, vol. xx (Cleveland: Arthur H. Clark, 1905), 76–77; Babcock, *Apache Adaption to Hispanic Rule*, 125, 252–53; González Quiroga, *War and Peace of the Rio Grande*, 14–15. Canutillo is approximately fifty-five miles from Jiménez according to Google Maps, but because the hacienda was so large and its specific parameters in 1804 are unknown, the location of Rafael's raid cannot be determined with certainty. The hacienda would later become home to Pancho Villa. González Quiroga notes that illegal trade sometimes occurred directly with wealthy Spaniards, but also through poor intermediaries known as *tratantes*. In New Mexico, such traders were known as Comancheros. Contraband trading with plains Indians continued into the late eighteenth century because it was profitable. Apaches would sometimes trade multiple horses for a pound of sugar or salt. See also James Blackshear, *Fort Bascom: Soldiers, Comancheros, and Indians in the Canadian River Valley* (Norman: University of Oklahoma Press, 2016); Silvio R. Duncan Baretta and John Markoff, "Civilization and Barbarism: Cattle Frontiers in Latin America," *Comparative Studies in Society and History* 20 (October 1978): 604–605; Mary W. Helms, "Matrilocality, Social Solidarity, and Culture Contact: Three Case Histories," *Southwestern Journal of Anthropology* 26 (Summer 1970): 200–201.

5. Santiago, *A Bad Peace and a Good War*, 94; Babcock, *Apache Adaptation to Hispanic Rule*, 125.

6. "Sucinta relación que manifiesta las muertes, cautiverios, robos y demás atrocidades causadas por los indios apaches Rafael y sus compañeros," Incident 1–4 (quotation in Incident 1); Moorhead, *The Presidio*, 62–63; Babcock, *Apache Adaptation*

to Hispanic Rule, 110. The report is somewhat unclear when and where this attack took place, but the "day 3" identifier indicates that it was the third day after they left Guajoquilla.

7. Jones, *Los Paisanos*, 4; "Sucinta relación que manifiesta las muertes, cautiverios, robos y demás atrocidades causadas por los indios apaches Rafael y sus compañeros," Incident 1–3; Barbara L. Voss, *The Archaeology of Ethnogenesis: Race and Sexuality in Colonial San Francisco* (Berkeley: University of California Press, 2008), 254; Cortés, *Views from the Apache Frontier*, 59; Matson and Schroeder, "Cordero's Description of the Apaches, 1769," 339–40. Because paisanos were generally subsistence-level farmers and ranchers, they posed little threat to the Apaches and there was little to gain monetarily from their deaths.

8. "Sucinta relación que manifiesta las muertes, cautiverios, robos y demás atrocidades causadas por los indios apaches Rafael y sus compañeros," Incident 2 (quotation); Pfefferkorn, *Sonora: A Description of the Province*, 146–50; Relación de los individuos en la quarta compañía volante, May 12, 1802, Revistas de inspección, Provincias Internas, Archivo General de Simancas, digitized on *pares.mcu.es* (hereafter cited as SGU), L7047.

9. "Compañía Volante de S. Cárlos de Parras," *Gazeta de México* June 12, 1799; Larramendi Service Record, August 10, 1816, AGN-PI, L254, R248; Pedro Ruiz de Larramedi to Bernardo Bonavía, November 1, 1804, AHED, MF492, R58; "Sucinta relación que manifiesta las muertes, cautiverios, robos y demás atrocidades causadas por los indios apaches Rafael y sus compañeros," Incident 2.

10. "Sucinta relación que manifiesta las muertes, cautiverios, robos y demás atrocidades causadas por los indios apaches Rafael y sus compañeros," Incident 1–3 (quotation in Incident 2). Salcedo, *Instrucción reservada de don Nemesio Salcedo y Salcedo comandante general de provincias internas a su sucesor*, 40–41. The order of events in this section is confusing, and it is possible that some of the incidents took place on different dates or in a different chronological order than it is presented here.

11. Jesús de la Teja (ed.), "Murillo's Plan for the Reform of New Spain's Defenses," *Southwestern Historical Quarterly* 107 (April 2004): 502–504, 514 (quotation on 514). The soldiers' uniforms would have differed if they were from a standard presidio company or a flying company. For more on uniform requirements for the Spanish military, see Moorhead, *The Presidio*, 185–89.

12. Weber, *The Spanish Frontier in North America*, 217; Moorhead, *The Presidio*, 185–86; De la Teja, "Murillo's Plan for the Reform of New Spain's Defenses," 502–504, 514 (quotation on 514).

13. "Sucinta relación que manifiesta las muertes, cautiverios, robos y demás atrocidades causadas por los indios apaches Rafael y sus compañeros," Incident 3; Report of Captain of the Primera Compania Volante November 6, 1804, AHED, MF492, R58. Lance R. Blyth in his dissertation, "The Presidio of Janos: Ethnicity, Society,

Masculinity, and Ecology in Far Northern Mexico," includes an in-depth analysis of the racial composition of the presidio companies of northern New Spain. In 1800, for example, he found that the number of mestizo soldiers in the presidio of Janos to be around 50 percent. This number remained fairly consistent over the next decade. See Lance R. Blyth, "The Presidio of Janos: Ethnicity, Society, Masculinity, and Ecology in Far Northern Mexico, 1685–1858," PhD diss., Northern Arizona University, Flagstaff, 2005, 35–38.

14. "Sucinta relación que manifiesta las muertes, cautiverios, robos y demás atrocidades causadas por los indios apaches Rafael y sus compañeros," Incident 3.

15. Ibid., Incident 3 (quotation); Martínez García, *Indios, mineros, peones y maestros*, 24.

16. "Sucinta relación que manifiesta las muertes, cautiverios, robos y demás atrocidades causadas por los indios apaches Rafael y sus compañeros," Incident 4.

17. Ibid.; Octavio Fernández Perea, *Jiménez en la historia y en la leyenda* (Chihuahua: La Universidad Autónoma de Chihuahua, 2008), 34.

18. Pfefferkorn, *Sonora: A Description of the Province*, 101, 147 (quotation on 147); Fernández Perea, *Jiménez en la historia y en la leyenda*, 34; Andy Adams, *The Log of a Cowboy: A Narrative of the Old Trail Days* (Cambridge: Riverside Press, 1903), 140–51. Adams wrote *The Log of a Cowboy* as a work of fiction, but because he had based the story on his own personal experiences as a cattle driver for many years, many historians consider the work to be one of the best resources for history of cattle drives.

19. John and Wheat, "Views from a Desk in Chihuahua," 155–56 (quotation on 156); Matson and Schroeder, "Cordero's Description of the Apaches, 1769," 345–46; Thwaites, *Early Western Travels*, vol. xx, 75.

20. John and Wheat, "Views from a Desk in Chihuahua," 155–56; Pike, *The Expeditions of Zebulon Montgomery Pike*, vol. 2, 751; Adams, *The Log of a Cowboy*, 211–12; "Sucinta relación que manifiesta las muertes, cautiverios, robos y demás atrocidades causadas por los indios apaches Rafael y sus compañeros," Incident 4.

21. Wislizenus, *Memoir of a Tour to Northern Mexico*, 46.

22. Comprobantes de gastos y lista de los indios apaches establecidos de paz en el presidio del Carrizal, 1800, Indiferente Virreinal, Carceles y Presidios, AGN, C0583; John and Wheat, "Views from a Desk in Chihuahua," 166; Griffen, *Apaches at War and Peace*, 63; Comprobantes de gastos de apaches establecidos de paz de la primera compañía volante, 1800, Indiferente Virreinal, Carceles y Presidios, AGN, C0583. Records for Carrizal show the rancheria of Yculidillin at Guajoquilla in 1800.

23. "Sucinta relación que manifiesta las muertes, cautiverios, robos y demás atrocidades causadas por los indios apaches Rafael y sus compañeros," Incident 19 (quotation); Hendricks and Timmons, *San Elizario*, 33, 38; Griffen, *Apaches at War and Peace*, 90–91; Babcock, *Apache Adaptation to Hispanic Rule*, 125; Wislizenus, *Memoir of a Tour to Northern Mexico*, 46; Merrill, "La Economía Política de las Correrías,"

644–45; Velsaco, *Noticias estadísticas del estado de Sonora*, 268–69. Horses were the most desired commodity for Apaches. It was said that in Apache culture, "the value of any article is regulated by the number of horses which it may bring." See Cremony, *Life Among the Apaches*, 247.

24. "Sucinta relación que manifiesta las muertes, cautiverios, robos y demás atrocidades causadas por los indios apaches Rafael y sus compañeros," Incident 5. The spelling of Maynez's name varies from one source to the next. Merino writes it as "Maines," while Babcock uses "Maynez." Different variations including "Maynes" are found in primary sources.

25. Babcock, *Apache Adaption to Hispanic Rule*, 255–56, 275, 282; Griffen, *Apaches at War and Peace*, 90–91; "Sucinta relación que manifiesta las muertes, cautiverios, robos y demás atrocidades causadas por los indios apaches Rafael y sus compañeros," Incident 5. Merino does not list Ultin at being a chief at Carrizal in 1804. This could be because Ultin was a lesser chief, Merino was using outdated information, or Ultin had only become a chief after Merino completed his report. Ultin may also have been a derivation of the name "Ycugidillin" or the Apache name for Chief Manta Negra. See John and Wheat, "Views from a Desk in Chihuahua," 166. For another example of an Apache stealing a wife of another Apache see, W. Michael Farmer, *Apacheria: True Stories of Apache Culture* (Guilford, Conn: Twodot, 2017), 52, 100.

26. "Sucinta relación que manifiesta las muertes, cautiverios, robos y demás atrocidades causadas por los indios apaches Rafael y sus compañeros," Incident 5.

27. Ibid., Incident 5, 8, 13.

28. Cortés, *Views from the Apache Frontier,* 65 (quotation); Nelson A. Miles, *Personal Recollections of Observation of General Nelson A. Miles* (Chicago: Werner Company, 1896), 454–55; Martín Luis Guzmán, *Memoirs of Pancho Villa*, Virginia H. Taylor trans. (Austin: University of Texas Press, 1965), 6, 18. Pancho Villa once also used Cabeza de Oso as a hideout.

29. "Sucinta relación que manifiesta las muertes, cautiverios, robos y demás atrocidades causadas por los indios apaches Rafael y sus compañeros," Incident 8.

30. "Noticias ulteriores del Apache," *Diario de México*, February 1, 1808. This is the only detailed description of the type of technique Rafael used to catch his victims off guard. I suspect the ploy was more in depth, and he had more variations of the technique than what is presented in the article.

31. "Sucinta relación que manifiesta las muertes, cautiverios, robos y demás atrocidades causadas por los indios apaches Rafael y sus compañeros," Incident 7. For a definition of a "mozo," see R. F. Grigsby, *R. F. Grigsby's Sierra Madre Journal, 1864* (Sebastopol, Calif: Pleasant Hill Press, 1976), 25.

32. Lucas Valenzuela Service Record, 1817, AGN-PI, L256, R250 (first, second, and third quotations); Blyth, "Presidio of Janos," 47; Lista de individuos que toman, June 3, 1812, Janos Collection, Folder 20, Section 4; Destinos y presios de surprendas,

April 20, 1812, Janos Collection, Folder 20, Section 4; Revista de primera compañía volante, 1803, Provincias Internas, SGU, L7047. Valenzuela's service records list him as holding the informal "honrada," status meant to indicate that he was not from a noble family but had earned prestige through his actions in life.

33. Lucas Valenzuela Service Record, 1817, AGN-PI, L256, R250; Of the three Apache auxiliaries who have taken up with Lucas Valenzuela, July 3, 1800, Indifferent Virreinal, AGN, C0583.

34. "Sucinta relación que manifiesta las muertes, cautiverios, robos y demás atrocidades causadas por los indios apaches Rafael y sus compañeros," Incident 7, 8, 9 (first quotation in 8; second quotation in 7).

35. Martínez García, *Indios, mineros, peones y maestros*, 24; "The Apache Kid" *The Evening Bee*, January 16, 1897 (quotation).

36. Lucas Valenzuela Service Record, 1817, AGN-PI, L256, R250; Francisco Minjares Service Record, December 1812, Janos Collection, Folder 20, Section 4; Pike, *The Expeditions of Zebulon Montgomery Pike*, vol. 2, 752 (quotation).

37. "Sucinta relación que manifiesta las muertes, cautiverios, robos y demás atrocidades causadas por los indios apaches Rafael y sus compañeros," Incident 10, 13; Pfefferkorn, *Sonora: A Description of the Province*, 149 (quotation).

38. "Sucinta relación que manifiesta las muertes, cautiverios, robos y demás atrocidades causadas por los indios apaches Rafael y sus compañeros," Incident 10–13, 43 (quotation in Incident 11). The officer reporting these incidents says that the Apaches took four hostages on March 25. I believe he is confusing one event with two and that the Apaches only had three total hostages (four counting Ultin's wife), the mozo they captured on March 18 and the two they captured on March 25. The mozo would later say that it was only him, La India, Rafael, José Antonio, and Chinche for six days. Bustamante believed he was lying because of this discrepancy, but I believe he is telling a version of the truth. The two captives on March 25 would not have traveled with them for long before being liberated.

39. "Sucinta relación que manifiesta las muertes, cautiverios, robos y demás atrocidades causadas por los indios apaches Rafael y sus compañeros," Incident 43; Gary Clayton Anderson, *The Indian Southwest, 1580–1830: Ethnogenesis and Reinvention* (Norman: University of Oklahoma Press, 2009), 27; Cheryl English Martin, *Governance and Society in Colonial Mexico* (Stanford, Calif.: Stanford University Press, 1996), 152 (quotation).

40. Conrad, "Captive Fates," 46–47; Morris Edward Opler, *An Apache Life Way: The Economic, Social, and Religious Institutions of the Chiricahua Indians* (Lincoln: University of Nebraska Press, 1996), 349–51.

41. "Sucinta relación que manifiesta las muertes, cautiverios, robos y demás atrocidades causadas por los indios apaches Rafael y sus compañeros," Incident 12.

42. Pike, *The Expeditions of Zebulon Montgomery Pike*, vol. 2, 751.

43. "Sucinta relación que manifiesta las muertes, cautiverios, robos y demás atrocidades causadas por los indios apaches Rafael y sus compañeros," Incident 11, 12 and 13. Incident 13 contains information given to the Spanish by one of the captives. Although numbers in Bustamante's collection often do not add up, especially concerning stolen animals, the math appears to add up in this section. At the beginning of this round of raids, the Apaches had one horse. They then stole two in one raid and ten in another. Leal recovered nine, meaning that each member escaped with one horse.

44. "Sucinta relación que manifiesta las muertes, cautiverios, robos y demás atrocidades causadas por los indios apaches Rafael y sus compañeros," Incident 14. Laicano says that he was with the Apache band for twenty-two days. Because Rafael's band captured him on March 25, this indicates that he was the child riding with them in April, but Bustamante does not give an indication of when he was freed. It is possible that Laicano was among those rescued by Valenzuela, and the child on the horse was another unknown captive. There is also the possibility that Bustamante or the reporting soldiers provided the wrong dates. One report came secondhand from a cowboy who said only that the event occurred on "23," but he does not clarify if this was March 23 or April 23.

Chapter 3

1. Weber, *Spanish Frontier in North America*, 224–26.

2. Weber, *Spanish Frontier in North America*, 227–30; Escudero, *Observaciones sobre el estado actual del departamento de Chihuahua*, 14–16; Pekka K. Hämäläinen, *The Comanche Empire* (New Haven, Conn: Yale University Press, 2009), 131–32; Zuñiga, *Rápida ojeada al estado de Sonora*, 14 (first quotation); Matson and Fontana, *Friar Bringas Reports to the King*, 122 (second quotation). For an in depth look at two commandant generals with different ideas about Apache policy, see Moorhead, *The Apache Frontier*, 239–74.

3. Weber, *Spanish Frontier in North America*, 224–26.

4. James Alexander Robertson (ed.), *Louisiana under the Rule of Spain, France, and the United States, 1785–1807: Social, Economic, and Political Conditions of the Territory Represented in the Louisiana Purchase*, vol. 1 (Cleveland: Arthur H. Clark, 1911), 139–45; Luis Navarro García, *Las Provincias Internas en el siglo XIX* (Seville: Escuela de Estudios Hispano-Americanos, 1965), 26–30; Salcedo, *Instrucción reservada de don Nemesio Salcedo y Salcedo comandante general de provincias internas a su sucesor*, 42–44; "Casa Calvo to Salcedo, March 5, 1804" in Donald Jackson (ed.), *Letters of the Lewis and Clark Expedition, with Related Documents, 1783–1854* (Urbana: University of Illinois Press, 1978), 184–85; Isaac Joslin Cox, *The Early Exploration of Louisiana* (Cincinnati: University of Cincinnati Press, 1906), 23–24; John L. Kessell, "To Stop

Captain Merry: Spanish Efforts to Intercept Lewis and Clark," *New Mexico Historical Review* 81 (Spring 2006): 125, 128–30.

5. Denis Holladay Damico, "The Cebolleta Land Grant: Multicultural Cooperation and Contention," *Natural Resources Journal* 48 (Fall 2008): 966–67; Frank Driver Reeve, *Navajo Foreign Affairs, 1795–1846* (Tsaile, Ariz.: Navajo Community College Press, 1983), 109–11.

6. Griffen, *Apaches at War and Peace*, 91–92.

7. Reeve, *Navajo Foreign Affairs*, 113–14; Frank McNitt, *Navajo Wars: Military Campaigns, Slave Raids, and Reprisals* (Albuquerque: University of New Mexico Press, 1972), 41–43. There are two accounts of the battle. In Narbona's version, the occupants of the cave were primarily Navajo warriors who were actively fighting the Spanish. The second version says the cave occupants were old men, women, and children who wished to surrender to the Spanish, but Narbona ignored them. The Spanish employed a similar strategy years before when attacking a group of Mescaleros who had taken shelter in a cave, and Americans did the same later for a different group of Apaches. See Santiago, *A Bad Peace and A Good War*, 137–38; George Alexander Forsyth, *The Story of the Soldier* (New York: D. Appleton, 1909), 282–83.

8. Salcedo, *Instrucción reservada de don Nemesio Salcedo y Salcedo comandante general de provincias internas a su sucesor*, 40–41; Salcedo to Captains and Commanders of Nueva Vizcaya, November 19, 1804, AHED, MF492, R58 (quotation). Unfortunately, this document is severely damaged, so it is unclear if Salcedo's orders were specifically for Rafael, or if this was a general proclamation concerning all Apaches.

9. Salcedo Proclamation, April 5, 1805, AHP, R1791a.

10. Cutter, *The Legal Culture of Northern New Spain*, 54–56, 130–31, 137–38. Cutter cites a study where only 1 person in 265 criminal cases in 1798 received the death penalty; Yoakum, *History of Texas*, vol. I, 412–16; Ernest R. Liljegren, "Zalmon Coley: The Second Anglo-American in Santa Fe," *New Mexico Historical Review* 62, no. 3 (July 1987): 277–78. To choose the American among the first group who would die, Salcedo had the remaining prisoners roll dice on a drum. Salcedo required the conspirators to serve in frontier presidios instead of facing the death penalty. Of course, Salcedo would later become famous for overseeing revolutionary leader Miguel Hidalgo's trial and subsequent execution by firing squad, so he was willing to authorize a death penalty. He just preferred to avoid it.

11. Pliny Earle Goddard, *Jicarilla Apache Texts* (New York: The Trustees, 1911), 270; Edmund Andrews, "Military Surgery among the Apache Indians," *The Chicago Medical Examiner* 10 (1869), 599–601; Barrett, *Geronimo's Story of His Life*, 24.

12. Goddard, *Jicarilla Apache Texts*, 270; Andrews, "Military Surgery among the Apache Indians," 599–601; Barrett, *Geronimo's Story of His Life*, 23–24 (quotation on 23).

13. "Sucinta relación que manifiesta las muertes, cautiverios, robos y demás atrocidades causadas por los indios apaches Rafael y sus compañeros," Incident 16. Considering that these dates are based on when soldiers learned of the incidents, it is possible that these series of attacks happened in a different chronological order. Bustamante indicates that Mendoza was captured later in October and that there was only one person killed in the attack. However, death records show "Apaches" as having killed Bernardo and Ramón Mendoza by October 2, 1805. I suspect that the reason for this discrepancy is that Spanish officials learned about the deaths secondhand at a later time. It is possible, although unlikely, that these Mendozas were unrelated to the kidnapped José Rafael Antonio, they died in a separate incident from the kidnapping, or they were killed by different Apaches. See Bernardo Mendoza Burial Record, October 2, 1805,, Satevó, Chihuahua, Defunciones, FHL and Ramón Mendoza Burial Record, October 2, 1805, Satevó, Chihuahua, Defunciones, FHL.

14. Ibid. Santa Cruz de Valerio was likely today's Santa Cruz, Chihuahua.

15. Ibid., Incident 17. Prudencio Baca Burial Record, October 13, 1805, San Pedro, Chihuahua, Defunciones, FHL; Adulto no conocido Burial Record, October 13, 1805, San Pedro, Chihuahua, Defunciones, FHL; Salvador de los Santos Burial Record, October 14, 1805, Cerro Gordo, Chihuahua, Defunciones, FHL; Antonio Delgado Burial Record, October 14, 1805, Cerro Gordo, Chihuahua, Defunciones, FHL; Albino Trejo Burial Record, October 14, 1805, Cerro Gordo, Chihuahua, Defunciones, FHL. Unfortunately, this section of Bustamante's report is very confusing about geography. Bustamante says their attacks occurred near "la Boquilla, cerca de la Laguna." There is the region of Laguna, and there are multiple lakes this could be referring to, as well as multiple towns in Chihuahua with "Boquilla" and "Laguna" in their names. Because of the previous references to Carrizal and Carmen, and that a home nearby was called Eusinillas, I believe this to be Lake Encinillas. For more on the geography of the area, see John Russell Bartlett, *Personal Narrative of Exploration and Incidents in Texas, New Mexico, California, Sonora, and Chihuahua*, vol. 2 (New York: D. Appleton, 1854), 406–18.

16. "Sucinta relación que manifiesta las muertes, cautiverios, robos y demás atrocidades causadas por los indios apaches Rafael y sus compañeros," Incident 15, 17; Michael P. Marshall, "Journal of Reconnaissance of the Camino Real," in *El Camino Real de tierra adentro*, vol. 2 (Santa Fe, NM: Bureau of Land Management, 1999), 25. There are multiple haciendas in Chihuahua named "Carmen" and multiple place names that contain the word "Carmen." I believe this refers to the hacienda just outside of Carrizal. Carrizal sat just south of El Paso and Nueva Vizcaya's border with New Mexico, with some officials regarding the small settlement as part of New Mexico.

17. Bernardo Bonavía to Justicias de la Cordillera, October 29, 1805, AHP, R1791a; Bernardo Bonavía to Justicias de la Cordillera, November 5, 1805, AHP, R1791a.

18. Ibid. (quotation).

19. "Sucinta relación que manifiesta las muertes, cautiverios, robos y demás atrocidades causadas por los indios apaches Rafael y sus compañeros," Incident 15; Salcedo, *Instrucción reservada de don Nemesio Salcedo y Salcedo comandante general de provincias internas a su successor*, 40–41, 73. Whenever conducting criminal investigations, Spanish officials generally asked witnesses to describe in detail the circumstances of any crimes they had seen committed, and these answers were recorded and used when sentencing perpetrators. It is possible that Bustamante used a testimony from Ultin to fill out his report. As will be discussed in following chapters, the Spanish treated Apache captives differently than they treated non-Apaches. See Cutter, *The Legal Culture of Northern New Spain*, 116.

20. Griffen, *Apaches at War and Peace*, 90–91, 95 (quotation on 91).

21. Salcedo, *Instrucción reservada de don Nemesio Salcedo y Salcedo comandante general de provincias internas a su sucesor*, 20.

22. For a version of the bell story, see Francisco Mendiola Galván, *El arte rupestre en Chihuahua expresión cultural de nómadas y sedentarios en el norte de México* (Chihuahua: Instituto Chihuahuense de la Cultura, 2002), 66. There is a similar story about a Sierra del Tambor, so named because Apache drums would resonate off the mountains and could be heard in the town of Santa Ysabel below. See "A Trip from Chihuahua to the Sierra Madre," *Putnam's Monthly Magazine*, July to December 1854, 412. There is a cave in the Sierra la Campana near Encinillas called Cueva del Indio. Local legends describe Rafael as having frequented a "Cueva del Indio" during his raids, but it is unclear if this is the same cave, as there is also a "Cueva del Indio" closer to Torreón that is a more likely candidate. Because the first recorded story of Rafael's cave comes from the early twentieth century, the legend may be untrue, and Rafael may not have used either cave. See Eduardo Guerra, *Historia de la Laguna, Torreón, su origen y sus fundadores* (Torreón: Impresora de Coahuila, 1932), 326

23. Jackson, *Following the Royal Road*, xi, xvi–xvii; Max L. Moorhead, *New Mexico's Royal Road: Trade and Travel on the Chihuahua Trail* (Norman: University of Oklahoma Press, 1958), 3.

24. Pedro Bautista Pino, *The Exposition on the Province of New Mexico, 1812* (Albuquerque: University of New Mexico Press, 1995), 54; Moorhead, *New Mexico's Royal Road*, 28–29, 32–33, 41–46; George Wilkins Kendall, *Narrative of the Texas Santa Fe Expedition Comprising a Description of a Tour through Texas and across the Great Southwestern Prairies, the Comanche and Caygüa Hunting-Grounds, with an Account of the Sufferings from Want of Food, Losses from Hostile Indians and Final Capture of the Texans, and Their March, as Prisoners, to the City of Mexico*, vol. 2 (New York: Harper and Brothers, 1845), 43–44.

25. Wislizenus, *Memoir of a Tour to Northern Mexico*, 42–43; Humboldt, *Political Essay on the Kingdom of New Spain*, vol. IV, 1–3, 14. Things were even more difficult for

the mules. They often carried 300 pounds of goods and, owing to the dry environment of New Mexico and Nueva Vizcaya, they had to go long distances with little in the way of pasturage and water. For a description of hacienda stores, see Kendall, *Narrative of the Texas Santa Fe Expedition*, vol. 2, 44, 112 and Frederick Schwatka, *In the Land of the Cliff Dwellers* (Boston: Educational Publishing, 1899), 72–73.

26. Humboldt, *Political Essay on the Kingdom of New Spain*, vol. IV, 1–3, 14; "Sucinta relación que manifiesta las muertes, cautiverios, robos y demás atrocidades causadas por los indios apaches Rafael y sus compañeros," Incident 17; Moorhead, *New Mexico's Royal Road*, 43. Moorhead says that the fair came into operation in 1806, but a letter written by Salcedo indicates that it happened before this date. See Salcedo Proclamation, April 10, 1804, Béxar Archives Microfilm Collection at the University of Texas at Arlington (hereafter cited as BA), R34; Edward K. Flagler, "Comercio y ferias de trueque: España y los indios de Nuevo México," *Revista Española de Antropología Americana* 37, no. 1 (2007): 51–65.

27. Salcedo, *Instrucción reservada de don Nemesio Salcedo y Salcedo comandante general de provincias internas a su sucesor*, 40–41; "Sucinta relación que manifiesta las muertes, cautiverios, robos y demás atrocidades causadas por los indios apaches Rafael y sus compañeros," Incident 17, 18. For an example of a traveling party sending muleteers ahead to procure supplies, see Josiah Gregg, *Commerce of the Prairies*, vol. 2 (New York: Henry G. Langley, and Astor House, 1844), 123–24 and Pino, *Exposition on the Province of New Mexico*, 54–55.

28. "Sucinta relación que manifiesta las muertes, cautiverios, robos y demás atrocidades causadas por los indios apaches Rafael y sus compañeros," Incident 18. Bustamante reported that they captured two additional prisoners here and one was let go. I suspect one of the prisoners was the same one Bustamante lists as captured at San Andres.

29. Ibid.

30. Pike, *The Expeditions of Zebulon Montgomery Pike*, 751.

31. "Sucinta relación que manifiesta las muertes, cautiverios, robos y demás atrocidades causadas por los indios apaches Rafael y sus compañeros," Incident 19; Daniel and Fuenta, "Diary of Pedro José de la Fuente," 278 (quotation); Lockwood, *The Apache Indians*, 18. The poor range of soldiers' muskets and the inability of military leadership to provide soldiers with efficient weapons and sufficient ammunition would continue to be a problem for those combating Apaches throughout most of the nineteenth century. As one observer noted, "The musket is second hand, and seldom serviceable for sharp-shooting, the only method effectual against the Indian. The red man feels reverence for the rifle only. This disadvantage in the arming of the soldiers, which might be partly bettered by their naturally keen eyesight, is increased by the little practice Government allows them for becoming good marksmen. Ball-cartridges are never plentiful with them, and they are economised to be almost entirely thrown away in action." See Von Tempsky, *Mitla*, 88.

32. "Sucinta relación que manifiesta las muertes, cautiverios, robos y demás atrocidades causadas por los indios apaches Rafael y sus compañeros," Incident 19.

33. Charles P. Elliott, "An Indian Reservation under General George Crook," *Military Affairs* 23 (Summer 1948): 101 (first quotation); Miles, *Personal Recollections of Observations of General Nelson A. Miles*, 446–47 (second quotation on 447). Henrietta Stockel argued that Apaches turning on their kin was not the norm until the Spanish offered a reward for bringing in the head of any Apache who refused to enter the establecimientos. The killing was less about the reward and more of a realization that additional Apaches at the establecimientos meant fewer rations for those who were already there. See Stockel, *On the Bloody Road to Jesus*, 93–94.

34. "Sucinta relación que manifiesta las muertes, cautiverios, robos y demás atrocidades causadas por los indios apaches Rafael y sus compañeros," Incident 19.

35. Ibid. La Noria was a nearby cattle ranch. See Lawrence Kinnaird, *The Frontiers of New Spain: Nicolas de Lafora's Description* (Berkeley, Calif.: Quivira Society, 1958), 139.

36. Pfefferkorn, *Sonora: A Description of the Province*, 149; Matson and Fontana, *Friar Bringas Reports to the King*, 120.

37. Matson and Fontana, *Friar Bringas Reports to the King*, 120. See also Mathew Babcock, "Turning Apaches into Spaniards: North America's Forgotten Indian Reservations," PhD diss., Dallas, Texas, Southern Methodist University, 2008, 212–13.

38. "Sucinta relación que manifiesta las muertes, cautiverios, robos y demás atrocidades causadas por los indios apaches Rafael y sus compañeros," Incident 20; Jones, *Los Paisanos*, 92. Humboldt, *Political Essay on the Kingdom of New Spain*, vol. II, 247-51

39. "Sucinta relación que manifiesta las muertes, cautiverios, robos y demás atrocidades causadas por los indios apaches Rafael y sus compañeros," Incident 20. For a nineteenth-century recipe for marquesotes de rosa, see *Diccionario de cocina, o el Nuevo cocinero Mejicano, en forma de diccionario* (Mexico D. F.: Imprenta de I. Cumplido, 1845), 59, 575–76, 587.

40. Jorge Chávez Chávez, "Retrato del Indio Bárbaro. Proceso de Justificación de la Barbarie de los Indios del Septentrión Mexicano y Formación de la Cultura Norteña," *New Mexico Historical Review* 73, no. 4 (October 1998): 415–16 (quotations on 415 and 416). Chávez Chávez goes more in depth when explaining the shift from killing for vengeance and material goods to killing for survival. He marks the time when the Spanish government placed a bounty on Rafael as the point this took place, and he seems to indicate that the Apaches only killed when bounty hunters sought them out or when they needed items for survival. I see no evidence that any shift happened at this time, as Rafael and José Antonio would kill numerous women and children who had little to offer them in terms of survival and who posed no threat to the band. Perhaps with more evidence this argument could be made about the band after 1808, but not in 1805–1806 as Chávez Chávez argues.

41. Francisco Velasco, *Noticias estadísticas del estado de Sonora*, 266–67; Guzmán, *Memoirs of Pancho Villa*, 5. Apache women were usually the ones who planted and picked corn, so it is unclear if the three men knew the basics of agriculture. Even if they did, it is doubtful they could have conducted a successful harvest while on the run.

42. Hämäläinen, *Comanche Empire*, 31–32; Grant D. Brinkworth, Jonathan D. Buckley, Manny Noakes, Peter M. Clifton, Carlene J. Wilson, "Long-Term Effects of a Very Low-Carbohydrate Diet and a Low-Fat Diet on Mood and Cognitive Function," *Archives of Internal Medicine* 169 (November 9, 2009): 1873–1880; Guzmán, *Memoirs of Pancho Villa*, 10–11 (quotation on 10). The incident upset Villa, and he refused to ride with Solís any longer. If Rafael, José Antonio, and Chinche were able to eat protein but not carbohydrates, they may have experienced protein poisoning, which occurs when protein makes up more than 40 percent of a person's dietary intake. Hämäläinen, contends that, in many ways, the conflict between the Comanches, Apaches, and Spanish can be explained as a war for access to carbohydrates.

43. Francisco Velasco, *Noticias estadísticas del estado de Sonora*, 266. Francisco Velasco borrows heavily from Antonio Cordero and José Cortés's descriptions of the Apaches in Matson and Schroeder, "Cordero's Description of the Apaches, 1769," 338; and Cortés, *Views from the Apache Frontier*, 58. However, he adds the description about personally witnessing what an Apache could eat in a single sitting. See also John and Wheat, "Views from the Apache Frontier," 58; José Francisco Velasco, *Sonora: Its Extent, Population, Natural Productions, Indian Tribes, Mines, Mineral, Lands, etc., etc.* William F. Nye (trans.) (San Francisco: H. H. Bancroft, 1861), 159; and Edwin Eastman, *Seven and Nine Years among the Camanches and Apaches: An Autobiography* (Jersey City, NJ: Clark Johnson, M.D., 1874), 240–41. Eastman said of the Apaches' propensity to overeat: "I often thought how happy those brutes would be if they were only endowed with the wonderful attributes of that little sea monster, the polyp, who, when his body is cut in half, suffers no inconvenience, but gormandizes as much as ever, with this advantage, that the food, instead of remaining in his stomach, passes out at the other end; thus allowing him to indulge in the pleasure of gluttony, without the inconvenience of being gorged" (quotation on 241).

44. "Sucinta relación que manifiesta las muertes, cautiverios, robos y demás atrocidades causadas por los indios apaches Rafael y sus compañeros," Incident 21, 22, 23; Lucas Valenzuela to Nemesio Salcedo, January 4, 1806, AHP, R1791a; Ygnacio Ontio Burial Record, Archivo de la parroquia de Santo Cristo de Burgos, Defunciones, FHL (quotation); "Sucinta relación que manifiesta las muertes, cautiverios, robos y demás atrocidades causadas por los indios apaches Rafael y sus compañeros," Incident 21, 22, 23, 24; Lucas Valenzuela to Nemesio Salcedo, January 4, 1806, AHP, R1791a. The Hacienda de Dolores was an eighty-nine-thousand-acre, government run ranch that Spain had expropriated from the Jesuits following their expulsion in 1767. The

hacienda provided cattle for rations for estableicimientos de paz. In 1806, it was run by the same Juan José Ruiz de Bustamante who would later assemble the report on Rafael's activities. There is some discrepancy between Bustamante and other sources. Bustamante gives the date of the attack as January 7 and says that the Apaches killed two people. Bustamante has three reports from January 7, two from Valenzuela and one from Mariano Varela. Varela reported that the Apaches had killed a cowboy and kidnapped a boy at Zanja. The first Valenzuela report indicates that the Apaches killed a cowboy at Zanja but says nothing about a kidnapping. The second says they killed a cowboy and kidnapped a child but does not give the location as Zanja. For whatever reason, Bustamante understood that Valenzuela was talking about the same person in his letters, but he did not make the connection that the man from the Varela report might be the same person reported by Valenzuela. This is seemingly confirmed by the Valenzuela letter in the Parral archives that only mentions one death and the Parish records from Guajoquilla that only list "Ygnacio Ontio," likely Ignacio Ontiveros, as having died around this date. However, considering that Bustamante was actually in charge of the Hacienda de Dolores at the time of the murder, it is possible that he recorded two murders because he had personal knowledge that a second one had occurred. See H. Bradley Benedict, "Hacienda Management in Late Colonial Northern Mexico: A Case Study of Juan Bustamante and the Hacienda of Dolores, 1790–1820," *Proceedings of the American Philosophical Society* 123, no. 6 (December 1979): 391–92.

45. Lucas Valenzuela to Nemesio Salcedo, January 4, 1806, AHP, R1791a; Mariano Varela Ramírez would later escort American Zebulon Pike to the United States, become lieutenant governor of Nueva Vizcaya, and help capture Miguel Hidalgo. See Lucas Martínez Sánchez, *Hidalgo y los insurgentes en la provincia de Coahuila* (Saltillo: Consejo Editorial del Estado, 2015), 509–10.

46. Lucas Valenzuela to Nemesio Salcedo, January 4, 1806, AHP, R1791a (quotations); "Sucinta relación que manifiesta las muertes, cautiverios, robos y demás atrocidades causadas por los indios apaches Rafael y sus compañeros," Incident 21, 22, 23.

47. "Sucinta relación que manifiesta las muertes, cautiverios, robos y demás atrocidades causadas por los indios apaches Rafael y sus compañeros," Incident 21, 22, 23; Lucas Valenzuela to Nemesio Salcedo, January 4, 1806, AHP, R1791a (quotations). Valenzuela's exact words were "por lo que cada uno esponga a serca del asunto."

48. Salcedo to José Perfecto Garnica, February 16, 1806, AHP, R1791a.

49. Lockwood, *The Apache Indians*, 19; Salcedo, *Instrucción reservada de don Nemesio Salcedo y Salcedo comandante general de provincias internas a su sucesor*, 34–35; Babcock, "Turning Apaches into Spaniards," 274. Since at least 1761, Spanish officials had been calling for Spain to provide presidio soldiers with "guns of long range" to be dispatched to New Spain for service against the Apaches.

50. W. Michael Mathes, "Arms for the Defense of the Eastern Provincias Internas of New Spain: A Mountain Cannon," *Colonial Latin American Historical Review* 6,

no. 3 (1997): 272–73; Stephen Harding Hart and Archer Butler Hulbert (eds.), *The Southwestern Journals of Zebulon Pike* (Albuquerque: University of New Mexico Press, 2006), 218.

51. Mathes, "Arms for the Defense of the Eastern Provincias Internas," 271–72 (quotation on 272); Salcedo, *Instrucción reservada de don Nemesio Salcedo y Salcedo comandante general de provincias internas a su sucesor,* 34–35.

52. Salcedo, *Instrucción reservada de don Nemesio Salcedo y Salcedo comandante general de provincias internas a su sucesor,* 34–35. For more on the difficulties in arming the people of the Internal Provinces, see Alonso Domínguez Rascón, "Autonomia, Insurgencia y oligarquía: Las Provincias Internas y la formación de los estados septentrionales," *Historia Mexicana* 66, no. 3 (2017): 1023–1075, and Juan Ramón de Andrés Martín, "La reacción realista en las Provincias Internas de Oriente ante el inicio del proceso de independencia de México (1808–1810)," *Aportes* 86, no. 3 (2014): 14.

Chapter 4

1. "Sucinta relación que manifiesta las muertes, cautiverios, robos y demás atrocidades causadas por los indios apaches Rafael y sus compañeros," Incident 24.

2. Cordero, "Cordero's Description of the Apaches," 353; Cortés, *Views from the Spanish Frontier*, 52, 58–60, 71–72.

3. "Sucinta relación que manifiesta las muertes, cautiverios, robos y demás atrocidades causadas por los indios apaches Rafael y sus compañeros," Incident 22, 24; Santiago, *A Bad Peace and a Good War*, 98.

4. "Sucinta relación que manifiesta las muertes, cautiverios, robos y demás atrocidades causadas por los indios apaches Rafael y sus compañeros," Incident 24.

5. Sucinta relación que manifiesta las muertes, cautiverios, robos y demás atrocidades causadas por los indios apaches Rafael y sus compañeros," Introduction, Conclusion.

6. José de la Cruz Pacheco Rojas, *Durango: historia breve* (Mexico City: Fondo de Cultura Económica 2001), chapter VIII; Ochoa Zazueta, *Apostillas de los Tepehuanes*, 68–70; Paul Conrad, "Empire through Kinship," 637–38. Pacheco Rojas may be confused between El Indio Rafael and El Cautivo Rafael, who was supposedly a Spaniard who had been captured and raised by either Apaches or Comanches and then abandoned when he developed arthritis. For a version of the El Cautivo Legend, see Carlos Sotelo, *Ensalada de historias y cuentos* (Bloomington, Ind.: Palibrio, 2012), 63. Sucinta relación que manifiesta las muertes, cautiverios, robos y demás atrocidades causadas por los indios apaches Rafael y sus compañeros," Introduction, Conclusion.

7. John and Wheat, "Views from a Desk in Chihuahua," 166. Enrique Vega Galindo, "El Indio Rafael," *Primera Plana* (Hermosillo), December 17, 2015; "Noticias ulteriores

del Apache," *Diario de México*, February 1, 1808 (quotation); Matson and Schroeder, "Cordero's Description of the Apache," 336; Sweeney, *Mangas Coloradas*, 4. At the time of this assessment, all European nations used longitude to mark their maps, but they could not agree upon where to begin counting. The British advocated a Greenwich Meridian because it was in their home country, but the Spanish refused to recognize the Greenwich Meridian established by the British and instead followed the Dutch practice of using the Spanish-controlled Canary Islands as a longitude marker. In addition, the Dutch only counted longitude east from Tenerife, not east and west as the British did with the Greenwich Meridian. These coordinates stretch from Taos, New Mexico in the north; Truth or Consequences, New Mexico in the west; Roswell, New Mexico to the east; and a still largely unpopulated area of the state of Chihuahua to the south. It is possible that Rafael was a White Mountain Apache considering that there was a White Mountain Apache with a very similar Apache name to Rafael's. The chief was prominent long after Rafael's death, so he was not Rafael, but members of the same band sometimes use the name of those who came before. See Radbourne, "Great Chief: Hashkeedasillaa of the White Mountain Apaches," 7–8. Linguist Willem De Reuse thinks Rafael's Apache name might indicate that he was a Cibecue Apache, although he noted the near impossibility in determining a specific nation of Apache based only on the Spanish spelling of Rafael's name. See Willem De Reuse to Bradley Folsom January 16, 2020 (email).

8. "Sucinta relación que manifiesta las muertes, cautiverios, robos y demás atrocidades causadas por los indios apaches Rafael y sus compañeros," Conclusion (quotation); Bethel Coopwood, "Route of Cabeza de Vaca: Part III," *Quarterly of the Texas State Historical Association* 3 (April 1900), 236; Juan Pedro Walker, "Map of the Route Through New Mexico," 1805, Huntington Manuscripts (Huntington Library, San Marino, California), 2049; Luis Alfonso Velasco, *Geografía y estadística de la republica Mexicana*, vol. XIX (México D. F.: Oficina Tipográfica de la Secretaría de Fomento, 1897), 23–26, 111–12 (quotation on p. 25). The untranslated text in the conclusion is from Merino, not Bustamante. He says "en la sierra de Cívolo, al Este del Estado, situada en el desierto oriental, que hoy pertenece á los Estados Unidos del Norte." Merino was located in Chihuahua when he assembled *Apuntes historicos* in 1856, and shortly before that time, the United States had annexed Texas and then taken what are now parts of Texas, New Mexico, Arizona, and California from Mexico in the U.S.-Mexico War. I suspect that the name Sierra Diablo, which continues to be used for a mountain range in West Texas is a misreading of "Cíbolo." For example, the "C" in Walker's 1805 map can easily be misconstrued as a "D." Because of this, it is also possible that Rafael was born in the Sierra Diablo, north of the Davis Mountains. Luis Alfonso Velasco's *Geografía y estadística de la republica Mexicana* from the nineteenth century notes that "las Sierras del Cibolo, which form irregular groups from the Rio Grande to Puente de Riesgo, north of the Sierra del Burro, and in it is

the great gap (quiebra) called Puente del Cíbolo, where the Arroyo of the same name passes." For a Walker map with Cibolo Creek labeled, see Israel Mendoza Levario, *A Brief Chronicle of Presidio del Norte: Homeland of the Jumano* (Austin: La Junta Press, 2012), 11. Also speaking to a Mescalero origin, Rafael would later inquire about an Apache named "Esquilnote" when speaking with a Spanish officer, indicating that the two were acquaintances. The word ES-KAL-TIN means chief in Mescalero and the name Esquilnote bears a resemblance to a Mescalero Apache chief named Esquin-yóe who lived in the area where Rafael was reported to have originated. See, "Sucinta relación que manifiesta las muertes, cautiverios, robos y demás atrocidades causadas por los indios apaches Rafael y sus compañeros," Incident 27; Santiago, *A Bad Peace and a Good War*, 64

9. Cortés, *Views from the Apache Frontier*, 137 (quotation); Matson and Schroeder, "Cordero's Description of the Apache," 351–55.

10. Martínez García, *Indios, mineros, peones y maestros*, 25–26; "Sucinta relación que manifiesta las muertes, cautiverios, robos y demás atrocidades causadas por los indios apaches Rafael y sus compañeros," Incident 24; Grenville Goodwin, *The Social Organization of the Western Apache* (Tucson: University of Arizona Press, 1969), 84–85.

11. "Sucinta relación que manifiesta las muertes, cautiverios, robos y demás atrocidades causadas por los indios apaches Rafael y sus compañeros," Incident 24.

12. Radbourne, "Great Chief: Hashkeedasillaa of the White Mountain Apaches," 7–8 (first quotation on 7; second and third quotations on 8).

13. "Sucinta relación que manifiesta las muertes, cautiverios, robos y demás atrocidades causadas por los indios apaches Rafael y sus compañeros," Incident 24; Martínez García, *Indios, mineros, peones y maestros*, 25–26. Unfortunately, this particular section of Bustamante's report is very brief and devoid of detail, so this encounter may have happened differently than it is portrayed here. I assumed that Rafael and José Antonio escaped on a Mescalero horse because the report mentions that they left with some of the Mescalero's firearms and ammunition. It is possible they acquired this ammunition through trade before the fighting began, and a disagreement over trading might have led to the violence.

14. "Sucinta relación que manifiesta las muertes, cautiverios, robos y demás atrocidades causadas por los indios apaches Rafael y sus compañeros," Incident 24–25; Lisa M. Hodgetts, "Faunal Evidence from El Zurdo," *Kiva* 62, no. 2 (1996): 149. The specific area is described as the Puerto de los Magueyes.

15. "Sucinta relación que manifiesta las muertes, cautiverios, robos y demás atrocidades causadas por los indios apaches Rafael y sus compañeros," Incident 25.

16. Ibid., Incident 25, 26.

17. Cortés, *Views from the Apache Frontier*, 77–78 (quotations on 78). Apaches also mourned by conducting a funeral. This sometimes involved placing the deceased in a gully and covering the body with stone, while other times, they scattered sticks on the

deceased until only its eyes were visible and lit the pyre on fire. Although this would not have been an option for Rafael and José Antonio, they may have cut their hair in misery and gone for days refusing to eat or speak Chinche's name.

18. Warren King Moorehead, *The American Indian in the United States, Period 1850–1914* (Freeport, NY: Books for Libraries Press, 1969), 235.

19. "Sucinta relación que manifiesta las muertes, cautiverios, robos y demás atrocidades causadas por los indios apaches Rafael y sus compañeros," Incident 26.

20. Ibid.

21. Ibid., Incident 27.

22. Martínez García, *Indios, mineros, peones y maestros*, 26; "Sucinta relación que manifiesta las muertes, cautiverios, robos y demás atrocidades causadas por los indios apaches Rafael y sus compañeros," Incident 27 (quotation).

23. "Sucinta relación que manifiesta las muertes, cautiverios, robos y demás atrocidades causadas por los indios apaches Rafael y sus compañeros," Incident 27.

24. Ibid.; Stern, "Social Marginality and Acculturation," 339–40.

25. Martínez García, *Indios, mineros, peones y maestros*, 26; "Sucinta relación que manifiesta las muertes, cautiverios, robos y demás atrocidades causadas por los indios apaches Rafael y sus compañeros," Incident 27 (quotation).

26. Ibid. The source does not say that Rafael left his captive with Valenzuela, but the next time Rafael and José Antonio appear they are alone. It would make sense that Valenzuela ensured that the captive stayed with him after the Apaches left, but it is also possible that the captive later escaped from the Apaches or that Rafael and José Antonio killed him. If he returned with Valenzuela to Guajoquilla, he may have been Luíz de la Cruz as parish records from that location mention a Luíz de la Cruz who "was known as El Cautivo, for having been captured by the enemy Apaches." This De la Cruz went to live with priest Juan José Sída in the parish church until his death in 1809. It also says that De la Cruz left the Apaches voluntarily when they were near the Hacienda Tierra Blanca near Guajoquilla. See Luíz de la Cruz Burial Record, 1809, Archivo de la parroquia de Santo Cristo de Burgos, Defunciones, FHL.

27. "Sucinta relación que manifiesta las muertes, cautiverios, robos y demás atrocidades causadas por los indios apaches Rafael y sus compañeros," Incident 28, 29, 30, 42. This may be what is today Rancho de Peña, Chihuahua. This portion of Bustamante's text is disorganized. Although I believe they took the boy in this encounter as a captive, they may have captured a different male child in another raid.

28. Ibid., Incident 31, 32, 33.

29. Ibid., Incident 34, 36. For more on the Hacienda de Ramos see Erasmo Sáenz Carrete, *Haciendas y minas: una historia de Santa María del Oro y su región* (Durango: Universidad Juárez del Estado de Durango, 1999), 133–34.

30. Velasco, *Noticias estadísticas del estado de Sonora*, 244–45; Oakah L. Jones Jr., *Nueva Vizcaya: Heartland of the Spanish Frontier* (Albuquerque: University of New

Mexico Press, 1988), 215–16. Like Salcedo, Bonavía was intelligent and progressive in many ways. He established a public school system in Durango, wanted the government to mint copper coins to better control money supply, and he established a school for weavers and a textile factory in Durango. Bonavía was apparently so free from oversight that it allowed him to engage in corruption for his personal financial gain. Peter Guardino, *The Time of Liberty: Popular Political Culture in Oaxaca, 1750–1850* (Durham, NC: Duke University Press, 2005), 97–98, 102–103. For a good summary of the difference between intendant governors, governors, and commandant generals, see Marc Steven Simmons, "Spanish Government in New Mexico at the End of the Colonial Period" (PhD. diss., University of New Mexico, Albuquerque, 1965), 59–61.

31. Fabius Dunn, "The Administration of Don Antonio Cordero, Governor of Texas, 1805–1808" (PhD diss., University of Texas, Austin, 1979), 73, 78–86, 99–102, 110–11; J. Edward Townes, *Invisible Lines: The Life and Death of a Borderland* (Fort Worth: Texas Christian University Press, 2008), 146–48; Carlos Casteñeda, *Our Catholic Heritage in Texas*, vol. V (Austin: Von Boeckmann-Jones, 1942), 260–61 (quotation on 261); Weber, *The Spanish Frontier in North America*, 294–95; Odie B. Faulk, *The Last Years of Spanish Texas, 1778–1821* (The Hague: Mouton, 1964) 121–22; Navarro García, *Las Provincias Internas en el siglo XIX*, 33–34; Salcedo to Viceroy, April 9, 1806, AGN-PI, L239, R235; Salcedo to Viceroy, April 9, 1806, AGN-PI, L239, R235.

32. "Sucinta relación que manifiesta las muertes, cautiverios, robos y demás atrocidades causadas por los indios apaches Rafael y sus compañeros," Incident 35.

33. Ibid., Incident 8, 35; Stockel, *On the Bloody Road to Jesus*, 91.

34. "Sucinta relación que manifiesta las muertes, cautiverios, robos y demás atrocidades causadas por los indios apaches Rafael y sus compañeros," Incident 33.

35. Sherry Robinson, *Apache Voices: Their Stories of Survival As Told to Eve Ball* (Albuquerque: University of New Mexico Press, 2003), 40 (quotation); "Sucinta relación que manifiesta las muertes, cautiverios, robos y demás atrocidades causadas por los indios apaches Rafael y sus compañeros," Incident 37.

36. "Sucinta relación que manifiesta las muertes, cautiverios, robos y demás atrocidades causadas por los indios apaches Rafael y sus compañeros," Incident 38.

37. Ibid., Incident 39 (quotation); Cremony, *Life Among the Apaches*, 227–28. Although insightful in many regards, Cremony can be highly biased and racist. For Apache counterpoints to his arguments about captivity and torture, see Eve Ball, Nora Henn, and Lynda Sanchez, *Indeh, an Apache Odyssey* (Norman: University of Oklahoma Press, 1988), 20, 83. For a general discussion of Plains Indian treatment of captives, see Brooks, *Captives and Cousins*, 185–88.

38. Miles, *Personal Recollections of Observation of General Nelson A. Miles*, 445 (first quotation); Ball, Henn, and Sanchez, *Indeh, an Apache Odyssey*, 83; Robert N. Watt, *Apache Warrior, 1860–1886* (New York: Osprey Publishing, 2014), 59 (second quotation).

39. "Sucinta relación que manifiesta las muertes, cautiverios, robos y demás atrocidades causadas por los indios apaches Rafael y sus compañeros," Incident 39.

40. Ibid., Incident 38–41. There are discrepancies in how many shepherds were
injured in Bustamante's account. One entry says that they captured the boy in San
Javier, likely referring to San Javier, Durango, but subsequent entries say that the boy
was from San Gregorio. The two locations were close to each other, so those reporting
the incident may have confused the locations or the boy originated from San Gregorio
but was taken captive while in San Javier.

41. "Sucinta relación que manifiesta las muertes, cautiverios, robos y demás atrocidades causadas por los indios apaches Rafael y sus compañeros," Incident 41, 67, 71.
Bustamante's calculations for the number of captives seems to be off here, but there
appear to be three captives. Whichever of the two girls was Josefa, she would remain
with the band until the following September.

42. Steven W. Hackel, *Children of Coyote, Missionaries of Saint Francis: Indian-Spanish Relations in Colonial California, 1769–1850* (Chapel Hill: University of North Carolina Press, 2005), 323–26; "Sucinta relación que manifiesta las muertes, cautiverios,
robos y demás atrocidades causadas por los indios apaches Rafael y sus compañeros,"
Incident 94; Pike, *The Expeditions of Zebulon Montgomery Pike*, vol. 2, 752. Rafael
may have used Catholicism as a means to justify his attacks. In some areas of northern
Mexico, especially those that did not receive regular teachings or those ministered by
sinful priests, parishioners adopted a form of Catholicism where they believed that they
could commit all acts, including murder and rape, and still go to heaven as long as they
asked forgiveness for their crimes from a priest before they died. As one observer noted
of this attitude, "believing in the priest's power to forgive, and the ease with which this
forgiveness may be obtained, not only weakens all moral restraints, but gives positive
encouragement to the indulgence of the meanest passions, and the perpetration of the
vilest crimes. He stabs with the assassin's hand his fellowmen to-day, and to-morrow,
should the law demand his life, the holy confessor, with prayer and crucifix and shrine,
sends him on to glory. Future punishment has no terrors for him, for his mediator can
change by his transforming power, scarlets sins into innocence and purity." See Flippin,
Sketches from the Mountains of Mexico, 30–31 (quote 31).

43. Hackel, *Children of Coyote, Missionaries of Saint Francis*, 323–26.

44. Ball, Henn, and Sanchez, *Indeh, an Apache Odyssey*, 5, 13–14, 56–57; Francisco
Velasco, *Noticias estadísticas del estado de Sonora*, 279–80.

45. Francisco Velasco, *Noticias estadísticas del estado de Sonora*, 279–80 (quotations
on 279); Babcock, *Apache Adaption to Hispanic Rule*, 19, 21–23, 70–74. Babcock
mentions that in the 1600s, many Apaches seemed receptive to certain elements of
Catholicism, but he argues that the Spanish did not follow through with conversion
efforts, and many of the priests who were supposed to be promoting Catholic beliefs
themselves engaged in sin.

46. Martínez García, *Indios, mineros, peones y maestros*, 28. For an explanation of the process by which Catholic priests baptized Tarahumaras in remote towns, see Schwatka, *In the Land of the Cave and Cliff Dwellers*, 349–50; Donald Harris Burgess, "Missionary Efforts among the Tarahumara Indians" (MA thesis, Texas Western College, El Paso, 1963), 39.

47. "Sucinta relación que manifiesta las muertes, cautiverios, robos y demás atrocidades causadas por los indios apaches Rafael y sus compañeros," Incident 42. The burial records pertaining to the years 1804 to 1812 have been ripped out of the Balleza ledger. See Archivos de la Parroquia de San Pablo Balleza, Chihuahua, Defunciones, FHL.

48. Ibid., Incident 42, 71 (quotation in Incident 42). Juana María would later escape on August 16, 1807 and claim that during her time with the band they had killed two captives, although sources do not clarify who the captives were.

49. Alberto Maynez to Bernardo Bonavía, October 26, 1806, AHED, MF492, R58 (quotation); Fernández Perea, *Jiménez en la historia y en la leyenda*, 34; Maynez to Bonavía, December 16, 1806, AHED, MF492, R58.

50. Dunn, "The Administration of Don Antonio Cordero," 134–35, 138–39, 142–43; Weber, *The Spanish Frontier in North America*, 294–95; Robert Bruce Blake Research Collection, Center for American History, Austin, vol. XLVI, 305–6.

51. Carlos Hernández, *Durango gráfico: Obra completa que da á conocer detalladamente la historia del estado de Durango, su geografía, su hidrografía, su minería, la estadística de su población en las distintas épocas de su desarrollo y sus poderosos elementos de riqueza en todas sus manifestaciones* (Durango: Talleres de J. S. Rocha, 1903), 44; Martin, *Governance and Society in Colonial Mexico*, 25.

52. Francisco Gabriel de Olivares Pronouncement, October 28, 1806 in Martínez García, *Indios, mineros, peones y maestros*, 28.

53. Fernández Perea, *Jiménez en la historia y en la leyenda*, 34 (quotation); Maynez to Bonavía, December 16, 1806, AHED, MF492, R58.

Chapter 5

1. Jones, *Nueva Vizcaya*, 216; "Sucinta relación que manifiesta las muertes, cautiverios, robos y demás atrocidades causadas por los indios apaches Rafael y sus compañeros," Incident 43; Deeds, *Defiance and Deference in Mexico's Colonial North*, 27–28.

2. Deeds, *Defiance and Deference in Mexico's Colonial North*, 27–28, 133–36, 165; Santiago, *A Bad Peace and a Good War*, 79; Jack S. Williams, "The Evolution of the Presidio in Northern New Spain," *Historical Archeology* 38, no. 3 (2004): 150–53. There had previously been presidios in the region to prevent uprisings by mission Indians, but these had been shuttered as missions became secularized.

3. "Sucinta relación que manifiesta las muertes, cautiverios, robos y demás atrocidades causadas por los indios apaches Rafael y sus compañeros," Incident 43; Carl Lumholtz, *Unknown Mexico*, vol. 1 (London: Macmillan, 1902), 448.

4. H. Bradley Benedict, "El Saqueo De Las Misiones De Chihuahua, 1767–1777," *Historia Mexicana* 22, no. 1 (1972): 24–33, 24–27; Deeds, *Defiance and Deference*, 195–96.

5. Sara Ortelli, *Trama de una guerra conveniente: Nueva Vizcaya y la sombra de los Apaches, 1748–1790* (Mexico City: Colegio de Mexico, 2007), 113–15; Lockwood, *The Apache Indians*, 20; Conrad, "Empire through Kinship," 636–38; Deeds, *Defiance and Deference in Mexico's Colonial North*, 185–86; Babcock, *Apache Adaptation to Hispanic Rule*, 125.

6. "Sucinta relación que manifiesta las muertes, cautiverios, robos y demás atrocidades causadas por los indios apaches Rafael y sus compañeros," Incident 43. Whether or not Rafael received help from disgruntled Tarahumaras and Tepehuanes is unclear, but the Spanish would continue to suspect this to be the case in spite of the Tarahumaras themselves being targets of Rafael.

7. Deeds, *Defiance and Deference in Mexico's Colonial North*, 136–37, 195.

8. "Sucinta relación que manifiesta las muertes, cautiverios, robos y demás atrocidades causadas por los indios apaches Rafael y sus compañeros," Incident 44–45, 47; Sarabia, "El Indio Rafael," 56. Bustamante's notes are ambiguous at this point, and he may have written that the January 27 attack occurred on February 27. Pachón was likely San José del Pachón.

9. Sarabia, "El Indio Rafael," 57. Colomo made this remark on February 1, 1807, but it is unclear if this is the same date he discovered the camp.

10. Matson and Schroeder, "Cordero's Description of the Apaches, 1769," 347.

11. John and Wheat, "Views from a Desk in Chihuahua," 155; Morris Edward Opler, *An Apache Life Way* [as cited in references], 346 (quotation). As described in Opler, "sometimes they tie a piece of something on a tree and then on another so that they can be trailed by friends who are looking for these signs. The pieces may be a whole day's journey apart. But the Chiricahua is looking for it as he goes along, for the agreement has been made, and he knows what the sign will be. Or they might agree that a stone pointing in a certain way will be a sign. Lines on the ground are also made to indicate which way they are turning on the trail. Dropping a stick in the direction in which you are traveling is another way."

12. Carta dirigida a los capitulares del Ayuntamiento de Parral, a los hacenderos y vecinos de la jurisdicción de Parral, February 23, 1807, Fondo Colonial, Archivo Histórico Municipal de Parral, digitized at *Rootspoint.com* (hereafter cited as AHMP) (quotations); Salcedo, *Instrucción reservada de don Nemesio Salcedo y Salcedo comandante general de provincias internas a su sucesor,* 40–41.

13. Weber, *The Spanish Frontier in North America*, 294–95; Dunn, "The Administration of Don Antonio Cordero," 143–52, 427; Julio Sánchez Bañón, "El septentrión novohispano: La comandancia general de las provincias internas" (PhD diss., Universidad Complutense de Madrid, 2015), 410–11; John Francis Hamtramck Claiborne, *Mississippi, as a Province, Territory, and State* (Baton Rouge: Louisiana State University Press, 1964), 268 (quotation); Salcedo, *Instrucción reservada de don Nemesio Salcedo y Salcedo comandante general de provincias internas a su sucesor,* 40–41. For examples of Apache attacks while Salcedo was away in Texas, see Joseph Manríquez Report, January 10, 1807, JMA, R14; Joseph Manríquez Report, January 28, 1807, JMA, R14; and Joseph Manríquez Report, January 29, 1807, JMA, R14.

14. "Sucinta relación que manifiesta las muertes, cautiverios, robos y demás atrocidades causadas por los indios apaches Rafael y sus compañeros," Incident 48; Fernando Operé, *Indian Captivity in Spanish America: Frontier Narratives* (Charlottesville: University of Virginia Press, 2008), 156–58.

15. "The 'Apache Kid'" *The Evening Bee*, January 16, 1897.

16. John and Wheat, "Views from a Desk in Chihuahua," 155; B. A. Botkin, *A Treasury of Western Folklore* (New York: Crown Publishers, 1975), 239.

17. "Sucinta relación que manifiesta las muertes, cautiverios, robos y demás atrocidades causadas por los indios apaches Rafael y sus compañeros," Incident 46, 47, 48. For an account of how these escapes may have been carried out, see James Hobbs, *Wild Life in the Far West: Personal Adventures of a Border Mountain Man* (San Francisco: Wiley, Waterman, Eaton, 1873), 325.

18. "A Trip from Chihuahua to the Sierra Madre," *Putnam's Monthly Magazine*, July to December 1854, 409 (quotation); "Sucinta relación que manifiesta las muertes, cautiverios, robos y demás atrocidades causadas por los indios apaches Rafael y sus compañeros," Incident 46–48. Felix Colomo reported that the child from Por was "apparently" captured on February 9 and the "muchacho left on February 13," but it is unclear if he is saying the child left Rafael on February 13 or if he left Colomo's care on that date. Although it is quite possible that there were two or maybe even three separate escape attempts, the ambiguity and uncertainty of Colomo's phrasing and the unlikelihood of success for three staggered escape attempts leads me to conclude that this was a single escape. According to Bustamante, the boy from Por returned home, Agustin Nájera made his way to the Hacienda de San Nicolás, and the boy captured in the vicinity of San Gregorio made his way to the Talamantes Ranch, where a cowboy found him.

19. "Sucinta relación que manifiesta las muertes, cautiverios, robos y demás atrocidades causadas por los indios apaches Rafael y sus compañeros," 52; Martin, *Governance and Society in Colonial Mexico*, 152; Pfefferkorn, *Sonora: A Description of the Province*, 150 (quotation). These declarations reveal the patriarchal nature of Spanish society,

wherein women were expected to be sexually restrained and one of the greatest fears held by Spanish men was that their wives and daughters would become concubines for Indian braves. This phenomenon will be discussed in a later chapter.

20. "Sucinta relación que manifiesta las muertes, cautiverios, robos y demás atrocidades causadas por los indios apaches Rafael y sus compañeros," Incident 49, 50.

21. Campbell W. Pennington, *The Tarahumar of Mexico: Their Environment and Material Culture* (Salt Lake City: University of Utah Press, 1963), 167–72. For an entertaining, albeit sensationalized account of Tarahumara running practices, see Christopher McDougall, *Born to Run: A Hidden Tribe, Superathletes, and the Greatest Race the World Has Never Seen* (New York: Random House, 2009).

22. "Sucinta relación que manifiesta las muertes, cautiverios, robos y demás atrocidades causadas por los indios apaches Rafael y sus compañeros," Incident 49, 50; Burgess, "Missionary Efforts among the Tarahumara Indians," 39; "José Manuel Quiros Service Record, AGN-PI, R253. Bustamante lists Rafael as having injured one person in two separate occasions on or around this date. This may be the case, but because of the similarities in location and time frame, I suspect it is the same incident.

23. Cremony, *Life Among the Apaches*, 180, n41 (first quotation); Robert N. Watt, "Raiders of a Lost Art? Apache War and Society," *Small Wars & Insurgencies* 13, no. 3 (2002): 11–12 (first quotation on 11; second quotation on 12).

24. "Sucinta relación que manifiesta las muertes, cautiverios, robos y demás atrocidades causadas por los indios apaches Rafael y sus compañeros," Incident 55 (quotation); José Manuel Quiros Service Record, AGN-PI, L254, R248. Quiros's service record says this happened March 31, so the date may be slightly off. The location of the ambush is also unclear, as Bustamante's report indicates that it happened in the Sierra de Camerones while Quiros says Sierra de la Piedra Lumbre (possibly near Maguarichi, Chihuahua). I believe these are just recording errors, but it is possible that these were two separate ambushes.

25. José Manuel Quiros Service Record, AGN-PI, L254, R248 (first quotation); Pfefferkorn, *Sonora: A Description of the Province*, 146 (second quotation); Grenville Goodwin, *Western Apache Raiding and Warfare*, ed. Keith H. Basso (Tucson: University of Arizona Press, 1971), 62; "Sucinta relación que manifiesta las muertes, cautiverios, robos y demás atrocidades causadas por los indios apaches Rafael y sus compañeros," Incident 55.

26. Watt, "Raiders of a Lost Art?," 12; "Sucinta relación que manifiesta las muertes, cautiverios, robos y demás atrocidades causadas por los indios apaches Rafael y sus compañeros," Incident 55–56; José Manuel Quiros Service Record, AGN-PI, L254, R248. Fortunately for them, Salcedo does not appear to have been upset by the outcome of the battle as he would promote Quiros not long after this incident took place. For more on Apaches targeting horses, see Watt, *Apache Tactics*, 53.

27. "Sucinta relación que manifiesta las muertes, cautiverios, robos y demás atrocidades causadas por los indios apaches Rafael y sus compañeros," Incident 52. No date is given for this attack. However, because it was reported on April 13, and it happened in the same general area as the other attacks, it likely occurred at around the same time.

28. Ibid., Incident 51, 53; Juan Francisco Martinez Burial Record, April 12, 1807, Guanaceví, Immaculada Concepción, Defunciones, FHL (quotation). This burial record may instead refer to the thirteen-year-old killed by Rafael on April 11.

29. Ibid., Incident 53; Martínez García, *Indios, mineros, peones, y maestros*, 29; (first quotation); José Miguel Callenos Burial Record, June 9, 1807, Santa María del Oro, FHL (second and third quotations).

30. For examples of Apaches mutilations and a discussion of the frequency with which they occurred, see González Quiroga, *War and Peace of the Rio Grande*, 14–15; Santiago, *The Jar of Severed Hands*, 84; Ball, Henn, and Sanchez, *Indeh, an Apache Odyssey*, 20–21, 83.

31. Farmer, *Apacheria: True Stories of Apache Culture*, xxii; Miles, *Personal Recollections of Observation of General Nelson A. Miles*, 446 (quotation); James L. Haley, *Apaches: A History and Culture Portrait* (Norman: University of Oklahoma Press, 1997), 381.

32. Santiago, *The Jar of Severed Hands*, 84; Pfefferkorn, *Sonora: A Description of the Province*, 149 (quotation).

33. Ball, Henn, and Sanchez, *Indeh, an Apache Odyssey*, 20–21, 81.

34. "Sucinta relación que manifiesta las muertes, cautiverios, robos y demás atrocidades causadas por los indios apaches Rafael y sus compañeros," Incident 76, 97, 98; "El Lic. D. Josef Flores Alatorre, escribe á su apoderado desde Sombrerete, como diximos en el número 818," *Diario de México*, December 30, 1807.

35. "Sucinta relación que manifiesta las muertes, cautiverios, robos y demás atrocidades causadas por los indios apaches Rafael y sus compañeros," Incident 54. The two muleteers were likely Ventura Flores and José Trinidad Carrera, as they are listed as having been killed by "el Indio Barbaro Rafael" on April 22. Ventura Flores Death Record, April 22 Ventura Flores Burial Record, April 22, 1807, Guanaceví, Immaculada Concepción, Defunciones, FHL; José Carrera Burial Record, April 22, 1807, Guanaceví, Immaculada Concepción, Defunciones, FHL.

36. "Sucinta relación que manifiesta las muertes, cautiverios, robos y demás atrocidades causadas por los indios apaches Rafael y sus compañeros," Incident 56, 57.

37. Pike, *The Expeditions of Zebulon Montgomery Pike*, vol. 2, 753 (quotation); Arizpe, *Report That Dr. Miguel Ramos De Arizpe Presents to the August Congress*, 31–32. Citizens who disobeyed soldiers could also face criminal charges. In the Internal Provinces, the commandant general and governors appointed judges to oversee

civilian trials, and because these judges were usually military men themselves, they often ruled in favor of soldiers over civilians.

38. "Sucinta relación que manifiesta las muertes, cautiverios, robos y demás atrocidades causadas por los indios apaches Rafael y sus compañeros," Incident 59, 60, 61. It was at this point that Rafael and his band killed six horses and left fourteen poorly treated on the nearby hill of Trinchera.

39. Haggard, *Handbook for Translators of Spanish Historical Documents*, 109–11.

40. "Sucinta relación que manifiesta las muertes, cautiverios, robos y demás atrocidades causadas por los indios apaches Rafael y sus compañeros," Incident 62.

41. Ibid., Incident 58–63 (first quotation in Incident 60; second quotation in Incident 61; third and fourth quotations in Incident 59; fifth, sixth, and seventh quotations in Incident 58). Bustamante records two deaths at the Velázquez Ranch, one unnamed and one the son of Ramón Vaca. Reading his summary, it seems possible that these were the same person. Bustamante also explains that on the fourth they killed someone at the Ranch of Santa Inés, captured a boy, and stole four horses from Captain Don Roque de Orozco. On June 5, they killed another near Basnuchil. On June 6, they killed a Tarahumara Indian in the Sierra de Papigochi. Again, Bustamante's account is confusing. He says that the band captured a boy. If they did, they may have killed him as an escaped captive would later indicate that by late summer, Rafael and José Antonio were the only male members of the band.

42. Schwatka, *In the Land of the Cave and Cliff Dwellers*, 178. See also, "Schwatka in Mexico," *The Indianapolis News*, June 1, 1889.

43. "Sucinta relación que manifiesta las muertes, cautiverios, robos y demás atrocidades causadas por los indios apaches Rafael y sus compañeros," Incident 63 (quotation); Deeds, *Defiance and Deference in Mexico's Colonial North*, 185–88. Bustamante writes the name of the town as Temaichi, but no town with this spelling exists on modern maps, although there are several similarly named towns. I believe that Bustamante is referring to the town of Tomochi, but I leave the original spelling in case this is incorrect.

44. "Sucinta relación que manifiesta las muertes, cautiverios, robos y demás atrocidades causadas por los indios apaches Rafael y sus compañeros," Incident 63; Paul Vanderwood, *The Power of God Against the Guns of Government: Religious Upheaval in Mexico at the Turn of the Nineteenth Century* (Stanford, Calif.: Stanford University Press, 1998), 319–20 (quotation 320).

45. Pennington, *The Tarahumar of Mexico*, 97–98; "Sucinta relación que manifiesta las muertes, cautiverios, robos y demás atrocidades causadas por los indios apaches Rafael y sus compañeros," Incident 63. Bustamante's report says that eight Tarahumara died around the time of the battle. It seems that two died shortly before or after the fight and six during, but owing to the ambiguity of the source, it is possible that these numbers are off.

46. Pfefferkorn, *Sonora: A Description of the Province*, 150–51.

Chapter 6

1. Pike, *The Southwestern Journals of Zebulon Pike,* 211; Julie M. Fenster, *Jefferson's America: The President, the Purchase, and the Explorers Who Transformed a Nation* (New York: Crown Publishers, 2016), 355, 359–60; Jared Orsi, *Citizen Explorer: The Life of Zebulon Pike* (New York: Oxford University Press, 2017), 226–27.

2. David Narrett, "Geopolitics and Intrigue: James Wilkinson, the Spanish Border-lands, and Mexican Independence," *William and Mary Quarterly* 69 (2012): 125–26; Pike, *Southwestern Journals of Zebulon Pike,* 178, 211; Rosalind Z. Rock, "Dying Quijote: Nemesio Salcedo and the Last Years of Spain in the Internal Provinces" (PhD diss., University of New Mexico, Albuquerque, 1981), 184; Orsi, *Citizen Explorer,* 132–33, 226–27. Time has still not revealed the true purpose of Pike's journey, but most historians believe that, for the most part, he was being honest to Salcedo, and his mission resembled that of Lewis and Clark's. General Wilkinson had sent Pike to acquire geographic information about the newly purchased Louisiana Territory, as well as scientific knowledge about its plants, animals, and geology. However, as Salcedo suspected, Pike also wanted to befriend the various Indian tribes he encountered in the North American West, which might be useful if the United States went to war with Spain over the limits of Louisiana. Any information that Pike could acquire about Spanish defenses would be beneficial for these purposes. However, Pike was probably not a vanguard for an imminent invasion and, more than likely, he had no part in Burr's plans to take over the Internal Provinces. For an alternate take on Pike's objectives, see Andro Linklater, *An Artist in Treason: The Extraordinary Double Life of General James Wilkinson Commander in Chief of the U.S. Army and Agent 12 in the Spanish Secret Service* (New York: Walker Publishing, 2009), 242–43. Linklater contends that Wilkinson wanted Pike to intentionally be captured by the Spanish, so Wilkinson could then use his imprisonment as justification for the United States Army to invade the Internal Provinces. Linklater believes Pike was aware of the plan.

3. Pike, *Southwestern Journals of Zebulon Montgomery Pike,* 211–20.

4. Ibid., 222–23 (quotation on 223). Pike even personally witnessed this destitution while being escorted back to the United States, and he saw how the war could be harmful to those Apaches who refused to make peace. While traveling through one small settlement, he witnessed a group of captured Apaches destined for Cuba. He saw "an officer arrived from St. Rosa with 24 men and two Apaches in irons. They were noble looking fellows, of large stature, and appeared by no means cast down by their misfortunes, although they knew their fate was transportation beyond the sea, never more to see their friends and relations."

5. Pike, *The Expeditions of Zebulon Montgomery Pike,* vol. 2, 752 (quotation); Orsi, *Citizen Explorer,* 229–30. While in Chihuahua, Pike had long conversations with Alberto Maynez, the commander of the Carrizal Presidio, and Maynez doubtlessly

informed Pike about the recent difficulties the Spanish had had in preventing the Carrizal Apaches from contraband trading. Mariano Varela Ramírez would also escort Pike to the United States, and he had served with Lucas Valenzuela in pursuing Rafael. While on his return trip to the United States, Pike spent three days in Guajoquilla where he interacted with many Spanish officers, at least some of whom had spent the past two-and-a-half years pursuing Rafael. See also Lucas Valenzuela to Nemesio Salcedo, January 4, 1806, AHP, R1791a.

6. Pike, *The Expeditions of Zebulon Montgomery Pike*, vol. 2, 752.

7. Ibid., xxxv–xxxvi; vol. 2, 752; Orsi, *Citizen Explorer*, 226–30; Pike, *Southwestern Journals of Zebulon Montgomery Pike*, 211, 213. Pike, *The Expeditions of Zebulon Montgomery Pike*, Vol. 2, 752; Andy Doolen, "Captive in Mexico: Zebulon Pike and the New American Regionalism," in *Mapping Region in Early American Writing*, eds. Edward Watts, Keri Holt, and John Funchion (Athens: University of Georgia Press, 2015), 127–28. Bustamante lists the number of dead at the end of June 1807 at 119. It is unclear what type of gambling Rafael enjoyed, but Apaches often raced horses, and they learned a number of games of chance from the Spanish, including card games and a version of hopscotch. See Virginia Wayland, "Princeton's Apache Playing Cards," *Princeton University Library Chronicle* 34 (Spring 1973): 147–57. The psychology behind the human tendency to exaggerate the threat of violence during times of tragedy is beyond the scope of this project. For more on this phenomenon, see Benjamin H. Friedman, "Managing Fear: The Politics of Homeland Security," *Political Science Quarterly* 126, no. 1 (2011): 77–106. Friedman points out that in 2007, 47 percent of Americans were "very or somewhat worried that they or someone in their family would become a physical victim of terrorism," although there was less than a one in two million chance of dying of terrorism on an annual basis.

8. "Sucinta relación que manifiesta las muertes, cautiverios, robos y demás atrocidades causadas por los indios apaches Rafael y sus compañeros," Incident 67, 69, 71. Bustamante is either confused in his count of captives in these sections or the witnesses, for whatever reason, lied about how many captives were in camp. One source says that Juana María escaped on August 16 and another August 18. Neither of these dates makes sense because Juana María would say that when she left Rafael, the only ones in camp were Rafael, José Antonio, and Josefa.

9. "Sucinta relación que manifiesta las muertes, cautiverios, robos y demás atrocidades causadas por los indios apaches Rafael y sus compañeros," Incident 64, 85. For an explanation of the usage of the term "baciero," see Charles H. Harris, *A Mexican Family Empire: The Latifundio of the Sánchez Navarro Family, 1765–1867* (Austin: University of Texas Press, 1975), 65.

10. James F. Brooks, "Served Well by Plunder: La Gran Ladronería and Producers of History Astride the Río Grande," *American Quarterly* 52, no. 1 (March 2000): 41–43; Eastman, *Seven and Nine Years among the Camanches and Apaches*, 114–15,

215–17; Opler, *An Apache Life Way*, 351 (first quotation); R. B. Stratton, *Captivity of the Oatman Girls: Being an Interesting Narrative of Life among the Apache and Mohave Indians* (New York: Carlton & Porter, 1857), 138 (second quotation). For a general overview of operant psychology, see J. A. Jones, "Operant Psychology and the Study of Culture," *Current Anthropology* 12, no. 2 (1971): 171–218; Rob Robin, "Prison Camps and Culture Wars: The Korean Brainwashing Controversy," in *The Making of the Cold War Enemy: Culture and Politics in the Military-Intellectual Complex* (Princeton, NJ: Princeton University Press, 2001), 162–82.

11. Jones, "Operant Psychology and the Study of Culture," 174–75; "Sucinta relación que manifiesta las muertes, cautiverios, robos y demás atrocidades causadas por los indios apaches Rafael y sus compañeros," Incident 69, 85. See also Dave Grossman, *On Killing: The Psychological Cost of Learning to Kill in War and Society* (Boston: Little, Brown, 1996).

12. "Sucinta relación que manifiesta las muertes, cautiverios, robos y demás atrocidades causadas por los indios apaches Rafael y sus compañeros," Incident 65, 66, 68, 85 (quotation in Incident 68).

13. Ibid., Incident 65, 66, 68, 70, 85. Bustamante seems to be counting Incident 66 and 68 as two separate occurrences. I believe that this is an error. The two attacks appear almost identical, and Nevares does not mention a second attack in his account of his time with the band in incident 85. Bustamante likely mistook Cerra de Piedras and Corral de Piedras and the date of September 5 and September 8. I have tried to make sense of the numbers from the three accounts, but there may have been more or less deaths and injuries than indicated.

14. José María Ochoa Burial, Parroqia de San Bartolomé de Allende, Defunciones, FHL (quotation); "Sucinta relación que manifiesta las muertes, cautiverios, robos y demás atrocidades causadas por los indios apaches Rafael y sus compañeros," Incident 72, 73, 74, 75.

15. "Sucinta relación que manifiesta las muertes, cautiverios, robos y demás atrocidades causadas por los indios apaches Rafael y sus compañeros," Incident 65, 66, 67, 68; Robert L. Snow, *Deadly Cults: The Crimes of True Believers* (Westport, Conn.: Greenwood Publishing, 2003), 179–82. Sources are unclear about who escaped and when, but the escapees likely were the recently captured woman from Las Cuevas, Nevares, the Tarahumara girl taken on August 27, and Josefa. It is possible that the escapes occurred at slightly different times. If this were the case, the initial escape probably at least inspired the subsequent escapes. Perhaps some of the captives escaped and Josefa, having been trusted to watch the captives, felt it was in her best interest to leave rather than face Rafael or José Antonio's ire. Sources say that the captive from "Sarca," which would indicate Josefa, escaped on October 18 when Rafael and José Antonio went to raid the Hacienda de Iturraldi. See also, Salcedo, *Instrucción reservada de don Nemesio Salcedo y Salcedo comandante general de provincias internas a su sucesor,* 40–41.

16. "El Lic. D. Josef Flores Alatorre, escribe á su apoderado desde Sombrerete, como diximos en el número 818," *Diario de México*, December 30, 1807.

17. Pfefferkorn, *Sonora: A Description of the Province*, 147 (quotation); Charles P. Stone, *Notes on the State of Sonora* (Washington, DC: Henry Polkinhorn Printer, 1861), 23. These numbers are based on a search of Bustamante's report for specific mentions of evening or night attacks. The phase of the moon of the given date was determined by consulting https://www.moonpage.com.

18. Jack Jackson, *Los Mesteños: Spanish Ranching in Texas, 1721–1821* (College Station: Texas A&M Press, 2006), 370–71; Rafael Pacheco to Manuel de Espadas, December 29, 1789, BA, R20; "Sucinta relación que manifiesta las muertes, cautiverios, robos y demás atrocidades causadas por los indios apaches Rafael y sus compañeros," Incident 74.

19. José Perfecto Hernandez Burial, Parroqia de San Bartolomé de Allende, Defunciones, FHL; Pedro José Hernandez Burial, Parroqia de San Bartolomé de Allende, Defunciones, FHL; "Sucinta relación que manifiesta las muertes, cautiverios, robos y demás atrocidades causadas por los indios apaches Rafael y sus compañeros," Incident 74 (quotation). Burial records show the two brothers were interred at the same time. Perfecto's record says he "did not receive the sacrament because he was killed by the Indians." Pedro's has "also killed by the Indians" scratched out for an unexplained reason.

20. "Sucinta relación que manifiesta las muertes, cautiverios, robos y demás atrocidades causadas por los indios apaches Rafael y sus compañeros," Incident 81, Conclusion.

21. Ingstad, *The Apache Indians*, 31; Salcedo, *Instrucción reservada de don Nemesio Salcedo y Salcedo comandante general de provincias internas a su sucesor,* 40–41. At one point, María Martina convinced Rafael and José Antonio to spare a captive they had determined to kill. See "Sucinta relación que manifiesta las muertes, cautiverios, robos y demás atrocidades causadas por los indios apaches Rafael y sus compañeros," Conclusion. One Spanish witness later described with shock that Martina and other female captives went about "with hats and mounted to horses like the men"; see Sarabia, "El Indio Rafael," 60.

22. "Sucinta relación que manifiesta las muertes, cautiverios, robos y demás atrocidades causadas por los indios apaches Rafael y sus compañeros," Incident 76, 80, 98.

23. Ibid., Incident 76; "El Lic. D. Josef Flores Alatorre, escribe á su apoderado desde Sombrerete, como diximos en el número 818," *Diario de México*, December 30, 1807; Pfefferkorn, *Sonora: A Description of the Province*, 150 (quotation).

24. "Sucinta relación que manifiesta las muertes, cautiverios, robos y demás atrocidades causadas por los indios apaches Rafael y sus compañeros," Incident 76, 97, 98; "El Lic. D. Josef Flores Alatorre, escribe á su apoderado desde Sombrerete, como diximos en el número 818," *Diario de México*, December 30, 1807.

25. "Sucinta relación que manifiesta las muertes, cautiverios, robos y demás atrocidades causadas por los indios apaches Rafael y sus compañeros," Incident 76, 97, 98; "El

Lic. D. Josef Flores Alatorre, escribe á su apoderado desde Sombrerete, como diximos en el número 818," *Diario de México*, December 30, 1807. Compounding problems, many of the official reports during this time originate from a week or more after an event was supposed to have occurred, and some contain only secondhand information. Bustamante estimates that the band killed around twenty-seven during this time, while a different source puts the number at nineteen.

26. "Sucinta relación que manifiesta las muertes, cautiverios, robos y demás atrocidades causadas por los indios apaches Rafael y sus compañeros," Incident 76, 79, 86. Bustamante's report labels this town as Tumachi. I believe this is Turuachi because it is adjacent to a "Chinaty," but owing to similarities in Raramuri town names, this may not be the case. The two deaths referred to in Incident 79, and the two deaths referred to in Incident 86 may be the same.

27. Josiah Conder, *Mexico and Guatemala* (London: J. Duncan, 1831), 62 (quotation); "Sucinta relación que manifiesta las muertes, cautiverios, robos y demás atrocidades causadas por los indios apaches Rafael y sus compañeros," Incident 77.

28. "Sucinta relación que manifiesta las muertes, cautiverios, robos y demás atrocidades causadas por los indios apaches Rafael y sus compañeros," Incident 87; R. W. H. Hardy, *Travels in the Interior of Mexico in 1825, 1826, 1827, & 1828* (London: Henry Colburn and Richard Bentley, 1829), 489 (quotation).

29. "Juan Josef Flores escribe á su apoderado desde Sombrete, en carta de 1 de Diciembre, entre otras cosas el párrafo siguiente," *Diario de México*, December 26, 1807; "Sucinta relación que manifiesta las muertes, cautiverios, robos y demás atrocidades causadas por los indios apaches Rafael y sus compañeros," Incident 87, 92, Conclusion; Farmer, *Apacheria: True Stories of Apache Culture*, xxii; "Ghastly Trails of Indian Raiders in the Southwest," *San Francisco Examiner*, December 29, 1895; "El Lic. D. Josef Flores Alatorre, escribe á su apoderado desde Sombrerete, como diximos en el número 818," *Diario de México*, December 30, 1807. Amóles is near Jicoro, the location that Laicano says José Antonio forced him to kill José Bernardo Abad Léon, so it is likely that the execution took place around this time. See also, José Reyes Service Record AGN-PI, R274.

30. José Reyes revista de inspección November 5, 1803, SGU, L7047; "Sucinta relación que manifiesta las muertes, cautiverios, robos y demás atrocidades causadas por los indios apaches Rafael y sus compañeros," Incident 81, 87, 88, 93; "Juan Josef Flores escribe á su apoderado desde Sombrete, en carta de 1 de Diciembre, entre otras cosas el párrafo siguiente," *Diario de México*, December 26, 1807. Those spotted likely included Rafael, José Antonio, José Salvador Bueno Laicano, María Martina, and two recent captives. Bustamante reports that many of these attacks took place at the beginning of January, not December, but I believe that there is confusion about dates and locations in some of these instances. Owing to similarities in the reports, it is possible that the two men killed on December 8 and the two men killed on December

9 were the same victims, but Bustamante believed them to be different. Bustamante says that the two Hacienda del Toro cowboys died on January 4, the two peasants in the vicinity of San Salvador on the modern border of Durango and Zacatecas on January 6, and the paisano on January 7. I believe these events happened in December considering that Rafael's location in January would make the attacks difficult to accomplish geographically. In addition, Bustamante reports Reyes as having found a dead horse on January 1, 1808, when a newspaper published on December 26, 1807 says that an unnamed officer found a dead horse on December 1, 1807. It is possible that two different reports specifically mention finding a dead horse on the first of the month, but confusion over the dates seems more likely.

31. "Juan Josef Flores escribe á su apoderado desde Sombrete, en carta de 1 de Diciembre, entre otras cosas el párrafo siguiente," *Diario de México*, December 26, 1807 (quotation); "Sucinta relación que manifiesta las muertes, cautiverios, robos y demás atrocidades causadas por los indios apaches Rafael y sus compañeros," Incident 88. As mentioned in the previous footnote, it is likely that Reyes found the horse on December 1, 1807, not January 1, 1808. The article does not specifically say that it was Reyes who found the horseshoes, but I believe he was responsible considering that he was the one chasing after Rafael and that this is the only mention of a dead horse at this point in the records.

32. "Juan Josef Flores escribe á su apoderado desde Sombrete, en carta de 1 de Diciembre, entre otras cosas el párrafo siguiente," *Diario de México*, December 26, 1807.

33. "Noticias ulteriores del Apache," *Diario de México*, February 1, 1808; Pfefferkorn, *Sonora: A Description of the Province*, 145–47 (quotation on 147); LaVerne Harrell Clark, *They Sang for Horses: The Impact of the Horse on Navajo and Apache Folklore* (Tucson: University of Arizona Press, 1966), 138; Laverne Harrell Clark, "Early Horse Trappings of the Navajo and Apache Indians," *Arizona and the West* 5, no. 3 (1963): quote on 246–48. The Apache-designed leather pouch shoes prevented lameness in horses, something that was especially problematic when traveling through mountainous terrain.

34. "Noticias ulteriores del Apache," *Diario de México*, February 1, 1808. For an explanation of the shoeing process in Mexico, see Gregg, *Commerce of the Prairies*, vol. 2, 94–95. By the late nineteenth century, Apaches had begun to emulate Europeans in creating metal traditional-style horseshoes, but there is no record of them creating rawhide or metal horseshoes in the European style before this time. See Clark, "Early Horse Trappings of the Navajo and Apache Indians," 247.

35. Jerry Williams, "Referential Shadows on New World Relations: Notes on Moors, Blacks, Jews and 'The Other,'" *Afro-Hispanic Review* 8, no. 1/2 (1989): 15–19.

36. For an excellent summary of the sistema de castas, see Llona Katzew, *Casta Painting: Images of Race in Eighteenth-Century Mexico* (New Haven, Conn.: Yale University Press, 2005), 39–45. According to art historian Emanuel Ortega, "Indios

bárbaros, indios mecos, chichimecas, and Apaches were some of the classificatory terms used to determine the lowest category of humans that appeared in casta paintings." See Emanuel Ortega, "Testimonies of Violence: Images of Franciscan Martyrs in the Provinces of New Spain" (PhD diss., University of New Mexico, Albuquerque, 2017), 150.

37. S. R. Tulkin and M. J. Konner, "Alternative Conceptions of Intellectual Functioning," *Human Development* 16, no. 1/2 (1973): 33–52.

38. Antonio García Cubas, *Diccionario geográfico, histórico y biográfico de los Estados Unidos Mexicanos*, vol. V (México, D. F.: Oficina Tipográfica de la Secretaría de Fomento, 1891), 206; "Sucinta relación que manifiesta las muertes, cautiverios, robos y demás atrocidades causadas por los indios apaches Rafael y sus compañeros," Incident 26, 81.

39. "Sucinta relación que manifiesta las muertes, cautiverios, robos y demás atrocidades causadas por los indios apaches Rafael y sus compañeros," Incident 81; "El Lic. D. Josef Flores Alatorre, escribe á su apoderado desde Sombrerete, como diximos en el número 818," *Diario de México*, December 30, 1807 (quotation).

40. Alonso Domínguez Rascón, *Estado, Frontera, y Ciudadanía* (Ciudad Juárez: Universidad Autónoma de Ciudad Juárez, 2017), 265, 269, 272, 275–85. Zacatecas was part of the larger province of Nueva Galicia.

41. Isabel Gil Sánchez, *Descripciones, económicas, regionales de Nueva España: provincias del Norte*, 1790–1814 (México, D. F.: Instituto Nacional de Antropología e Historia, 1976), 105; Williams, "The Evolution of the Presidio in Northern New Spain," 150–53; "Sucinta relación que manifiesta las muertes, cautiverios, robos y demás atrocidades causadas por los indios apaches Rafael y sus compañeros," Incident 81, 82; "El Lic. D. Josef Flores Alatorre, escribe á su apoderado desde Sombrerete, como diximos en el número 818," *Diario de México*, December 30, 1807.

42. "Sucinta relación que manifiesta las muertes, cautiverios, robos y demás atrocidades causadas por los indios apaches Rafael y sus compañeros," Incident 84. The Hacienda de Sauceda appears to be modern Saucillo just north of the contemporary border between Zacatecas and Durango.

43. "Sucinta relación que manifiesta las muertes, cautiverios, robos y demás atrocidades causadas por los indios apaches Rafael y sus compañeros," Incident 83.

44. Ibid., Incident 90–91, 93–94 (first quotation in Incident 90; second quotation in Incident 94).

45. Ibid., Incident 95. The captive was likely the fourteen-year-old or the Chinatu woman.

46. Ibid., Incident 93, 94, 96, 97; Sarabia, "El Indio Rafael," 57–58. As mentioned, there are a number of discrepancies in Bustamante's report, and Sarabia seems to have gotten some of his dates wrong. Bustamante contends that the boy from Jicorica was the one killed by Laicano. Because the *Diario de México* reported Laicano's rescue as having happened before this, Rafael, José Antonio, or an unnamed member of their

band likely killed this child. Bustamante suspects that Rafael may have killed an additional person at the Gogojito Ranch. It is unclear if the number of killed should also include three who Sarabia reports died at the estancia de Acatita on February 6, 1808. It is possible that these were already reported deaths from January, but they may also refer to three who Rafael's band would kill in 1809, and Sarabia put the incorrect year.

47. Ibid., Incident 98.

48. "An Englishman's Views of Mexico and the Mexicans," *American Flag*, May 7, 1848.

49. Von Tempsky, *Mitla*, 83 (first quotation); Ochoa Zazueta, *Apostillas de los Tepehuanes*, 68 (second quotation).

Chapter 7

1. "Juan Josef Flores escribe á su apoderado desde Sombrete, en carta de 1 de Diciembre, entre otras cosas el párrafo siguiente," *Diario de México*, December 26, 1807. The *Diario* accepted letters from anyone who wanted their information printed without charge, but it did not pay authors. Therefore, it is likely that Alatorre wrote the letter to the *Diario* as a public service or to simply provide an interesting story to readers. For more on colonial Mexican journalism, see Lillian Estelle Fisher, *The Background of the Revolution for Mexican Independence* (Boston: Christopher Publishing House, 1934), 68; Henry Lepidus, "The History of Mexican Journalism," *University of Missouri Bulletin* 29, no. 4 (January 1928): 19–23. As noted by Lepidus, at this time, New Spain only had two newspapers in regular publication. The *Diario de México* had begun publication in 1805 under the editorship of Carlos María de Bustamante, who would later become famous for writing an extensive history of Mexico. The *Gazeta de México* had been published since 1784, and its editor Juan López Cancelada hated the new rival paper and would do whatever he could to either discredit or one up the stories published in the *Diario*.

2. "El Lic. D. Josef Flores Alatorre, escribe á su apoderado desde Sombrerete, como diximos en el número 818," *Diario de México*, December 30, 1807.

3. "Noticias ulteriores del Apache," *Diario de México*, February 1, 1808 (quotation); Ruth Wold, "The Mexican Arcadia," *Hispania* 52, no. 3 (1969): 478–480; Bancroft, *History of the North Mexican States and Texas*, 595; Jorge Ruedas de la Serna, "Gracia, erotismo y originalidad en un poeta de la Arcadia mexicana," *Revista ALPHA Revista da Faculdade de Filosofia Ciências e Letras de Patos de Minas* 7 (2006): 200. Little is known about Arezi, but he appears to have been well acquainted with Rafael's background. At the time, pseudonyms were common when writing to the *Diario*, and it is likely that Arezi was actually an older man named Ramírez who was a member of a poetry society called the Mexican Arcadia and a frequent contributor to the *Diario*

de México. One member of the arcadia described Arezi as "chasing shepherdesses in spite of his age." Most of what is known about Rafael's early life comes from this letter. Based on Nevares's involvement in the Guajoquilla community, his records for baptizing Apache children, and Bancroft's suggestion that a priest had educated Rafael, I had already concluded that Rafael Nevares had raised Rafael prior to finding this article, so the letter appears to be dependable.

4. Raymond Carr, *Spain, 1808–1975* (New York: Oxford University Press, 1982), 81–94; Emilio Ocampo, *The Emperor's Last Campaign: A Napoleonic Empire in America* (Tuscaloosa: University of Alabama Press, 2009), xvi–xviii. Fortunately for Salcedo, war with France meant that he no longer had to watch for an invasion from Britain as Napoleon's actions had led to an alliance between Britain and Spain, but this attention now had to be devoted to watching the French. For example, Salcedo gathered money to support the fight against Spain in Iberia. Rafael Nevarez contributed 10 pesos to the cause. See Guillermo Cervantes, "De un presidio colonial a una ciudad, Santa María de las Caldas hoy Jiménez, Chihuahua," (PhD diss., Universidad Autónoma de Ciudad Juarez, 2009), 140. For one of numerous reports in the *Diario* concerning Napoleon and the situation in Spain, see "Fernando Septimo Rey de España y de las Indias, y en su nombre la Suprema Junta de ambas," *Diario de México*, August 2, 1808.

5. Salcedo, *Instrucción reservada de don Nemesio Salcedo y Salcedo comandante general de provincias internas a su sucesor,* 40–41 (quotation on 40); Marc Simmons, *Spanish Government in New Mexico* (Albuquerque: University of New Mexico Press, 1968), 43; Orozco, *El estado de Chihuahua en el parte de la nación,* 304; Rock, "Dying Quijote," 228–29. It is unclear when Salcedo first developed this plan. Since at least 1804, Salcedo had been complaining about his health deteriorating and asking for permission to retire. Spanish officials had granted this request at some point in 1807 or 1808, prompting Salcedo to begin working on a record of his tenure as commandant general to turn over to his successor. The resulting, *Instrucción reservada de don Nemesio Salcedo y Salcedo comandante general de provincias internas a su sucesor* is a lengthy document that features Salcedo's thoughts on a variety of topics including the economic situation in northern New Spain, the problems the commandant general had faced with the United States, and, of course, his dealings with the various unincorporated Indians of the Internal Provinces. As part of this last section, Salcedo included a lengthy explanation of his plans to locate and capture Rafael and José Antonio. Indeed, the commandant general devoted more words to explaining the difficulties he had faced with the two Apaches than he did for any individual Indian group, other than the Apaches as a whole.

6. Simmons, *Spanish Government in New Mexico,* 67–68 (quotation on both pages).

7. Salcedo, *Instrucción reservada de don Nemesio Salcedo y Salcedo comandante general de provincias internas a su sucesor,* 34–35; Pike, *The Expeditions of Zebulon Montgomery Pike,* vol. 2, 767; Alonso Domínguez Rascón, "Autonomía Insurgencia

y oligarquía," 1027–48; Mathes, "Arms for the Defense of the Eastern Provincias," 271–72 (quotation on 271). By 1810, Salcedo had received a return on his investment, paid back the money he had borrowed from the veteran companies of Nueva Vizcaya to fund the factory, and produced some seven hundred smooth bore muskets. Salcedo was so proud of the weapons that he even sent one to the viceroy and one to the head of the Royal Corps of Engineers of New Spain along with blueprints so that they could follow his design.

8. Orozco, *El estado de Chihuahua en el parte de la nación*, 304 (quotation); Sánchez Bañón, "El septentrión novohispano," 410–12.

9. Grant Shepherd, *The Silver Magnet: Fifty Years in a Mexican Silver Mine* (New York: E. P. Dutton, 1938), 37–38. For another example of this lookout system, see Cave Johnson Couts, *Hepah, California! The Journal of Cave Johnson Couts from Monterey, Nuevo Leon, Mexico, to Los Angeles, California, during the Years, 1848–1849* (Tucson: Arizona Pioneers' Historical Society, 1961), 42–43.

10. Francisco Minjares Service Record, 1803, Janos Collection, Folder 20, Section 4; "Juan Josef Flores escribe á su apoderado desde Sombrete, en carta de 1 de Diciembre, entre otras cosas el párrafo siguiente," *Diario de México*, December 26, 1807; Salcedo, *Instrucción reservada de don Nemesio Salcedo y Salcedo comandante general de provincias internas a su sucesor*, 40–41; Ugarte to Cordero, March 7, 1809, BA, R40; Babcock, *Apache Adaption to Spanish Rule*, 110. Salcedo does not give a date as to when he assigned soldiers to various outposts, but Bustamante's report shows that soldiers started reporting from haciendas in September 1807.

11. Miles, *Personal Recollections of Observation of General Nelson A. Miles*, 480–81 (first quotation on 480; second quotation on 481); Forsyth, *The Story of the Soldier*, 274–75 (third quotation on both pages).

12. Salcedo, *Instrucción reservada de don Nemesio Salcedo y Salcedo comandante general de provincias internas a su sucesor*, 41 (first and second quotations); Pfefferkorn, *Sonora: A Description of the Province*, 210; David A. Yetman, *The Ópatas: In Search of a Sonoran People* (Tucson: University of Arizona Press, 2010), 50–51, 209; Cortés, *Views from the Apache Frontier*, 26; A. F. Bandelier, *Final Report of Investigations Among the Indians of the Southwest* (Cambridge, Mass.: University Press, 1890), 241–42. Zebulon Pike likely witnessed one of the first Ópata companies arriving from Sonora. He said of this group, "I saw a detachment of them at Chihuahua who appeared to be fine, stout, athletic men, and were the most subordinate and faithful troops I ever knew, acting like a band of brothers and having the greatest attachment for their officers." Pike, *Expeditions of Zebulon Montgomery Pike*, vol. 2, 773.

13. "Sucinta relación que manifiesta las muertes, cautiverios, robos y demás atrocidades causadas por los indios apaches Rafael y sus compañeros," Conclusion. For additional information on the treatment of Ópata captives in Apache society, see Paul R. Nickens and Kathleen M. Nickens, "Victor of Old San Carlos: Portrait of a

Captive Mexican and Apache Tag Band Chief," *The Journal of Arizona History* 56, no. 3 (2015): 278–79.

14. Sarabia, "El Indio Rafael," 57–58 (quotations on 57); "Sucinta relación que manifiesta las muertes, cautiverios, robos y demás atrocidades causadas por los indios apaches Rafael y sus compañeros," Incident 99, 102.

15. Ibid. 57–59 (quotation on 57).

16. José Aguallo y José Maria García Burial Record, February 14, 1808, Santa María del Oro, Defunciones, FHL; Two whose life was ended by the Indian Rafael, February 18, 1808, Santa María del Oro, Defunciones, FHL (quotation). The first two are listed as having been killed on February 6 at Tinaja. No date is given for the unidentified victims, but their death location says "las cansas."

17. Sarabia, "El Indio Rafael," 57–58; "Sucinta relación que manifiesta las muertes, cautiverios, robos y demás atrocidades causadas por los indios apaches Rafael y sus compañeros," Incident 99, 102. Sarabia likely refers to don Antonio Sanchez's muleteers who Bustamante reported killed in Incident 102.

18. "Sucinta relación que manifiesta las muertes, cautiverios, robos y demás atrocidades causadas por los indios apaches Rafael y sus compañeros," Incident 99; Sarabia, "El Indio Rafael," 57–58 (quotation on 58). Sarabia says that Pedro Pérez was the one to liberate the captives. It is possible that Pérez and Juárez arrived at the same time or that they were a part of the same unit. Sarabia might also be citing a different battle.

19. Sarabia, "El Indio Rafael," 58–59 (quotation on 59); José de la Cruz Pacheco Rojas and Joseph P. Sánchez, *Memorias de Coloquio Internacional El Camino Real de Tierra Adentro* (México D. F.: Instituto Nacional de Antropología e Historia, 2000). Bernardo Bonavía also learned of Rafael's recent attacks and dispatched three "golpes de fuerza" of forty men each to track down the band.

20. "Sucinta relación que manifiesta las muertes, cautiverios, robos y demás atrocidades causadas por los indios apaches Rafael y sus compañeros," Incident 101; Sarabia, "El Indio Rafael," 59.

21. Deeds, *Defiance and Deference in Mexico's Colonial North*, 145, 159; Sarabia, "El Indio Rafael," 59; Sara Ortelli, "Vivir en los márgenes: Fronteras porosas y circulación de población en la Nueva Vizcaya tardo colonial," *Anuario de Historia Regional y de las Fronteras* 19, no. 1 (January 2004): 52–53; Sara Ortelli, "Entre desiertos y serranías: Población, espacio no controlado y fronteras permeables en el Septentrión novohispano tardocolonial," *Revista d'História Moderna* 32 (2014): 98–99. Deeds lists a town nearby San Gregorio as "Suibupa." This is likely the "Soyupa," but I went with the spelling in Sarabia.

22. Sara Ortelli, "Del discurso oficial a las fuentes judiciales el enemigo y el proceso de mestizaje en el norte novohispano tardocolonial," *Memoria Americana* 13 (2005): 76.

23. Sarabia, "El Indio Rafael," 59.

24. Causa criminal de oficio contra los indios del pueblo de San Gregorio de la jurisdicción de San Andres, 1808, Juzgado Criminal, Archivo Histórico del Gobierno del Estado de Durango (hereafter cited as AHD), Caja 25, Exp., 148; Tania Celiset Raigosa Gómez, "La Justicia Criminal en Durango, Nueva Vizcaya, 1750–1824" (PhD diss., Universidad de Sevilla, Seville, May 2017), 283–84 (quotation on 284); María Guadalupe Rodríguez López (ed.), *Historia de Durango*, vol. 2 (Durango: Universidad Juárez del Estado de Durango, 2013), 263, 602. There was also speculation that residents spent two or three days with Rafael at a place named Colorado, and that they brought him to the Cordon de los Anteojos.

25. Ortelli, "Vivir en los márgenes," 52–53; Deeds, *Defiance and Deference in Mexico's Colonial North*, 145, 159; López, *Historia de Durango*, vol. 2, 263, 602 (first quotation on 263, n212); Causa criminal de oficio contra los indios del pueblo de San Gregorio de la jurisdicción de San Andres, 1808, Juzgado Criminal, AHD, Caja 25, Exp., 148 (second quotation).

26. Causa criminal de oficio contra los indios del pueblo de San Gregorio de la jurisdicción de San Andres, 1808, Juzgado Criminal, AHD, Caja 25, Exp., 148.

27. López, *Historia de Durango*, vol. 2, 601. Prisons in the Internal Provinces were notoriously bad. Some of the Americans who had been captured as members of Philip Nolan's outfit faced near starvation, with one complaining that the only food he received for months was a chicken head and neck. See Yoakum, *History of Texas,* 422.

28. "Sucinta relación que manifiesta las muertes, cautiverios, robos y demás atrocidades causadas por los indios apaches Rafael y sus compañeros," Conclusion.

29. Ibid.," Incident 102, 103, 104; Moorhead, *New Mexico's Royal Road*, 52–54; The men may have been resupplying a garrison of soldiers that Salcedo had placed in Guanaceví. Soldiers often had to escort pay, horses, and needed supplies to nearby presidios or garrisons every three to four months. Although Spain had been using private companies to ship supplies throughout the Internal Provinces, soldiers often served as escorts, especially for specie. For more on the Spanish supply system, see Roland Rodriguez, "'I Was Nothing but a Lender of What I Was Ordered to Supply . . .': Francisco Amangual, Trustee of the Presidio *Las Compañías Volantes* in the Spanish Borderlands, 1701–1812" (PhD diss., University of Texas, El Paso, 2015); Moorhead, *The Presidio*, 196–97.

30. Gonzalo M. Quintero Saravia, *Bernardo De Gálvez: Spanish Hero of the American Revolution* (Chapel Hill: University of North Carolina Press, 2018), 59 (quotation); "Sucinta relación que manifiesta las muertes, cautiverios, robos y demás atrocidades causadas por los indios apaches Rafael y sus compañeros," Incident 102, 103, 104.

31. "Sucinta relación que manifiesta las muertes, cautiverios, robos y demás atrocidades causadas por los indios apaches Rafael y sus compañeros," Incident 102, 103, 104.

32. Ibid.

33. Ibid., Incident 62, 67, 102, 103, 104.

34. Ibid.

35. Ibid., Incident 105, 106, 107.

36. Ibid., Incident 106

37. Ibid., Incident 106, 107, 108; Sarabia, "El Indio Rafael," 59–60. Along the way, they may have killed a vecino and another soldier, as a priest in Parral reported rumors of this happening nearby. While this would make sense geographically, as the purported location was on the way to their next sighting, Spanish officials concluded that the information concerned previous assaults. Castillo remained a captive of the group until January 1809.

38. "Sucinta relación que manifiesta las muertes, cautiverios, robos y demás atrocidades causadas por los indios apaches Rafael y sus compañeros," Incident 108; Sarabia, "El Indio Rafael," 59–60.

39. "Sucinta relación que manifiesta las muertes, cautiverios, robos y demás atrocidades causadas por los indios apaches Rafael y sus compañeros," Incident 108, 109. Sarabia, "El Indio Rafael," 60.

40. Ibid., Incident 110–11 (first quotation in Incident 110; second quotation in Incident 111); José Acosta Burial Record, November 28, 1808, Encinillas, San Juan Bautista, Defunciones, FHL (fourth quotation); Patricia Bargas Burial Record, November 28, 1808, Encinillas, San Juan Bautista, Defunciones, FHL (third quotation); Lorenzo Mendoza Burial Record, December 5, 1808, Encinillas, San Juan Bautista, Defunciones, FHL (fifth quotation). Burial records say "Lorenzo Mendoza" instead of "Lorenzo Herrera." This may be a different person, but the first name and the location and date of the murder indicate that either Bustamante or the priest performing the burial gave an incorrect last name.

41. Pike, *The Expeditions of Zebulon Montgomery Pike*, vol. 2, 768.

42. Francisco Velasco, *Noticias estadísticas del estado de Sonora*, 268; "Sucinta relación que manifiesta las muertes, cautiverios, robos y demás atrocidades causadas por los indios apaches Rafael y sus compañeros," Incident 112, Conclusion. The initial report said that Francisca was between four to five years old, but a report written approximately two years later said she was between nine to ten years old. I took the high end of the initial estimate and the low end of the later estimate to reach the five to seven approximation. Therefore it is possible that the child was slightly younger or slightly older than the age given here. It is also possible that the Apache child mentioned in the end report was captured at a later date, and this is different girl, not Francisca.

43. Botkin, *A Treasury of Western Folklore*, 238–39 (quotation); Herbert Heywood, "The Terror of the Border," *Leslie's Weekly*, April 25, 1895.

44. "A Trip from Chihuahua to the Sierra Madre," 412; Bancroft, *History of the North Mexican States and Texas*, 595.

45. "España, "*Gaceta de la Regencia de España é Indias*, February 7, 1811 (quotation); "El Sr. Brigadier . . . ," *Gazeta del Gobierno de México*, December 5, 1811;

Salcedo, *Instrucción reservada de don Nemesio Salcedo y Salcedo comandante general de provincias internas a su sucesor,* 40–41; Orozco, *El estado de Chihuahua en el parte de la nación,* 304.

46. Samuel Chamberlain, *My Confession: Recollections of a Rogue* (Austin: Texas State Historical Association, 1997), 254–57, 260, 290 (first quotation on 254; second quotation on 257). Chamberlain's narrative is particularly disjointed in this section of his book as he portrays a number of locations that are distant from one another as being in close proximity. A copy of Chamberlain's sketch is located on page 255. Unfortunately, owing to Chamberlain's propensity for exaggeration and because so much time had passed between the war and when he wrote his memoirs, much of the narrative contains inaccuracies and embellishments. Indeed, historian Brian DeLay calls Chamberlain "at once the most brutally honest and maddeningly inventive chronicler of the war," so it is unclear what elements of his story are true and which are fiction. Therefore, the story of the Great Chief and his Indian and white wives may refer to Rafael, another famous Indian leader, a fictional legend, or it was a product of Chamberlain or someone else's imagination. See DeLay, *War of a Thousand Deserts,* 261.

47. Orozco, *Las guerras indias en la historia de Chihuahua,* 152; Enrique Vega Galindo, "El Indio Rafael," *Primera Plana* (Hermosillo), Edición 11, December 17, 2015.

48. "Sucinta relación que manifiesta las muertes, cautiverios, robos y demás atrocidades causadas por los indios apaches Rafael y sus compañeros," Incident 113; Riva Palacio, *Mexico a través de los siglos,* vol. 4, 778; "El Sr. Brigadier. . . ," *Gazeta del Gobierno de México,* December 5, 1811.

49. "Sucinta relación que manifiesta las muertes, cautiverios, robos y demás atrocidades causadas por los indios apaches Rafael y sus compañeros," Incident 42, 43, 91–93. Chávez Chávez, "Retrato del Indio Bárbaro," 415–16. Chávez Chávez argues that the reason the number of deaths went down is because Rafael and José Antonio went to Durango and Zactecas where fewer people were trying to kill them because of the reward. The author provides no evidence other than Bustamante's report. He also seems to be unaware of Rafael's use of disguises or the fact that Rafael and José Antonio had already spent a lot of time in Durango prior to 1810 and that they would spend much of their time from 1808 to 1810 in Chihuahua and Coahuila.

Chapter 8

1. "Sucinta relación que manifiesta las muertes, cautiverios, robos y demás atrocidades causadas por los indios apaches Rafael y sus compañeros," Incident 114.

2. The Laguna region is generally considered to be the fertile area between the Naza and Aguanaval Rivers. For a general appraisal of the economic prospects of the Laguna region, see Harris, *A Mexican Family Empire,* 171, 184–85, 200–201.

3. Ibid., 6–9; Vito Alessio Robles, *Coahuila y Texas en la época colonial* (Saltillo: Ed. Cultura, 1938), 506; Pike, *Southwestern Journals of Zebulon Montgomery Pike*, 224–25 (first and second quotations on 225).

4. Kinnaird, *The Frontiers of New Spain*, 139; Pike, *Southwestern Journals of Zebulon Montgomery Pike*, 224–25 (quotation on 225).

5. "Sucinta relación que manifiesta las muertes, cautiverios, robos y demás atrocidades causadas por los indios apaches Rafael y sus compañeros," Incident 115; Martínez García, *Indios, mineros, peones, y maestros*, 30–31.

6. "Sucinta relación que manifiesta las muertes, cautiverios, robos y demás atrocidades causadas por los indios apaches Rafael y sus compañeros," Incident 115; Martínez García, *Indios, mineros, peones, y maestros*, 30–32; Sarabia, "El Indio Rafael," 60. Bustamante spells Zambrano as "Sambrano" but he is almost certainly referring to Juan Zambrano of Coahuila. Sombreretillo is located near modern-day Matamoros, Coahuila, in southwestern Coahuila.

7. "Sucinta relación que manifiesta las muertes, cautiverios, robos y demás atrocidades causadas por los indios apaches Rafael y sus compañeros," Incident 110, 115 (quotation in Incident 115); Sarabia, "El Indio Rafael," 60; Martínez García, *Indios, mineros, peones, y maestros*, 30–32. Bustamante says only "diaries and news correspondence in the months of February and part of March report that Rafael and his companion Antonio executed seven and took one captive." Although he would later mention an additional three deaths for February, bringing the recorded deaths to ten.

8. Martínez García, *Indios, mineros, peones y maestros*, 30–31; Contreras Palacios, *Antecedentes históricos a la fundación de el Torreón*, 141. As will be shown in a later chapter, at least one of those that Contreras lists Rafael as having killed, Inocente Perales, occurred during a later foray into Coahuila, and Bustamante did include him in his count. Priests often demanded exorbitant burial fees to bury the dead. This forced many family members to abandon the bodies of the deceased so that priests would have to perform funerals free of charge. See Gregg, *Commerce of the Prairies*, vol. 2, 263–64.

9. Sarabia, "El Indio Rafael," 60.

10. Ibid.

11. Ibid.

12. Pfefferkorn, *Sonora, A Description of the Province*, 209–10 (first quotation on 209); Sarabia, "El Indio Rafael," 60 (second quotation).

13. Sarabia, "El Indio Rafael," 60; Ugarte to Cordero, March 7, 1809, BA, R40 (first and second quotations); Moorhead, *The Apache Frontier*, 272. Salcedo had recently reassigned Ugarte after the officer attended a ceremony recognizing United States control of Natchitoches, Louisiana. See Townes, *Invisible Lines*, 122–24.

14. Babcock, *Apache Adaptation to Hispanic Rule*, 189–90, 193–94; Griffen, *Apaches at War and Peace*, 91–93; Christopher J. Huggard and Terrence M. Humble, *Santa Rita del Cobre: A Copper Mining Community in New Mexico* (Boulder: University Press

of Colorado, 2012), 16–17; Hendricks and Timmons, *San Elizario*, 40–41; Nemesio Salcedo to Governor of New Mexico, July 16, 1810, Spanish Archives of New Mexico Microfilm Collection, University of New Mexico at Albuquerque (hereafter cited as SANM), R17, F148–49.

15. Rodriguez, "I Was Nothing but a Lender," 65. Dunn, "The Administration of Don Antonio Cordero," 413–15. This happened in October 1808.

16. Mathis, "Arms for the Defense of the Eastern Provincias Internas," 274–77 (quotation on 274). Salcedo had been complaining about a lack of mobile cannons and trained artillerymen since at least 1804, and he originally tried asking officials in Mexico City to send him five or six lighter cannon and trained artillerymen who knew how to use them, but the viceroy could not meet these requests. While on campaign, Salcedo's new cannon would sit on the mule's back in an assembly constructed from the same rollers and pack saddles that muleteers used when hauling cargo. A second mule would carry an additional rig consisting of a full gun carriage and two wheels. In cases where soldiers needed greater precision, they could remove this assembly and place the cannon on top of it, thereby creating a more traditional cannon. The wheels on this assembly were smaller than a regular cannon so as not to rub the haunches of the mule during transport. The second assembly also contained removable boxes for munitions that could be taken off during travel to lighten the load on the mule.

17. "Sucinta relación que manifiesta las muertes, cautiverios, robos y demás atrocidades causadas por los indios apaches Rafael y sus compañeros," Incident 116 (first quotation); José Guadalupe Rodríguez, April 18, 1809, Archivo de la parroquia de San Bartolomé, Defunciones, FHL; Miguel Portillo, April 18, 1809, Archivo de la parroquia de San Bartolomé, Defunciones, FHL; Juan Antonio Fiero, April 18, 1809, Archivo de la parroquia de San Bartolomé, Defunciones, FHL; José María Peña, April 18, 1809, Archivo de la parroquia de San Bartolomé, Defunciones, FHL (second quotation). "José Antonio Cardenas, October 1809, Archivo de la parroquia de Santo Cristo de Burgos, Defunciones, FHL (third quotation); José Manuel Calletana de los Relles, October 1809, Archivo de la parroquia de Santo Cristo de Burgos, Defunciones, FHL (fourth quotation).

18. Almada, *Resumen geográfico del municipio de Jiménez*, 39; Fuentes Rebolloso, "El Santo Cristo de Burgos," 12.

19. Mathis, "Arms for the Defense of the Eastern Provincias Internas," 271–74 (first and second quotations on 272). Details on the campaign in the Sacramento Mountains are sparse. A brief summary can be found in Lorena Gallegos Renova, "La vida en el presidio de Janos: relcciones sociales de los tiempos coloniales a los primeros años independientes" (MA thesis, Escuela Nacional de Antropología e Historia, Chihuahua, 2012), 99.

20. "Sucinta relación que manifiesta las muertes, cautiverios, robos y demás atrocidades causadas por los indios apaches Rafael y sus compañeros," Incident 118.

21. Ibid., Incident 117.

22. Ibid. Juan de Urquidi may have been a member of the Urquito family to which Rafael Nevares's sister-in-law belonged. He was perhaps the same Juan Urquida who John Russell Bartlett would later describe in his memoirs of his travels through Mexico. Bartlett, *Personal Narrative of Explorations and Incidents in Texas, New Mexico, California, Sonora, and Chihuahua*, vol. 2, 459–62.

23. "Sucinta relación que manifiesta las muertes, cautiverios, robos y demás atrocidades causadas por los indios apaches Rafael y sus compañeros," Incident 119.

24. Ibid., Incident 120; Martínez García, *Indios, mineros, peones, y maestros*, 31. I believe this location is today's Vallecillo.

25. "Sucinta relación que manifiesta las muertes, cautiverios, robos y demás atrocidades causadas por los indios apaches Rafael y sus compañeros," Incident 120; L. W. Powell, "The Pueblo Indians," *Potter's American Monthly*, 1878, 228. Pueblo Indians sometimes built entrances to their homes on their roofs to make things even more difficult for would-be Apache raiders.

26. "Sucinta relación que manifiesta las muertes, cautiverios, robos y demás atrocidades causadas por los indios apaches Rafael y sus compañeros," Incident 120.

27. Martínez García, *Indios, mineros, peones y maestros*, 30–31; "Sucinta relación que manifiesta las muertes, cautiverios, robos y demás atrocidades causadas por los indios apaches Rafael y sus compañeros," Incident 125. This is located near modern-day Chorreras, Chihuahua, former site of the San Carlos Presidio.

28. "Sucinta relación que manifiesta las muertes, cautiverios, robos y demás atrocidades causadas por los indios apaches Rafael y sus compañeros," Incident 125.

29. Ibid.

30. Ibid., Incident 121, 125 (quotation in Incident 121). Bustamante only counts this as three deaths, perhaps because the one who José Dionisio killed happened afterward. I believe it is at this time that the band captured José Tomás Matías Ochoa. Later José Dionisio mentions that Rafael took Ochoa three months after his own capture. Since Dionisio was captured in September, the dates line up.

31. Ibid., Incident 122, 124 (quotation in Incident 122); Policarpo Vázquez Burial Record, February 9, 1810, Aldama San Gerónimo Chihuahua, Defunciones, FHL.

32. "Sucinta relación que manifiesta las muertes, cautiverios, robos y demás atrocidades causadas por los indios apaches Rafael y sus compañeros," Incident 122, 123, 124, 126. Francisco Minjares Service Record, April 14, 1812, Janos Collection, Folder 20, Section 4.

33. "Sucinta relación que manifiesta las muertes, cautiverios, robos y demás atrocidades causadas por los indios apaches Rafael y sus compañeros," Incident 123. The report does not specify who was assisting the Apaches only that he was a male. Considering that he had participated in previous raids and he had been with the band for some time the helper was almost certainly Dionisio, but it might also have been

Ochoa. The wording in this section is somewhat confusing, and it is possible that the passage does not translate to the Apaches pushing the mules from the mountain. The death records for both Domínguez and Visuaño say "killed by the Indian Rafael in the Sierra del Carriso." Urbano Domínguez, February 14, 1810, Meoqui, San Pablo, Defunciones, FHL; Roberto Visuaño Burial Records, February 14, 1810, Meoqui, San Pablo, Defunciones, FHL.

34. Ibid.

35. Jones, *Los Paisanos*, 145–46. Apaches even served as mail carriers from 1802 to 1804. Given this and Rafael's knowledge of the Internal Provinces, I would not be surprised if uncovered documents revealed that at one time, Rafael, José Antonio, or Chinche served as mail carriers.

36. "Sucinta relación que manifiesta las muertes, cautiverios, robos y demás atrocidades causadas por los indios apaches Rafael y sus compañeros," Incident 125.

37. Ibid.

38. Ibid., Incident 125.

39. Ibid., Incident 127.

40. Ibid.; Von Tempsky, *Mitla*, 39. Apaches often left inferior firearms, with "ammunition being most wanted."

41. Juan Núñez Burial Record, April 3, 1810, Encinillas, San Juan Bautista, Defunciones, FHL; Manuel Núñez Burial Record, April 3, 1810, Encinillas, San Juan Bautista, Defunciones, FHL (first quotation); "Sucinta relación que manifiesta las muertes, cautiverios, robos y demás atrocidades causadas por los indios apaches Rafael y sus compañeros," Incident 128–29; Pfefferkorn, *Sonora: A Description of the Province*, 148 (second quotation). There are two entries for Manuel Núñez, one on April 3 and one on April 5. It is possible that this was a clerical error or that there was an additional victim.

42. "Sucinta relación que manifiesta las muertes, cautiverios, robos y demás atrocidades causadas por los indios apaches Rafael y sus compañeros," Incident 129.

Chapter 9

1. "Sucinta relación que manifiesta las muertes, cautiverios, robos y demás atrocidades causadas por los indios apaches Rafael y sus compañeros," Incident 130; John and Wheat, "Views from a Desk in Chihuahua," 166; Griffen, *Apaches at War and Peace*, 88; Moorhead, *The Presidio*, 70; Lundwall, *Copper Mining in Santa Rita*, 58, 133–34. The commandant general also assigned Apache bands to only hunt in particular regions. Hendricks and Timmons, *San Elizario: Spanish Presidio to Texas County Seat*, 41.

2. "Sucinta relación que manifiesta las muertes, cautiverios, robos y demás atrocidades causadas por los indios apaches Rafael y sus compañeros," Incident 130.

3. Ibid., Incident 130, 137. It is possible that the second captive was Francisca, not the Apache child captured in the raid the previous year. If that were the case, the fate of the girl from the previous attack on establecimiento Apaches is unknown.

4. Ibid., Incident 131; This may be the same Dolores mine described in V. Pender "Some Reminiscences of Old Dolores," *Engineering and Mining Journal* (June 1910): 1329–30. The author describes Apaches as having killed workers at the mine in the nineteenth century. However, because he does not use Rafael and José Antonio's names, and considering that there were multiple mines in the area, there is no way to definitively tie the two instances together.

5. "Sucinta relación que manifiesta las muertes, cautiverios, robos y demás atrocidades causadas por los indios apaches Rafael y sus compañeros," Incident 132.

6. Ibid., Incident 133.

7. Ibid., Incident 134, 135, Conclusion.

8. Orozco, *El estado de Chihuahua en el parte de la nación*, 304; Cortés, *Views from the Apache Frontier*, 26; Santiago, *A Bad Peace and a Good War*, 100–101; "Sucinta relación que manifiesta las muertes, cautiverios, robos y demás atrocidades causadas por los indios apaches Rafael y sus compañeros," Introduction, Conclusion.

9. "Sucinta relación que manifiesta las muertes, cautiverios, robos y demás atrocidades causadas por los indios apaches Rafael y sus compañeros," Incident 136, Conclusion; Pfefferkorn, *Sonora: A Description of the Province*, 210 (quotation).

10. Cortés, *Views from the Apache Frontier*, 26 (quotation); Arreola, "Chiricahua Apache Homeland in the Borderland Southwest," 119.

11. "Sucinta relación que manifiesta las muertes, cautiverios, robos y demás atrocidades causadas por los indios apaches Rafael y sus compañeros," Incident 136.

12. Bernal Vázquez, *Jiménez: 250 Años en lucha contra la adversidad*, 83–84.

13. "Sucinta relación que manifiesta las muertes, cautiverios, robos y demás atrocidades causadas por los indios apaches Rafael y sus compañeros," Incident 137.

14. Ibid.; "España," *Gaceta de la Regencia de España é Indias*, February 7, 1811; "El Sr. brigadier" *Gaceta del Gobierno de México*, December 5, 1811; Francisco Javier Sánchez Moreno, "Los Indios 'Bárbaros' en la frontera noreste de Nueva España entre 1810 y 1821," *Americanistas*, 26 (2011), 30–31. Lending credence to the suggestion that Comanches assisted in the effort, earlier in the month, Comanches joined Spanish soldiers on a campaign against Mescalero Apaches. Nemesio Salcedo to Governor of New Mexico, July 16, 1810, SANM, R17, F148–49.

15. "Sucinta relación que manifiesta las muertes, cautiverios, robos y demás atrocidades causadas por los indios apaches Rafael y sus compañeros," Incident 137. The location "Cerros de Acatita" does not exist on modern maps, but it likely refers to the low elevation mountains near the infamous Wells of Baján.

16. Ibid.

17. "España," *Gaceta de la Regencia de España é Indias*, February 7, 1811; "El Sr. brigadier" *Gazeta del Gobierno de México*, December 5, 1811; "Sucinta relación que manifiesta las muertes, cautiverios, robos y demás atrocidades causadas por los indios apaches Rafael y sus compañeros," Incident 137.

18. Watt, "Raiders of a Lost Art?," 11 (quotation); "Sucinta relación que manifiesta las muertes, cautiverios, robos y demás atrocidades causadas por los indios apaches Rafael y sus compañeros," Incident 137.

19. "Continuación de los donativos para zapatos y otros socorros en beneficio de los soldados del exército de la península," *Gaceta del Gobierno de México*, August 17, 1810; "España," *Gaceta de la Regencia de España é Indias*, February 7, 1811; "El Sr. Brigadier . . . ," *Gazeta del Gobierno de México*, December 5, 1811.

20. Riva Palacio, *Mexico a través de los siglos*, vol. 4, 778 (first quotation); Cremony, *Life Among the Apaches*, 227–28 (second quotation on 227); "El Sr. Brigadier . . . ," *Gazeta del Gobierno de México*, December 5, 1811; Orozco, *El estado de Chihuahua en el parte de la nación*, 304; "Sucinta relación que manifiesta las muertes, cautiverios, robos y demás atrocidades causadas por los indios apaches Rafael y sus compañeros," Incident 137. Orozco's account aligns with Bustamante's in some aspects but not others. For example, Orozco says that the final battle took place in the Balleza zone and that Chinche was still alive when it occurred.

21. Orozco, *El estado de Chihuahua en el parte de la nación*, 304 (first quotation); "Sucinta relación que manifiesta las muertes, cautiverios, robos y demás atrocidades causadas por los indios apaches Rafael y sus compañeros," Incident 137 (second quotation).

22. Stockel, *On the Bloody Road to Jesus*, 85. The practice of cutting off Apache extremities to serve as trophies or proof of a kill continued under Mexico and the United States. See for example, Donna J. Guy and Thomas E. Sheridan, eds. *Contested Ground: Comparative Frontiers on the Northern and Southern Edges of the Spanish Empire* (Tucson: University of Arizona Press, 1998), 90; John L. Kessell, *Friars, Soldiers, and Reformers: Hispanic Arizona and the Sonora Mission Frontier, 1767–1856* (Tucson: University of Arizona Press, 2016), 313; Martínez García, *Indios, mineros, peones y maestros*, 34.

23. Von Tempsky, *Mitla*, 77.

24. Kessell, *Friars, Soldiers, and Reformers*, 160; J. Frank Dobie, *Apache Gold and Yaqui Silver* (Austin: University of Texas Press, 1985), 194 (quotation).

25. "Sucinta relación que manifiesta las muertes, cautiverios, robos y demás atrocidades causadas por los indios apaches Rafael y sus compañeros," Incident 137.

26. Ibid.; "A Trip from Chihuahua to the Sierra Madre," 412; Bancroft, *History of the North Mexican States and Texas*, 595 (quotation).

27. Ibid.

28. "Sucinta relación que manifiesta las muertes, cautiverios, robos y demás atrocidades causadas por los indios apaches Rafael y sus compañeros," Incident 137 (quotation); Martínez García, *Indios, mineros, peones y maestros*, 34.

29. "Continuación de los donativos para zapatos y otros socorros en beneficio de los soldados del exército de la península," *Gaceta del Gobierno de México*, August 17, 1810 (quotation); *Gaceta de la Regencia de España é Indias*, February 7, 1811.

30. "España, "*Gaceta de la Regencia de España é Indias*, February 7, 1811.

31. Salcedo, *Instrucción reservada de don Nemesio Salcedo y Salcedo comandante general de provincias internas a su sucesor,* 40–41; "El Lic. D. Josef Flores Alatorre, escribe á su apoderado desde Sombrerete, como diximos en el número 818," *Diario de México*, December 30, 1807; "España" *Gaceta de la Regencia de España é Indias*, February 7, 1811; Julio Guerrero, *La génesis del crimen en México: estudio de psiquiatría social* (Paris: Imprenta de La Vda de Ch. Bouret, 1901), 232–33 (quotation on 232–33).

32. Endfield, "Decades of Drought, Years of Hunger," 155–57; Wislizenus, *Memoir of a Tour to Northern Mexico*, 65. Salcedo may also have selected Bustamante for this service because when he was younger, he had served in the military, fought against Apaches, and commanded Ópata soldiers. See Daniel and Fuenta, "Diary of Pedro José de la Fuente," 269.

33. "Sucinta relación que manifiesta las muertes, cautiverios, robos y demás atrocidades causadas por los indios apaches Rafael y sus compañeros," Conclusion.

34. Ibid., Incidente 132, Conclusion.

35. Ibid., Incidente 137, Conclusion.

36. Ibid.

37. Martínez García, *Indios, mineros, peones y maestros*, 34; "Sucinta relación que manifiesta las muertes, cautiverios, robos y demás atrocidades causadas por los indios apaches Rafael y sus compañeros," Conclusión (quotation); Conrad, "Captive Fates," 259–60. Conrad does not record a convoy of Apache captives destined for Mexico City for the next six years, so perhaps the two remained in the Internal Provinces.

38. Juliana Barr, *Peace Came in the Form of a Woman: Indians and Spaniards in the Texas Borderlands* (Chapel Hill: University of North Carolina Press, 2007), 262–63.

39. "Sucinta relación que manifiesta las muertes, cautiverios, robos y demás atrocidades causadas por los indios apaches Rafael y sus compañeros," Conclusion.

40. Brooks, *Captives and Cousins*, 69–70; Barr, *Peace Came in the Form of a Woman*, 262–63; Shelton, *For Tranquility and Order*, 53, 102; Peter Stern, "The White Indians of the Borderlands," *Journal of the Southwest* 33 (Autumn 1991): 270 (quotation).

41. "Sucinta relación que manifiesta las muertes, cautiverios, robos y demás atrocidades causadas por los indios apaches Rafael y sus compañeros," Conclusion.

42. Ibid.

43. Ibid.

44. Ibid.

45. Ibid. See also Orozco, *El estado de Chihuahua en el parte de la nación*, 304.

46. "Sucinta relación que manifiesta las muertes, cautiverios, robos y demás atrocidades causadas por los indios apaches Rafael y sus compañeros," Conclusion.

47. Ibid.

48. Joaquín Befarano Burial Record, August 23, 1804, Archivo de la parroquia de Santo Cristo de Burgos, Defunciones, FHL (first quotation); José Ricardo Silva Burial Record, October 4, 1804, Archivo de la parroquia de Santo Cristo de Burgos, Defunciones, FHL (second quotation); Martínez García, *Indios, mineros, peones y maestros*, 30–31; Contreras Palacios, *Antecedentes históricos a la fundación de el Torreón*, 141; Gregg, *Commerce of the Prairies*, 263–64.

49. "Sucinta relación que manifiesta las muertes, cautiverios, robos y demás atrocidades causadas por los indios apaches Rafael y sus compañeros," Incident 21, 22, 23, 24.

50. Ibid.; Lucas Valenzuela to Nemesio Salcedo, January 4, 1806, AHP, R1791a; Ygnacio Ontio Burial Record, Archivo de la parroquia de Santo Cristo de Burgos, Defunciones, FHL.

51. See Appendix B and "Sucinta relación que manifiesta las muertes, cautiverios, robos y demás atrocidades causadas por los indios apaches Rafael y sus compañeros," Conclusion. The 35 percent is based on a random sample of twenty available burial records. The deaths in August 1804 cannot be attributed to Rafael with existing evidence, but it is possible that he committed them prior to being put on trial. There is no record of Rafael having attacked anyone in June 1809, and it was during this time that many Apaches were in rebellion against the Spanish, meaning that the deaths in this month were likely not Rafael. Considering that the four August 1810 victims were interred after Rafael's death, he was likely not responsible, but considering that his band was nearby shortly before this, and that it often took weeks for soldiers and family members to return bodies for burial, this cannot be said for sure. These numbers actually serve to show how few Apache attacks unrelated to Rafael that there were during this time.

52. "Sucinta relación que manifiesta las muertes, cautiverios, robos y demás atrocidades causadas por los indios apaches Rafael y sus compañeros," Conclusion.

Chapter 10

1. Henry Charles Lea, "Hidalgo and Morelos," *American Historical Review* 4 (July 1899): 636–38; Enrique Krauze, *Mexico: Biography of Power* (New York: HarperCollins, 1997), 91, 93–94; Hugh M. Hamill Jr., *The Hidalgo Revolt: Prelude to Mexican Independence* (Gainesville: University Press of Florida, 1996), 192 (quotation); Hugh M. Hamill, "Early Psychological Warfare in the Hidalgo Revolt," *Hispanic American Historical Review* 41 (May 1961): 207–209.

2. MacLachlan and Beezley, *Mexico's Crucial Century*, 14; Hamill, "Early Psychological Warfare in the Hidalgo Revolt," 209–10; Eric Van Young, *The Other Rebellion: Popular Violence, Ideology, and the Mexican Struggle for Independence, 1810–1821*

(Stanford, Calif.: Stanford University Press, 2001), 21. For a brief historiographical discussion of revolution in New Spain and Mexico, see Will Fowler, "Understanding Individual and Collective Insurrectionary Action in Independent Mexico, 1821–1876," in *Malcontents, Rebels, and Pronunciados: The Politics of Insurrection in Nineteenth-Century Mexico*, ed. Will Fowler (Lincoln: University of Nebraska Press, 2012), xvii–xxxvi.

3. Domínguez Rascón, *Estado, Frontera, Ciudanía*, 273; Julia Kathryn Garrett, *Green Flag over Texas: A Story of the Last Years of Spain in Texas* (New York: Cordova Press, 1939), 36; Bradley Folsom, *Arredondo: Last Spanish Ruler of Texas and Northeastern Mexico* (Norman: University of Oklahoma Press, 2017), 41–42, 74–75.

4. Navarro García, *Las Provincias Internas en el siglo XIX*, 63–64; Elizabeth H. John, "The Riddle of Mapmaker Juan Pedro Walker" in *Essays on the History of North American Discovery and Exploration*, Stanley H. Palmer and Dennis Reinhartz, eds. (College Station: Texas A&M University Press, 1988), 123–25; Domínguez Rascón, *Estado, Frontera, y Ciudanía*, 222, 225, 265–66; Van Young, *The Other Rebellion*, 172–73.

5. Jorge Chávez Chávez, *Visiones históricas de la frontera* (Juárez: El Colegio de Chihuahua, 2013), 56.

6. Hamill, "Early Psychological Warfare in the Hidalgo Revolt," 209–12; Krauze, *Mexico*, 97; Timothy J. Henderson, *The Mexican Wars for Independence* (New York: Hill and Wang, 2009), 97–104.

7. Henderson, *The Mexican Wars for Independence*, 101–102; Garrett, *Green Flag over Texas*, 211–12; Isidro Vizcaya Canales, *En los albores de la independencia: las Provincias Internas de Oriente durante la Insurrección de don Miguel Hidalgo y Costilla, 1810–1811* (Monterrey: Publicaciones del Instituto Tecnológico y de Estudios Superiores de Monterrey, 1976), 154–55, 230–31; Casteñeda, *Our Catholic Heritage in Texas*, vol. VI, 32–33; Martínez Sánchez, *Hidalgo y los insurgentes en la provincia de Coahuila*, 160; "El Sr. Brigadie . . . ," *Gazeta del Gobierno de México*, December 5, 1811 (quotation). The fact that Longinos responded to both incidents indicates that Rafael must have been killed very close to the spot of Elizondo's trap.

8. Orozco, *El estado de Chihuahua en el partido de la nación*, 304; Bancroft, *History of the North Mexican States and Texas*, 277–82, 780–81; Rock, "Dying Quijote," 225.

9. Contreras Palacios, *Antecedentes históricos de la fundación de el Torreón*, 141; Simmons, *Spanish Government in New Mexico*, 43; Rock, "Dying Quijote," 228–29.

10. Isabel Olmos Sánchez, *La sociedad mexicana en vísperas de la independencia, 1787–1821* (Murcia: Universidad de Murcia, 1989), 68; Nombramiento de Caballero Gran Cruz de la Orden de Isabel la Católica a Nemesio Salcedo, March 24, 1815, Archivo Histórico Nacional, Madrid, digitized at pares.mcu.es; "Salcedo" *Gaceta de Madrid*, December 10, 1816. Those to be honored included viceroys, high ecclesiastical officials, intendents, and commandant generals.

11. William Spencer Robinson, *Iturbide of Mexico* (Durham, NC: Duke University Press, 1952), 63–64, 72; Henderson, *The Mexican Wars for Independence*, 166–70; Timothy E. Anna, "Francisco Novella and the Last Stand of the Royalist Army in New Spain," *Hispanic American Royalist Review* 51 (February 1971), 95–96, 103, 106–109.

12. Folsom, *Arredondo*, 210, 222; Griffen, *Apaches at War and Peace*, 91–93, 119–22.

13. Folsom, *Arredondo*, 224; Joel Roberts Poinsett, *Notes on Mexico Made in the Autumn of 1822* (London: J. Miller, 1825), 315–16, 346. Poinsett estimated that the cost of "Frontier posts, and expenses of the Apaches Indians" to be $119,850, with the "pay and expenses of the army" of all of Mexico being $1,957,377 (quotations 346). For an example of the difficulties former establecimientos faced, see Couts, *Hepah, California!*, 42–43

14. Escudero, *Observaciones sobre el estado actual del departamento de Chihuahua*, 241–43 (quotation on 243); Couts, *Hepah, California!*, 59; James O. Pattie, *The Personal Narrative of James O. Pattie of Kentucky, during an Expedition from St. Louis, through the Vast Regions between that Place and the Pacific Ocean* (Cincinnati: E. H. Flint, 1833), 175. In 1827, a group of Spanish-speaking Apaches attacked American James O. Pattie. For more discussion on Indians using knowledge gained through interaction with Hispanic settlements to then attack these settlements, see Conrad, "Captive Fates," 155–56.

15. William H. C. Whiting, "Journal of William H. C. Whiting," in Philip Saint George Cooke, et al., *Exploring Southwestern Trails, 1846–1854* (Glendale, Calif.: Clark, 1938), 271 (first quotation); "A Trip from Chihuahua to the Sierra Madre," 409 (second quotation); Griffen, *Utmost Good Faith*, 44. For more on Compa, see William B. Griffen, "The Compás: A Chiricahua Apache Family of the Late 18th and Early 19th Centuries," *American Indian Quarterly* 7, no. 2 (Spring 1983): 21–49.

16. Von Tempsky, *Mitla*, 101.

17. Michael James Box, *Captain James Box's Adventures and Explorations in New and Old Mexico* (New York: J. Miller, 1869), 185–87; Contreras Palacios, *Antecedentes históricos a la fundación de el Torreón*, 163; Von Tempsky, *Mitla*, 46–47; Bandelier, *Final Report of Investigations Among the Indians of the Southwest*, 494 (quotation). For a summary of the onset of the post-independence Apache raids and an impassioned plea for the Mexican people to address the issues facing the northern frontier, see Escudero, *Observaciones sobre el estado actual del departamento de Chihuahua*, 7–24. See also DeLay, *War of a Thousand Deserts*.

18. Almada, *Resumen geográfico del municipio de Jiménez*, 23; Gregg, *Commerce of the Prairies*, vol. 2, 133–34; "Indios Barbaros," *El Siglo Diez y Nueve*, April 11, 1848 (quotation).

19. Bandelier, *Final Report of Investigations Among the Indians of the Southwest*, 494; Poinsett, *Notes on Mexico*, 315 (first quotation); Velasco, *Noticias estadísticas del estado de Sonora*, 255 (second quotation).

20. Lumholtz, *Unknown Mexico*, vol. I, 25; Brooks, "Served Well by Plunder," 41.

21. For the effect that the international border would have on Indian raids into Mexico, see Delay, *War of a Thousand Deserts*.

22. Martínez García, *Indios, mineros, peones y maestros*, 34; Orozco, *Las Guerra indias en la historia de Chihuahua*, 196 (quotation); "Sucinta relación que manifiesta las muertes, cautiverios, robos y demás atrocidades causadas por los indios apaches Rafael y sus compañeros," Conclusion. The fate of the child placed in the care of don Juan de Dios Calderón is unknown.

23. "Historia," *Diario de Colima*, October 24, 1993; Enrique Vega Galindo, "El Indio Rafael," *Primera Plana*, Edición 11, December 17, 2015.

24. Enrique Vega Galindo, "El Indio Rafael," *Primera Plana*, Edición 11, December 17, 2015; "Historia," *Diario de Colima*, October 24, 1993.

25. Ochoa Zazueta, *Apostillas de los Tepehuanes*, 69 (first quotation); Contreras Palacios, *Antecedentes históricos de la fundación de el Torreón*, 141 (second quotation). For another misunderstanding of Rafael's death, see López, *Historia de Durango*, vol. 2, 330.

26. Guerra, *Historia de la Laguna, Torreón, su origen y sus fundadores*, 326–27 (quotation on 326–27); Martínez García, *Indios, mineros, peones y maestros*, 35. Guerra does not give a specific date for "Rafael's" reemergence but implies that it was around 1860. It is possible that an attack by any Indian group would prompt this response, as Geronimo mentions a similar occurrence when his group of Chiricahua Apaches attacked a Sonoran town in 1863. As soon as the people of the town learned that his group of Apaches was in the area, they fled, allowing Geronimo's Apaches to loot the empty homes and stores. See Barrett, *Geronimo's Story of His Life*, 72. It is also possible that the people of El Refugio or La Loma feared another bandit or Indian leader named Rafael who operated closer to their time, but either the author or the storyteller confused this person with the Rafael from the early nineteenth century.

27. Guerra, *Historia de la Laguna, Torreón, su origen y sus fundadores*, 327.

28. Ibid., 326.

29. Haldeen Braddy, "Pancho Villa's Hidden Loot," *Western Folklore* 12, no. 2 (1953): 77–84 (quotations on 77). For more on Apaches and rumors of treasure in the Sierra Madre, see Ingstad, *The Apache Indians*, 87–88, 122, 133–35. There were also rumors that Francisco "Pancho" Villa hid one million pesos worth of gold pieces near Chihuahua City at the turn of the twentieth century. Others place Villa's treasure near Ysleta, Texas, and still others El Paso. Making the Rafael story plausible is that there appears to have been some truth to the rumor that Villa hid some of his money. A reliable eyewitness described a time where he accompanied Villa to Santa Cecilia and watched as Villa dug up a wine box containing gold bars that he had hidden there years earlier. Villa then used this money to fund improvements to his hacienda at Canutillo. Treasure hunters also search for specie that Geronimo supposedly hid in Arizona or northern Mexico.

30. "Sucinta relación que manifiesta las muertes, cautiverios, robos y demás atro-cidades causadas por los indios apaches Rafael y sus compañeros," Incident 34, 120, Conclusion. At the time, northwestern New Spain was experiencing a substantial increase in the amount of metal extracted from mines, so even poor paisanos might carry silver and gold.

31. Neil Goodwin, *Like a Brother: Grenville Goodwin's Apache Years, 1928–1939* (Tucson: University of Arizona Press, 2004), 212 (quotation); Sotomayor Garza, *Anales Laguneros*, 43; "Extracto El Agente, Jesús Mier," *Periodico Oficial*, February 8, 1904.

32. Guerra, *Historia de la Laguna, Torreón, su origen y sus fundadores*, 326 (quota-tion on 326); "Extracto El Agente, Jesús Mier," *Periodico Oficial*, February 8, 1904. It is unclear from the text if Reyes is referring to the Treasury of Mexico, the Treasury of Coahuila, the city treasury or some other body.

33. Braddy, "Pancho Villa's Hidden Loot," 84 (quotation on 84).

Conclusion

1. Although it is beyond the scope of this project, those interested will find a well-informed discussion of the origins of the "noble savage" trope in the introduc-tion of Terry Jay Ellingson, *The Myth of the Noble Savage* (Berkeley: University of California Press, 2001), 1–8.

2. C. L. Sonnichsen, "The Ambivalent Apache," *Western American Literature* 10, no. 2 (1975): 99–102. For a look at the changing public perception of Indians, see Linnete Manrique, "Dreaming of a Cosmic Race: José Vasconcelos and the Politics of Race in Mexico, 1920s–1930s," *Cogent Arts & Humanities* 3 no. 1 (2016): 1–13.

3. Rocío Galicia, "*Apaches* de Victor Hugo Rascón Banda: identidad y represent-ación del septentrión entre indios y mexicanos," *Latin American Theatre Review* 42, no. 9 (Spring 2009): 17–18; Bob Boze Bell, "Ay Chihuahua!" *True West Magazine* (April 2016), accessed January 20, 2020, https://truewestmagazine.com/ay-chihua-hua-spanish-equivalent-yikes/ (quotation).

4. Enrique Vega Galindo, "El Indio Rafael," *Primera Plana*, Edición 11, December 17, 2015.

5. Sweeney, *Mangas Coloradas*, 11.

6. Nicholas A. Curott and Alexander Fink, "Bandit Heroes: Social, Mythical, or Ra-tional?," *American Journal of Economics and Sociology* 71, no. 2 (2012): 470–71 (quotation on 470); Eric Hobsbawm, *Primitive Rebels: Studies in Archaic Forms of Social Movement in the 19th and 20th Centuries* (Manchester: Manchester University Press, 1959), 12–14.

7. Henderson, *The Mexican Wars for Independence*, 216–22.

8. Campa Mendoza, *Las insurrecciones de los pueblos indios en México*, 67–68 (first quotation). See also, Antonio Bertan "Ideas e historias que viajaban en mula," *Mural*

(Guadalajara), December 13 1999: 12; Enrique Vega Galindo, "El Indio Rafael," *Primera Plana*, Edición 11, December 17, 2015 (second quotation); Ángel Trejo, "Las rebeliones previas al Grito de Independencia," *Buzos de la noticia: Revista de análisis político*, September 2011, 45. For another example of Rafael as a revolutionary, see, Raigosa Gómez, "La Justicia Criminal en Durango," 283–84.

9. Chávez Chávez, *Visiones históricas de la frontera*, 55 (quotation).

10. Curott, and Fink, "Bandit Heroes: Social, Mythical, or Rational?," 470–73; Chávez Chávez, *Visiones históricas de la frontera*, 55–56.

11. Curott, and Fink, "Bandit Heroes: Social, Mythical, or Rational?," 473; Chávez Chávez, *Visiones históricas de la frontera*, 56–57 (first quotation); James David Nichols, "A 'Great System of Roaming': Runaway Debt Peons and the Making of the International Border," in *The Limits of Liberty: Mobility and the Making of the Eastern U.S.-Mexico Border* (Lincoln: University of Nebraska Press, 2018), 83 (second quotation). Curott and Frink argue that some bandits earned legendary status because they served as a check on state power, and they provided rules when the local government refused to do so. There is no evidence of the latter in regard to Rafael and little evidence for the former. Indeed, it seems that the Spanish government became more restrictive, passing laws limiting movement between towns. It is possible that some on the periphery received relief from government-imposed restrictions because soldiers were needed to pursue Rafael, but this conclusion is a stretch. Perhaps hacienda owners gave their workers more leeway or allowed them more time off, but extant evidence does not support this conclusion. A counterargument to Rafael being detrimental to the revolutionary cause could be applied to the area that is today Sonora and Sinaloa because at the time of Hidalgo's uprising, a number of soldiers from these areas were deployed to Nueva Vizcaya to stop Apaches, and, considering how slowly armies moved at the time, it is likely that many of the soldiers from these regions sent to look for Rafael had yet to return by September 1810. As Alejo García Conde stated at the time, "due to the lack of urban and provincial militia; all kinds of weapons; trained officers, who were involved in war with the barbarian Indians; a shortage of aid; suspicious natives and vecinos; [Hidalgo] could incline them to adopt the seductive maxims of the insurrection." Alejo García Conde quoted in José Marcos Bustos and María del Valle Borrero Silva, "La crisis de la monarquía hispánica en la intendencia de Arizpe, insurgencia y contrainsurgencia," *Americanistas* 28 (2012): 6.

12. Juan Josef Flores, "Juan Josef Flores escribe á su apoderado desde Sombrerete, en carta de 1 de Diciembre, entre otras cosas el párrafo siguiente," *Diario de México*, December 26, 1807.

13. Antonio Bertan, "Ideas e historias que viajaban en mula," *Mural* (Guadalajara), December 13 1999: 12; Salcedo, *Instrucción reservada de don Nemesio Salcedo y Salcedo comandante general de provincias internas a su sucesor*, 40–41 (quotation).

14. Guerrero, *La génesis del crimen en México*, 232–33. For a contemporary assessment of the Spanish officers, see William Davis Robinson, *Memoirs of the Mexican Revolution, Including a Narrative of the Expedition of General Xavier Mina; to Which Are Annexed Some Observations on the Practicability of Opening a Commerce between the Pacific and Atlantic Oceans, through the Mexican Isthmus, in the Province of Oaxaca, and at the Lake of Nicaragua; and the Vast Importance of Such Commerce to the Civilized World* (London: Lackington, Hughes, Harding, Mavor & Lepard, 1821), 23–24, 35 and Poinsett, *Notes on Mexico Made in the Autumn of 1822*, 256–57.

15. Hugh Pendexter, "The Gate through the Mountain Part I," *Adventure*, February 3, 1920; Hugh Pendexter, *The Gate through the Mountain* (New York: A. L. Burt, 1929), 308–12 (quotation on 301). Based on publication dates, it appears that Pendexter assembled his articles for *Adventure* as a standalone work in 1929. To explain the time difference between when Rafael was committing his robberies in Mexico and when the fictional California thefts occur, the author leaves open the possibility that the Ralph in the story was the original Ralph's son or someone who took up his mantle after the original died.

16. Stephen T. Holmes, *Contemporary Perspectives on Serial Murder* (Thousand Oaks, Calif.: Sage Publications, 1998), 1–2. Holmes defines serial killing as "the killing of three or more people over a period of more than 30 days, with a significant cooling-off period in between the murders." Because Rafael and José Antonio had numerous cooling off periods, sometimes for multiple months, they clearly meet this definition. Holmes argues that serial killers murdered for lust, thrill, power, and creature comforts, placing food and money in the latter category. Available sources indicate that at one point or another Rafael and José Antonio fit into all of these categories.

17. Ralph Adam Smith, *Borderlander: The Life of James Kirker, 1793–1852* (Norman: University of Oklahoma Press, 1999), 170. H. H. Holmes is often cited as one of the most prolific serial killers in United States history. His grotesque methodology has led some to estimate that he killed more than two hundred people, but authorities only definitively tied him to seven deaths.

18. Bernal Vázquez, *Jiménez: 250 Años en lucha contra la adversidad*, 83. Poetic license was taken with the translation to emulate the syntax of English language nursery rhymes.

19. Frank J. Dobie, *Tongues of the Monte* (Austin: University of Texas Press, 1980), 100–101 (first quotation); "Historia" *Diario de Colima*, October 24, 1993 (second quotation).

20. For an example of a popular history that only mentions Rafael in a few lines, see Vizcaya Canales, *En los albores de la independencia*, 154, 273.

21. For a version of the El Cautivo Legend, see Sotelo, *Ensalada de historias y cuentos*, 63.

22. Herbert Heywood, "The Terror of the Border," *Leslie's Weekly*, April 25, 1895.

BIBLIOGRAPHY

Archival Sources

Archivo de Hidalgo del Parral Microfilm Collection, Southern Methodist University (cited as AHP)

Archivo General de las Indias, https://pares.culturaydeporte.gob.es (cited as AGI)

Archivo General de la Nación, México, https://archivos.gob.mx/guiageneral/ (cited as AGN) Cárceles y Presidios

Archivo Histórico del Gobierno del Estado de Durango Microfilm Collection, University of Texas at El Paso (cited as AHED)

Archivo Histórico del Gobierno del Estado de Durango (cited as AHD) Juzgado Criminal

Archivos Históricos del Arzobispado de Durango Microfilm Collection, University of Texas at El Paso (cited as AHAD)

Archivos Históricos del Arzobispado de Durango, Durango

Archivo Histórico Municipal de Parral https://www.rootspoint.com/fondo-colonial (cited as AHMP)

Archivo General de la Nación Microfilm Collection, University of New Mexico at Albuquerque Provincias Internas (cited as AGN-PI)

Archivo General de Simancas, https://pares.culturaydeporte.gob.es (cited as SGU)

Benson Latin American Collection, University of Texas at Austin, Janos Presidio Collection (cited as Janos Collection)

Béxar Archives Microfilm Copy, University of Texas at Arlington (cited as BA)

Ciudad Juárez Cathedral Archives Microfilm Collection, University of Texas at El Paso (cited as JCA)

Ciudad Juárez Municipal Archives Microfilm Collection, University of Texas at El Paso (cited as JMA)

Family History Library of the Church of Jesus Christ of Latter-Day Saints (cited as FHL)

Spanish Archives of New Mexico Microfilm Collection, University of New Mexico at Albuquerque (cited as SANM)

Newspapers and Periodicals

Adventure
American Flag
Bicentario, el ayer y hoy de México
Buzos: Revista de análisis político
Diario de Colima
Diario de México
The Evening Bee
Gaceta del Gobierno de México
Gaceta de Madrid
Gazeta de México
Gaceta de la Regencia de España é Indias
The Indianapolis News
Leslie's Weekly
Mural (Guadalajara)
Periodico Oficial
Potter's American Monthly
Primera Plana (Hermosillo)
Putnam's Monthly Magazine
San Francisco Examiner
El Siglo Diez y Nueve
Sobre todo la fe: revista mensual de la diócesis de Parral

Books and Articles

Adams, Andy. *The Log of a Cowboy: A Narrative of the Old Trail Days.* Cambridge: Riverside Press, 1903.

Andrews, Edmund. "Military Surgery among the Apache Indians." *The Chicago Medical Examiner* 10 (1869), 599–601.

Algier, Keith Wayne. "Feudalism on New Spain's Northern Frontier: Valle de San Bartolomé, A Case Study." PhD diss., University of New Mexico, 1966.

Almada, Francisco R. *Resumen geográfico del municipio de Jiménez.* Ciudad Juárez: Editorial el Labrador, 1961.

Anderson, Gary Clayton. *The Indian Southwest, 1580–1830: Ethnogenesis and Reinvention.* Norman: University of Oklahoma Press, 2009.

Anna, Timothy E. "Francisco Novella and the Last Stand of the Royalist Army in New Spain." *Hispanic American Royalist Review* 51 (February 1971): 92–111.

Arizpe, Miguel Ramos de. *Report That Dr. Miguel Ramos De Arizpe Presents to the August Congress on the Natural, Political, and Civil Condition of the Provinces of Coahuila, Nuevo León, Nuevo Santander, and Texas.* New York: Greenwood Press, 1969.

Arreola, Daniel D. "Chiricahua Apache Homeland in the Borderland Southwest." *Geographical Review* 102, no. 1 (2012): 111–31.

Babcock, Mathew. *Apache Adaptation to Hispanic Rule.* Cambridge: Cambridge University Press, 2016.

———. "Turning Apaches into Spaniards: North America's Forgotten Indian Reservations." PhD diss., Dallas, Texas, Southern Methodist University, 2008.

Ball, Eve, Nora Henn and Lynda Sanchez. *Indeh, an Apache Odyssey.* Norman: University of Oklahoma Press, 1988.

Bancroft, Hubert H. *The Works of Hubert Howe Bancroft: History of the North Mexican States and Texas.* San Francisco: Bancroft, 1886.

Bandelier, A. F. *Final Report of Investigations Among the Indians of the Southwest.* Cambridge, Mass.: University Press, 1890.

Barakat, Robert A. "Juan Tigre: A Mexican Folktale." *Journal of Popular Culture,* 4, no. 1 (1970): 230–39.

———. "Wailing Women of Folklore." *Journal of American Folklore,* 82, no. 325 (1969): 270–72.

Barr, Juliana. *Peace Came in the Form of a Woman: Indians and Spaniards in the Texas Borderlands.* Chapel Hill: University of North Carolina Press, 2007.

Barrett, Stephen Melvil. *Geronimo's Story of His Life.* New York: Duffield & Co., 1906.

Bartlett, John Russell. *Personal Narrative of Exploration and Incidents in Texas, New Mexico, California, Sonora, and Chihuahua,* vol. 2. New York: D. Appleton, 1854.

Bazant, Mílada. *Bestiality: The Nefarious Crime in Mexico, 1800–1856.* Oakland: University of California Press, 2016.

Bell, Bob Boze. "Ay Chihuahua!" *True West Magazine* (April 2016). Accessed January 20, 2020, https://truewestmagazine.com/ay-chihuahua-spanish-equivalent-yikes/.

Benedict, H. Bradley. "El Saqueo De Las Misiones De Chihuahua, 1767–1777." *Historia Mexicana* 22, no. 1 (1972): 24–33

———. "Hacienda Management in Late Colonial Northern Mexico: A Case Study of Juan Bustamante and the Hacienda of Dolores, 1790–1820." *Proceedings of the American Philosophical Society* 123, no. 6 (December 1979): 391–409.

Bernal Vázquez, Héctor M. *Jiménez: 250 Años en lucha contra la adversidad.* n.p., 2003.

Betzinez, Jason. *I Fought with Geronimo.* Harrisburg, Penn.: Stackpole, 1959.

Blackshear, James. *Fort Bascom: Soldiers, Comancheros, and Indians in the Canadian River Valley.* Norman: University of Oklahoma Press, 2016.

Blyth, Lance. *Chiricahua and Janos: Communities of Violence in the Southwestern Borderlands, 1680–1880.* Lincoln: University of Nebraska Press, 2012.

——. "The Presidio of Janos: Ethnicity, Society, Masculinity, and Ecology in Far Northern Mexico, 1685–1858." PhD diss., Northern Arizona University, Flagstaff, 2005.

Botkin, B. A. *A Treasury of Western Folklore*. New York: Crown Publishers, 1975.

Box, Michael James. *Captain James Box's Adventures and Explorations in New and Old Mexico*. New York: J. Miller, 1869.

Braddy, Haldeen. "Pancho Villa's Hidden Loot." *Western Folklore* 12, no. 2 (1953): 77–84.

Brinkworth, Grant D., Jonathan D. Buckley, Manny Noakes, Peter M. Clifton, Carlene J. Wilson. "Long-Term Effects of a Very Low-Carbohydrate Diet and a Low-Fat Diet on Mood and Cognitive Function." *Archives of Internal Medicine* 169 (November 9, 2009): 1873–1880.

Brooks, James F. *Captives and Cousins: Slavery, Kinship, and Community in the Southwest Borderlands*. Chapel Hill: University of North Carolina Press, 2011.

——. "Served Well by Plunder: La Gran Ladronería and Producers of History Astride the Río Grande." *American Quarterly* 52, no. 1 (March 2000): 23–58.

Burgess, Donald Harris. "Missionary Efforts among the Tarahumara Indians." MA thesis, Texas Western College, El Paso, 1963.

Casteñeda, Carlos. *Our Catholic Heritage in Texas*, vol. V. Austin: Von Boeckmann-Jones, 1942.

Castro, Rafaela. *Chicano Folklore: A Guide to the Folktales, Traditions, Rituals, and Religious Practices of Mexican Americans*. New York: Oxford University Press, 2001.

Campa Mendoza, Victor. *Las insurrecciones de los pueblos Indios en México*. Durango: Ediciones Fondo Internacional de Becas para Estudiantes Indígenas, 2001.

Carr, Raymond. *Spain, 1808–1975*. New York: Oxford University Press, 1982.

Cervantes, Guillermo. "De un presidio colonial a una ciudad, Santa María de las Caldas hoy Jiménez, Chihuahua." PhD diss., Universidad Autónoma de Ciudad Juárez, 2009.

Chamberlain, Samuel. *My Confession: Recollections of a Rogue*. Austin: Texas State Historical Association, 1997.

Chanthaphonh, Chip Colwell. *Massacre at Camp Grant*. Tucson: University of Arizona Press, 2007.

Chávez Chávez, Jorge. "Retrato del Indio Bárbaro. Proceso de Justificación de la Barbarie de los Indios del Septentrión Mexicano y Formación de la Cultura Norteña." *New Mexico Historical Review* 73, no. 4 (October 1998): 389–425.

——. *Visiones históricas de la frontera*. Juárez: El Colegio de Chihuahua, 2013.

Claiborne, John Francis Hamtramck. *Mississippi, as a Province, Territory, and State*. Baton Rouge: Louisiana State University Press, 1964.

Clark, LaVerne Harrell. "Early Horse Trappings of the Navajo and Apache Indians." *Arizona and the West* 5, no. 3 (1963): 233–48.

———. *They Sang for Horses: The Impact of the Horse on Navajo and Apache Folklore.* Tucson: University of Arizona Press, 1966.

Conder, Jósiah. *Mexico and Guatemala.* London: J. Duncan, 1831.

Conrad, Paul T. "Captive Fates: Displaced American Indians in the Southwest Borderlands, Mexico, and Cuba, 1500–1800." PhD diss., University of Texas, Austin, 2011.

———. "Empire through Kinship: Rethinking Spanish-Apache Relations in Southwestern North America in the Late Eighteenth and Early Nineteenth Centuries." *Early American Studies* 14, no. 4 (2016): 626–60.

Contreras Palacios, Gildardo. *Antecedentes históricos a la fundación de el Torreón.* Torreón, Coah.: Ayuntamiento de Torreón, 1992.

Cook, Leah Candolin. "The Last Apache 'Broncho': The Apache Outlaw in the Popular Imagination, 1886–2013." MA thesis, University of New Mexico, Albuquerque, 2014.

Coopwood, Bethel. "Route of Cabeza de Vaca: Part III." *Quarterly of the Texas State Historical Association* 3 (April 1900): 229–64.

Cortés, José. *Views from the Apache Frontier: Report on the Northern Provinces of New Spain.* Norman: University of Oklahoma Press, 1989.

Couts, Cave Johnson. *Hepah, California! The Journal of Cave Johnson Couts from Monterey, Nuevo Leon, Mexico, to Los Angeles, California, during the Years, 1848–1849.* Tucson: Arizona Pioneers' Historical Society, 1961.

Cox, Isaac Joslin. *The Early Exploration of Louisiana.* Cincinnati: University of Cincinnati Press, 1906.

Cremony, John Carey. *Life Among the Apaches: The Classic History of Native American Life on the Plains.* San Francisco: A. Roman, 1868.

Curott, Nicholas A., and Alexander Fink. "Bandit Heroes: Social, Mythical, or Rational?" *American Journal of Economics and Sociology* 71, no. 2 (2012): 470–97.

Cutter, Charles R. *The Legal Culture of Northern New Spain, 1700–1810.* Albuquerque: University of New Mexico Press, 2001.

Damico, Denis Holladay. "The Cebolleta Land Grant: Multicultural Cooperation and Contention." *Natural Resources Journal* 48 (Fall 2008): 963–81.

Daniel, James M., and Pedro José de la Fuenta. "Diary of Pedro José de la Fuente, Captain of the Presidio of El Paso del Norte, August–December, 1765." *Southwestern Historical Quarterly* 83, no. 3 (January 1980): 259–78.

Deeds, Susan M. *Defiance and Deference in Mexico's Colonial North: Indians under Spanish Rule in Nueva Vizcaya.* Austin: University of Texas Press, 2003.

De la Teja, Jesús (ed.). "Murillo's Plan for the Reform of New Spain's Defenses." *Southwestern Historical Quarterly* 107 (April 2004): 501–34.

De la Torre Curiel, José Refugio. *Twilight of the Mission Frontier: Shifting Interethnic Alliances and Social Organization in Sonora, 1768–1855.* Stanford, Calif.: Stanford University Press, 2012.

Delay, Brian. *War of a Thousand Deserts: Indian Raids and the U.S.-Mexican War.* New Haven, Conn.: Yale University Press, 2008.

Diccionario de cocina, o el Nuevo cocinero Mejicano, en forma de diccionario. Mexico D. F.: Imprenta de I. Cumplido, 1845.

Dobie, Frank J. *Apache Gold and Yaqui Silver.* Austin: University of Texas Press, 1985.

———. *Tongues of the Monte.* Austin: University of Texas Press, 1980.

Doolen, Andy. "Captive in Mexico: Zebulon Pike and the New American Regionalism." In *Mapping Region in Early American Writing.* Edited by Edward Watts, Keri Holt, and John Funchion. Athens: University of Georgia Press, 2015.

Domínguez Rascón, Alonso. "Autonomía Insurgencia y oligarquía: Las Provincias Internas y la formación de los estados septentrionales." *Historia Mexicana* 66, no. 3 (2017): 1023–1075.

———. *Estado, Frontera, y Ciudadanía.* Ciudad Juárez: Universidad Autónoma de Ciudad Juárez, 2017.

Duncan Baretta, Silvio R., and John Markoff. "Civilization and Barbarism: Cattle Frontiers in Latin America." *Comparative Studies in Society and History* 20 (October 1978): 587–620.

Dunn, Fabius. "The Administration of Don Antonio Cordero, Governor of Texas, 1805–1808." PhD diss., University of Texas, Austin, 1979.

Dye, Nancy Schrom, and Daniel Blake Smith. "Mother Love and Infant Death, 1750–1920." *Journal of American History* 73 (September 1986): 329–53.

Eastman, Edwin. *Seven and Nine Years among the Camanches and Apaches: An Autobiography.* Jersey City, NJ: Clark Johnson, M.D., 1874.

Ellingson, Terry Jay. *The Myth of the Noble Savage.* Berkeley: University of California Press, 2001.

Elliott, Charles P. "An Indian Reservation under General George Crook." *Military Affairs* 23 (Summer 1948): 91–103.

Escudero, José Agustín de. *Observaciones sobre el estado actual del departamento de Chihuahua.* Mexico City: Juan Ojeda, 1839.

Farmer, W. Michael. *Apacheria: True Stories of Apache Culture.* Guilford, Conn: Twodot, 2017.

Faulk, Odie B. *The Last Years of Spanish Texas, 1778–1821.* The Hague: Mouton, 1964.

Fenster, Julie M. *Jefferson's America: The President, the Purchase, and the Explorers Who Transformed a Nation.* New York: Crown Publishers, 2016.

Fernández Perea, Octavio. *Jiménez en la historia y en la leyenda.* Chihuahua: La Universidad Autónoma de Chihuahua, 2008.

Fisher, Lillian Estelle. *The Background of the Revolution for Mexican Independence.* Boston: Christopher Publishing House, 1934.

Flagler, Edward K. "Comercio y ferias de trueque: España y los indios de Nuevo México." *Revista Española de Antropología Americana* 37, no. 1 (2007): 51–65.

Flippin, J. R. *Sketches from the Mountains of Mexico*. Cincinnati: Standard Publishing, 1889.

Florescano, Enrique, and Isabel Gil Sánchez (eds.). *Descripciones económicas regionales de Nueva España: Provincias del Norte, 1790–1814*. Mexico City: Instituto Nacional de Antropología e Historia, 1976.

Folsom, Bradley. *Arredondo: Last Spanish Ruler of Texas and Northeastern Mexico*. Norman: University of Oklahoma Press, 2017.

Forsyth, George Alexander. *The Story of the Soldier*. New York: D. Appleton, 1909.

Fowler, Will. "Understanding Individual and Collective Insurrectionary Action in Independent Mexico, 1821–1876." In *Malcontents, Rebels, and Pronunciados: The Politics of Insurrection in Nineteenth-Century Mexico*. Edited by Will Fowler. Lincoln: University of Nebraska Press, 2012.

Francisco Velasco, José. *Noticias estadísticas del estado de Sonora*. Hermosillo: Gobierno del Estado de Sonora, 1985.

——. *Sonora: Its Extent, Population, Natural Productions, Indian Tribes, Mines, Mineral, Lands, etc., etc.* Translated by William F. Nye. San Francisco: H. H. Bancroft, 1861.

Friedman, Benjamin H. "Managing Fear: The Politics of Homeland Security." *Political Science Quarterly* 126, no. 1 (2011): 77–106.

Froebel, Julius. *Seven Years' Travel in Central America, Northern Mexico, and the Far West of the United States*. London: Richard Bentley, 1859.

Fuentes Rebolloso, Rosa María. "El Santo Cristo de Burgos." *Sobre todo la fe: revista mensual de la diócesis de Parral* 1, no. 7 (August 2013): 12.

Galicia, Rocío. "*Apaches* de Victor Hugo Rascón Banda: identidad y representación del septentrión entre indios y mexicanos." *Latin American Theatre Review* 42, no. 9 (Spring 2009): 17–40.

Gallegos Renova, Lorena. "La vida en el presidio de Janos: relaciones sociales de los tiempos coloniales a los primeros años independientes." MA thesis, Escuela Nacional de Antropología e Historia, Chihuahua, 2012.

García Cubas, Antonio. *Diccionario geográfico, histórico y biográfico de los Estados Unidos Mexicanos*, vol. V. México, D. F.: Oficina Tipográfica de la Secretaría de Fomento, 1891.

García Torres, Vicente. *Documentos para la historia eclesiástica y civil de la Nueva Vizcaya*. Mexico, D. F.: Imprenta de Vicente García Torres, 1857.

Garrett, Julia Kathryn. *Green Flag over Texas: A Story of the Last Years of Spain in Texas*. New York: Cordova Press, 1939.

Gerhard, Peter. *The North Frontier of New Spain*. Norman: University of Oklahoma Press, 1993.

Goddard, Pliny Earle. *Jicarilla Apache Texts*. New York: The Trustees, 1911.

González Quiroga, Miguel Ángel. *War and Peace of the Rio Grande, 1830–1880*. Norman: University of Oklahoma Press, 2020.

Goodwin, Grenville. *The Social Organization of the Western Apache*. Tucson: University of Arizona Press, 1969.

———. *Western Apache Raiding and Warfare*. Edited by Keith H. Basso. Tucson: University of Arizona Press, 1971.

Goodwin, Neil. *Like a Brother: Grenville Goodwin's Apache Years, 1928–1939*. Tucson: University of Arizona Press, 2004.

Green, Thomas A. *Latino American Folktales*. Westport, Conn.: Greenwood Press, 2009.

Gregg, Josiah. *Commerce of the Prairies*, vol. 2. New York: Henry G. Langley and Astor House, 1844.

Griffen, William B. *Apaches at War and Peace: The Janos Presidio, 1750–1858*. Norman: University of Oklahoma Press, 1988.

———. "The Compás: A Chiricahua Apache Family of the Late 18th and Early 19th Centuries." *American Indian Quarterly* 7, no. 2 (Spring 1983): 21–49.

———. *Utmost Good Faith: Patterns of Apache-Mexican Hostilities in Northern Chihuahua Border Warfare, 1821–1848*. Albuquerque: University of New Mexico Press, 1988.

Grigsby, R. F. *R. F. Grigsby's Sierra Madre Journal, 1864*. Sebastopol, Calif.: Pleasant Hill Press, 1976.

Grossman, Dave. *On Killing: The Psychological Cost of Learning to Kill in War and Society*. Boston: Little, Brown, 1996.

Guardino, Peter. *The Time of Liberty: Popular Political Culture in Oaxaca, 1750–1850*. Durham, NC: Duke University Press, 2005.

Guerra, Eduardo. *Historia de la Laguna, Torreón, su origen y sus fundadores*. Torreón: Impresora de Coahuila, 1932.

Guerrero, Julio. *La génesis del crimen en México: estudio de psiquiatría social*. Paris: Imprenta de La Vda de Ch. Bouret, 1901.

Guy, Donna J., and Thomas E. Sheridan, eds. *Contested Ground: Comparative Frontiers on the Northern and Southern Edges of the Spanish Empire*. Tucson: University of Arizona Press, 1998.

Guzmán, Martín Luis. *Memoirs of Pancho Villa*. Translated by Virginia H. Taylor. Austin: University of Texas Press, 1965.

Hackel, Steven W. *Children of Coyote, Missionaries of Saint Francis: Indian-Spanish Relations in Colonial California, 1769–1850*. Chapel Hill: University of North Carolina Press, 2005.

Haggard, J. Villasana. *Handbook for Translators of Spanish Historical Documents*. Austin: University of Texas Archives Collection, 1941.

Haley, James L. *Apaches: A History and Culture Portrait*. Norman: University of Oklahoma Press, 1997.

Hämäläinen, Pekka. *The Comanche Empire*. New Haven, Conn: Yale University Press, 2009.

Hamill, Hugh M. "Early Psychological Warfare in the Hidalgo Revolt." *Hispanic American Historical Review* 41 (May 1961): 206–35.

———. *The Hidalgo Revolt: Prelude to Mexican Independence*. Gainesville: University Press of Florida, 1996.

Hardy, R. W. H. *Travels in the Interior of Mexico in 1825, 1826, 1827, & 1828*. London: Henry Colburn and Richard Bentley, 1829.

Harper, Ernest Bouldin. "Personality Types: A Note on Sociological Classification." *Social Science* 1, no. 1 (1925): 26–29.

Harris, Charles H. *A Mexican Family Empire: The Latifundio of the Sánchez Navarro Family, 1765–1867*. Austin: University of Texas Press, 1975.

Hart, Stephen Harding, and Archer Butler Hulbert eds. *Southwestern Journals of Zebulon Pike*. Albuquerque: University of New Mexico Press, 2006.

Helms, Mary W. "Matrilocality, Social Solidarity, and Culture Contact: Three Case Histories." *Southwestern Journal of Anthropology* 26 (Summer 1970): 197–212.

Henderson, Timothy J. *The Mexican Wars for Independence*. New York: Hill and Wang, 2009.

Hendricks, Rick, and W. H. Timmons. *San Elizario: Spanish Presidio to Texas County Seat*. El Paso: Texas Western Press, 1998.

Hernández, Carlos. *Durango gráfico: Obra completa que da á conocer detalladamente la historia del estado de Durango, su geografía, su hidrografía, su minería, la estadística de su población en las distintas épocas de su desarrollo y sus poderosos elementos de riqueza en todas sus manifestaciones*. Durango: Talleres de J. S. Rocha, 1903.

Hobbs, James. *Wild Life in the Far West: Personal Adventures of a Border Mountain Man*. San Francisco: Wiley, Waterman, Eaton, 1873.

Hobsbawm, Eric. *Primitive Rebels: Studies in Archaic Forms of Social Movement in the 19th and 20th Centuries*. Manchester: Manchester University Press, 1959.

Hodgetts, Lisa M. "Faunal Evidence from El Zurdo." *Kiva* 62, no. 2 (1996): 149–70.

Holmes, Stephen T. *Contemporary Perspectives on Serial Murder*. Thousand Oaks, Calif.: Sage Publications, 1998.

Hudson, Wilson M. *The Healer of Los Olmos and Other Mexican Lore*. Dallas: Southern Methodist University Press, 1951.

Huggard, Christopher J., and Terrence M. Humble. *Santa Rita del Cobre: A Copper Mining Community in New Mexico*. Boulder: University Press of Colorado, 2012.

Humboldt, Alexander von. *Political Essay on the Kingdom of New Spain*. London: Longman, Hurst, Rees, Orme and Brown, and H. Colburn, 1811.

Ingstad, Helge. *The Apache Indians: In Search of the Missing Tribe*. Lincoln: University of Nebraska Press, 2004.

In the Matter of the Claim of Certain Mexican Citizens to Lands on the Rio Grande Known by the Name of District of "El Chamizal." Mexico D. F.: Secretary of Foreign Relations, 1905.

Ives, Ronald L., "The Sonoran 'Primer Montezuma' Legends." *Western Folklore,* 9, no. 4 (1950): 321–25.

Jackson, Hal. *Following the Royal Road: A Guide to the Historic Camino Real de Tierra Adentro.* Albuquerque: University of New Mexico Press, 2006.

Jackson, Jack. *Los Mesteños: Spanish Ranching in Texas, 1721–1821.* College Station: Texas A&M Press, 2006.

Jackson, Donald (ed.). *Letters of the Lewis and Clark Expedition, with Related Documents, 1783–1854.* Urbana: University of Illinois Press, 1978.

Jackson, Robert H. *Frontiers of Evangelization: Indians in the Sierra Gorda and Chiquitos Missions.* Norman: University of Oklahoma Press, 2017.

John, Elizabeth H. "The Riddle of Mapmaker Juan Pedro Walker." In *Essays on the History of North American Discovery and Exploration.* Edited by Stanley H. Palmer and Dennis Reinhartz. College Station: Texas A&M University Press, 1988.

———., and John Wheat, eds., "Views from a Desk in Chihuahua: Manuel Merino's Report on Apaches and Neighboring Nations, ca. 1804." *Southwestern Historical Quarterly* 95, no. 2 (1991): 138–76.

Jones, J. A. "Operant Psychology and the Study of Culture." *Current Anthropology* 12, no. 2 (1971): 171–218.

Jones, Oakah L., Jr. *Los Paisanos: Spanish Settlers on the Northern Frontier of New Spain.* Norman: University of Oklahoma Press, 1996.

———. *Nueva Vizcaya: Heartland of the Spanish Frontier.* Albuquerque: University of New Mexico Press, 1988.

Katzew, Llona. *Casta Painting: Images of Race in Eighteenth-Century Mexico.* New Haven, Conn.: Yale University Press, 2005.

Kendall, George Wilkins. *Narrative of the Texas Santa Fe Expedition Comprising a Description of a Tour through Texas and across the Great Southwestern Prairies, the Comanche and Caygüa Hunting-Grounds, with an Account of the Sufferings from Want of Food, Losses from Hostile Indians and Final Capture of the Texans, and Their March, as Prisoners, to the City of Mexico.* New York: Harper and Brothers, 1845.

Kessell, John L. *Friars, Soldiers, and Reformers: Hispanic Arizona and the Sonora Mission Frontier, 1767–1856.* Tucson: University of Arizona Press, 2016.

———. "To Stop Captain Merry: Spanish Efforts to Intercept Lewis and Clark." *New Mexico Historical Review* 81 (Spring 2006): 125–40.

Kinnaird, Lawrence. *The Frontiers of New Spain: Nicolas de Lafora's Description.* Berkeley, Calif.: Quivira Society, 1958.

Krauze, Enrique. *Mexico: Biography of Power.* New York: HarperCollins, 1997.

Lea, Henry Charles. "Hidalgo and Morelos." *American Historical Review* 4 (July 1899): 636–38.

Lepidus, Henry. "The History of Mexican Journalism." *University of Missouri Bulletin* 29, no. 4 (January 1928): 19–23.

Liljegren, Ernest R. "Zalmon Coley: The Second Anglo-American in Santa Fe." *New Mexico Historical Review* 62, no. 3 (July 1987): 263–86.

Linklater, Andro. *An Artist in Treason: The Extraordinary Double Life of General James Wilkinson Commander in Chief of the U.S. Army and Agent 12 in the Spanish Secret Service.* New York: Walker Publishing, 2009.

Lockwood, Frank C. *The Apache Indians.* Lincoln: University of Nebraska Press, 1987.

Marshall, Michael P. "Journal of Reconnaissance of the Camino Real." In *El Camino Real de tierra adentro,* vol. 2 (Santa Fe, NM: Bureau of Land Management, 1999), 25.

Lumholtz, Carl. *Unknown Mexico,* vol. 1. London: Macmillan, 1902.

MacLachlan, Colin M., and William H. Beezley, *Mexico's Crucial Century, 1810–1910: An Introduction.* Lincoln: University of Nebraska Press, 2010.

Manrique, Linnete. "Dreaming of a Cosmic Race: José Vasconcelos and the Politics of Race in Mexico, 1920s–1930s." *Cogent Arts & Humanities 3 no. 1 (2016):* 1–13.

Marcos Bustos, José, and María del Valle Borrero Silva. "La crisis de la monarquía hispánica en la intendencia de Arizpe, insurgencia y contrainsurgencia." *Americanistas* 28 (2012): 1–22.

Martin, Cheryl English. *Governance and Society in Colonial Mexico.* Stanford, Calif.: Stanford University Press, 1996.

Martínez García, Roberto. *Indios, mineros, peones y maestros: ensayos y breves relatos.* Torreón, Coahuila: Universidad Iberoamericana, 2001.

Martínez Peñas, Leandro, and Manuela Fernández Rodríguez. "La guerra contra los Apaches bajo el mando de Ramón de Castro y Pedro de Nava en las Provincias Interiores." *Revista de Historia Militar,* 111 (July 2012): 119–58.

Martínez Sánchez, Lucas. *Hidalgo y los insurgentes en la provincia de Coahuila.* Saltillo: Consejo Editorial del Estado, 2015.

Mathes, Michael W. "Arms for the Defense of the Eastern Provincias Internas of New Spain: A Mountain Cannon." *Colonial Latin American Historical Review* 6, no. 3 (1997): 267–77.

Matson, Daniel S., and Albert H. Schroeder, eds. "Cordero's Description of the Apaches, 1769." *New Mexico Historical Review* 32, no. 4 (1957): 335–56.

———. and Bernard L. Fontana, eds., *Friar Bringas Reports to the King: Methods of Indoctrination on the Frontier of New Spain, 1796–1797.* Tucson: University of Arizona Press, 2017.

McDougall, Christopher. *Born to Run: A Hidden Tribe, Superathletes, and the Greatest Race the World Has Never Seen.* New York: Random House, 2009.

McKanna, Clare V., Jr. *White Justice in Arizona: Apache Murder Trials in the Nineteenth Century*. Lubbock: Texas Tech University Press, 2005.

McNitt, Frank. *Navajo Wars: Military Campaigns, Slave Raids, and Reprisals*. Albuquerque: University of New Mexico Press, 1972.

Mendiola Galván, Francisco. *El arte rupestre en Chihuahua expresión cultural de nómadas y sedentarios en el norte de México*. Chihuahua: Instituto Chihuahuense de la Cultura, 2002.

Mendoza Levario, Israel. *A Brief Chronicle of Presidio del Norte: Homeland of the Jumano*. Austin: La Junta Press, 2012.

Merrill, William L. "La economía política de las correrías: Nueva Vizcaya al final de la época colonial." In Marie-Areti Hers, José Luis Mirafuentes, María de los Dolores Soto, and Miguel Vallebueno, eds., *Nómadas y sedentarios en el norte de México: Homenaje a Beatriz Braniff*. México: Universidad Nacional Autónoma de México, 2000: 623–68.

Michno, Gregory. *Encyclopedia of Indian Wars: Western Battles and Skirmishes, 1850–1890*. Missoula, Mont.: Mountain Press Publishing, 2003.

Miles, Nelson A. *Personal Recollections of Observation of General Nelson A. Miles*. Chicago: Werner Company, 1896.

Mirafuentes Galván, José Luis. "Los dos mundos de José Reyes Pozo." *Estudios de Historia Novohispana* 21 (2009): 67–105.

Moorehead, Warren King. *The American Indian in the United States, Period 1850–1914*. Freeport, NY: Books for Libraries Press, 1969.

Moorhead, Max L. *The Apache Frontier: Jacobo Ugarte and Spanish-Indian Relations in Northern New Spain, 1769–1791*. Norman: University of Oklahoma Press, 1968.

———. *New Mexico's Royal Road: Trade and Travel on the Chihuahua Trail*. Norman: University of Oklahoma Press, 1958.

———. *The Presidio: Bastion of the Spanish Borderlands*. Norman: University of Oklahoma Press, 1991.

Mörner, Magnus. *Race Mixture in the History of Latin America*. Boston: Little, Brown, 1975.

Narrett, David. "Geopolitics and Intrigue: James Wilkinson, the Spanish Borderlands, and Mexican Independence." *William and Mary Quarterly* 69 (2012).

Navarro García, Luis. *Las Provincias Internas en el siglo XIX*. Seville: Escuela de Estudios Hispano-Americanos, 1965.

Nichols, James David. "A 'Great System of Roaming': Runaway Debt Peons and the Making of the International Border." In *The Limits of Liberty: Mobility and the Making of the Eastern U.S.-Mexico Border*. Lincoln: University of Nebraska Press, 2018.

Nickens, Paul R., and Kathleen M. Nickens. "Victor of Old San Carlos: Portrait of a Captive Mexican and Apache Tag Band Chief." *Journal of Arizona History* 56, no. 3 (2015): 277–322.

Ober, Frederick Albion. *Travels in Mexico and Life Among the Mexicans*. Boston: Estes & Lauriat, 1887.

Ocampo, Emilio. *The Emperor's Last Campaign: A Napoleonic Empire in America*. Tuscaloosa: University of Alabama Press, 2009.

Ochoa Zazueta, Jesús Ángel. *Apostillas de los Tepehuanes*. Mexico D. F.: Nueva Hispanidad, 1967.

Olmos Sánchez, Isabel. *La sociedad mexicana en vísperas de la independencia, 1787–1821*. Murcia: Universidad de Murcia, 1989.

Operé, Fernando. *Indian Captivity in Spanish America: Frontier Narratives*. Charlottesville: University of Virginia Press, 2008.

Opler, Morris Edward. *An Apache Life Way: The Economic, Social, and Religious Institutions of the Chiricahua Indians*. Lincoln: University of Nebraska Press, 1996.

Orozco, Victor. *El estado de Chihuahua en el parto de la nación, 1810–1831*. Mexico City: Plaza y Valdés, 2007.

———. *Las Guerra indias en la historia de Chihuahua*. Ciudad Juárez: Universidad Autónoma de Ciudad Juárez, 1992.

Orsi, Jared. *Citizen Explorer: The Life of Zebulon Pike*. New York: Oxford University Press, 2017.

Ortega, Emanuel. "Testimonies of Violence: Images of Franciscan Martyrs in the Provinces of New Spain." PhD diss., University of New Mexico, Albuquerque, 2017.

Ortelli, Sara. "Del discurso oficial a las fuentes judiciales el enemigo y el proceso de mestizaje en el norte novohispano tardocolonial." *Memoria Americana* 13 (2005): 53–81.

———. "Entre desiertos y serranías: Población, espacio no controlado y fronteras permeables en el Septentrión novohispano tardocolonial." *Revista d'Història Moderna* 32 (2014): 85–107.

———. *Trama De Una Guerra Conveniente: Nueva Vizcaya y La Sombra De Los Apaches, 1748–1790*. Mexico City: Colegio de Mexico, 2007.

———. "Vivir en los márgenes: Fronteras porosas y circulación de población en la Nueva Vizcaya tardo colonial." *Anuario de Historia Regional y de las Fronteras* 19, no. 1 (January 2004): 39–57.

Pacheco Rojas, José de la Cruz. *Durango: historia breve*. Mexico City: Fondo de Cultura Económica, 2001.

———. *El Proceso de Independencia en Durango: Periodo de la insurgencia, 1808–1812*. Durango: Universidad Juárez del Estado de Durango, 2010.

———. and Joseph P. Sánchez, *Memorias de Coloquio Internacional El Camino Real de Tierra Adentro*. México D. F.: Instituto Nacional de Antropología e Historia, 2000.

Palmer, Jessica D. *The Apache Peoples: A History of All Bands and Tribes Through the 1800s*. Jefferson, N.C: McFarland, 2013.

Pattie, James O. *The Personal Narrative of James O. Pattie of Kentucky, during an Expedition from St. Louis, through the Vast Regions between that Place and the Pacific Ocean*. Cincinnati: E. H. Flint, 1833.

Pender V. "Some Reminiscences of Old Dolores." *Engineering and Mining Journal* (June 1910): 1329–30.

Pendexter, Hugh. *The Gate through the Mountain*. New York: A. L. Burt, 1929.

Pennington, Campbell W. *The Tarahumar of Mexico: Their Environment and Material Culture*. Salt Lake City: University of Utah Press, 1963.

Perez, Domino R. *There Was a Woman: La Llorona from Folklore to Popular Culture*. Austin: University of Texas Press, 2008.

Pfefferkorn, Ignaz. *Sonora: A Description of the Province*. Translated by Theodore E. Treutlein. Albuquerque: University of New Mexico Press, 1949.

Pike, Zebulon. *The Expeditions of Zebulon Montgomery Pike: To Headwaters of the Mississippi River, Through Louisiana Territory, and in New Spain, During the Years 1805–1807*. New York: Francis P. Harper, 1895.

Pino, Pedro Bautista. *The Exposition on the Province of New Mexico, 1812*. Albuquerque: University of New Mexico Press, 1995.

Poinsett, Joel Roberts. *Notes on Mexico Made in the Autumn of 1822*. London: J. Miller, 1825.

Quintero Saravia, Gonzalo M. *Bernardo De Gálvez: Spanish Hero of the American Revolution*. Chapel Hill: University of North Carolina Press, 2018.

Radbourne, Allan. "Great Chief: Hashkeedasillaa of the White Mountain Apaches." *Journal of Arizona History* 50 (Spring 2009): 1–58.

Raigosa Gómez, Tania Celiset. "La Justicia Criminal en Durango, Nueva Vizcaya, 1750–1824." PhD diss., Universidad de Sevilla, Seville, May 2017.

Ramos-Kittrell, Jesús A. *Playing in the Cathedral: Music, Race, and Status in New Spain*. New York: Oxford University Press, 2016.

Reeve, Frank Driver. *Navajo Foreign Affairs, 1795–1846*. Tsaile, Ariz.: Navajo Community College Press, 1983.

Reséndez, Andrés. *The Uncovered Story of Indian Enslavement in America*. Boston: Houghton Mifflin Harcourt, 2016.

Riva Palacio, Vicente. *Mexico a través de los siglos*, vol. 4. Mexico: D. F.: J. Ballescá y Compañía, 1888.

Rivera, Pedro de, Thomas H. Naylor, and Charles W. Polzer. *Pedro De Rivera and the Military Regulations for Northern New Spain, 1724–1729: A Documentary History of His Frontier Inspection and the Reglamento De 1729*. Tucson: University of Arizona Press, 1988.

Rivers, Claudia. "JUAREZ ARCHIVES," *Handbook of Texas Online*. Accessed June 5, 2020, http://www.tshaonline.org/handbook/online/articles/lcjo4, last modified on June 15, 2010.

Robertson, James Alexander (ed.). *Louisiana under the Rule of Spain, France, and the United States, 1785–1807: Social, Economic, and Political Conditions of the Territory Represented in the Louisiana Purchase*, 2 vols. Cleveland: Arthur H. Clark, 1911.

Robin, Rob. "Prison Camps and Culture Wars: The Korean Brainwashing Controversy." In *The Making of the Cold War Enemy: Culture and Politics in the Military-Intellectual Complex* (Princeton, NJ: Princeton University Press, 2001), 162–82.

Robinson, Sherry. *Apache Voices: Their Stories of Survival as Told to Eve Ball*. Albuquerque: University of New Mexico Press, 2003.

Robinson, William Spencer. *Iturbide of Mexico*. Durham, NC: Duke University Press, 1952.

Robinson, William Davis. *Memoirs of the Mexican Revolution, Including a Narrative of the Expedition of General Xavier Mina; to Which Are Annexed Some Observations on the Practicability of Opening a Commerce between the Pacific and Atlantic Oceans, through the Mexican Isthmus, in the Province of Oaxaca, and at the Lake of Nicaragua; and the Vast Importance of Such Commerce to the Civilized World*. London: Lackington, Hughes, Harding, Mavor & Lepard, 1821.

Robles, Vito Alessio. *Coahuila y Texas en la época colonial*. Saltillo: Ed. Cultura, 1938.

Rock, Rosalind Z. "Dying Quijote: Nemesio Salcedo and the Last Years of Spain in the Internal Provinces." PhD diss., University of New Mexico, Albuquerque, 1981.

Rodríguez López, María Guadalupe (ed.). *Historia de Durango*, vol. 2. Durango: Universidad Juárez del Estado de Durango, 2013.

Rodriguez, Roland. "'I Was Nothing but a Lender of What I Was Ordered to Supply . . .': Francisco Amangual, Trustee of the Presidio *Las Compañías Volantes* in the Spanish Borderlands, 1701–1812." PhD diss., University of Texas, El Paso, 2015.

Ruedas de la Serna, Jorge. "Gracia, erotismo y originalidad en un poeta de la Arcadia mexicana." *Revista ALPHA Revista da Faculdade de Filosofia Ciências e Letras de Patos de Minas* 7 (2006): 200.

Ruxton, George F. *Adventures in Mexico and the Rocky Mountains*. London: J. Murray, 1849.

Sáenz Carrete, Erasmo. *Haciendas y minas: una historia de Santa María del Oro y su región*. Durango: Universidad Juárez del Estado de Durango, 1999.

Salcedo, Nemesio, and Canales I. Vizcaya. *Instrucción reservada de don Nemesio Salcedo y Salcedo comandante general de provincias internas a su sucesor*. Chihuahua, Chih., México: Centro de Información del Estado de Chihuahua, 1991.

Sánchez, Isabel Gil. *Descripciones, económicas, regionales de Nueva España: provincias del Norte, 1790–1814*. México, D. F.: Instituto Nacional de Antropología e Historia, 1976.

Sánchez Bañón, Julio. "El septentrión novohispano: La comandancia general de las provincias internas." PhD diss., Universidad Complutense de Madrid, 2015.

Sánchez Moreno, Francisco Javier. "Los Indios 'Bárbaros' en la frontera noreste de Nueva España entre 1810 y 1821." *Americanistas*, 26 (2011): 20–47.

Santiago, Mark. *A Bad Peace and a Good War: Spain and the Mescalero Apache Uprising of 1795–1799*. Norman: University of Oklahoma Press, 2018.

———. *Jar of Severed Hands: Spanish Deportation of Apache Prisoners of War, 1770–1810*. Norman: University of Oklahoma Press, 2011.

Sarabia, Atanasio G. "El Indio Rafael," *Investigaciones históricas*, I (October 1938): 53–61.

Schwatka, Frederick. *In the Land of the Cliff Dwellers*. Boston: Educational Publishing, 1899.

Shelton, Laura M. *For Tranquility and Order: Family and Community on Mexico's Northern Frontier, 1800–1850*. Tucson: University of Arizona Press, 2010.

Shepherd, Grant. *The Silver Magnet: Fifty Years in a Mexican Silver Mine*. New York: E. P. Dutton, 1938.

Simmons, Marc Steven. *Spanish Government in New Mexico*. Albuquerque: University of New Mexico Press, 1968.

———. "Spanish Government in New Mexico at the End of the Colonial Period." PhD. diss., University of New Mexico, Albuquerque, 1965.

Smith, Ralph Adam. *Borderlander: The Life of James Kirker, 1793–1852*. Norman: University of Oklahoma Press, 1999.

Snow, Robert L. *Deadly Cults: The Crimes of True Believers*. Westport, Conn.: Greenwood Publishing, 2003.

Sonnichsen, C. L. "The Ambivalent Apache." *Western American Literature* 10, no. 2 (1975): 99–102.

Sotelo, Carlos. *Ensalada de historias y cuentos*. Bloomington, Ind.: Palibrio, 2012.

Sotomayor Garza, Jesús G. *Anales Laguneros*. Torreón: Ayuntamiento de Torreón, 1992.

Stern, Peter. "Social Marginality and Acculturation on the Northern Frontier of New Spain." PhD diss., University of California, Berkeley, 1984.

———. "The White Indians of the Borderlands." *Journal of the Southwest* 33 (Autumn 1991): 262–81.

Stockel, H. Henrietta. *On the Bloody Road to Jesus: Christianity and the Chiricahua Apaches*. Albuquerque: University of New Mexico Press, 2004.

Stockel, H. Henrietta. *Salvation through Slavery: Chiricahua Apaches and Priests on the Spanish Colonial Frontier*. Albuquerque: University of New Mexico Press, 2008.

Stone, Charles P. *Notes on the State of Sonora*. Washington, DC: Henry Polkinhorn Printer, 1861.

Stratton, R. B. *Captivity of the Oatman Girls: Being an Interesting Narrative of Life among the Apache and Mohave Indians*. New York: Carlton & Porter, 1857.

Sweeney, Edwin R. *Cochise: Chiricahua Apache Chief.* Norman: University of Oklahoma Press, 1995.

———. "Mangas Coloradas and Apache Diplomacy: Treaty-Making with Chihuahua and Sonora, 1842–1843." *Journal of Arizona History* 39, no. 1 (1998): 1–22.

———. *Mangas Coloradas: Chief of the Chiricahua Apaches.* Norman: University of Oklahoma Press, 2011.

———. "One of Heaven's Heroes: A Mexican General Pays Tribute to the Honor and Courage of a Chiricahua Apache." *Journal of Arizona History* 36, no. 3 (1995): 209–32.

Taylor, William B. *Theater of a Thousand Wonders: A History of Miraculous Images and Shrines in New Spain.* New York: Cambridge University Press, 2016.

Terrazas, Silvestre. *Curiosidades históricas.* Chihuahua: El Correo de Chihuahua, 1909.

Thwaites, Reuben Gold. *Early Western Travels, 1748–1846,* vol. xx. Cleveland: Arthur H. Clark, 1905.

Townes, J. Edward. *Invisible Lines: The Life and Death of a Borderland.* Fort Worth: Texas Christian University Press, 2008.

Tulkin, S. R., and M. J. Konner. "Alternative Conceptions of Intellectual Functioning." *Human Development* 16, no. 1/2 (1973): 33–52.

Valenzuela Arce, José Manuel. *Entre la mágica y la historia.* Tijuana: Programa Cultural de las Fronteras, El Colegio de la Frontera Norte, 1992.

Vanderwood, Paul. *The Power of God Against the Guns of Government: Religious Upheaval in Mexico at the Turn of the Nineteenth Century.* Stanford, Calif.: Stanford University Press, 1998.

Van Young, Eric. *The Other Rebellion: Popular Violence, Ideology, and the Mexican Struggle for Independence, 1810–1821.* Stanford, Calif.: Stanford University Press, 2001.

Velasco, Luis Alfonso. *Geografía y estadística de la republica Mexicana,* vol. XIX. México D. F.: Oficina TipoGráfica de la Secretaría de Fomento, 1897.

Vizcaya Canales, Isidro. *En los albores de la independencia: las Provincias Internas de Oriente durante la Insurrección de don Miguel Hidalgo y Costilla, 1810–1811.* Monterrey: Publicaciones del Instituto Tecnológico y de Estudios Superiores de Monterrey, 1976.

Von Tempsky, G. F. *Mitla: A Narrative of Incidents and Personal Adventures on a Journey in Mexico, Guatemala, and Salvador in the Years of 1853 to 1855.* Edited by J. S. Bell. London: Longman, Brown, Green, Longmans, & Roberts, 1858.

Voss, Barbara L. *The Archaeology of Ethnogenesis: Race and Sexuality in Colonial San Francisco.* Berkeley: University of California Press, 2008.

Voss, Stuart F. *On the Periphery of Nineteenth-Century Mexico: Sonora and Sinaloa.* Tucson: University of Arizona Press, 1982.

Watt, Robert N. *Apache Tactics 1830–1886.* New York: Osprey, 2014.

———. *Apache Warrior, 1860–1886*. New York: Osprey, 2014.

———. "Raiders of a Lost Art? Apache War and Society." *Small Wars & Insurgencies* 13, no. 3 (2002): 11–12.

Wayland, Virginia. "Princeton's Apache Playing Cards." *Princeton University Library Chronicle* 34 (Spring 1973): 147–57.

Weber, David. *The Spanish Frontier in North America*. New Haven, Conn.: Yale University Press, 1992.

Weddle, Robert S. *The San Sabá Mission*. College Station: Texas A&M University Press, 1999.

Whiting, William H. C. "Journal of William H. C. Whiting." In Philip Saint George Cooke, *Exploring Southwestern Trails, 1846–1854*. Edited by Ralph P. Bieber and Averam B. Bender. Glendale, Calif.: Arthur H. Clark, 1938.

Williams, Jack S. "The Evolution of the Presidio in Northern New Spain." *Historical Archaeology* 38, no. 3 (2004): 6–23.

Williams, Jerry. "Referential Shadows on New World Relations: Notes on Moors, Blacks, Jews and 'The Other.'" *Afro-Hispanic Review* 8, no. 1/2 (1989): 15–19.

Wislizenus, Frederick Adolph. *Memoir of a Tour to Northern Mexico: Connected with Col. Doniphan's Expedition, in 1846 and 1847*. Washington, DC: Tippin & Streeper, 1848.

Wold, Ruth. "The Mexican Arcadia." *Hispania* 52, no. 3 (1969): 478–80.

Worcester, Donald Emmet. *The Apaches: Eagles of the Southwest*. Norman: University of Oklahoma Press, 1992.

Yetman, David A. *The Ópatas: In Search of a Sonoran People*. Tucson: University of Arizona Press, 2010.

Yoakum, Henderson K. *History of Texas: From Its First Settlement in 1685 to Its Annexation to the United States in 1846*. New York: Redfield, 1855.

Zuñiga, Ignacio. *Rápida ojeada al estado de Sonora: dirigida y dedicada al supremo gobierno de la nación*. Mexico City: Impreso por Juan Ojeda, 1835.

Page numbers in italic type indicate maps.

Baján, Wells of, 158
Bancroft, Hubert Howe, 147, 240–41n3
Báro, José, 29–30
Barraza, Pedro, 40
Barrozo, Juan Ignacio, 89
Bautista de las Casas, Juan, 157
Befarano, Juaquín, 10
Bernal Vázquez, Héctor M., 14
Bonaparte, Joseph, 112, 156
Bonaparte, Napoleon, 4, 112, 148, 159
Bonavía y Zapata, Bernardo: and
  bounty for Rafael's band, 70–71, 83;
  and Hidalgo's rebellion, 157; and
  pursuit of Rafael's band, 76, 117–18;
  as governor of Durango, 37, 70, 224–
  25n30; as Salcedo's successor, 159
Burciaga, Pedro, 119–21
Burr, Aaron, 94
Bustamante, Juan José Ruiz de: and
  Hidalgo's trial, 158; as researcher on
  Rafael's band, 6–7, 91–92, 115, 128,
  149–55, 196n17; background and
  experience, 149, 219–20n44, 253n32.
  See also documentation of Rafael's
  band
Bustamante, Narciso Díaz de, 122

Calderón, Juan de Dios, 150, 257n22
California, 163
Calleja, Félix, María, 158
Calletana de los Relles, José Manuel, 132
Camino Real, 49–51, *50*
cannons, 4, 131–32, 140, 248n16
Cañon de Fernándes, 129–30
Cantera, 67
captives of Apaches. *See* Apache
  captives
captives of Rafael's band: and escaping,
  47, 67, 83–84, 97–98, 100, 136; as
  messengers, 67–69; as witnesses,

75–76; conditioning and initiation,
38, 88–89, 98–99; female, 124–25,
129–30, 133, 140–41; rescue of, 107,
147–48; torture and execution of,
72–73, 103, 109, 142; value of, 39, 57.
See also Apache captives
captives of Spanish, 13, 54. *See also*
  Indians adopted by Spanish
Cárdenas, José Antonio, 132
Cárdenas, José Manuel de, 143
Cárdenas, Juan de Dios, 150
Carrasco, Manuel, 52–54
Carrera, José Trinidad, 231n35
Carrizal Apaches: and connection
  to Guajoquilla, 17; and illegal
  trade, 34–35, 152, 233–34n5; and
  Mimbreños origin, 203n21; and
  Navajo revolt, 44; and Rafael, 48, 53,
  65–66, 123–24, 140; and second La
  India, 123; and third La India, 141;
  and Ultin's wife (La India), 35
Carrizal Presidio: and pursuit of
  Rafael's band, 47–48; description of,
  27, 34, 215n16
Carrulo, Magdaleno, 143–44
Castillo, José, 122, 126. *See also* captives
  of Rafael's band
Castillo, Rafael, 101
Ceballos, Agustín, 116
Cebolleta, New Mexico. *See* Navajo
  revolt; New Mexico (Spanish)
Cerda, Juan Antonio, 128
Cerro Cabeza de Oso, 36
Cerros de Acatita, 144, 147, 251n15
Chamberlain, Samuel, 124–25
Charles IV, 112
Chávez, Francisco, 108
Chávez, Hilario, 122
Chávez Chávez, Jorge, 55–56, 157–58, 171

CPSIA information can be obtained
at www.ICGtesting.com
Printed in the USA
BVHW071839071022
648927BV00010B/1006

9 780806 190686